Psychology in Human Context

Sigmund Koch

Psychology in Human Context

Essays in Dissidence and Reconstruction

Edited and with a Preface by
David Finkelman *&* Frank Kessel

The University of Chicago Press
Chicago and London

David Finkelman is associate professor of psychology at St. Mary's College of Maryland. **Frank Kessel** is a program director at the Social Science Research Council in New York City.

The University of Chicago Press, Chicago 60637
The University of Chicago Press, Ltd., London
© 1999 by The University of Chicago
All rights reserved. Published 1999
Printed in the United States of America
08 07 06 05 04 03 02 01 00 99   1 2 3 4 5

ISBN: 0-226-44930-0 (cloth)
ISBN: 0-226-44931-9 (paper)

Library of Congress Cataloging-in-Publication Data

Koch, Sigmund.
    Psychology in human context : essays in dissidence and reconstruction / Sigmund Koch ; edited and with a preface by David Finkelman and Frank Kessel.
        p.   cm.
    ISBN 0-226-44930-0 (alk. paper). — ISBN 0-226-44931-9 (pbk : alk. paper)
    1. Psychology.   I. Finkelman, David.   II. Title.
BF121.K54   1999
150—dc21   98-52008
                                                                                         CIP

Contents

PART THREE: **Studies in the Pathology of Knowledge**

Editors' Preface

This volume contains a collection of writings by one of the twentieth century's most penetrating and wide-ranging scholar-critics, the psychologist Sigmund Koch.

When Koch died in August 1996, the preparation of this collection was close to complete. This had been a lengthy process, beginning—in one respect—roughly twenty years ago when, with the assistance of one of us (D.F.), Koch put together a tentative collection of his papers. As he himself explains in his introduction, these were seen as a "surrogate volume 7," in place of Koch's long-planned "postscript" to the monumental six-volume *Psychology: A Study of a Science*, which he edited and which was published between 1959 and 1963. (See Robinson 1998 and Wertheimer 1998 for two illuminating "retrospective reviews" of that overall project, with particular emphasis on Koch's editorial role.) In reality, he had been working in one way or another on volume 7 ever since the *Study* was published. But ultimately it was this collection that took the most definite shape, most significantly in the form of an extensive eighty-three-page "proposal," produced in 1983, that came to be known as "The Red Book" (reflecting its binding). In those pages Koch not only laid out a selection of essays corresponding closely to the present form, but also provided an extensive rationale for each. Beyond that, he had written a foreword for many of the essays.

Thus our task as editors—a role we came to share a couple of years before his death—was considerably aided and guided by Koch's own detailed plans. And we have seen our responsibility as that of bringing the volume into the published light of day in a form as close as possible to those plans and his wishes, subject primarily to space constraints (although as Koch himself says in the introduction, the University of Chicago Press — and David Brent in particular — have all along been singularly supportive of this project).

What, then, have we done as editors? First, we constructed forewords for the chapters that did not already have them, working from text Koch had written in the Red Book. Second, we shortened the manuscript in a number of ways. As chapter 2 we substituted "Psychology and Emerging Conceptions of Knowledge as Unitary" (delivered at a symposium at Rice University in 1963) for a considerably longer historical chapter on "The Age of Theory" (originally prepared for volume 7 of the *Study*). Although we did so reluctantly, Koch himself had expressed some reservations regarding length, and in the Red Book had suggested the Rice Symposium paper as a possible alternative. We are satisfied that this essay does present some of the historical context contained in the original "Age of Theory" chapter, albeit in abbreviated form. Also we are content in the knowledge that that chapter, as well as the rest of the original manuscript for volume 7, is available to scholars in the collection of Koch's papers on deposit at the Archives of the History of American Psychology at the University of Akron. The same applies to an essay on "Scientism and Government" that Koch had written in 1968 and proposed in the Red Book; we eliminated that chapter, partly because it is somewhat dated, but mainly because of space constraints. (In reaching this editorial decision, along with several others, we were guided by a particularly perceptive and sympathetic reading of the original manuscript by an anonymous reviewer.)

We also shortened several other chapters. From chapter 3 we eliminated a section on "systems theory as an integrating paradigm" (where "systems theory" referred to the version promulgated by von Bertalanffy in the late 1960s). Chapter 5 — "A Theory of Definition: Implications for Psychology, Science, and the Humanities" — was reduced by about 20 percent, primarily by condensing the discussion of the historical background. Chapter 6 — "The Concept of 'Value Properties' in Relation to Motivation, Perception, and the Axiological Disciplines" — was similarly shortened, and the original manuscript combined with some text from a published version. And redundancies with other chapters were eliminated from chapters 8 and 9 — "Ameaning in the Humanities" and "Psychology and Its Human Clientele: Beneficiaries or Victims?" — thereby saving several pages each.

Which is not to say that we have eliminated all redundancies among the chapters. Here we were largely guided by Koch's own considered wishes and arguments. Most notably, we were convinced by his view — as expressed in the Red Book — that "a [repeated] 'module' creeps into many of my papers; this is the fate of even mildly idiosyncratic thinkers when seeking to extend their positions to a variety of issues. In preparing the manuscript, I shall try to hold such repetitiousness to a minimum, but I do not think the *total* elimination of these position-reprises desirable in a book of *essays*. It is well that both boredom and space be reduced, but it is also important that each essay be self-contained." And as a central corollary, in deciding which passages to delete or retain, we have sought to ensure that Koch's distinctive style and voice are essentially unaltered.

Conversely, we also added some material. Most notably, we included as chapter 14 a more recent essay (published in 1992, after the Red Book had been prepared) on the physicist-philosopher Percy W. Bridgman. In this paper Koch shows how the ideas of the originator of the term *operational definition* were seriously misinterpreted and misused by psychologists. This, in our view, not only constitutes a characteristically caustic analysis of "cognitive pathology" in psychology, but also reflects Koch's respect for the contrary, namely, the kind of depth and sensibility of thought Bridgman exemplified.

Also, to the intellectual autobiography in chapter 1 we have added a brief appendix describing the "Aesthetics Research Project" that engaged Koch for much of the last years of his life. Taken from talks he gave in the early 1990s, these pages convey the essence of a "reconstructive" project that brought Koch back to his earliest roots in literature and the arts.

Finally, we scrutinized the fairly large number of temporal references that occur in the original papers (e.g., "twenty years ago"; "in the last thirty years"). In most cases, the phrases were amended to make the point of reference 1995, when Koch was last able to give attention to the manuscript. In three chapters, however, the point of reference remains the date on which the chapter was written. As conveyed in their respective forewords, chapter 1 was delivered as an address in 1977, chapter 2 presented in 1963, and chapter 8 an address delivered in 1969. In a similar spirit, we amended some but not all period-specific references to gender (e.g., the use of *he* and *him* as generic pronouns).

It remains only to convey that we regard it as a signal honor to have known Sigmund Koch, to have counted him as a personal friend and professional inspiration, and thus to have played a small role in bringing this book into being. Suffice it to say that, in the 1960s, the incisiveness and range of his ideas — expressed in rhetorically rich and unique style — engaged the minds of two undergraduate students of psychology who came upon the Rice Symposium presentation (chapter 2) in places as far apart as the University of Cape Town and the City College of New York. These students, having coincidentally received their Ph.D.s from the same institution (the University of Minnesota), subsequently discovered that they—along with numerous others of their generation of psychologists—could recount, by memory, which of Sig's powerful passages had excited them the most; and they could speak with great gratitude and feeling of how the penetrating, critical gaze of his essays on the foundational issues of psychology had—almost paradoxically—strengthened their own faith in and commitment to a scholarly endeavor that so often seemed anemic, if not lifeless. This collection, we trust, will not merely reveal the continuing currency of his essential ideas but, more, keep Sig's inspirational spirit alive for generations to come, providing intellectual and moral signposts for future travelers in the irreducibly rich terrain of the psychological studies.

Frank Kessel and David Finkelman

Introduction

This book is a critique of the modern psychological enterprise which I have developed over a forty-year span. Since I am primarily a psychologist, it is a critique "from within"—but not a parochial one, for I have increasingly seen certain dysfunctionalities (indeed, perversities) of psychological inquiry as endemic to modern thought in virtually all areas. Most of the attitudes underlying the critique came together in the mid-fifties, when I was directing the ambitious study of the status of psychology that resulted in the six volumes of *Psychology: A Study of a Science*. During those years, I began to engage a set of themes (both in connection with the *Study* and independently of it) which I have pursued ever since. The work has been animated by a coherent set of attitudes towards the nature of inquiry, creative effort, and knowledge—but it is difficult to define these attitudes in terms more succinct than the entirety of the book.

It is also hard to define the character of this book. It is more organic than a collection of essays; less so than a systematically deployed treatise. It is colligation, rather more than collage. About three-quarters of it derives from previously published articles in scattered sources; the rest has not before been published.

Much of the material derives from my draft towards a personal "postscript" volume to *Psychology: A Study of a Science*. The manuscript for the projected volume 7 of that *Study* was on the verge of completion more times than I care to remember; a succession of career changes created so long a delay between the *Study* proper and its postscript that I ultimately decided not to carry it through. There is a sense, though, in which the present volume can be read as a "surrogate" volume 7, for it carries forward a line of thinking that in large part originated in my attempt to see a pattern in the detailed retrospective analyses of their own systematic efforts contributed by the ninety distinguished participants in that *Study*.

As a "surrogate volume 7," the present book is a good exchange for the original: not only does it sample the development of ideas that were incipient (or had not yet inhabited my head) thirty years ago, but in the present context I am freed of the compulsion to align my ideas with the detailed trends of the contributions to the *Study*. I think those trends to have been illuminating to me—and, indeed, to many who have read or sampled the six volumes of the *Study*. But the freedom to be idiosyncratic is a precious gift—one that is too rarely given under conditions of modern scholarship. Thus, mainly, this book is *not* a volume 7. It is a report of the non-heroic odyssey of a confused, bemused, and (occasionally) amused wanderer through some small part of the terrain of modern thought: primarily psychological and philosophical terrain, but including a few side trips here and there.

How place the character of that report? On a superficial level, the book can be seen (and correctly so!) as a contribution toward a post-positivist psychology and a post-positivist world. (Despite the impressions of some, neither has quite arrived.) On a less superficial level, it can be seen as an effort to localize a deeper and more general pathology in modern thought, of which the positivistic sensibility is but one manifestation.

What I have in mind by this "deeper pathology" can here be only allusively suggested. One may begin to get warm by noting (re scholarship) the unquenchable need within almost all sub-groupings of inquirers (even the most libertarian or counter-mainstream) for the rapid erection of pre-congealed methodic orthodoxies; the huddling together of scholars in defensively imperialistic cells protected by such orthodoxies; the instrumental and bureaucratized relations between ideas and their votaries ("thoughts" as negotiable products, rather than *thinking* as intrinsically motivated process!); and—here we are getting warmer—the propensity to embrace group-justifying or -aggrandizing *delusions* to an extent which converts scholarship into a form of utilities-seeking role-playing.

The important point to emphasize is that such tendencies as I have just vaguely adumbrated are as characteristic of phenomenologists, neo-Kantians, advocates of Westernized versions of Zen and other Eastern philosophies, the uncontainably proliferating sub-groupings of neo-Wittgensteinians, etc., as they are (or at one time were) of *logical positivists*. They are as characteristic of "cognitive science" theorists, developmental "stage theorists," humanistic psychologists, psycholinguists, and reality therapists as they are of the most stolidly unregenerate, positivistically buttressed *behaviorists*. One can see the same tendencies, perhaps in more splendid amplitude, within the lush dispersion of sub-groupings in the social sciences. And, indeed, the same tendencies are discernible in the humanities: take current "hermeneutics," structuralism, deconstructionism, and semiotics just for starters. And, yes, the same holds for the *arts*, whether in "modernist" or "post-modernist" collectivities of camps comprehending — by this late date in the century — intricacies of subspeciation that transcend the resources of taxonomy.

Criticisms of the foundations of modern culture — whether leveled against particular fields or of general cast — have of course been mounted throughout this century. A polytonal cacophony of Marxist refrains has been sung — with rather visible effects in certain parts of the West and East — ever since the second half of the *nineteenth* century. But we must not forget the occasional Ortega y Gassets, Spenglers, Vaihingers, Krauses, Musils, Mauthners, Kafkas, Jasperses, and their ilk, who made their dire diagnoses of modern sensibility early in the century, and their predecessors like Kierkegaard, Büchner, Schopenhauer, Nietzsche, Dostoyevsky in the nineteenth. Self-determining, prophetic, and idiosyncratic thinkers of this cast (and their ranks could be multiplied) have certainly found a hearing, thought not always in their own time. Nevertheless, it is fair to say that the actual grotesqueries of mainstream modern intellectual, artistic, and practical life were very little mitigated by these sporadically occurring critiques.

The syndrome that some have called scientism and others positivism has remained the most pervasive feature of Western sensibility from the late nineteenth century through the present (conceivably transitional) day. Challenges to this syndrome, however powerful the analysis or rhetoric in which they were housed, were infrequent and little heeded during the first half of this century. At some point in the early to mid-fifties, critiques of the positivist world view, mounted from a motley variety of perspectives, became numerous, and from that point on, reappraisals of the nature of knowledge and creative activity continued to burgeon.[1] That incipient tide

---

1. The scope of the attrition upon regnant views of science and of knowledge that had emerged in the 1950s was addressed in my 1964 Rice Symposium paper (written in 1962), "Psychology and Emerging Conceptions of Knowledge as Unitary" (reprinted here as chapter 2). At that point, it was already easy to select, more or less casually, significant recent work of about thirty individuals in support of my contention that "an era in thought-about-thought

of interest in the reinspection of the nature of knowledge received a powerful increment in visibility, if not in substance, from C. P. Snow's 1959 Rede Lecture, which advanced his (rather belated) discovery of the cross-purposeful "gap" between the "two cultures" (scientific and humanist) in the modern world. The ensuing wave of international concern with gap-reduction strategies — though not much less superficial than Snow's initial analysis — made broadly popular (even among university administrators!) a sense that there might be something off-center, perhaps distorted, in humankind's perception of the nature of its own intellectual artifacts. But during that Snow-flurry and ever since, there have emerged, increasingly, rather more muscular dissidents and reconstructionists in every area of scholarly, creative, and practical activity, who have been challenging foundation assumptions, methodic stratagems, concepts, theoretical rationales, subject-matter delimitations, and values which had been in place for most of the century, and in some instances had remained stable since the Enlightenment.

By the present phase — now that we self-consciously see ourselves as fin-de-siècle creatures — reassessments of the intellectual presuppositions of this century have become epidemic; though, one must hasten to add, not ragingly so, for the earlier mainstream presuppositions are everywhere still visible. One should also note that many of the reassessments themselves bear certain of the traits of the tendencies under criticism. Moreover, the associated reconstructive proposals range in tenor from the responsible through the boldly conjectural to the wild, and beyond that, the weird.

Almost all the critiques offer a fast therapy based (say) on an extrinsic selection from the history of ideas, whether ancient or modern (e.g., Taoism, Aristotelianism, neo-Kantianism, or philosophical phenomenology); or on a "new" reading of the import of physics (e.g., "implicate order" or "neo-thermodynamics"); or on a re-reading of older minority views within science (e.g., "emergent," or "creative" evolution); or on an unlimited hypersufficiency of interpretations of the nature and limits of knowledge

---

is breaking up." After I joined the Ford Foundation in 1964, I was instrumental in establishing an international "study group" that put about fifty of the scholars working in this vein into continuing communication. Few psychologists were aware of the mushrooming critique of the very model of science that they held sacrosanct. Kuhn, of course, became visible (and influential) within psychology not long after the publication of his 1962 *Structure of Scientific Revolutions*. But he was not — and still is not — seen in relation to the already large body of cognate critical analyses that preceded his book (cf. chapter 3).

based on linguistic analysis; or on some one of a plethora of "new" methodologies (e.g., systems theory, catastrophe theory, chaos theory), or on someone's latest version of humans qua subtle floppy disc programs.

Against the preceding background, perhaps I can locate the character of my own critical effort. It has been a modest one. I have sought first and foremost to invite people in my own field to *think,* and to help create conditions under which they might be liberated from a set of profession-wide constraints, both epistemological and substantive, within which authentic, problem-responsive thinking was, if not impossible, at least illegal. I offer no panacea; no therapy — other, perhaps, than my own brand of cognitive therapy. Non-spurious knowledge — especially in the human studies — is in my view achievable only in very small, fragile, and sensibility-dependent increments. If I have offered anything *re*constructive, it has been based on my dogged pursuit of two themes: a theory of "definition," which begins to give a glimmer of insight into how, in fact rather than in stipulation, communication takes place both in and out of science; and an "objective" theory of value (perhaps "pre-theory" would be the better term), which adduces psychological grounds for a belief in the utter interpenetration of the putative "realms" of "fact" and "value."

In the course of analyzing issues connected with the constraints upon significant inquiry in psychology, it soon became apparent that the conclusions which came my way held, in one degree or another, for many other disciplinary and informal contexts in which thinking takes place. Perhaps what I see in those other contexts are but chimeras of my own intellectual imperialism, but certain of my conjectures are at least confirmed by dissidents within those areas who have developed views convergent with my own.

I will have been perceived as somewhat arch in discussing the tenor of my views at some length, but not their content. But an introduction must not usurp the rights of the book to follow. An overview of my work — and something of its early genesis — is the topic of the "intellectual autobiography" that forms chapter 1. At this juncture, however, I would like to say a few things about the genesis of my "philosophical" stance, and my philosophical influences, which are not covered in quite the same way in the first chapter.

Though I am a psychologist and, secondarily, philosopher of science, I have also sustained (with frequent guilty interruptions) a lifelong interest in the arts and humanities. Most of my work has been done from *within* psychology—where, beginning in the late 1930s, I have concentrated on problems of "theoretical" cast. During the initial decade of my career, I also did experimental work in the psychology of learning and of motivation. It should be noted that my career as student and, a little later, contributor joined the stream of psychological history towards the beginning of the period marked by the hegemony of neobehaviorism. I should add that, during this novitiate phase, I was a confirmed (though not totally enslaved) logical positivist who felt that the sophisticated technical insight into the nature of scientific theory imparted by my philosophical training could be put to splendid use in guiding my psychologist colleagues towards the realization of theoretical and methodological objectives they had already themselves acquired—rather more through osmosis than competent scholarship—from the neopositivists. All these matters—along with the development of my attitudes both toward my own work and my field—are readdressed in more detail in chapter 1.

Suffice it to say here that my attitude toward what I found myself doing was, from the very beginning, strangely ambivalent. It was as if I were living in a hypnotic trance but in at least occasional touch with emanations from a previously awake existence. Psychology at that time was one of the purest instances in history of an academic enclave dominated by a group delusion: in hindsight it could almost be *defined* as the institutionalization of a delusion.

In essence, the delusion could be characterized as the presumption that this most ambitious—if ill delimited—subject in the history of scholarship was at the very verge of total conquest of its problems before it had gotten under way. The simplistic philosophy of science originating (circa the mid-1920s) in the logical positivism of the Vienna Circle (augmented by what appeared to be cognate methodic proposals deriving from operationism and neopragmatism) was universally interpreted by psychologists as an infallible codex, rote allegiance to which would guarantee the "construction" of predictively powerful psychological theory adequate to the entire domain (whatever that might be!) of the "science." It should be added that the psychologists of the day were ill prepared even to understand the *technical* formulations of the philosophic and methodic ideas that so inspired them.

Another prevailing conviction of that day held that the inductive base of the grand, hypothetico-deductive theory which virtually all thought imminent need not even involve observational or empirical work with *human beings;* it was sufficient that the *general* principles of "behavior" be based on the study of some "representative high-order mammal" — preferably a conveniently fecund and portable species, the environment of which was "rigorously" and easily controllable. In practice, this turned out to be the white rat. From the "fundamental" behavioral laws to be garnered from the study of such subjects in a few "standard" apparatus-determined situations (e.g., mazes, discrimination boxes, various forms of the Skinner box) designed to tease out "determinants" of learning, were to be *deduced particular* behavioral relationships adequate to the entire domain of psychology, *including* human psychology. One might, of course, have to face up to a mild complication if one envisaged the possibility, or possible importance, of individual and species *differences*. No problem! Merely work out ways of determining individual-specific and species-specific "values" for certain of the "empirical constants" in the appropriate general laws.

I have called the period to which I here allude psychology's "Age of Theory." The brief description of its atmosphere here given verges on caricature, but caricature is the only mode in which a delusional system of the magnitude at issue — which largely controlled the history of psychology from roughly 1930 to 1960 — can be addressed. In the heyday of the Age of Theory (what I have called its "Classic Phase," circa 1935–1945), it was not unusual for a psychologist literally to believe that the *task* of the science would be completed within ten or fifteen years — and this, despite the fact that the period was a highly polemical one, marked by continuous competition among a half-dozen or so major theorists (cum their respective followerships). The unbridled optimism of these competing groups was based on a common conception of *method*. And this consensus, as I now see it, was buttressed by an autistic magic which is perhaps definitive of twentieth-century sensibility: the belief, at some deep level, that the agent of inquiry can transfer the *responsibility* for inquiry to a set of self-corrective *rules*. More than that — a kind of comforting cognitive scotoma for the obvious fact that *rules* are not inhabited by entelechies which render them *self*-applying.

As I have already suggested, in my earliest years qua psychologist I was myself victim to the delusion-complex I have sought to describe. But between 1942 (when I started to teach at Duke University) and the early 1950s, the scales fell gradually from my eyes.

The ten-year progress of my disaffection from the prevailing delusional system was based on the particularistic work that I was doing within that system, not on any disposition to reexamine my general philosophical commitments. Nor was I much influenced by the attrition upon positivism that began to become evident, toward the end of that interval, in philosophic and other contexts external to psychology. Initially, my restiveness was based on an incipient feeling that the dominating theories of the pre-war era and their post-war successors were disappointingly unproductive of knowledge that was worth having; that the fashionable tide of methodological law-making and discussion was neither enriching the theoretical enterprise nor leading to increased clarity about the methodic concepts under consideration; that the prevailing method-fetishism was acting as a stifling constraint on the ranges of curiosity asserted in inquiry; that the truly interesting work in progress, of which psychology has never been utterly devoid, was done at the price of punishing stresses against canon law, and sometimes vitiated by the divigations and ritual circumlocutions thereby occasioned. The question for me was, specifically and in detail, what were the conditions *within* psychology responsible for this state of affairs; this encouraged, still working from within, constant and perhaps rather jaundiced analytic re-scrutiny of particular methodological issues: e.g., the doctrine of "intervening variables"; problems of "operational" and empirical definition; questions concerning the limits of generality; analyses of theoretical formulations with a view towards determining which of the governing methodological assumptions checked out in practice and which did not; problems connected with variable identification, with measurement and strategies of mathematization; and so on.

At a certain phase—it is impossible to say when—it became clear that what was "wrong" could not be set right by piecemeal readjustments of local methodological doctrines, no matter how varied and subtle. Rather, what was wrong seemed in the over-all procedural picture: the image of science, its goals, and the modes of its making, which served as governance for psychological inquiry. At *such* a point, one was forced to reexamine one's philosophical commitments, for the simple reason that psychology had imported this image of science from the very same body of doctrine that had fathered those commitments.

Even the most casual pursuit of that policy began to make it evident that the dominant recent images of science, both at technical and lay levels, had all but excluded the *agent* of inquiry. This comes about as an inevitable byproduct of the modern concentration on the "logic of science." What results from this single-minded pursuit of "rational reconstruction" rather than empirical description of the particularities of the scientific enterprise is a view which progressively attenuates the human inquirer into an abstraction—ultimately a coincidental one, whose presence can seem a mere unhygienic complication. Thus one arrives at a conception which can suggest, even if it does not explicitly hold, science to be a disembodied set of rules having the happy property of "self-correctiveness." And this begets the impression, widely shared over a wide swath of this century, that science means linear, continuous, preguaranteed advance.

The obvious corrective—one which seems to have occurred to not a few individuals at about the same point in history—is to restore science to its human agency. The *stuff* of science is in the first instance human activity of the problem-oriented sort known as inquiry. Certainly this circumstance had not gone unnoticed earlier in the century. Among philosophers in the pragmatic tradition, Dewey was outstanding in his disposition to see much of the task of philosophy, especially that of epistemology and logic, as the analysis of inquiry. Positivists had joined with neopragmatists since the mid-1930s in allocating an entire branch of philosophic effort to "pragmatics"—conceived as an area largely concerned with particularities of inquiry. But Dewey, though his analysis of inquiry has still not had the impact it deserves, had failed sufficiently to stress the difference of incidence between his effort (so richly cognizant of the history, psychology, and sociology of ideas) and that of the logical positivists. (He in fact tended to stress the rather superficial convergences in the two viewpoints.) And among those in the positivist-neopragmatist grouping, concentration on the formal problems of syntactics and, later, semantics, left pragmatics an almost wholly empty field.

My earliest thinking about this defect of balance, of stress, in the modern view of science was a disposition unrelentingly to unpack the meaning of some such innocent proposition as *"science is the work of humans."* A useful way to give initial insight into the position to be taken in this book—a position meant to be open and *not* systematic, and thus one that must be misrepresented in any tidy précis—might be to reach embarrassingly far back in time and quote from the earliest draft towards volume 7 of *Psychology: A Study of a Science* my summary of what an unpacking of such a proposition might involve.

> In order to unpack the meaning of these words, it is merely necessary to do this: We must pack into "work" everything that we know about the nature of human performances; and into "humans" we must pack everything that we know about the nature of that quaint species. We must exercise very special vigilance against attributing to human performances any qualities

that we do not attribute to their human agents. And we must be obsessively careful not to attribute to "science," either its results or its methods, anything incompatible or in any way inconsonant with the predicate expression. I submit that the meaning of such a sentence has never been fully—or fully enough—explored in accordance with such criteria.

If we bring to bear on the human being as scientist all that we have long known about humans as such, certain obvious things follow.

Human beings show the same characteristics in the scientific situation as in others. They are the carriers of culture-determined and individually filtered values; they are the victims of autisms and obsessions; they are responsive to persuasion and propaganda and can be the conscious or unwitting agents thereof. They have drives towards security, prestige, self-aggrandizement. They are responsive to socially, institutionally, and professionally manipulated rewards, and they easily fall into institutionalized role-playing sets.

Conceptual parsimony is not the only economy in human thought: there is an absolute parsimony in its occurrence. Human beings, even as scientists, rarely press intellectual activity past the demands of immediate and limited problem-contexts, and the character of their solutions is often better adjusted to professionally or conventionally established standards of acceptability than to the demands of the problem. Human beings, even when scientists, are exceedingly reluctant to scrutinize critically or reappraise their own basic values, foundation beliefs, metatheories—personal or scientific. Human communication, even when scientific, is too often monologue, and when dialogue, too often dual monologue.

It is far from my intention to submerge science in some impenetrable Hobbesian gloom. I would in fact submit it to be a central paradox of modern thought that, although psychological and social science has rather overstressed the murky Hobbesian shadows in its portrait of humankind, science of science has produced a view of one aspect of human work which seems to suppose its agent to be all sweetness and light. The point is not to urge any need for a more cynical view of the race, but to suggest that more of the evidence which makes such views plausible in some degree be given its place in the analysis of scientific activity.

For humans are also partly reasonable — capable in some miraculous way of arriving at knowledge which is somehow adjusted to the character of the world, and their own relations to it. Moreover, I think there are excellent empirical grounds — both "common sense" and scientific — for asserting that human beings are partly reasonable, constructive, creative in a positive way, and not *merely* as an illusory by-product of the whirring Hobbesian machine. If one is to use a language of "drives," let us mark it down emphatically that people have "cognitive" and "aesthetic" drives in addition to the standard gastrointestinal and gonadal complement, and that they are apparently provided with the equipment for backing up such "drives" in action. If a person's behavior is determined by his or her role as *socius,* it is also susceptible to regulation by the perception of objective values. Humans may be intellectually lazy, but they also may be said to live for the occasional moments when they find it possible to transcend that laziness. Humans may work for socially and institutionally manipulated "rewards," but the history of ideas is a succession of rejections of such rewards. Human communication, even when monologue, can be exquisite monologue. Redundancy can be a safeguard of communication, as well as the mark of an inflated message.

Though I dislike this language of double personality in attempts to describe the human condition, I do not see how its use can be avoided when the problem is one of balancing a perspective. One, of course, hopes that ultimately the ladder will be thrown away, that it will give way to a differentiated view of humankind which will capture the balance, not by schizophrenic apposition, but via a conceptual net which catches the subtle interpenetrations. Despite many claims to the contrary, such a view is unfortunately in the distant future, if at all attainable.

On the basis, then, of what feeble and banal descriptive resources we have, we can conclude that scientific activity must represent a blend of the "rational" and the "extrarational." Whatever *else* scientific activities and their results may involve, they must represent some function of rational and extrarational determinants.

Such statements are indeed very loose, but it is not difficult to explicate them: Specify for me a criterion of rational procedure, of "warranted assertability," as Dewey might say, of efficient problem solution, of soundly and judiciously entertainable knowledge. Make this criterion normative and absolute or descriptive and contingent; let it register an ideal for the best practice of science, or let it be a generalization of that practice. I will then point out that this criterion, once stated, can only be *approximated* in action. If this is merely the tautological consequence of what is meant by "criterion," or "rule," it is an important tautology, one worth bearing in mind. But more strongly to the point, I will show that rule-regulated behavior is far more inconstant, impure, qualified, multi-leveled, extra–rule determined, than science of science, as recently written, will prepare you to expect. I will show this for the *typical* case of criterion-regulated activity, and I will show it for the *best* extant "realization" of any criterion than you care to specify.

Furthermore, I will show that though the rules may be "guides" to action, they cannot be *recipes* for action. Rules may be said to be "rational," depending on the efficacy of their instrumental relations to the ends they are designed to bring about. Action may be assessed as "rational" in terms of its degree of approximation to specified rules considered rational. But whatever degree of approximation *is* achieved, is more the story of the action than the rule. If rules are determinants of action, the causal distance is very great, and the underdetermination immense. Rules, at best, are templates through which action is somehow squeezed, and in this process of squeezing, the templates themselves are continually bent and twisted — sometimes in ways which make apparent the need for new ones.

One could continue to quote from this thirty-five-year-old draft, but it was written in another mood, which found its own style. The present mood would lead to a different statement but, I fear, a rather more discursive one — perhaps not much shorter than the entirety of this book.

It should already be obvious that what was said in the above extract about *scientific* inquiry holds, so far as it goes, for inquiry in any field, not excluding the several "humanities." Indeed, when one holds in view the *stuff* of inquiry, rather than its presumed regulative criteria, it rapidly becomes apparent that it is far easier to identify pervasive and general features than those — certainly of commensurate importance — specific to particular disciplines or problem-areas. A responsible interest in the texture of knowledge can be implemented only by detailed and painstaking empirical study of both the relatively general features of inquiry and the differential ones imposed by varying problematic locales.

A perspective of the sort suggested in the preceding paragraphs had already settled into my head by the time the project which issued as *Psychology: A Study of a Science* entered its planning phase (late 1952). It was such a perspective that animated both the design of the *Study* (as essentially a massive collaborative assessment of psychology's prevailing model of method), and my long years of effort in the implementation of the project and the analysis of its import. Under the stimulus of the project activities — and in some degree the corroborative impact of the contributors' analyses as these arrived over time — my "dissident" perspective expanded, differentiated, and matured along the lines reflected in the essays of this book.

During those years of working on the project and developing in privacy my then-outré ideas, I was a lonely person. But in 1959 I discovered a remarkable ally. I picked up a copy of Michael Polanyi's *Personal Knowledge* (1958), and had the strange experience of reading, at many junctures in this work, precisely my own thoughts but in more profound, energetically elaborated, and erudite form. A brief comparison of my own point of view with that of Polanyi's will do the double duty of celebrating my association with him (for I soon came to know him well), and providing a context for some further clarification of the philosophic incidence of this book.

Since Polanyi's work, though far from unknown, has still not received the recognition it deserves, let me commence by saying that I consider *Personal Knowledge* to be the most sustained, eloquent, and devastating critique of regnant modern views of the nature of knowledge that has yet been written and, further, that the boundless intellectual energy and range of this work qualifies it as one of the great books of this century. As Bertrand de Jouvenel has said (1961, 131), he "has moved from a great career as a scientist to a great career as a philosopher. Given the exceptional powers required for this duality of achievements, the former experience afforded exceptional material for the latter preoccupation." Polanyi has been outstanding in his disposition to do justice to the empirical particularities of inquiry and to carry out an analysis of knowledge in a way that slights neither its range, fine structure, nor the more pervasive features of its generative processes. Comparing my own feeble effort to Polanyi's, the most general observation I would have to make is that while I tend to distrust philosophic *systems* of large architecture, Polanyi aims at a certain systematic philosophic finality and moves towards that aim with a kind of élan that will brook no gaps. He thus sometimes tries to disgorge more from extant knowledge about inquiry, and from his own experience, than these can reasonably be expected to contain.

Nevertheless, there is a marked parallelism in our general approaches, especially in respect to the critique of modern dominant conceptions of knowledge (conceptions, the prototypical forms of which are registered in logical positivism and analytic philosophy), and in the disposition to reconceive the theory of knowledge in a way which places the human inquirer at its center. Both accounts would base analysis of problems hitherto treated within the traditional resources of epistemology, or of logic, on the detailed empirical characteristics of the human agent in process of inquiry or knowing; both would thus grant the psychology, sociology, and history of inquiry, scientific and otherwise, a far more decisive role in the pursuit of epistemological questions than has been customary.

Among the more detailed correspondences is an inclination to see as one of the chief distortions in the modern view of inquiry an excessive emphasis on regulation by *rule;* a largely convergent reanalysis of the meaning of "objectivity" in its relation to inquiry; a radical demur against the conventionalistic and linguistic emphases of recent fashion, together with a conviction that empirically apt examination of knowledge shows it to have, in specifiable senses, ontological content; consonant analyses of the dependence of communication on extra-articulate processes, and thus analyses of language and meaning which are convergent at not a few points. I point to these similarities in full humility and with no implication that my own treatment of the respective issues is based on so formidable a range of competences as is Polanyi's. But these coincidences are instructive, I think, in pointing towards a change in intellectual climate to which individuals widely separated in place and personal history were responding in comparable ways.

Perhaps the outstanding general difference between Polanyi's and the present approach is that I prefer to emphasize *on principle* the tentativeness and openness of whatever can currently be said about many of the vital aspects of human cognition and, more generally, of inquiry and its fruits. As a psychologist, I am poignantly apprised that the knowledge in my field about these matters is limited and, where it exists (or seems to), is often trivial or beside the point. Thus I see my role as that of tentatively circumscribing a few relevant questions and inviting interest in their continuing specification and analysis. I say "continuing" because I do not conceive of these questions as having conclusive answers. Inquiry about inquiry must surely go forward for as long as must inquiry in its first-order sense. And challenging as are the problems of first-order inquiry, the study of inquiry itself cannot well be less challenging. It would be unfair to suggest that Polanyi was not cognizant of such considerations. But he seems the type of thinker who prefers to batter his way into challenging problems, even when the available weapons are frangible in the extreme. Thus, for instance, he will occasionally borrow — as in his analyses of perception and of learning — rather more from psychology than it has to offer. And one feels that, unconventional philosopher though he be, there remains a rather generous residue of the philosophic drive towards systematic completeness.

An overview of the more concrete ideas which emerged over time from the working attitudes I have been trying to characterize in the preceding pages will be the burden of the initial section of chapter 1. And the autobiographic mode of that chapter will also add some literal detail to the story of my transformation from mainstream psychologist-novitiate to groping gadfly. Chapter 1 may thus serve as a very concise introductory prefiguration of the main themes to be explored in the book. At *this* point, however, I should like to supplement the table of contents by giving brief rationales for the sequencing of the remaining chapters.

Part 1: The Prospects and Limits of a Significant Psychology. This part of the book discusses some of the central issues of the psychological enterprise. Chapters 2, 3, and 4 are of a genre halfway between intellectual history and critical methodological analysis. They seek to isolate and chart the effects of the main metatheoretical decisions which have controlled the history of "fundamental" psychology over the past half-century. At the most general level, the attitudes regulating inquiry can be ordered to two metaphors definitive of the ends of systematic effort: *theory* in a special sense deriving from the "rational reconstructions" of early logical positivism, and the *paradigm* in a somewhat corrupted sense of Thomas Kuhn's notion. It is thus possible to discriminate an "Age of Theory" extending from circa 1930 to the early 1960s (and perhaps still residually in force), and an "Age of the Paradigm," which began to displace certain of the Age of Theory attitudes shortly after the publication of Kuhn's *The Structure of Scientific Revolutions* in 1962. These successive, but partially overlapping, periods are discussed in chapter 2, "Psychology and Emerging Conceptions of Knowledge as

Unitary," and Chapter 3, "The Age of the 'Paradigm.'" Chapter 2 only glancingly discusses the Age of Theory in the context of a critique of behaviorism.[2] Chapter 3 more directly analyzes the concept of the paradigm as it has functioned in recent and current psychological theorizing. Against this fifty-year historical backdrop, chapter 4, "Psychology versus the Psychological Studies," presents my own critique of any presumption that psychology can be a coherent discipline, and my arguments—both of historical and "in principle" cast—to the effect that the definitive analytic methods of natural science are not applicable to most psychological questions worthy of interest. Instead, it is suggested that the methods of "the psychological studies" (other than biological psychology and its various subspecifications) might be more fruitfully seen as akin to those of the humanities.

Part 2: Steps toward Reconstruction. Chapters 5, on "A Theory of Definition," and 6, on "The Concept of 'Value Properties,'" represent reconstructive efforts which attempt to clear the way for the pursuit of "the psychological studies." Chapter 5 provides a liberating reformulation of perhaps the most deep-seated and congealed body of methodological lore—that concerning empiricist and "operational" criteria of definition—which has sustained the objectivistic scientism of the past half-century. Chapter 6 considers a central set of substantive issues—those converging on value—in such a way as to show the essential interrelatedness of psychological and humanistic analysis and, indeed, the need for collaboration between psychologists and humanists on major issues of psychological import.

Part 3: Studies in the Pathology of Knowledge. It will become evident in chapter 1—and perhaps is already evident—that I believe there to be certain perversities of cognitive function endemic to the human condition which stem from efforts to court security in the face of uncertainty. Part 3 explores the broad dispersion of such "passionately courted cognitive disutilities" within the inquiring practices of the psychological and social sciences and—to some extent—the humanities as well. The tendency for psychology to "enact" science rather than seek knowledge, and to subordinate inquiry to superficially assessed but reassuringly "fail-safe" methodologies borrowed from extrinsic sources, will have been developed in histori-

---

2. As discussed in our preface, this chapter substitutes for the chapter originally intended here on "The Age of Theory." *Eds.*

cal context in part 2. It is now addressed more focally — and with the intent to understand the deeper human and historical bases for such misfirings of the inquiring impulse.

The attempt to render intelligible the "epistemopathic" proclivities so conspicuous in the history of modern *psychology* must acknowledge from the outset that such tendencies in psychology are but special manifestations of a syndrome shared by virtually all fields of scholarly and creative activity in this century. I do not exclude sectors of the natural and biological sciences from that generalization, but part 3 concentrates upon the more specifically human studies. And, of these latter, it is perhaps psychology which illustrates the dysfunctional trends at issue in purest form.

The root pathology that I see as the source of the epistemopathic syndrome that I think so pervasive is a mode of cognition that I call *ameaningful thinking*. I will defer even a preliminary delineation of what I have in mind by "ameaningful thinking" until chapter 1, where its identification in very brief compass is attempted. Suffice it to say here that it is a method-dominated, routine, "lazy" mode of cognition that has been within the repertoire of all persons at all times, but its incidence — relative to the passionately problem-embracing and authentic modes of meaningful cognition that are also within the powers of all persons — has markedly increased in the modern period. It is a prime purpose of part 3 to explore the nature, conditions, and consequences of ameaningful thinking in detail.

Chapter 7 is the foundation chapter of part 3: It develops the notion of ameaningful thinking in extenso, explores its manifestations in the recent history of psychology, and introduces a few speculations concerning the historical basis for the increased incidence of ameaning in this century. Chapter 8 extends the analyses of the preceding one to the arts and humanities.

Chapters 9 and 10 trace the impact of ameaningful modes of thought within psychology and the social sciences upon a variety of application-contexts of those disciplines having great importance to human beings. Chapter 9 examines certain of the received opinions within psychology concerning its actual and potential contributions to "human welfare." Chapter 10 explores the ameaningful paradoxes implicit in the efforts of those "humanistic psychologists" who would release "human potential" via the technology of the "encounter group movement."

Part 3 continues with a triad of very brief chapters which address the work of three psychologists — two of them of great fame (Clark Hull, chapter 11; B. F. Skinner, chapter 12), while the third (Karl Zener, chapter 13) is known by only a few. The ameaningful basis and texture of Hull's form of "neobehaviorism" and of Skinner's "radical behaviorism" can be seen to have a special significance when it is considered that these two men are among the half-dozen or so figures who have had the greatest impact upon psychology in this century. Chapter 13 is a memoir of Karl Edward Zener, a colleague of mine at Duke University for twenty-five years, whose career can be seen as a contrast case to those of Hull and Skinner (and innumerable other psychologists of this century), and as a reassuring reminder that history is not its record. Karl Zener was a man who withstood the blandishments of ameaning absolutely — and this during an era when the penalties for rejecting the official delusion-system of his discipline were very great. [For reasons explained in our preface, we have added a chapter 14 to part 3, on the physicist-philosopher P. W. Bridgman. *Eds.*]

The book concludes with a coda (chapter 15) entitled "The Limits of Psychological Knowledge: Lessons of a Century qua 'Science.'" This chapter picks up much of the rationale of the critique of psychology developed earlier in the book and seeks to extend that rationale to deeper levels. The human context of the ameaning syndrome is seen to lie in the "antinomal" structure of human experience: the circumstance — discerned by Kant in his analysis of those "antinomies of pure reason" that disenfranchise dogmatic metaphysics, but not generalized by him — that there is a class of questions which have intense meaning to all human beings but which "transcend the competence of human reason." The pervasiveness of such meaningful yet (strictly) undecidable issues in experience leads to forms of cognitive denial that fuel ameaningful thinking. The chapter considers certain implications of such an analysis for the century-old conception of psychology as an "independent, experimental science."

The problems of editing are especially agonizing when "editor" and author happen to be one and the same — and even more so when compounded by the need to select from a scattered oeuvre composed over a long time-span. One arbitrary restriction I have made is to exclude materials written before the 1960s, even though there is much from the preceding decade that I think still to have current significance. Another was to work toward an organically coherent volume; certain of my pieces were not good fits relative to the architecture I ultimately thought best to adopt. A third constraint was space. The University of Chicago Press was generous in its allotment of that expensive commodity, but (understandably) not suicidally so. In consequence of these circumstances, some of my favorite work is not represented in this volume — but who am I to judge whether this might not be a boon to its readers?

Most of the chapters are presented in a form quite close to the original publications or manuscripts on which they are based. In a few instances (e.g., chapters 3 and 6), the presentation integrates materials deriving from two or more sources. The provenance of each chapter is indicated in its foreword.

There are inevitable problems of overlap in a collection of writings which develops long-term intellectual preoccupations incrementally over time. This is especially so when those preoccupations are in any degree idiosyncratic: one is always having to prepare the way for a new step by a reprise of the previous ones. I have sought to reduce such overlaps in the chapters of this book but not utterly to eliminate them. A certain amount of repetition can facilitate communication — not only in pedagogical contexts but even among adepts (perhaps especially among the latter!). And — knowing full well that some readers will not peruse the book sequentially (or in toto) — I felt it desirable that each chapter be relatively self-contained.

Finally, a book that was not written in a single inspired episode ending yesterday poses the problem of "updating." When I was young, I was obsessive about the requirement that anything I published be developed to a "last-minute" state of currency, both in content and bibliography. *Now,* I am less a fetishist about such matters. I hope myself not deluded in thinking that all essays (whether historic or analytic in objective) drawn upon by this book have current relevance. I think that there have been many developments in the psychology and philosophy of the past twenty or twenty-five years which are supportive — in spirit and sometimes letter — of certain of my views. If I were to "update" by addressing all such developments, the book would become interminable, and the contours of my own views would dissolve into a vaguely libertarian conceptual gel.

I have, however, employed three devices which will serve to align the chapters of this book (especially those based on "older" writings) with subsequent developments: Newly written forewords explaining the place of each chapter in the development of my thinking, the context in which its source materials were written, the relation of the chapters to others in the book, and so on; occasional new footnotes which update the text in relation either to history or changes in my own thinking; and occasional afterwords to chapters which require more such commentary than can be compressed into footnotes.

Key persons who influenced my intellectual development are identified in the introductory chapter. To those persons I should like to add a number of other significant individuals who generously encouraged certain of my ideas during the transitional years of my break with orthodoxy. They include Karl Muenzinger (a psychologist of self-determining and penetrating cast who, like Karl Zener, deserves a far more visible entry on the historic record), Donald K. Adams, Helge Lundholm, Karl Lashley, Henry A. Murray, Edward Chace Tolman, Edwin R. Guthrie, Wolfgang Köhler, Egon Brunswik, Robert Leeper, and Donald Marquis. I should add that I received not only encouragement from these men but much stimulation from their work.

This book could not have happened without the technical help, loving nurturance, and angelic resistance to boredom by my prose, of my wife, Lys Dunlap Koch. She compounded the bad luck of having superb secretarial skills with the bad luck of marrying a man who "wrote" via tape recorder. For thirty-five years, she transcribed every word I put on tape into impeccable typescript. More importantly, she was an accomplished professional editor, who applied her faultless command of English (which happened to be English English) to the taming of my metaphors, and the doctoring of my hyper-volubility.

Another person who has expended too much of herself on the care, coddling, and control of this author is my friend and former secretary, Rosalie Carlson. She has been responsible for the final typescript of many of the papers that have been tapped for this book. Paul Guay, Research Assistant for the Program in which I work (the Boston University "University Professors Program") is the most erudite bibliographer I have ever known. Indeed, he knows more about the literature of the varied fields pursued by the members of the Program than do any of us know about our *own* fields. His generous help has been indispensable to this project.

And, finally, Dr. David Brent of the University of Chicago Press is the most intelligent, amiable, patient, and helpful editor I have ever worked with. I would add "discriminating" to my list of adjectives, were that not construable as an immodesty.

1

Vagrant Confessions of an Asystematic Psychologist: An Intellectual Autobiography

Foreword

It is not within my nature spontaneously to initiate the project of an "intellectual autobiography." I am serious about my efforts to *think,* but have tended to take the agent of that process rather lightly. A dialectic between lightness (sometimes flippancy) of tone and seriousness of content was thus the only mode in which I could address the task. In content, the following paper is as felicitous an introduction to this book as anything I might write de novo. I considered changing its "voice" towards something more like the sober modulations of written scholarship; but soon realized that tonality is central to my message, even when I "write" in "written voice." I have therefore modified the paper very little for the present purpose; it was originally delivered as an invited address to the Divisions of Philosophical Psychology and of the History of Psychology of the American Psychological Association, at the association's annual convention in San Francisco in 1977. Further information about the paper's genesis is contained in its opening paragraphs.

«

It was two years ago that I found myself melting with embarrassing alacrity at Dr. Barbara Ross's suggestion that I tender a deposition concerning my career to Division 26 (History of Psychology) at a future American Psychological Association convention. Ten seconds later I was appalled at the idea and ten months later relieved that it had not been pursued. But at the last APA, I found Dr. Michael Wertheimer equally irresistible when he suggested that I address Divisions 24 (Philosophical Psychology) and 26 on "what had made Sigmund Koch." Ten seconds later I was appalled and at this moment I have an odd impulse to swallow myself—shoes first.

What I think motivated these two lapses of taste—and has certainly sustained my ambivalent and unsteady course to this podium—is awareness that psychology is populated by a vast hypersufficiency of *heroes* but as yet not a single *anti-hero*. I mean "anti-hero" in the literal, *literary* sense: the type of endemically misplaced person, forensic fathead, hyper-inept Quixote, that dominates the novel (and English play) of the last twenty years. It is important that someone step in to fill the anti-heroic void in psychology. I herewith submit my credentials.

But how? There is no strong story line in the life of an anti-hero; nor even the idle, intricate order of an oriental carpet. His objectives are *found,* not chosen; he floats supine on a sea of adventitiousness; he limps slowly to the sound of an extraordinarily arrhythmic drummer; he assigns time and energy to enterprises in totally maladaptive ways. Whatever might prove instructive about the anti-hero could be conveyed only by haphazard and unending iteration, or a method of massive collage.

In the assigned speck of time, I shall try to give: (1) a necessarily skeletal status report of my current thinking concerning besetting problems of our turmoiled discipline; (2) an intellectual origin point which I will arbitrarily reconstruct from the first decade or so of my sentient life (i.e., college years through early post-doctoral period); and (3) *not* an orderly account or even précis of the journey from origin point to current clinical condition but, rather, a few vagrant confessions concerning humiliating lessons I learned along the way. The overarching question—as is fitting for anti-heroes and clowns—will be that of *dignity.* How discover—over a certain time-swath in this century—one's dignity in a field like psychology? How discover the dignity of the field?

Current Geography of Our Hero's Head

I was one of the early psychologists to bring a background in the philosophy of science to bear on the analysis of methodological and theoretical problems. For good measure, during the initial ten years of my career, I was a dauntless and virile rat-runner, concentrating on the differential testing of rival theories of learning and on the empirical determination of learning-motivation relationships. After that I directed, under the sponsorship of the American Psychological Association, a massive assessment of fundamental psychology at midcentury—a study which brought me into contact with most of the influential psychological theorists of our times.

In the course of long years of detailed analytical work, my early enthusiasm for methodological work of the sort that provides pre-manufactured norms for the construction and justification of "theory" (or of "rigorous" systematic formulations, by any other name) gradually diminished. For the past twenty years or so, I have vigorously argued that a fetishistic emphasis upon method has been a principal constraint upon the quality of psychological, social-scientific, and—in some reaches—humanistic thought in this century. As early as the mid-1950s, I began to mount an attack upon the presuppositions of scientism—which I see as no less antithetical to the spirit of science than to that of the psychological, social, and humanistic studies—in senses markedly convergent with the thought of Michael Polanyi, though my thinking and his developed in total independence. An early sympathy for the tenets of logical positivism, along with serious attentiveness to the claims of some behaviorist thinkers, long ago gave way to stringent apostasy.

I wish I could assume that my current attitudes were broadly known, but it is my jaundiced impression that there is little correlation between the visibility of heroic names (let alone anti-heroic ones) and the perceptual salience of the mental pearls generated by their owners. I must, then, identify a few of the coordinates of my headpiece, current shape, even at the risk of a level of generality that will make me seem as vacuous as I *am* crotchety.

For some years I have argued that psychology has been misconceived, whether as science or any kind of coherent discipline devoted to the empirical study of man. That psychology *can* be an integral discipline is the nineteenth-century myth that motivated its baptism as an independent science—a myth which can be shown to be exactly that, both by a priori and empirico-historical considerations (cf. Koch 1971; chapter 4).

On an a priori basis, nothing so awesome as the total domain comprised by the functioning of all organisms (not to mention persons) could possibly be the *subject matter* of a coherent discipline. If *theoretical* integration be the objective, it should be considered that such a condition has never been attained by any large subdivision of inquiry—including physics. When the details of psychology's one-hundred-year *history* are consulted, the patent tendency is towards theoretical and substantive fractionation (and increasing insularity among the "specialties"), not integration. Almost forty years ago, Heinrich Klüver was enthusiastically looking forward to the "impending dismemberment of psychology." No prediction ever made by a psychologist has been so fulsomely confirmed! As for the larger quasi-theoretical "paradigms" of psychology, history shows that the hard knowledge accrued in one generation typically disenfranchises the regnant analytical frameworks of the last.

My position suggests that the *noncohesiveness* of psychology finally be acknowledged by replacing it with some such locution as "the psychological studies." The psychological studies, if they are really to address the historically constituted objectives of psychological thought, must range over an immense and disorderly spectrum of human activity and experience. If significant knowledge is the desideratum, problems must be approached with humility, methods must be contextual and flexible, and anticipations of synoptic breakthrough held in check. Moreover, the conceptual ordering devices, technical languages ("paradigms," if you prefer) open to the various psychological studies are—like all human modes of cognitive organization—perspectival, sensibility-dependent relative to the inquirer, and often non-commensurable. Such conceptual incommensurabilities will often obtain not only between contentually different psychological studies but between perspectivally different orderings of the "same" domain. Characteristically, psychological events are multiply-determined, ambiguous in their human meaning, polymorphous, contextually environed or embedded in complex and vaguely bounded ways, evanescent and labile in the extreme. This entails some obvious constraints upon the task of the inquirer and limits upon the knowledge he can hope to unearth. Different *theorists* will—relative to their different analytical purposes, predictive or practical aims, perceptual sensitivities, metaphor-forming capacities, preexisting discrimination repertoires—make asystematically different perceptual cuts upon the same domain. They will identify variables of markedly different grain and meaning contour, selected and linked on different principles of grouping. The cuts, variables, concepts, that is, will in all likelihood establish different universes of discourse, even if loose ones.

Corollary to such considerations, it should be emphasized that "paradigms," theories, models (or whatever one's label for conceptual ordering devices) can never prove *preemptive* or preclusive of alternate organizations. That is so for any field of inquiry, but conspicuously so in relation to the psychological and social studies. The presumption on the part of their promulgators that the gappy, sensibility-dependent, and often arbitrary paradigms of psychology *do* encapsulate preemptive truths is no mere cognitive blunder. Nor can it be written off as an innocuous excess of enthusiasm. It raises a grave moral issue reflective of a widespread moral bankruptcy within psychology. In the psychological studies, the attribution to any paradigm of a preemptive finality has the force of telling human beings precisely what they are, of fixing their essence, defining their ultimate worth, potential, meaning; cauterizing away that quality of ambiguity, mystery, search, that makes progress through a biography an adventure. Freud's tendency to view dissidents and critics in *symptomatic* terms — and to resolve disagreement by excommunication — is no circumscribed failing, but indeed renders problematic the character of his entire effort, not only morally but cognitively. One is tempted to laugh off the ludicrous prescriptionism of self-anointed visionaries like Watson, Skinner, and even certain infinitely confident prophets of the theory of finite automata — but their actual impact on history is no laughing matter.

Because of the immense range of the psychological studies, different areas of study will not only require different (and contextually apposite) methods, but will bear affinities to different members of the broad groupings of inquiry as historically conceived. Fields like sensory and biological psychology may certainly be regarded as solidly within the family of the biological and, in some reaches, natural sciences. But psychologists must finally accept the circumstance that extensive and important sectors of psychological study require modes of inquiry rather more like those of the humanities than the sciences. And among these I would include areas traditionally considered "fundamental" — like perception, cognition, motivation, and learning, *as well as* such more obviously rarified fields as social psychology, psychopathology, personology, aesthetics, and the analysis of "creativity."

Much of what I have proposed is grounded on an analysis, on which I have been working for twenty years, of the functioning of lexical units in natural and technical languages. The work suggests a sensible alternative to the absurdities of the definitional schemata of logical positivism and operationalism, and leads, I think, to fresh insights into problems of inquiry and of knowledge. This analysis shows that definition of abstract, general, or referentially "rich" concepts upon any delimited base of "epistemic simples" (such as a putative class of "physical thing predicates" or of verifying "operations") simply does not work. Such reductive definitional schemata confound symptom and meaning: if taken seriously they denude the universe of everything worth talking, or indeed thinking, about.

Analysis of the conditions of actual communication will show that effective definition is essentially a perceptual *training process.* The definer seeks to guide the addressee towards perception of the intended property, relation, or system thereof. If the referent is a subtle, delicately contoured, or embedded one (which it often is), such guidance may be very difficult indeed. The addressee may not possess preexisting discriminations requisite to perceiving "the point." The event manifolds which "carry" the referent may be too fleeting, complex, or variable for ready segregation of the constancy in question. In the ideal case, definition would be a form of ostension via a perceptual display that exhibits the referent in its purest, least masked, most sharply contoured form. Scientific experiment may be interpreted in that light. It is often difficult to approximate the ideal form. Verbal definitions, though limited by their surrogate character, depend for their efficacy on the definer's skill at mobilizing relevant components of the addressee's discrimination repertoire. And whether (and with what precision) the communication actually takes place will depend on the fineness and nicety of the discriminations within the addressee's repertoire. Definition is thus sensibility-dependent and probabilistic: nothing says that the intended property or relation will be noted — or brought into comparable resolution — by all addressees.

This analysis suggests that all definition is *real definition:* a definition tags and preserves the discrimination of *something* within the world flux — however embedded or intricately contoured that something may be. Moreover, *what* is tagged is no more stable than the discriminal activities and powers of appliers of the term. Processes of *metaphor* — i.e., the perception in new settings of relational characters which overlap (or are similar to) the characters tagged by an "old term" — are ubiquitous in language use. Though metaphor can lead to debased usages when the discrimination is less differentiated than a previously established use (or overlaps it only vaguely), in *creative* uses of language the meaning of a word can be sharpened and enriched by attaching it to contexts in which the original relational characters are more purely or richly exhibited. Man has the capacity for effortful perceptual search for subtle overlaps that can refine and extend established meanings. When such efforts towards creative metaphor are successful, then *knowledge* has been extended!

This perceptual theory of definition has many consequences — including certain of the judgments made in the earlier paragraphs of this status report. But I have yet to underline one obvious set.

It should already be apparent that this account stresses the continuity between precise, differentiated, and subtle discriminations upon the human universe within the resources of natural language and *technical* knowledge — even of the most abstruse character. It emphasizes the circumstance that the so-called technical languages — whether of science, the psychological and social studies, or the "hard" humanities—develop as differentiations from natural language, and always continue to depend on their embedding context in natural language for their interpretation and use. Particulate and nice *description* is no lowly or easy task; it is in fact the very basis—indeed, the flesh—of all non-spurious knowledge.

There is a strong sense in which psychology was already "established" before it commenced as a science. Once we appreciate the vast resources of psychological knowledge coded in the natural language, and internalized in the sensibilities of those who use it well, it should become a paramount matter of intellectual responsibility for those who explore the human condition to ensure that this knowledge not be degraded, distorted, or obliterated in their technical conceptualizations. Such a responsibility cannot be met by experientially impoverished or functionally illiterate persons. Since the task of the psychological studies is not to *supplant* the cognitive achievements stabilized within the natural language, but to refine and extend that knowledge, it is incumbent upon its inquirers that they have *extraordinary* capacities for discriminating upon the inner and outer world, and for the precise and supple mapping of language to their discriminations. Indeed, the requirements for such capacities are so stringent as to render problematic the very idea of a massively populated profession. And *meaningful* pursuit of the widely varied psychological studies will demand of the inquirers in each area rich and specialized sensibilities relevant to the particular phenomenal domain at issue. This means that the psychological studies taken together requires a workforce of more heterogeneous character (relative to the backgrounds and skills of its members) than does any other currently institutionalized branch of inquiry.

The judgments thus far made received their most extended development to date in my lengthy contribution to the 1975 *Nebraska Symposium* volume (1976a; cf. chapters 3 and 5). Before leaving this report on the mental geography of our anti-hero, I must make reference to an entire continent not yet represented in the cartography. Many years ago, I began to talk—first in jest, then in earnest—about the need for a field called *the pathology of inquiry* (or, more baroquely, *cognitive pathologistics*). Decades of inquiry into the inquiry of others—and into germane processes inside my own head—have induced in me a sense of awe at the plenitude of *homo sapiens'* gift for the mismanagement of its own mind. It is perhaps the ultimate genius of the race!

The notion of cognitive pathology is developed in a number of places later in this volume, most notably chapters 7 and 15; at this juncture, let me simply say that from such a perspective, it now occurs to me that I have worked as a cognitive pathologist throughout my mature career. My 10-year dedication to *Psychology: A Study of a Science* (1959b, 1962b, 1963) was largely an exercise in cognitive pathology—or, more precisely, cognitive therapeutics. The bulk of my editorial effort went towards helping to free brilliant and creative men from the straitjacket of an "official" epistemology which at some early point (and with one or another degree of cheerfulness) they had allowed themselves to be laced into. My extensive series of publications contra behaviorism—from the excruciatingly detailed and boresome analysis of Hull's theory in *Modern Learning Theory* (1954; cf. chapter 11), through the historically oriented generic analysis in the Rice Symposium volume (1964 [chapter 2]), to my recent review (1976b [chapter 12]) of Skinner's *About Behaviorism*—was also by way of fleshing out the cognitive pathological tradition. Here I might say parenthetically that one solid achievement of cognitive pathologistics is that on the basis of that series of analyses alone, rational men (if such there be) would have to conclude that behaviorism is finished. If there is residual motility, it is only that the corpse does not understand my arguments.

Two of my favorite papers—one published, the other not, and both equally known—present the metatheory and foundation postulates for the cognitive-pathologistic venture. The first of these (1965 [chapter 7]) pursues the extensive evidences of a syndrome that I call "ameaningful thinking" over a wide swath of psychological activity; the second (1969a [chapter 8]) extends the argument to the practice of the arts and humanities in this century. It is fitting that I conclude this "status" report with an outline of what cognitive pathologists mean by "ameaningful thinking," for I may have occasion to illustrate the concept—and very possibly the process—in the sequel.

Ameaningful thought or inquiry (the prefix has the same force as the *a-* in words like *amoral*) regards knowledge as the result of "processing" rather than discovery. It presumes that knowledge is an almost automatic result of a gimmickry, an assembly line, a methodology. It assumes that inquiring action is so rigidly and fully regulated by rule that in its conception of inquiry it often allows the rules totally to displace their human users. Presuming as it does that knowledge is generated by processing, its conception of knowledge is fictionalistic, conventionalistic. So strongly does it see knowledge under such aspects that at times it seems to suppose the object of inquiry to be an ungainly and annoying irrelevance. Detail, structure, quiddity are obliterated. Objects of knowledge become caricatures, if not faceless, and thus they lose reality. The world, or any given part of it, is not felt fully or passionately and is perceived as devoid of objective value. In extreme forms, ameaningful thought becomes obsessive and magical.

Throughout the recent history of the sciences, humanities, and (increasingly) the arts, there is lush and harrowing evidence of the play of ameaningful thinking.

Origin Point

Clad in his father's billowing Burberry, and tinted in a neurasthenic Proustian pallor, our slender anti-hero arrived at New York University in autumn, 1934. He was at the time a passionate (and self-conscious) litterateur, who had edited the literary section of his high school newspaper, won a national competition among high school poets for inclusion in an anthology of modern poetry, and won his graduating-class literary award with an essay in criticism. During the preceding summer, he had founded and begun to edit an independent "little" magazine (a not uncommon practice in those days among aspiring writers) and he, of course, already knew that his commitment to poetry and literary criticism was to be unswerving and eternal.

He early fell in with the campus literary lights, gravitating especially to Delmore Schwartz, who soon joined him in the editing of the still incipient magazine (*Mosaic*). The journal lasted for two issues, but it did place us in contact with certain of the giants and would-be giants of modern literature. Schwartz—who published his first pieces in *Mosaic*—went on to a distinguished literary career. He died in the mid-sixties, at the age of fifty—destroyed by the purity of his commitment and thus the unattainable altitude of his standards—but in recent years has become a posthumous culture-hero by virtue of Saul Bellow's having used him as the model for the central character in his novel, *Humboldt's Gift*.

My own purity (and no doubt talent) being inferior to Delmore's, I early proved seducible by other intellectual blandishments. The pattern was as follows: I started my college work with a concentration in English literature, but in a trice discovered that I needed no help from my professors. (To this day, I cannot understand the heads of literate students and intending writers who major in anything so expendable as academic English.) My mind being an essentially analytical one, I soon turned to philosophy. By 1934, logical positivism had largely captured philosophy on an international basis. The NYU department, though it included a few Deweyite pragmatists and Marxists, was no exception. In no time at all, I was a confirmed positivist, with confident answers to the conveniently narrow range of questions that the position accredited as "meaningful." It is well that I stand back for a moment and illustrate at my own expense one of the more obvious laws of cognitive pathologistics. From among the range of philosophical positions thrown up by a twenty-five-hundred-year history, I was able to arrive at a rational and mature choice in approximately two weeks. I fear that in all fields of scholarship such celerity of commitment is the rule: young persons enthusiastically plunge into their conceptual beds of Procrustes at the moment the sheet is turned down by someone they find admirable; often they do not emerge for the rest of their lives.

Because positivist creed found most statements of traditional philosophy to be trans-empirical and thus technical "nonsense," the legitimate roles of the philosopher were reduced to two: he could do work in pure logic or he could, qua applied logician, help clarify and hone the language of science. The latter task was seen mainly to involve the excision of residual metaphysical components but comprehended as well generous methodological guidance in relation to matters of theoretical form, rigor, and justifiability. I soon decided on this second role, having quickly discovered that though I was an able student of logic, I did not have the makings of a creative logician. But *which* science would I grace with my methodological sophistication? *Psychology* was an easy choice, for two unarguable reasons. First, it (i.e., the field) *was* easy, but also, what field in the panoply of scholarship seemed more desperately to *need* help? I had been appalled and insulted by the boresome triviality of my first few courses in psychology. The field came through to me as a collage of weird and conceptually rubbery insularities rendered in a patois of garbled and pedestrian neologisms. As I have somewhere said: "So massive an absurdity cried out for redress. Besides — an absurdity so massive could hardly hold its own against a little clear thinking." And so — I decided to supplement my "major" in philosophy with the equivalent of a second major in psychology. If the dignity of the field were to be salvaged (or discovered), then the boredom of studying it would simply have to be sustained.

The preceding insane rationale for what was to become my actual career choice was leavened by one bit of maturity. I was at least able to perceive that if one were to do philosophy of science, it was necessary for the doer to know one science well. I must, even as an undergraduate, have had an intimation that the then current atmosphere in philosophy would produce a crop of philosophers of science who, knowing virtually no physics (and with the traces of adolescent acne still decorating their faces), would be gravely informing their students that Einstein was "philosophically naïve." I suspect that even today one or two philosophers of science are still plying their craft in that way.

I do not remember a point at which I relinquished my literary ambitions (the presumption was that, come what may, I would continue to write genuine prose and perhaps poetry on the side), but I did persevere in the career choice just described. In 1938, I went for graduate work to the University of Iowa, mainly because Herbert Feigl—who at that time was the only member of the Vienna Circle concentrating on methodological problems of psychology—was there, and also because of the presence of Kurt Lewin. As a bonus, Kenneth Spence, too, materialized; it was his first year at Iowa. I worked closely with all three men, and to this day do not regret that circumstance. I came to reject, in different degrees, the ideas of all three, but men can be better than their ideas and *these* men were of high altitude. I learned much from them.

Though I enrolled at Iowa as a student in philosophy, I soon concluded that responsible methodological work concerning a discipline required not merely a high order of knowledge about that discipline but intimate immersion in its research processes from within. I therefore transferred to psychology at the end of my first semester. Whatever the anguish of association with our discipline, this is another of my early decisions which I regard as non-callow. If methodology is not pursued indigenously, it is worse than useless. I have believed that throughout my career—and have seen the point confirmed too fulsomely over the same interval.

My Master's thesis, written under Feigl, sought to convey to psychologists the logical positivist codification of scientific theory more accurately than had been done by the few psychologists who had already touched on this theme, and to show the power of the approach by applying it to the concept of "motivation" (with especial reference to the motivational thinking of Hull, Tolman, and Lewin). I could not have chosen a more felicitous topic. Psychology was already within what I have called in later writings its "Age of Theory." The period dominated by *classical behaviorism* had led to little more than an accumulation of particularistic and unrelated findings. By the early thirties, psychologists were learning from Hull (and, indirectly, from the philosophers of science) that there had been a slight oversight in the Watsonian program. It was, apparently, not enough to emulate the objectivistic experimentalism of physics; it was equally important to emulate its powerful and rigorous *theoretical* methods. Such admonitions were usually conjoined with the good news that certain philosophers of science had already rendered into easy pedagogical form the mysteries of the theoretical trade. Within this atmosphere, my thesis was rapidly seen as a graven message, which—though it had descended from the mount in the sweaty hands of a first-year graduate student—just could bring psychology into its long promised land.

Spence—who was then just beginning to establish his interest in methodology—was in my humble office virtually every afternoon during the writing of the thesis in quest of discussion and bibliographic advice. He advised me to publish the masterpiece at the earliest possible date, seeming actually to believe that the fate of psychology would be deeply affected by the event. I did publish it some two years later in the form of two articles in the *Psychological Review* entitled "The Logical Character of the Motivation Concept" (1941a, 1941b). Almost instantly, these papers began to appear on the required reading lists of advanced courses and proseminars in psychology departments around the country. Short of a diatribe that I addressed to the Encounter movement a few years ago (1973a), these papers stand up as the most widely read artifacts that have flown from my pen. To me, they also stand up as the silliest and most superficial documents I have ever written: they fall into a genre that could be characterized as falsetto stipulations of self-righteous but ignorant minds. A more conventional name for the genre is "manifestos on the technique of theory construction."

Having heard that Köhler was moving to Duke University (the rumor proved erroneous) and having been offered an attractive stipend there, I transferred from Iowa to Duke after the completion of my Master's. Immediately upon arrival in Durham (fall, 1939), I learned that Spence had been trying to reach me (I had spent a month or so in New York). Spence had shown my thesis to Hull at some point after my departure; Hull wanted the author at Yale; neither knew the author's whereabouts. I contacted Hull and was advised to stand by in Durham while the difficult problem of finding a stipend at that late date was addressed. For a few weeks I did not unpack, but the upshot was negative. A close miss! But now and then I have wondered where our anti-hero's head (and perhaps the rest of him) would be if that stipend had materialized.

Though I was staggered by the provinciality of life at Duke (to a degree in excess of the traumatic shock imparted to a callow New York intellectual by Iowa City), it has long been clear to me that the Duke association could not have been more fortunate. The Department was a cozy entity in those days, but it prided itself on its catholicity of purview and contained some people of exceptional quality. Its founder, William McDougall, had been responsible — as I early learned — for its intellectually open, nonmainstream tone, and from what I soon began to learn about him, I regret to this day that I never knew him. He had died the year before I arrived. The two men towards whom I early gravitated — and who ultimately became close colleagues — were not, and never did become, as well known as my mentors at Iowa, but Donald K. Adams and Karl E. Zener were, in my estimation, among the most gifted psychologists of the century. They were self-determining, cultivated, original, and utterly above those compromises of curiosity, intellectual dignity, and character which make for success in American scholarship. It is heartbreaking not to have the time to tell you a little about the quality and style of these men. I have, however, published a memoir of Karl Zener (1969b [chapter 13]) which I think the best thing I have written — for it describes a man whose emulation by psychologists could settle all doubts about the dignity of our field.

My main intent as a graduate student at Duke was to implement my resolve to plunge into the empiristic mud of research. Naturally, my companion in the venture was to be the rat. And it was equally natural that the problem be fraught with theoretical significance: indeed, it was to be a "differential test" of Hullian versus Lewinian theory. I will not even bother to describe the rather arbitrary performance situation selected as the arena for the differential test. In any case, "postulates" were established; theorem-pairs (some of them conflicting) were derived in quasi-Euclidian form; apparatus was constructed (by our fumbling anti-hero); rats were run for some four hours a day over some year and a half (the profound problem demanded a design that was time-extensive and labor-intensive); calculators were interminably cranked; and Lewin won — by a slight margin. The whole problem, of course, had been premised on the belief, reflected in every syllable of my Master's piece, that differential test of rival and properly formalized theories would automatically move psychology towards integration and consensus. But even as I wrote the dissertation, a large part of me knew that it was not Lewin who had won the competition with Hull; it was I. And was Hull, Hull? No. He, too, was me. Both theories were indeed far too gappy to be brought to bear on the concrete situation I had chosen — or indeed on any. And they were differentially gappy. Hull was Swiss cheese, the holes of which I had arbitrarily to fill. Lewin was Swiss cheese with no cheese; perhaps a little rind. Yet my belief in the infallible productiveness of the policy of formalization and differential test was hardly dented. Though all of my ensuing research experience (and much of my thinking) brought it harrowingly into question, it was some ten years before I explicitly renounced it.

Upon completion of the dissertation (summer, 1942), I was asked to stay on in the Department. It was war-time, and my heroic war contribution involved something close to round-the-clock teaching of a joint course in general and military psychology to Naval and Marine officer candidates in a program that had been instituted at Duke. Around the edges of this, I taught a few courses for non-military students (one of them in the field, corrupt as was its object, called "propaganda analysis" — which had a great currency during the war); I participated ineptly in some survey research for the Government; and I found some time for a little "serious" research and writing.

In a year or two, it was possible to reembrace the rat laboratory and to do occasional writing on theoretical themes. The research concentrated on problems involving the interrelations of motivational, learning, and performance "variables," and was prosecuted between (roughly) 1943 and 1952. Initially it was done in collaboration with William J. Daniel (a crisp experimentalist and a buoyant, witty man with a marvelously scatological tongue, who remained one of my dearest friends until his death in 1967), and later, in collaboration with a succession of graduate students.

The research sequence was rooted in the besetting theoretical issues of the day which, of course, inevitably meant "Hull versus X." While I was still a graduate student, Hull had sent me an early draft of what became *Principles of Behavior* (1943), and I had led a seminar for my fellow students on that material. By the time I commenced my post-doctoral research, I had developed a rich culling of implausibilities and lacunae in the theory which invited empirical determination. Daniel and I started with a measurement of "reaction potential" (responses to extinction in a Skinner box) under conditions of "maximal habit strength" (seventy previous reinforcements under a standard strong hunger) and "zero concurrent drive" (meaning hunger-satiation). Hull's cosmically general "postulate 7" purporting to define the role of all drives in their dynamogenic impact on all learning structures in determining the strength of all behavior for all organisms — and to state this "quantitatively" — had demanded an implausibly high value for the condition when there is no current drive whatsoever. This Homeric multi-variable function had been based on Skinner box data from a few groups of Yale-matriculated rats, and the zero-drive point was conspicuous among the infinite number of points representing pure extrapolation. In a study involving an obsessive replication of all ascertainable experimental conditions constitutive of Hull's induction base (and using a Yale-manufactured replica of the original apparatus), we found almost precisely zero reaction potential at zero drive.

In subsequent experiments, my collaborators and I did work on other "low" levels of hunger; on the so-called problem of "irrelevant drive"; on the role of drive in habit acquisition (in contradistinction to performance); on what Skinnerians had called "operant level" as a function of perceptual characteristics of the manipulandum; and on other matters. But for reasons which, at the time, I was reluctant to formulate even to myself, I had a sub-standard disposition to publish most of the findings. Nor, for that matter, did I ever get around to publishing my doctoral study.

The experiment with Daniel (Koch and Daniel 1945) and another study of similar cast involving weak intensities of hunger, with I. J. Saltzman (Saltzman and Koch 1948), *were* published. They received considerable attention in the literature, but the only acknowledgment from Yale (before 1951) was an article written by an assistant of Hull's which sought, by a wildly ornate and arbitrary argument, to explain the Koch-Daniel results away. However, when Hull massively revised the theory of *Principles of Behavior* in his subsequent book, *Essentials of Behavior* (1951) — in response not to evidence but to the dictates of a laborious "quantificational methodology" purporting to alleviate the purely illustrative character of the mathematical trim in the earlier theory — he *did* acknowledge our evidence. But *now*, its use was in *support* of the new (and, in the opinion of most, degraded) theory. Our spurious findings had become authentic ones as soon as the theory had evolved in such a way that their negativity became positivity!

Despite sub-surface qualms about my rat research, I continued in my early post-doctoral years to percolate happily as a comparative analyst of theory and sententious logical positivist law-giver. Or so it would appear if one had read the modest stream of my publications during that period, or taken my courses — especially my graduate courses in theoretical psychology, which I began to give immediately after the war had liberated me for matters higher than military psychology. My reputation burgeoned moderately in consequence of a number of book reviews written during this period, including a long review (1944) in the *Psychological Bulletin* of Hull's *Principles of Behavior.* They were written from a confident logical positivist bias, and were stridently critical of informal, sloppy, or indeed "literary" theorizing. The review of *Principles of Behavior* is an interesting artifact of my own cognitive pathology as then in force. Though I had more detailed insight into the empirical, and indeed conceptual, inadequacies of the theory than could have had other contemporary readers, the review was highly enthusiastic. After all, the author had met the terms of my overarching belief system: he had striven towards hypothetico-deductive explicitness and rigor; he had been bold in the right way. But amusingly, the brief *critical* section at the end of this largely expository review can be read almost as an outline for the devastating judgment's of Hull's effort that I was to come to in my analysis of 1954.

So much for a vignette of my origin point qua scholar. But scholarship in our time is a strange activity. It rarely engages the resources of the total person. In too many fields, security has come to be sought by evasive simplifications of the subject and aims of inquiry — sometimes to a degree tantamount to total evasion. Such a set produces a cascading of silly assumptions, silly profession-centered myths, silly questions. Soon, the backlog of these obscures whatever it was within the domain that invited interest. The novitiates in such fields, though some may see around the edges of the profession-sanctioned madness, have not the strength to challenge such authoritative madness. Funny things happen to the minds of young — and, too often, mature — scholars. The absurd becomes the profound; the silly, the deeply serious. I was inducted into a generation of scholars that did not bat an eyelash when Tolman closed his 1938 Presidential Address with the words:

> I believe that everything important in psychology (except perhaps such matters as the building up of a superego, that is everything save such matters as involve society and words) can be investigated in essence through the continued experimental and theoretical analysis of the determiners of rat behavior at a choice point in a maze.

For Tolman (by no means a simple-minded man), the parenthetical reservation perhaps registered guilt but had little impact on his theoretical behavior. For others — it is possible to believe that the properly tough-minded among them did not even note the qualification. As for me — in the preface to my doctoral dissertation I had gallantly acknowledged the existence of World War II by suggesting that the study to be reported, however esoteric, could well — by advancing fundamental psychology — diminish the chance of future wars. My response to a world in conflagration was to echo Tolman's point! But like it, my response expressed guilt — and perhaps doubt.

There was in me a severe malaise of spirit which I warded off by an excess of certitude; indeed, a jaunty crassness not uncommon among my peers and seniors. The most telling manifestation was that I became a divided being, *not* in a conflicted way (that would have been healthy!) but in an absolute and osmosis-proof way. My early passions for literature and the arts—and indeed other artifacts of the human universe—were, if not totally obliterated, hermetically sealed off. My *scientific* thinking was not to be vulgarized by such matters! Though I had been a voracious and venturesome reader between approximately my twelfth and twenty-first years, my excursions into literature all but disappeared except for occasional fugues when I would defect from science and read in a driven and guilty way for a week or two. The intention to continue with creative writing was utterly quashed. Though I had seen poetry as a central calling, it was no longer possible for me even to *read* poetry. I remain anaesthetic to poetry to this very day.

And this malaise of the spirit had an agonizing impact on the mode of my *scholarly* work. In short, I loathed the work, was embarrassed and even cynical about my identification with psychology. Though it is my good fortune never to have been an ambitious person, my work pattern became painfully sporadic; I tended to work in consuming bursts separated by long intervals of glazed vegetation. This pattern has not much changed over the years.

The story of my professional development is thus essentially that of the gradual growing together of the fragments of my fractured personhood: the rearticulation of whatever is human in me with my formal "calling."

Concluding

I conclude, then, at the beginning.

I have concentrated on the story of my professional "origin point" because I think it as much an account of an archetype as it is of an interval in the life of one anti-hero. Psychology can be nothing save a malign and deceitful joke if its scholars do not bring their full human resources to the process of inquiry. Yet its atmosphere—educational, cognitive, valuational—works towards attenuation and denial of the very qualities in its inquirers which could render their inquiry worthwhile. In each fumbling pilgrimage towards dignity, there is the chance of discovering—perhaps enlarging—the dignity of the field. I know that my own anti-heroic pilgrimage has been largely a failure. Whether it has been an utter one, I mercifully cannot know. But it is possible to hope that younger and more courageous pilgrims will find the initiation-archetype I have sought to convey instructive. Time, I fear, has not invalidated the applicability of that archetype.

It is far more important to sense the terms of one's career predicament qua psychologist than to know the particularities of any single journey towards its resolution. If I were some day to set down that part of the story, I should have to make some anti-heroic confessions that could serve as useful cautions to other travelers. A vagrant sampling follows:

• *Some* of those who do not think me a morally and mentally deteriorated defector from scientific purity see me as self-determining and possessed of some intellectual courage. Yet my movement towards rearticulation was slow, and not devoid of fear. The theory of my journey is, in a word, adventitiousness. At no point did I heroically invite the return of my walled-off oracles. Rather, I continued to ply my theoretical and analytical trade, and it was the attritional impact of psychological history upon my philosophical tools, and the frangibility of those tools in the very process of my using them, that rendered the walls breachable. The oracles stealthily crept back—in a condition so emaciated that often a return went long unnoticed.

By the mid-to-late-forties, I was fulsomely apprised of the deficiencies of the positivistic picture of science: its hyper-rule-saturated character; the untenability of the distinction between the context of justification and the context of discovery; its failure to arrive at an intelligent or intelligible analysis of the notion of "interpretation" of formal systems, and the corollary deficiencies in its analysis of empirical definition and of "cognitive significance"; its dogmatic and thin conception of the task and nature of philosophy. I was aware that these and many other failings were not corrigible inadequacies of detail but silly manifestations of a central—and total—neglect of the human context and agency of science. Yet I did not put the picture together in any figural way—whether in my head or in print—till the mid-fifties. Similarly, by the mid-forties I was apprised of the epistemological inadequacies of the behaviorist program; its quality of conceptual double entendre; its distorting impact on problem selection and trivializing impact on problem "solution." And indeed, by 1949 I was well into an analysis of Hull that showed there to be not a single determinate concept, or concept-linkage, within the entire—presumably rigorous—theoretical array. Yet the first time I declared the behaviorist program a failure in practice and infeasible in principle was in a rather fugitive contribution to a symposium held by the Minnesota Center for the Philosophy of Science in 1954. And, so far as I can recall, I did not publish that judgment before 1961 (reprinted as Koch 1965 [chapter 7]) — though there *were* strong innuendos concerning the matter in my 1954 assessment of Hull's theory, and in a paper of 1956.

• Would I have had the daring to depart from the mainstream to any appreciable extent if I had not enjoyed the intellectual freedom and security of the Duke Department, and the support and inspiration of the two exceptional colleagues whom I have mentioned? Karl Zener in particular set for me a model of trenchant and restive skepticism concerning central-tendency ideas and values, of investigative ardor and breadth, of relentlessness in the pursuit of *meanings* rather than verbal surrogates for knowledge, of personal wholeness and dignity both in and out of scholarship, which I could only feebly emulate. Of him I have said, "If I were a Plato, he would have been my Socrates. But I am no Plato."

• I have mixed feelings about my ten-year dedication to *Psychology: A Study of a Science* (Project A, as it was known before publication). They were the most vigorous years of my maturity, and one inevitably raises poignant historical "ifs" about the disposition of such years. I did, however, manage to lead a double life: full-time midwife to the ideas of others and part-time conceiver of my own. And the rate and depth of change in my thinking have certainly not been comparable in any other period of my life. Would such changes have happened if *not* for the exceptional challenge posed by the Project? And could I have allowed my thinking to become quite so outré, if not for the respectability loaned me by association with that augustly sponsored and glittering enterprise?

• Whatever dignity is achievable by analytic work alone — even a form of analysis meant to liberate and potentiate others for creative thinking — is a pallid thing. The bulk of my career has been given to analysis, and I have been derelict and cowardly in having given so little play to the creative oracles that conceivably lurk within me. My constructive work has been limited to two themes: the theory of definition (chapter 5) which I described towards the beginning of this talk (and which, not surprisingly, chose "dignity" as a prototype lexical unit in its initial formulation); and an empirical theory of value (chapter 6) which, via a radical reconception of the nature of motivational process, makes it difficult to doubt that value events occur as objective characters of experience, and are related in lawful ways to the biological and, ultimately, "stimulus" processes of which experience is a function. I joined both of these themes in the mid-fifties (apparently my best years) while Project A was in mid-course, and have returned

39

to them sporadically over the years. My work on them is certainly the best work I have done. The theory of definition, I boldly believe, takes one a decent distance towards a correct phrasing of the nature of inquiry and of knowledge. My work on "value properties" establishes a meaningful and researchable basis for aesthetics, and illuminates other axiological concerns such as the relations of science and value. Yet I have published only sparingly on them (1956, 1961b, 1965, 1969d, 1973a, 1976a), and indeed, did not publish a substantial treatment of the thinking that went into my 1959 paper on definition (1959b) until 1975 (1976a). And far worse, I have been derelict in not giving these ideas the effort and passion that their useful implementation might require.

• And I have been a cop-out in more significant ways. I have not only retreated from the labor of developing my few interesting ideas; I have on occasion retreated from psychology—and indeed, scholarship—altogether.

And finally: how does it add up at age sixty? I can find only two positive entries—both ambiguous—in the ledger.

First, *Psychology: A Study of a Science* did, I think, make some tenuous contribution towards the dignity of our field. At the time of the Project's design (circa 1952–53), American psychology was controlled by something much like an official "meta-methodological" covenant stipulating the one true path to scientific virtue. To some of us it seemed grievously clear that the attendant method-fetishism was acting as a stifling constraint on the ranges of curiosity asserted in inquiry, and that even the interesting work in progress (of which our field has never been devoid) was done at the price of punishing stresses against canon law. If liberation were possible, what better strategy than invite a large number of our most creative inquirers to test that epistemology—explicitly and in detail—against their own inquiring histories. The results did in fact subject the official "Age of Theory" premises to massive—and conspicuous—attrition. And, by training analytical attention on a wider range of theoretical activities than had been customary among practitioners of the "methodological" genre, the Study picked up—and by reflection augmented—many of the newer interests which by now have carried fundamental psychology far past its frenzied preoccupation with "learning." Did it *destroy* the old meta-theoretical armamentarium? That depends on how one reads! In historical terms, no. Hypothetico-deductive theories have given way to "models" and "models" to "paradigms." And these words do mark changes—often liberalizations—in conceptions of inquiring polity. But, sometimes overtly and sometimes in disguise, certain of the old icons survive. One of the more depressing laws of cognitive pathologistics is: "*sufficiently* bad ideas are immortal." Take the notion of "operational definition" as a triumphant example! But, in general, I think it can be said that *Psychology: A Study of a Science* did generate a rhetoric that helped make citizenship in psychology more tolerable.

Second, in the summer of 1964, I worked feverishly on volume 7 of *Psychology: A Study of a Science* in the hope of completion (dashed, I fear) before my departure-date for the Ford Foundation. Karl Zener was reading my material as it came off the typewriter. A few weeks before he died, he handed back the chapter entitled "Motivation and Value Properties" (which included a sustained analysis of the meaning-contour of "elegance" as a prototypical "objective" value property) and said with genuine enthusiasm: "Marvelous, you have *now* salvaged two words: 'dignity' and 'elegance.'" If Karl—who always overvalued me to an absurd degree—were right, I would be glad to rest my career on that two-word corpus. But even so, they are only words.

Afterword

Nothing has happened since 1977 that would disqualify the preceding account as an adequate prolegomenon to this book. Despite my advancing years, I have neither embraced nor "discovered" any messianic idea, "new" or old, that would unify or reorient psychology, or human knowledge in general, or provide a convenient key to the cosmic ontology, or an ultimate key to why such a key cannot be found. I have not even solved the mind-body problem. Many of my nonmainstream colleagues (of which the number burgeons) have achieved one, several, or all of the above—whether through the fast acquisition of a mantra or a rapid dip into advance-fringe interpretations of the "new" (i.e., *post*-post-classical) physics. Nor has my continuing—indeed, growing—sensitivity to the broad (and principled) constraints upon whatever can be called rational in human inquiry or creative performance given way to systematically "irrationalist" or "anti-rationalist" proclivities. My sense of the fragility, openness to revision, and necessary contextualism of any "method," and of the subtlety of the tacit skills upon which the meaningful application of any "rule" must depend, has not developed into the "anti-method" phobia that has recently inhabited some persons in philosophy whose views bear superficial similarities to certain of my own. Though at one time I was seen (if seen at all) as a candidate for incarceration in a rubber room, I am probably now more likely to be thought a somewhat inhibited libertarian.

Whatever *has* happened in my work since 1977 that might bear on the purposes of this book can be described on three fronts.

• Having abjured for all time the role of editor upon completion of the six-volume study of the status of psychology, I found myself adventitiously propelled into a second assumption of the role in 1979. In that year—when psychology's formal *centennial* as an "independent, experimental science" was being celebrated by the American Psychological Association—I happened to be president of two of its Divisions: General Psychology (Division 1) and Philosophical Psychology (Division 24). It seemed appropriate to devote the entirety of the annual convention programs for these Divisions to a series of symposia in which leading representatives of major fields of "fundamental" psychology would take a backward glance at how their fields had fared over the century. In the event, the papers were sufficiently probing, honest, and revelatory of attitudinal changes in psychology as a whole to render me susceptible to a second attack of the editorial affliction. With Dr. David Leary (who had served as program chairman for both Divisions) assisting, an anthology was projected—on the assumption that I could contain my obsessiveness to the extent of adjusting a few commas, and complete that process within a few months. It eventuated that there were also semi-colons to consider and, then, words, sentences, and other matters. Editorial obsessiveness *was* curtailed; manuscript went to the publishers within two years. (My earlier study of the status of psychology had required ten!)

The book that resulted, *A Century of Psychology as Science* (Koch & Leary 1992), can be seen as a miniature—and editorially less interventionistic—successor to the six-volume *Psychology: A Study of a Science,* which enables a second fix upon the status of the discipline two decades after the original one. The pooled verdict of the forty-two contributors to *A Century of Psychology as Science* can be seen to confirm and, more broadly and deeply to implement, trends that were already visible in the earlier study (cf. Koch 1959a). At surface levels, the "Age of Theory" attitude complex is a thing of the past. At sub-surface levels, the reading must be more ambiguous (cf. Koch 1992b, 962–67).

• My pursuit of themes related to the "pathology of knowledge" has not abated. This is reflected, in part, by further thinking concerning the impact of psychology on twentieth-century culture and sensibility (cf. chapter 9); by my speculations concerning the existential predicament that undergirds and fuels ameaningful thinking (cf. chapter 15); and by other concerns such as my reinspection of the scandalous history of what happened to P. W. Bridgman's ideas in psychology (chapter 14).

• In 1982, circumstances finally permitted me to mount a project on the arts which I had contemplated for twenty-five years. The "Aesthetics Research Center" at Boston University was based on the obvious, but hitherto bypassed, idea that those most intimately concerned with the creation of art might provide more authentic and differentiated insight into the conditions of its generation and apprehension than the externally situated aesthetician (whether philosophic or "experimental"). I hope it will be evident from the material in the following Appendix that many of the themes addressed in the Aesthetics Research Project are organically related to my views (cf. chapter 6) concerning the implications of the concept of "value properties" for aesthetics. In a sense, then, the Project can be seen as an implementation of a line of abstract thinking concerning central problems of psychology that I commenced many years ago. In another and more general sense, the Project is an illustration of the kind of collaboration between psychologists and humanists that I have long deemed requisite to the address of humanly important "phenomena" within the presumed purview of psychology. Whether the outcome be specifically allocatable to a "discipline" called psychology, or to some composite area for which there is no standard name in the map of scholarship, is of little moment.

Appendix: The Aesthetics Research Center[1]

The Aesthetics Research Center was inaugurated in January, 1983, to implement a program of systematic study of artistic endeavor and experience. Its primary aim was to secure the collaboration of major artists in studies

1. This material is drawn from some of Koch's unpublished writings, notably the texts of presentations to the American Psychological Association annual meeting in 1992 and 1993. One manuscript is entitled "The state of the art in the psychology of the arts," another, "Genesis and plan of the Aesthetics Research Project," and a third, "Some brief generalizations concerning the results of the Aesthetics Research Archive Project." The project is also presented in some detail in the November–December 1987 issue of the Boston University Magazine, *Bostonia* (Queijo 1987).

Partly in light of his writing above of having "hermetically sealed off" his "early passions for literature and the arts" (p. 37), it may be worth recording that—in one of his APA presentations—Koch reported that "while at Duke in the early sixties, [he] had formed the conception of a small Institute which would launch a program of research in the arts. . . . The main emphasis was to have been the elicitation from artists of detailed phenomenologies concerning matters of process and craft. Certain lines of more formal research—especially on problems relating perception psychology to the fine arts—were also envisaged. Two colleagues—Karl Zener and Mercedes Gaffron—were to have been associated with that enterprise." *Eds.*

of their own work. The Center brought to the University for extended conversations mature artists of very high caliber. During a pilot phase, two hour "research conversations" were conducted with four local artists, three of them faculty members of the Boston University School of the Arts: Jacques Cartier (theater director), Joseph Ablow (painter), and Joyce Mekeel (composer and music theorist). A fourth conversation was with Louise Vosgerchian, Professor of Music at Harvard (concert-pianist and music theorist). The discussions were intended to test particular modes and lines of questioning and to resolve technical problems of recording, situational ambience, etc. Typically there were three questioners, all familiar with the work of the artist under study.

The next step was to go on to four full-scale, but still exploratory studies with major artists. In each study, three co-inquirers (all artists or critics chosen for their knowledge of the work of the visiting artist) added their own perspectives to the conversations, but each in a different session. (It had already been determined that including more than three persons at a time in any conversation transformed the session into something more like a seminar than a conversation.) The participants were Virgil Thomson (composer and critic); Zelda Fichandler (founder and producing director of the Arena Stage, Washington, D.C.); Barbara Weisberger (founder and director of the Pennsylvania Ballet); and Phyllis Curtin (opera singer and voice teacher).

The full study was finally begun in 1986 with the help of a grant from the Ford Foundation. The grant derived from an allocation dedicated to archival studies in the arts—which meant that we had to accommodate our plans to the production of an archival outcome. We became the "Boston University Aesthetics Research Archive," and early on arranged with the special collections branch of Boston University's Mugar Library to deposit our material.

Accommodating to an archival interest had a minimal impact on our mode of work; mainly, we were impelled to improve our recording technique, and also the aesthetic dignity of the recording site. In any event, the plan involved a rather more crisp version of what had evolved during the pilot period. And since I had determined that a two-month interval was the optimal time for the spacing of studies, it was clear that only six or seven artists could be studied per year.

Emphasis in the selection of artists was placed on seniority and recognized excellence. In composing the group, a varied representation of arts was intended but not by any means a systematic representation. In any conflict between intrinsic excellence (or long-term impact) as the basis for selecting a person, versus the balancing of fields, the former criterion always prevailed.

Who were the participating artists? From January 1, 1986, through the end of 1988, we were able to complete twelve studies. I will list the artists in the order of their participation: Eric Hawkins (choreographer and dancer); Norman Dello Joio (composer); Edward Albee (playwright); Ulrich Franzen (architect); Saul Bellow (novelist); Mercedes Matter (visual artist and art educator); Arthur Miller (playwright); Milton Babbitt (composer); Toni Morrison (novelist); Richard Wilbur (poet); Edward Larabee Barnes (architect); Violette Verdi (ballerina and company director).

Each artist was invited to visit the University for two full days. Two research conversations (each of two hours' length) were held each day. The initial conversation was always conducted tête-à-tête with the project director; the others usually (but not always) involved the participation of a third person (whether artist, critic, or scholar) chosen on the basis of familiarity with the artist's oeuvre or field.

The areas of questioning — and particular questions — were chosen relative to detailed initial knowledge of the artist's oeuvre or background. Considerably before each study, I got from the artist as much personal and professional documentation as was available. I also immersed myself in everything the artist had published or recorded, and in the critical and biographical literature bearing on the artist. After such preparation, I worked out in advance a detailed discussion "scenario" for each of the four sessions which constituted a given study. This was not an interview checklist, but a detailed set of discussion themes designed to tap the artist's special knowledge in areas I anticipated to be maximally productive. The themes were used flexibly and in no fixed order during a given discussion. The aim was to allow for — indeed invite — organic development of each conversation.

The "expert discussants" who were brought in to join the conversations were selected early in the course of preparing for each study and were briefed in some detail concerning the plans for the sessions in which they were to participate. I might add that the "expert discussants" were of considerable stature in their own fields, and that they were always chosen subject to the suggestion, or the approval, of the artist.

I must stress that the atmosphere we sought to realize was not that of a sequence of interviews, but of *conversations*. The artists were not "subjects" who responded but collaborators who conversed. Discussants were encouraged not to shun disagreements or differences of perspective. The

45

occasional controversial interchanges were among the most productive interludes.

The content format for a typical study will show more clearly what we tried to do:

Session I: Personal and Professional Development. This conversation (two hours) was tête-à-tête between the artist and project director. An effort was made to supplement the established public record with information concerning factors that had helped form the artist's sensibility.

Sessions II and III: Process and Craft. These two sessions (four hours in all) formed a loose unit in which the artist addressed particularistically and in extenso his or her objectives, working methods and habits, craft emphases and discoveries, modes of preconceptualizing and executing given works. Typically, the discussion was organized around the artist's attempt to reconstruct the creative genesis ("life history" so to say) of one or more major works from the incubation phase through completion. This provided a line of continuity from which references to many other works in the artist's oeuvre could spin off. (Sessions II and III always included a third discussant deemed especially knowledgeable about the artist's work. The same discussant was usually included in both of these conversations.)

Session IV: Assessments of the Twentieth Century History and the Recent Status of the Artist's Field or Genre. In this conversation (two hours) the artist was asked to locate his or her own effort in relation to recent and current trends; to address the characteristic problems posed for his or her calling by this century; to extrapolate from present tendencies the prospects (in the near term and more remotely) for his or her field and for other arts. (A third discussant — whether artist, historian, or critic — believed to have a broad grasp of the modern history of the field in question was invited in this connection.)

Finally, some conclusions, generalizations, and perhaps even morals — relating to theory and method in the psychological studies — might be in order.

• All of the sixteen major studies (that includes the four ten-hour studies of the pilot) are, I have to believe, among the richest sources of artist-generated information concerning their own working methods, objectives, value-systems, "sensibility profiles" in history. And all, I think, are among the most vivid and comprehensive archival registrations of creative human beings in history. These are not my judgments alone; they are the judgments of many competent viewers.

• A guiding presumption of the Project was that artists have much tacit knowledge about the dynamics of their own operations—some of which can be rendered effable through particulate, far-ranging (and sympathetic) questioning. This presumption has been justified: the artist often arrives at insights which he or she had not previously formulated or "discovered"—sometimes insights and analyses of quite general significance which have not yet made their way into the corpus of human knowledge.

• A related, obvious, but not unimportant, conclusion is that artists are *not* a separate genus, but are persons who use in a special way faculties that all of us share.

• Artistic work requires frequent access to a particular mode of mental functioning often called the "creative state" (though I prefer a neutral designation like "State B"—cf. chapter 7). This is a hyper-energetic condition characterized by heightened mental fluency and spontaneity; totality of focus upon the work-context—indeed concentration to an extent that the "self" disappears: agent and problem (or object) fuse; thinking goes forward, so to say, autonomously. The detailed characteristics of this mode have been spelled out in remarkable unanimity by our artists. The ways of entering and sustaining this state vary widely, and the Project gives much concrete information about such matters.

• Though all of us are capable of "State B" interludes, few have learned to husband them for "creative" purposes, and some do not even note the difference between this condition and their more usual goal-oriented, daily striving. Our current culture, even our educational system, hardly acknowledges this distinction.

• The differences between artists and others are perhaps better characterized in *moral* terms than in the descriptive jargon of psychology. The artistic commitment requires enormous degrees of discipline, steadfastness, self-criticism, gallantry in the face of frustration, and indeed heroism in the disposition to confront and explore the full range of one's experience. There are many varieties and levels of *fear* associated with the work of artists.

At the present level of generality, most conclusions I have mentioned may not seem novel. The value of our studies is in the detail—and especially the source—of the findings. The Project's findings are not inferences from the "outside" made by scholars; they are the direct testimony of the artists themselves.

If these studies are seen as involving qualitative method, please note that my pilgrim's progress of collaboration with artists—though motivated by a strong but diffuse commitment—was almost wholly determined by adventitiously changing contexts, and that the ultimate modes of work were context-dependent choices. I did not lift a thing from any "qualitative method" rule book. Note further that, though I was seeking to determine the limits of making effable the tacit knowledge owned by human beings concerning their most complex and mysterious inner processes, I conducted myself as a *person,* not a psychologist, in this work. Any hint of psychodynamic eavesdropping or other professional voyeurism would have subverted the whole enterprise. In fact, I made no reference whatsoever to psychology during the conversations and never lapsed into jargon. The only references to psychological ideas were made by the artists (e.g., Albee on the "computer" model of memory)!

Yes, the "N" of this Project is very small. I had actually planned to include thirty artists, and further diversify the fields and modes of work represented. But each member of the "N" is precious; and the number (bearing in mind the specific occupants of my modest "N" of sixteen) is sufficient for a relevantly sensitive analyst to disembed important generalities concerning artistic work and, more importantly, the way these are qualified relative to the field of the artist, and unique characteristics of the artist's objectives and history.

And finally, I would like to assure all lonely workers in the idiom of qualitative research that the appropriately disciplined human mind is an enormously competent essence-extractor. You can take that figuratively or literally. Or you can perceive that the "figurative" often *is* the literal.[2]

2. Borrowing some of Koch's terms (see, for example, chapter 9, pp. 307–309), we believe that—as revealed through his interviews—the reflections of these disciplined connoisseurs have the potential to yield understanding of meaningful and creative human functioning that is not just ontology-respecting but also ontology-enhancing. *Eds.*

1

THE PROSPECTS AND LIMITS OF
A SIGNIFICANT PSYCHOLOGY

2

Psychology and Emerging Conceptions of Knowledge as Unitary[1]

Editors' Foreword

For reasons discussed in our preface, this chapter (Koch 1964) replaces Koch's original choice, a lengthy historical treatment of "The Age of Theory" that he had originally drafted for the postscript volume of *Psychology: A Study of a Science*. It contains what is perhaps his most vigorous and spirited critique of behaviorism, and also considers the role of neobehaviorism in the Age of Theory. This is set in the broader context of the relationship between the sciences and the humanities, and more generally, of a significant shift in the conception of knowledge that Koch saw under way in the late 1950s and early 1960s. It was one of the most influential of his writings.

The chapter was originally presented at a symposium at Rice University in 1963, which was published the following year under the title *Behaviorism and Phenomenology: Contrasting Bases for Modern Psychology* (University of Chicago Press). The other contributors were R. B. MacLeod, Norman Malcolm, Carl Rogers, Michael Scriven, and B. F. Skinner. For a scholarly volume, the book achieved a wide circulation.

I. Introduction

I can only believe that my title, submitted some months ago, was the product of a burst of sabbatical-induced euphoria. It would perhaps be well to neglect entirely what I had in mind by using this title, but that degree of

1. More detailed analyses of the history of behaviorism reflecting a point of view similar to the one taken in this paper may be found in Koch 1954, 1959a (esp. 733–49, 752–69), 1961a.

sobriety I cannot achieve. Behaviorism is a position whose implications transcend psychology. It is also one which has leaned heavily on extra-psychological sources of support and, indeed, owes its origin in large part to trends in the history of ideas that have formed modern man's general conception of the nature of knowledge. The career of behaviorism having thus been bound up with that of a widely deployed movement in recent culture, it is hardly likely that its fate will not be similarly bound. I propose, then, to honor the present title, if only to the extent of a few paragraphs which attempt to record what in some contexts is known to all of you but is not always sufficiently stressed in considerations of behaviorism: that there is currently taking place a sweeping redefinition by man of the nature of his own knowledge. An era in thought-about-thought is breaking up. A new one, with implications that justify the often abused adjective "revolu-tionary," is under way.

For more than a decade, processes of reappraisal have been going for-ward in almost every branch of intellectual activity, which, taken together, lend more than modest credence to the diagnosis just made. In science—despite a rate of technological and even fundamental advance almost in-credible relative to past history—a new humility has become evident. In both the natural and biological sciences there are conspicuous tendencies to perceive and point up limits; to acknowledge, in the very conception of inquiry, the importance of the uncodifiable; to view with respect other domains of cognitive activity, and to search for and recognize continuities with such domains. In literature, the congealed standards of the first half of the century are under scrutiny: some voices no longer fear to question the sententious judgmentalism of those who have defined "the modern tradition"; there is restiveness over certain consequences, if not always claims, of formalism and experimentalism; there is a disposition to surren-der some of the hypothetical riches of "ambiguity" for the austerities of meaning and to exchange the insularities of aesthetic cliquism for commit-tedness to life and its predicaments. One discerns similar evidences in the visual arts—even if more submerged by certain last-ditch assertions of the earlier twentieth-century values than in the case of literature. In reaction to the glut of "anti-art" produced by such noisy movements as abstract expressionism and action painting, voices here and there are beginning to decry the hegemony of "movements," and the restrictive aesthetic mys-tiques that have at once instigated and fed on them.

In the scholarly humanities, there is a new and constructive intransi-gence: a determination no longer to accept the indifference of a society whose values derive from idolatry of science; at the same time, a resolve not to find consolation in a philosophy of contempt for the uninitiate, but to re-examine rationales in such a way as to promote the spread of the humanist perspective in a world which much needs it and to discover the location and involvements of the humanities in the organism of knowledge. In education, there is much casting about — but in no direction so much as in that which seeks to embed particular knowledge in generality of purview, and to salvage that classical conception which sees knowledge not merely as instrumental or decorative, but as a terminal good.

In philosophy, the indications are perhaps most compelling of all. An era during which philosophy almost voted itself out of existence in its fervor for security is almost ended. Its surrender of its history, its shedding of metaphysics and axiology, its flight from substantive problems to those of method, its reduction of those of method to those of language — all these have come increasingly under question. Logical positivism is no longer with us. Analytic philosophy, which, on the surface, seemed to broaden the purview of positivism by extending analysis from scientific to natural languages but which at times achieved an even greater constriction by conceiving natural language as that of "common sense" per se, is in process of inviting back many of the recently proscribed fields and problems of philosophy. Ethics and value studies in general are back. Contraries of virtually every canonical resolution of specific epistemological problems, of the sort that held sway for thirty or forty years, are back. And they have been brought back in the hands of former logical positivists and current analytic philosophers — as well as by others.

Along with these local but cognate processes of reappraisal, interests in the total articulation of knowledge have been conspicuous for the past decade or so. Those asserting such interests have originated in each of the fields mentioned and in some few not noted. The area of concern is often couched in such terms as "the relations of the sciences and the humanities." It is widely supposed that *Year 1* of this concern commenced with C. P. Snow's Rede Lecture (Snow 1959), which gave currency to the phrase "the two cultures." One intends nothing invidious in noting that an explicit interest in similar problems has never been wholly absent since that point in history at which it became possible to discriminate "the sciences" from "the humanities," and further, that though such interests have been submerged during much of the present century, they were pursued with some ardor by the beginning of the fifties, if not before. In any event, there is by now more than a small literature (and in my opinion, a portentous one), the tendency of which is to seek reassessment of recently reigning conceptions of human knowledge in a way sensitized to the continuities within the processes that mediate inquiry in *all* fields and to the possible arbitrariness of such boundaries as those currently drawn to separate the major divisions of knowledge.

To this reinspection of the texture of knowledge, the major contributions have come, significantly enough, from physical scientists: outstandingly, Michael Polanyi (1951, 1958, 1959), but also men like Sir George Thompson (1961), J. Robert Oppenheimer (1955, 1962), J. B. Conant (1947, 1951), Gerald Holton (1952, 1960), Harold Gomes Cassidy (1962), and the Bridgman who wrote *The Way Things Are* (1959). The same context of thinking has been joined by scientists from other fields: e.g., the microbiologist René Dubos (1961), the paleontologist Loren Eiseley (1958, 1959, 1961), and the mathematician (also literary critic and historian of ideas) J. Bronowski (1951, 1959; Bronowski and Mazlish 1960). Again, this same context of thinking has been fed, perhaps less directly but with comparable significance, by those among the historians of science whose tendency—either explicit or implicit—has been to test reigning conceptions of the nature of science against the *facts* of inquiry (e.g., Alexandre Koyré [1939, 1957]; I. B. Cohen [1956]; Herbert Butterfield [1949]; Charles Coulston Gillispie [1960]; Thomas S. Kuhn [1962]), and those among the philosophers of science who seem most eager to adjust their view of science to the particularities of history, e.g., Stephen Toulmin (1953, 1961; Toulmin and Goodfield 1962) and N. R. Hanson (1958). This line of questioning has also received profit from the works of men who have sharply called recent philosophical orthodoxies into question, e.g., Brand Blanshard (1962) and Ernest Gellner (1959).

To such contributions there may of course be added those of the many individuals who have been drawn to a concern with "science-humanities relations" by Snow's controversial lecture (1959). The issue, as posed by Snow, has certainly become a cause célèbre. It has been the object of widespread comment in the popular and intellectual press and has set the topic for countless university symposia and pronouncements by educators. It has led to reassessments of the objectives of education by special study commissions (e.g., Leverhulme Study Group 1961), and inspired revisions—at the level of planning and sometimes of practice—of university curricula. It has even spawned several anthologies which seek to demonstrate the unity of knowledge by the culling of poems about science (e.g.,

Eastwood 1961), and at least one book which analyzes the artistic propensities of scientists as revealed in their technical drawings (Lapage 1961). One rather expects that the number of art exhibits sponsored by medical and dental associations is due for a sharp increase and that some enterprising theoretical physicists will soon be addressing the nature of things in the mode of Lucretius. Whatever the final value of this Snow-flurry, it is entirely evident that Snow had, in his phrase, "touched a nerve," indeed a massive and international one. And it would be unfair to leave any impression that the resulting discussion has been altogether fallow; not a few of the ideas have been constructive or clarifying.

While this wave of interest has gathered, psychology and the social sciences have stood on shore, almost untouched by the spray. Those who know the history of modern psychology (I will not speak for the social sciences, though I suspect that much of what I have to say is relevant) will find little cause for surprise in this. We are not known for our readiness to be in the wavefront of history. It could almost be maintained that modern psychology ran out of its independence at the moment of declaring it. In every period of our history, we have looked to external sources in the scholarly culture—especially natural science and the philosophy of science—for our sense of direction. And typically we have embraced policies long out of date in those very sources. What is unique about our present lag relative to the rest of scholarly culture is that each branch of the latter seems to be either working toward, or inviting into existence, a redefinition of knowledge based on an *empirical* analysis of inquiry of a sort which must largely depend on *psychological* modes of analysis. Indeed, extant efforts in this direction everywhere involve psychological commitments, often of a rough and ready sort. Yet psychology seems hardly cognizant of the challenge implicit in these circumstances. Or of the circumstances.

More curiously still, the emerging redefinition of knowledge is already at a phase, in its understanding of the particularities of inquiry, which renders markedly obsolete that view of science still regulative of inquiring practice in psychology. This can be said in utter literalness, for the view in question was imported, with undisguised gratitude, from the philosophy of science and related sources some three decades ago but, while remaining more or less congealed in psychology, was subjected to such attrition in the areas of its origin that in those areas it can no longer properly be said to exist. Psychology is thus in the unenviable position of standing on philosophical foundations which began to be vacated by philosophy almost as soon as the former had borrowed them. The paradox is now compounded: philosophy and, more generally, the methodology of science are beginning to stand on foundations that only psychology could render secure.

Strongest of all, the new interests in the particularities of inquiry and the interrelations of the resulting knowledge invite into existence precisely those curiosities, neglect of which has most thwarted the historically constituted aims of psychology. Whether these aims be stated in terms of the total functioning of the organism or in any others given by history, it is clear that problem selection has tended to be guided by simplistic presuppositions and that we have addressed only glancingly, if at all, those contexts of human function which are most valued by the judgment of civilization. It is precisely such knowledge which is now most wanted by the culture at large. But it is precisely such knowledge that is most wanting in psychology.

There is a strange circularity, then, in the predicament of psychology. Psychology has long been hamstrung by an inadequate conception of the nature of knowledge, one not of its own making. A world now in motion toward a more adequate conception begins to perceive that only psychology can implement it. Yet psychology is prevented from doing so because, almost alone in the scholarly community, it remains in the grip of the old conception. But this state of affairs could lead to a happy consequence: should psychology break out of the circle just described, it could at one and the same time assume leadership in pressing toward resolution of the central intellectual problem of our time *and* liberate itself for the engagement of bypassed, but important and intensely interesting, ranges of its own subject matter. Moreover, it can find courage to do these things in the circumstance that the very sources upon which it has most leaned for authority—physics and the philosophy of science—are, together with the rest of the scholarly community, urgently inviting them to be done.

Perhaps the most important *immediate* thing that could be done toward breaking out of this circle would be to lay to rest, once and for all, the incubus of behaviorism. In recent years, behaviorism has—reflexively as it were—almost accomplished such a maneuver on its own. But it has not gone at the matter with true élan. It needs help.

Behaviorism has been given a hearing for fifty years. I think this generous. I shall urge that it is essentially a role-playing position which has outlived whatever usefulness its role might once have had. If you expect me to support this statement via a final and crushing refutation of behaviorist epistemology, you will be disappointed. I suspect that there is a class of positions that are wrong but not refutable and that behaviorism may be in such a class. For many methodological proposals and for certain positions of metaphysical or even empirical import, I am not even sure what a "refutation" would mean. If behaviorism is advanced as a *metaphysical* thesis, I do not see what, in final analysis, can be done for a truly obstinate disbeliever in mind or experience, even by way of therapy. If it is advanced as a *methodological* thesis, I think it can be shown that (*a*) the conception of science which it presupposes (especially of concept definition and application and of verification) does not accord with practice even in those sciences which the position most wishes to emulate, and (*b*) that its methodic proposals have had extremely restrictive consequences for empirical problem selection and a trivializing effect upon the character of what are accepted as "solutions" by a large segment of the psychological community. More than this, I think that for both metaphysical and methodological variants of behaviorism (and I am not convinced that the methodological variety is quite so "uncontaminated" with metaphysics as stereotype would have it), the following can be said: These are essentially irrational positions (like, e.g., solipsism) which start with a denial of something much like a foundation-tenet of common sense, which *can,* in the abstract, be "rationally" defended for however long one wishes to persist in one's superordinate irrationality, but which cannot be *implemented* without brooking self-contradiction. The exhibition of such self-contradictions is, I think, as close to a "refutation" of behaviorism as one can reasonably get. But the task is made cumbrous, of course, by the behaviorist's tendency to cover up such discrepancies between precept and practice by artfully concealing both his analytic elisions and extra-systemic importations of experiential meanings (often effecting their invisibility even to himself). The usual device is a shifting use of an extraordinarily non-particulate and crassly defined technical ·vocabulary.

I cannot, in the present paper, develop all of the preceding lines of consideration or, indeed, any of them in the detail that would be desirable. I shall concentrate primarily on exhibiting the outmoded and inadequate character of the view of science to which most behaviorists still appeal in support of their epistemology and on certain of the pragmatic effects of that epistemology on problem selection and treatment. Since I have been asked to give my presentation a historical cast, I shall begin with a shamelessly abstract historical rundown of the chief phases of behaviorism in American psychology, and shall consider further topics via a medley of briefly considered illustrations, so that a broad historical picture may be suggested, if only dimly. If time remains, I should like to close with a few comments concerning phenomenological alternatives to behaviorism as they are currently shaping up.

II. Behaviorism
1. Historical

The story of the rise of behaviorism and of the neobehaviorist succession is familiar. But certain strands of it, especially if brought into relation with developments since about 1950, can yet be instructive. And the tendency of this latter interval—which can be called the period of neo-neobehaviorism—is perhaps not familiar, especially to the philosophers in the audience.

Classical Behaviorism

Classical behaviorism (1912–30) is best understood as a set of widely shared, if variably interpreted, orienting attitudes toward the business of psychology. As is well known, these included:

a) Objectivism. The insistence on objective techniques for securing data and the corollary disposition to (in Watson's phrase) "bury subjective subject matter." Again in the aseptic language of Watson, behaviorism "attempted to make a fresh, clean start in psychology, breaking both with current theories and with traditional concepts and terminology" (1929, 4). Only such observations were to be considered admissible as can be made by independent observers upon the same object or event—exactly as in physics or chemistry. Most of the time, Watson defended his central thesis on methodological grounds, but sometimes a metaphysical judgment to the effect that "mind" or "consciousness" does not exist is suggested. And there were other behaviorists in the classical interval, for example, A. P. Weiss, who were consistently and uncompromisingly metaphysical materialists.

b) S-R orientation. All lawful psychological statements are to be expressed in terms of stimulus and response. Watson's ambiguities in respect to the definition of these terms—his vagrant fluctuation between physical and molar-situational criteria of S and physiological versus molar-behavioral criteria of R—are notorious. The problems thereby raised plagued subsequent behaviorist writers, "classical" and "neo." As early as 1922, Tolman was exercised by such ambiguities and asserted his advocacy of a consistently "non-physiological behaviorism." Yet the issue received nothing re-sembling a consensus until the 1950s, and "resembling" is used advisedly.

c) Peripheralism. Watson's program necessitated that he consider how phe-nomena traditionally classed as "mental" might be treated in objective S-R terms. Most of his positive systematic ideas are thus attempts to show that processes formerly conceived as determined primarily by the brain could be better understood if allocated mainly to receptors, effectors, and their most direct nerve connections. Best known in this connection are Watson's motor theories of imagery and thinking, of feeling and of emo-tion. Somewhat more elaborated peripheralistic hypotheses were put for-ward during the classical interval by such writers as Smith and Guthrie (who, already in 1921, presaged, in such notions as the "maintaining stim-ulus," "pre-current response," and "readiness," peripheral mechanisms very much like Hull's S_D and r_G; see Smith and Guthrie 1921).

d) Emphasis on learning and on some form of S-R associationism as the basic laws of learning. Traditional psychology approached learning as subsidiary to sensory and perceptual problems. But an S-R psychology, by side-stepping perception, is prone to place central emphasis on learning. Moreover, by 1913 (the year that marks the formal advent of behaviorism), learning had proven a field eminently open to objective study. The story of how Watson came to fix on *conditioned reflex* principles as the basic laws of learning is of interest, from a "sociology of science" point of view. Some years ago, Lashley told it to Karl Zener and me on one of his visits to Duke. Watson spent much of the summer of 1916 in a frantic effort to obtain photo-graphic records of implicit speech movements. The hope was to present such pictures of the physical basis of thinking in his presidential address to the American Psychological Association which he was to give that fall. But about two weeks before the scheduled time for the address, it became ap-parent that success was not likely to be forthcoming. Watson rapidly shifted tack. Lashley, then a student in his laboratory, had been doing work on human salivary and motor conditioning. For his address, Watson (1916) hurriedly wrote up this research, along with a vigorous recommen-dation of the use of conditioning methods (then but slightly known out-side of Russia). Thereafter, he assigned progressively greater importance, not only to the utility of the *methods* (e.g., for the study of animal sensory acuity), but to the value of conditioning *principles* for the explanation of behavior. By 1924, he was prepared to phrase *all* problems of learning in terms of "conditioning."

e) Environmentalism. This hardly requires development. Watson's extreme position is well known. What is not comparably well known is that his unbridled assessment of the extent to which environmental "shaping" is possible did not become explicit in his writing until close to the end of his career as psychologist.

Neobehaviorism

Classical behaviorism had been an attempt to escape the stagnation of the subjectivist psychologies then prevailing by providing psychology with a *decision procedure,* which, it was hoped, would make forward movement inevitable. But though the position soon attained hegemony — Watson was correctly reporting the trend when, in 1924, he said, "Most of the younger psychologists realize that some such formulation as behaviorism is the only road leading to science" (p. vii) — it degenerated with comparable celerity into polemicism and inflated program-making. Neobehaviorism may be seen as a second attempt to provide psychology with a decision procedure — this time an effective one that would conserve the orienting attitudes of behaviorism but recast them in such a way as to give them teeth.

By the late twenties, there was much "objective" experimentation but few bodies of clearly stated predictive principles comparable to the crowning achievement of physics: its theories. Instead, experimentation seemed aimless, "theoretical" hypotheses but loosely related to data, and debate idle. The search for a "decision procedure" thus became a search for a formulary of the techniques for "constructing" *rigorous theory.* The incidence of the search for *objectivity* now shifts. Early behaviorism had primarily involved attempts to guarantee the objectivity of the descriptive (first-order) concepts used for empirical data. While not giving up this objective (and indeed trying to place its pursuit on a more secure footing), neobehaviorism sought to realize and implement objectivism at the level of theory. The idea was to ensure that all elements of a system language be "securely anchored" by explicit linkages to antecedent independent and consequent dependent variables and, in general, to effect a point-for-point correspondence of the logical properties of systematic formulations of psychology with those of psychology's traditional emulation-model, physics. In pursuit of these ends, psychology did not go directly to physics but turned instead for its directives to middlemen. These were, for the most part, philosophers of science (especially logical positivists) and a number of physical science methodologists who had been codifying a synoptic view of the nature of science and who, by the early thirties, were actively exporting that view from their specialties to the scholarly community at large. The view was based on a "rational reconstruction" of a few selected formulations in theoretical physics and put forward a detailed model of the scientific enterprise which came to be known as the "hypothetico-deductive method."

It would be revealing to reconstruct a little of the early history of this interaction between psychology and the "science of science." But I must hold myself to a few points:

The sources to which psychology turned in the early thirties for its model of science were primarily logical positivism, neopragmatism, and operationism. Because of objective consonances among these positions and certain sympathetic interactions among their holders, a complex and uneven fusion (to which the dominant contours were given by logical positivism) began to take place from the late twenties onward. It should be observed that psychology's selections from this cluster of formulations were spotty, adventitiously determined, and not supported by especially expert scholarship in the relevant sources.

The neobehaviorist period was ushered in by Hull's advocacy of hypothetico-deductive method. His advocacy, though fervent, was not sounded in the *technical* terms of the concurrent philosophical developments. Also, Hull's frequent recommendations and illustrations of axiomatic method during the early thirties tended not to include sustained consideration of problems of empirical definition. Though Bridgman's (1927) work had been cited by H. M. Johnson as early as 1930, it was not until the mid-thirties that a spate of articles on "operational definition" directed the attention of psychologists to empirical definition and produced the widespread impression that objectivism could be finally implemented only by careful "operational" practice. It was not until the late thirties that the preceding contexts of discussion were supplemented by analyses which explicitly took the logical-positivist model of science as regulative. Though initially recommendations of axiomatic method and discussions about operational strategy had tended to occur in somewhat separated contexts, both of these topics found an integrative framework in the formulations of logical positivism. Discussions and applications of positivistic meaning criteria soon began to appear in the literature side by side with operationist analyses. Throughout this entire sequence and down to this very day, no great clarity was achieved about these imported ideas: witness the tendency still prevailing on the part of many to use "logical positivism" and "operationism" interchangeably.

What in fact seems to have been the case is that psychology was enthralled by the apparent authority of these ideas, not their content. The large methodological literature by which they were conveyed from the glittering areas of their origin to psychology was prescriptive and zealous but, when written by psychologists, marked by modest orders of philosophical sophistication and, when written for psychologists by philosophers, vitiated by limited familiarity with the research problems of our science. What seems to have been imparted to the typical psychologist might be characterized as an ocean of awe surrounding a few islands of sloganized information, as for instance that a theory is an "interpreted formal system," that such systems are constituted by such and such "elements," that a theory makes contact with "observable states of affairs" via a specification of experimental "operations" or by means of a cryptic device known as the "reduction sentence."

Be all this as it may, psychology, in America at least, soon stabilized itself within the ambiance of the positivist-neopragmatist-operationist view of science (let us call it the "new view"). The hypothetico-deductive reconstruction of science that it put forward was open to the interpretation that properly rule-regulated scientific work was *self-corrective*, and thus it seemed to offer a more or less sure-fire instrumentality for scientific advance. Though neobehaviorists took the initiative in wiring the elements of this model into their scientific sensibilities, psychologists of other conceptual tendency followed suit in accepting the hypothetico-deductive model and other aspects of the "new view" in one or another degree.

A period of comparative optimism, which I have called in another connection the "Age of Theory," soon supervened: it was marked by a general feeling that psychology had finally arrived at the phase of progressive science. "Theory" tended to be conceived of as a *commodity*, the production of which could be scheduled by educating the work-force into the presumptive dictates of the "new view" of science. Theoretical publications in psychology tended increasingly to divide concern between translating the new view into stipulations of the objectives of "sound theory" for psychology and presentation of formulations intended to approximate such objectives.

It is hardly necessary to reconstruct the atmosphere of the Age of Theory, particularly that of its classical interval, say, from the mid-thirties to the mid-forties. The regulation of systematic work by the directives and imagery of hypothetico-deduction, the sub-culture surrounding operational definition, the lore concerning the intervening variable, the belief in the imminence (if not achievement) of precisely quantitative behavioral theory of comprehensive scope, the broadly shared judgments with respect to strategic foundation data, the belief in automatic refinement and convergence of theories by the device of "differential test," the fixed vocabulary for the comparative dissection and analysis of theory—all of these are easily recalled, if indeed recall is necessary. The rather stable geography of dominating theoretical positions and the standard contexts of apposition and opposition will also come easily to mind. These scattered fragments define an ideology not wholly discontinuous with that of the present.

In broad aspect, neobehaviorism may be seen as a marriage between the orienting attitudes of classical behaviorism and one or another interpretation of the "new" model of science. The general orienting attitudes are to be implemented by translation into theory, or theory-like formulations, in accord with the requirements of the model. As a result, the earlier attitudes are reasserted but in altered form. Thus, for instance, re *objectivism,* the metaphysical overtones of classical behaviorism are, at least by frequent asseveration, sloughed off and attempts are made in a variety of directions to find rationales for a consistently *methodological* objectivism. With respect to the earlier homogeneously *S and R framework,* it can be said that though S and R are retained as the end-terms of psychological analysis, most neobehaviorists sub-specify this framework at least to the extent of introducing into the causal equation for behavior certain concepts ("intervening variables") meant to represent "internal" behavior determinants. It is worth noting that in some neobehavioristic formulations there may be discerned a number of intervening variables (e.g., aspects of Hull's D, also I_R and $_sO_R$) which are not uniquely determined by (or inferable from) antecedent "stimulus" variables. In respect to the classical emphasis on *learning,* it is of course no secret that neobehaviorism preserved and perhaps heightened this emphasis, most neobehaviorist formulations being essentially "theories" of learning. At the same time, Watson's emphasis on Pavlovian *conditioning* principles gives way to a variety of emphases in which classical conditioning is subsumed under more general principles, supplemented, or reinterpreted. Most such emphases are further characterized by the attempt to achieve finer, more rigorous, and, hopefully, quantitative specification of the conditions of learning. The *peripheralism* of classical behaviorism is, of course, also retained, but with the difference that

63

attempts toward more particulate analyses of the consequences for behavior dynamics of certain peripheral "mechanisms" are made by some neobehaviorists, while the peripheralism of others of somewhat stronger "empty organism" predilection assumes the more purely methodological guise of restricting causal statements entirely to "observable events" at the periphery of the organism.

Adequate portrayal of neobehaviorism would, of course, demand lengthy development, not only of the preceding generalizations, but of others which would be needed to describe comparably definitive features. Here, however, I should like to expand very briefly upon a few characteristic aspects of neobehaviorism's defense of its *objectivist* epistemology, which topic is, after all, fundamental to assessment of the position.

Two of the outstanding contexts in which neobehaviorism has over the years tried to define and defend its *methodological objectivism* have been (*a*) a set of loose agreements concerning the legitimate *observation base* of psychology, and (*b*) the lore surrounding the *intervening variable paradigm* of theory construction.

a) Observation base. As already implied, the interval leading into the Age of Theory was marked by uneasiness over the mixed metaphysical-methodological grounds and the inconstant criteria developed by classical behaviorism in defense of its epistemology. Psychology needed a clear and, so to say, "connotationally uncontaminated" rationale for objectivism, a *consistently* methodological one. The "operational" criterion seemed to provide this, as did later certain other formulations of the empirical criterion of meaningfulness of the sort developed by logical positivism.

Though interpretations of technical meaning criteria imported from the philosophy of science were free and various, certain core beliefs concerning the legitimate observation base for psychological statements were common to all of them. It is significant that these commitments were historically prior to the importation of such criteria, and, after importation, they remained untouched by the frequent and radical changes in meaning theory which continued in normal course of professional epistemological scholarship.

Such rock-bottom commitments concerning the observation base may be suggested via the following reconstructions:

1. All lawlike statements of psychology containing *dependent variables* not expressible in, or reducible to, publicly verifiable and thus "objectively" observable *behavior* indexes are to be excluded as illegitimate. Such dependent variable terms are to be defined in the same observation terms as are

at the basis of physical science (weak form) and, perhaps, are even translatable into, or reducible to, actual descriptive and explanatory concepts of physics (strong form). The prototypical case of an admissible dependent variable is, of course, the notion of *response* or, more specifically, a "measurable" index of response, in some one of the varied, if often unspecified, meanings of "response."

2. Similarly, it is demanded that legitimate *independent variables* of psychology designate referents which can pass the test of independent, simultaneous observability *and* are definable in either the observation language of physical science or the concepts of physics. The prototypical case of an admissible independent variable is, of course, the notion of the *stimulus*, again in some one of many rather unseparated meanings. It should be noted that, in the case of the independent variable, the strong-form requirement of translatability into (or "connectability," in some strong sense, to) the concepts of physics has retained more general currency (as, e.g., in the "physical energy" criterion for the definition of the stimulus) than the analogous requirement for the dependent variable.

During the Age of Theory, these assumptions were embedded in, or rendered into the language of, the various "operational" or empirical meaning criteria imported from the methodology of science. The rather casual character of the relation between such technical criteria and these commitments concerning the observation base is indicated by the widespread presumption that the mere use of a language of stimulation and behavior, S and R, entails a built-in guarantee of semantic significance. Yet it must be noted that during most of the Age of Theory no great progress was made toward resolving the ambiguities in the definitions of S and R bequeathed by classical behaviorism. Hull, for instance, fluctuated between physicalistic and molar-behavioral (and in practice, experimenter-perceived) criteria of S and R as vagrantly as did Watson. Such tendencies are strikingly epitomized in Hull's theory by the fact that, though he carefully specified four response *measures* of the major dependent variables of his system (1943, 383), there is virtually no consideration of the R-term which the "measures" measure, nor is much concern given to estimating the empirical plausibility that the measures will co-vary. Guthrie was disposed to hold consistently to a physicalistic usage of S and R, but, as we shall see later, he himself makes clear in his last published article that his practice could not conceivably have been consistent with such usage. I am constantly told that Skinner has all along merited a clean bill of health in his "generic" concept of reflex and his analyses of the character of operant behavior. Perhaps this is so, but I must frankly confess that I have never been able to read his statements about his own scientific behavior in a univocal way and, further, that I suspect that though a definition of an R-class in terms of a physically specifiable "property upon which reinforcement is contingent" (1953, 66) may not create especial trouble when that class is apparatus-determined (as in the Skinner box), it can run into trouble in the context of such remote extrapolations of his principles as are involved in the analysis of "verbal behavior" and other citizenly pursuits.

b) The intervening variable paradigm. Nowhere is the intersection between the autisms of the Age of Theory and the "new view" of science better symbolized than in the *intervening variable paradigm.* Its appeal to Age of Theory systematists was twofold. First, it seemed to offer a guarantee of objectivism *at the level of theory.* The criterion of "firm anchorage" of theoretical concepts via explicit functional relations to antecedent and consequent "observables," beautifully fulfilled the yearning of the Age for a theoretical *decision procedure.* If inferred explanatory concepts were to be unequivocally linked to observables, no longer need there be fear of irresponsible constructions whose role within the theory is instant to the whim of the theorist (what Hull called "anthropomorphism . . . in behavior theory"). At the same time, the paradigm seemed to render into orderly and intelligible terms the problems confronting the psychological theorist: he needed three classes of variables; he needed the interconnecting "functions"; he needed a mode of inferring or constructing those functions; etc. Moreover, the schema was readily reconcilable with various elements of the "new view." The statements interlinking the three classes of variables could, if one so desired, be asserted as *postulates,* thereby making place for the paraphernalia and imagery of hypothetico-deductive method. The fervent drive toward *quantification* of systematic relationships could become the quest for quantitatively specified intervening variable functions. Of especial significance to our present concern, the demand for explicit linkages with observables could be equated with the demand for *operational* (or "satisfactory" empirical) *definition.* And, relative to all these happy desiderata, the schema included a built-in guarantor of success: a standard method—the "defining experiment"—for inferring postulates from experimental evidence. In briefest terms, the method was to select or design a series of experiments, the empirical variables of which would be placed in correspondence with (that is, "represent" or "realize") the *theoretical* variables whose relations were in question. Standard curve-fitting techniques were to be applied to the experimental data. The resulting equations or "curves" were then presumably to hold for the theoretical variables whose relations were at issue. Though such a strategy can be (and has been) elaborated in differing ways, its rationale has rarely been questioned.

Here we note only that the vocabulary and directives of intervening variable strategy were legislative for many during much of the Age of Theory. Originally proposed by Tolman (1932, 1935, 1936a, 1936b, 1938), it was taken over in modified form by Hull (1943) and the many under his influence (e.g., Spence [1944]; Miller [1951]). They (and others even outside the behaviorist tradition) attempted to conform to the paradigm in the arrangement of variables in their theories and in the specification of intervening variable functions. These latter were often of unrestricted generality and sometimes were put forward in mathematical, or apparently mathematical, form.

We will chronicle certain of the more recent vicissitudes of the ideology concerning the *observation base* and the *intervening variable paradigm* in the discussion of neo-neobehaviorism that follows.

Neo-neobehaviorism

Such general emphases of neobehaviorism as have been mentioned remained relatively stable until the mid-forties. But they came increasingly under question during the late forties and fifties. This resulted partly from the failure of neobehaviorist systems to realize the theoretical and practical objectives announced in the thirties. But more generally, this interval saw profound changes in psychology, in the course of which neobehaviorist positions were modified and liberalized. The pressures toward "liberalization" were partly internal to behaviorism, arising from the interaction between theory and research (especially where theoretical ideas were extended to man-pertinent problems). But many extrinsic developments invited or enforced modifications of neobehaviorism. These I can illustrate only in passing: e.g., a resurgence of interest in such bypassed areas as instinctive behavior, perception, complex motivational processes, and thinking; a revivified concern with the physiological basis of behavior, which both reflected and augmented significant new knowledge about the nervous system; a wider excursion of theoretical ideas than in previous decades (e.g., Hebb, Gibson); growth in influence of established nonbehaviorist formulations (e.g., Gestalt viewpoints, psychoanalytic and other personality theories stressing experiential analysis, for instance, Murray's and Rogers's); development of new approaches to behavioral analysis (e.g., sensory processes, communication, simple learning) via a wide range of formal and mathematical models drawing on systems-engineering and probability mathematics. In responding to such trends, "liberalized" neo-behaviorism all but lost its identifying characteristics. Certainly the position has so changed as to merit the addition of a new "neo" to its title. The changes are especially evident in the volumes of *Psychology: A Study of a Science* (especially Study 1 [Koch 1959b]), in which many influential theorists, including neobehaviorists, present detailed retrospective analyses of their positions. Major orienting attitudes of classical behaviorism and neo-behaviorist modifications thereof can be seen to be watered down to a point such that distinctiveness is threatened. I confine myself to a cursory sampling of evidences of the attenuation of attitudes which seek to enforce *objectivism,* in the two contexts that were broached a few paragraphs back: commitments concerning the *observation base* and the *intervening variable paradigm.*

a) Changing trends re objectivism. With respect to the *observation base,* among the more dramatic of these evidences is the radical re-analysis of S and R evident in many of the essays. Though S and R have in some sense always been under re-analysis, it is rare that the enterprise has proceeded with the present abandon. For instance, Guthrie, whose career overlaps classical and neobehaviorism, once and for all abandons the persistent behaviorist hope that stimuli may be uniformly reducible to *physical* description, and response, to "movement in space." Rather, "we find ourselves inevitably describing [stimuli] in perceptual terms"; moreover, "it is . . . necessary that they have *meaning* for the responding organism" (1959, 165; italics mine). With regard to response, "we cannot reduce the classes of psychological facts which . . . we must deal with to component movements in space" (1959, 165). In the same volume, Neal Miller points out, in a sweeping assessment of past practice, that "stimulus-response psychologists may be said to know and care relatively little about either stimuli or responses; they are specialists on the hyphen between the S and R and could more aptly be called 'hyphen psychologists,' or to use Thorndike's term, 'connectionists'" (1959, 242). By way of reconstruction, Miller presents, perhaps more sharply than in previous writings, his method of "functional behavioral definition," which holds that "a response is any activity by or within the individual which can become functionally connected with an antecedent event through learning; a stimulus is any event to which a response can be so connected" (1959, 239). In the same paper, Miller gives painstaking attention to *central processes,* and remains a peripheralist only to the extent of phrasing them in terms of the "central response," a type of "response" certainly not, either in fact or by Miller's intention, identifiable with muscle contraction or gland secretion. Indeed, he points out that this concept allows "the theory to exploit images, . . . perceptual responses, . . . and the possibility that central responses can contribute to the focusing of attention" (1959, 242). Tolman, in his contribution to Study 1 (1959), re-evaluates his objectivistic theory of purposive behavior, indicating repeatedly that his major theoretical concepts (intervening variables) come from his "own phenomenology," and expressing serious doubt as to whether such concepts can even be *applied* objectively (i.e., according to fixed rules which link them to behavioral "pointer readings"). This last illustration takes us by a natural transition to the topic of the *intervening variable paradigm.*

With respect to the *intervening variable paradigm,* it may be said that the trend of *Psychology: A Study of a Science* is to call it and much of the associated doctrine sharply into question; to do this in almost every sense in which questioning is possible. Thus, for instance, the originator of the doctrine, Tolman, has now come full circle relative to the feasibility of "standard" *defining experiments.* He now adduces strong grounds for doubting the trans-situational generality of any theoretical function based on the particularities (i.e., the obtained co-variations of empirical variables) of "standard" defining experiments. Moreover, Tolman's general conception of the significance of intervening variables in his theory has dramatically changed: no longer are they determinately linked to "the empirically stipulated independent and dependent variables" (i.e., observables, operational or reductive symptoms); rather, "they are merely an aid to thinking ('my thinking,' if you will)" — "a tentative logic (or psychologic) of my own" (1959, 148). Interestingly, Lazarsfeld (1959), in discussing the need for progress in the methodology of social science index formation, makes precisely the same evaluation of the defining experiment. Again, Neal Miller calls sharply into question the empirically warranted *generality* of all intervening variable functions thus far put forward by *any* theorist by making an acute analysis of "the experimental design required but seldom used to justify intervening variables" (1959, 276–80). The design stipulated by Miller (essentially use of two or more independent experimental "operations" and "measures," respectively) can be seen to require an exceedingly weak warrant of generality; yet it is only Miller himself who has applied this design, and this only at *qualitative* levels in a few simple situations where the "intervening variable" was a single primary drive like hunger or thirst. Moreover, even in such instances, Miller by no means always finds the necessary co-variation. All is not calm, even in the presumably unruffled area of sensory psychology. Thus Licklider (1959), in his analysis of auditory formulations, repeatedly points to the problem of indeterminacy in the linkage between his intervening variables and his final dependent variable as perhaps the most troublesome puzzle in his thinking.

b) Return of the repressed. Perhaps the single most conspicuous and significant change ushered in by neo-neobehaviorism is *the massive return to a concern with empirical problem areas long bypassed or only glancingly acknowledged because of their subjectivistic "odor"* (or, I would add, because of an entirely realistic appraisal of the difficulties of significant progress on these problems in an exclusively "objective" mode). A little of the more remote history here might be instructive. In his first publication on behaviorism (1913), Watson had said:

> The situation is somewhat different when we come to a study of the more complex forms of behavior, such as imagination, judgment, reasoning, and conception. . . . Our minds have been so warped by the fifty-odd years which have been devoted to the study of states of consciousness that we can envisage these problems only in one way. We should meet the situation squarely and say that we are not able to carry forward investigations along all of these lines by the behavior methods which are in use at the present time. . . . The topics have become so threadbare from much handling that they may well be put away for a time. (468)

But Watson was able to pursue this policy only until the end of the paragraph in which it was proposed. In the very next paragraph, we find an adumbration of his motor theory of "the so-called 'higher thought' processes." And in his eagerness to write a behavior psychology, "and never go back upon our definition," we find Watson conspicuously concerned, during the rest of his career as a psychologist, with attempts to show that the problems of subjectivistic psychology could find an objective resolution. In his efforts toward dramatic conquests along these lines, he, in effect, did something worse than neglect the problems at issue: he *liquidated* them via a series of the most arbitrary, simplistic, and ontology-distorting solutions. The reaction during the period of neobehaviorism to this (and to similar tendencies on the part of other classical behaviorists)

70

was, in effect, to eschew investigations of the "higher processes" and adopt a rationale which held that the laws of these would be forthcoming as secondary derivations from postulates asserting fundamental behavior principles based (typically) on learning data. In consonance with such a rationale, there is a shift from Watson's recommended tactic of extending conditioning methods to the analysis of *human* behavior, to the concentration upon determining general behavior laws via intensive application of conditioning methods to animals. But the point to stress is that with the exception of a few illustrative efforts made mainly by Hull in the earlier phases of the development of his theory (e.g., 1930a, 1935b) the promised "derivations" of perceptual, cognitive, and other "complex phenomena" were not forthcoming.

It is of the first significance, then, that beginning (roughly) in the late forties, one can detect a markedly increased disposition, especially among younger behaviorists, to give analytic and sometimes research attention to such formerly eschewed areas as perception, language behavior, thinking, and so-called mediational processes in general. Evidence of the dramatic growth of such interests may be found in the three volumes of Study II of *Psychology: A Study of a Science* (Koch 1962b, 1963). In this study, devoted to the interrelations of major subject matter areas of psychology, the tactic was to invite representatives of various areas to pursue the analysis of bridging relations between the given area and any others that the contributor might be interested in considering. *All* authors selected to represent the field of learning chose to consider relations with *perception*. Of the six authors in this group (two were collaborators), five would define themselves with little equivocation as neobehaviorists. Other authors of neobehaviorist cast, who had been invited to represent (as their field of primary affiliation) fields as broadly disparate as sensory psychology, motivation, social psychology, and psycholinguistics, also chose perception and cognitive process as important termini of their bridging interests. The result is an extensive sub-anthology on extensions of neobehaviorist theory to the long-forbidden areas—a kind of massive study in the return of the repressed.

I leave this audience to interpret the preceding extraordinarily fragmentary rundown of history. To me it suggests the story of the gradual attenuation of a position that was never *seriously* tenable, never consistent, based on thin and shifting rationales, and adopted more to serve needs for comfort and security than a passion for knowledge. Does this story of attenuation, attrition, and compromise "refute" behaviorist epistemology? Here I can only revert to my earlier observation that in certain connections "refutation" is an (unsystematically) ambiguous notion. I think that our story begins to suggest the unfruitfulness of the position, its restrictive effects on problematic curiosity, its scholastic character, perhaps most of all, its basic ludicrousness. Perhaps it is the last, which, in the end, will be the most compelling. When the ludicrousness of the position is made sufficiently plain, perhaps it will be laughed out of existence. Behaviorists have themselves done a pretty good job in rendering this quality apparent. Perhaps the following lines of consideration, which presuppose, but further specify, certain aspects of our historical outline, will carry the "*argumentum ab ludicrum*" a bit further. For me, these considerations are reasons for proposing that the position be considered once and for all defunct.

2. Behaviorism's Evaporating Methodological Support

I return now to a theme suggested in the preamble to this paper—the few pages in which I tried to justify its ornate title.

General Changes in the Philosophy of Science

For more than thirty years, the central—I think it fair to say "entire"—defense of behaviorist epistemology has been on methodological grounds. The neobehaviorists have *wanted* it this way. But the picture of scientific method now beginning to emerge among physicists, other natural scientists, many philosophers of science, and others challenges the behaviorist conception of science and the imported methodological views on which it was based, at virtually every point. The idea of behaviorism was that replicability of findings, reliability of prediction, and so on, could be purchased only by use of fixed linkages with "objective indicators"; by conformity to schemata which assumed that elaboration, application, and verification of a theory must take place in something like a wholly articulate, wholly stated context of *rules*. But for some years now, physicists and biologists, philosophers of science and historians of science have been converging upon a view of science which emphasizes the extent to which the scientific process is, in principle and at all stages, *under-determined by rule*. If one wishes defensively to fall back on the distinction between "context of discovery" and "context of justification," one falls back on a distinction that any empirically apt account of inquiry shows to be unsupportable and that, indeed, no longer receives support in many expert quarters. Any detailed analysis of the "justificatory" activities of scientists, for instance, will show justification at many points to depend as much on extra-rule-determined processes as does discovery.

Among the re-analyses of inquiry that are now shaping up there is no point-for-point consensus, but most agree in stressing the absurdity in principle of any notion of *full formalization,* in underlining the gap between any linguistic "system" of assertions and the unverbalized processes upon which its interpretation and application (not to mention its formulation) are contingent, in acknowledging the dependence of theory construction and use at every phase on individual sensibility, discrimination, insight, judgment, guess. The emerging redefinition of inquiry knocks away virtually every one of the props on which the strange caution-inspired epistemology of the behaviorist had leaned. Even the presumptive, borrowed prestige attaching to his views is gone.

If the behaviorist refuses to resonate to this emerging redefinition of inquiry (and I suspect that one or two will resist), he should then be reminded that he began to become bereft of his extracurricular methodological supports very shortly after he discovered them. Behaviorism has stood pat on a few issues dissected out of the methodology of science anywhere from twenty to thirty years ago. But philosophers and scientific methodologists have not stood pat. Debate, revision, and change have been continuous, and even among those philosophers and methodologists who in some residual sense hold on to a rule-saturated conception of science, not a single plank in the old positivist-neopragmatic scaffolding remains unaltered.

The traditional positivistic distinction between analytic and synthetic statements has been broadly questioned (by positivists among others). Continuing analysis of the nature of logical and mathematical systems has revealed new complexities; few would be content now with the view that regards formal statements as tautologies. Whatever can be meant by the "interpretation" of formal systems is now itself interpreted in markedly different ways than formerly. The verifiability theory of meaning (and cognate formulations) has long languished in dereliction. More generally, attempts to state criteria which establish the limits of cognitive meaningfulness are either given up as self-stultifying in principle or have been so liberalized (e.g., Carnap 1956) as to make them compatible with certain classes of metaphysical statements. As suggested in the preamble to this paper, even the analytic (or "ordinary language") philosophers, themselves in some ways a protest group to logical positivism, have for some time been defecting from the more positivistically flavored features of their program.

But even more directly relevant to the issues at hand, certain former positivists (e.g., Carnap, Feigl) have decreed — if only guardedly — a relegitimization of *introspection*. Thus Carnap, in 1956, rather grudgingly points out:

> Although many of the alleged results of introspection were indeed questionable, a person's awareness of his own state of imagining, feeling, etc., must be recognized as a kind of observation, in principle not different from external observation, and therefore as a legitimate source of knowledge, though limited by its subjective character. (70–71)

But the Bridgman of *The Way Things Are* (1959), a book that has yet received little mention in psychological literature, is far less grudging. There he takes an uncompromisingly anti-behaviorist position, insisting that "first-person report" is essential to significant operational analysis in principle and, in psychological and social contexts, mandatory in practice. The flavor of his general position may be sensed from the following quotations:

> Insistence on the use of the first person, either explicitly or implicitly, will inevitably focus attention on the individual. This, it seems to me, is all to the good. The philosophical and scientific exposition of our age has been too much obsessed with the ideal of a coldly impersonal generality. . . . Neglect of the role of the individual, with resulting overemphasis on the social, may well be one of the fundamental difficulties in the way the human race handles its mind. (5)

> Another word for which I believe the private aspect is much more important than ordinarily realized is "proof." . . . Here I shall only reiterate my opinion that a proper appreciation of this will alter the common picture of science as something essentially public into something essentially private. (237)

It might be pointed out in passing that a remarkable affinity exists between the position taken in this 1959 book and that of another book published at about the same time — Michael Polanyi's *Personal Knowledge* (1958).

Despite such far-flung developments as I have just tried to sample, some behaviorists will perhaps try to find aid and comfort in the circumstance that certain of the "ordinary language" philosophers find support, in their interpretations of linguistic "use," for what has been called "logical behaviorism." To such I would reply that this position is, in my impression, currently far less popular than it once was (say, shortly after the appearance of Ryle's *Concept of Mind* [1949]).

Newer Conceptions of Definition and Meaning

One topic which I would much like to discuss in substance, rather than merely in terms of historical trend, is the implications of certain newer ideas concerning definition, meaning, and language for the assessment of behaviorist epistemology. This I will try to do, if only in the most summary way.

Modern *philosophical* meaning theory has taken the form mainly of a search for a criterion of the cognitive significance of statements. The "solutions" or proposed criteria—though sub-groups fall into certain family relationships—have been most varied. Thus, taking logical positivism alone (and only a few examples at that), at various phases it has put forward criteria of significance (for a statement) in terms of "truth conditions," "complete verifiability," "falsifiability," "weak verifiability," "method of verification," "practical feasibility of verification," "verifiability in principle," "testability," "confirmability," etc. This samples the development through 1937; after that the "criteria" become more complex and more difficult to identify in a catch-phrase. Most such criteria were, of course, embedded in detailed technical analyses and became the subjects of much polemical writing.[2]

When, in the early thirties, the Age of Theory began its search for a set of decision procedures, it could have turned to any of the above criteria

---

2. Useful historically oriented analyses of positivist meaning criteria may be found in Hempel (1959) and Blanshard (1962, 189–248). It might be noted in passing that Hempel 1959 is a reprint of Hempel 1950 and includes a section of author's "remarks" as of 1958: in these latter, Hempel suggests that the "idea of cognitive significance . . . has lost its promise and fertility as an explicandum" (129).

Useful though the preceding references be, it is fair to say that no truly adequate history of modern philosophical meaning theories as yet exists. Such a history would have to start at least as early as the formulations of the pragmatism (James and Pierce) and the positivism (Mach, Avenarius, and Poincare) of the late nineteenth and early twentieth centuries. Especially in recent decades, issues in this field have become so intricately ramified, and differences in position so subtly shaded, as to pose a formidable challenge to historical scholarship. Such a book as L. J. Cohen's *The Diversity of Meaning* (1962), though not essentially a historical study, considers meaning-conceptions over a sufficiently broad spectrum to suggest the magnitude of the problem.

except the last two ("testability" and "confirmability," in the special senses defined by Carnap, did not become available until 1936–37) or, indeed, to many others. Instead, partly by historical accident, psychology focused on the early formulations of Bridgman's "operational criterion" of meaning, which, by phrasing the meaning of a scientific concept in terms of "corresponding" *experimental* and (ultimately) observational operations, offered attractive imagery to a science at once self-conscious of its newly won experimental status and eager to get experiment into tighter relation with theory. The historical accident was essentially that a few psychologists (*a*) happened to become apprised of Bridgman's work and (*b*) published on its implications for psychology. If they had done their outside reading in slightly different order, they might have focused on the proposals of Schlick, or of early mid-Carnap, or of the neopragmatist, C. I. Lewis, or, in fact, on a variety of other criteria having an intent similar to Bridgman's. In such a case the clang of the psychological literature re definition would today be different.

As I earlier indicated, the lore concerning operational definition soon began to fuse with the lore concerning logical positivism. Carnap (1936–1937) published, in "Testability and Meaning," what was quickly to become the most influential analysis of meaningfulness in the history of logical positivism. I believe that I was the first author (Koch 1941a) to discuss this analysis in the psychological literature and to examine its relation to operationism—but note that this was not until 1941. No presentation in the literature—including mine—has done justice to the technical detail of Carnap's treatment. However, the notions of the "disposition concept," the "reduction sentence," and "chains" thereof, soon entered the jargon of psychological commerce.

I ask you to note an interesting circumstance. Since 1937, there has been the lushest proliferation of philosophical discussions of meaning in history. Not only have Carnap (1956) and other positivists liberalized their meaning criteria out of all recognition, but analytic philosophers have uncovered new vistas of subtlety with their discriminations of such matters as "open-texture" and "language strata" (Waismann 1951, 1953) and a previously unanticipated complexity of "utterance" types in natural languages (e.g., Austin 1962). Yet very little of this has penetrated into psychology. The typical theoretically oriented psychologist, not excluding the behaviorist, still draws sustenance and security from a theory of definition (and more generally of science) over twenty years old, and moreover, one which its originators have largely abandoned.

Not only have the newer philosophical considerations of meaning made obsolete the older "supports" for behavioristic analyses of definition and, in general, the conditions of communication in our science, but they converge on a picture remarkably inconsonant with behaviorist views. I nevertheless have a feeling that there is a need for effective *psychological* analysis of the nature of language, especially such problems as those of definition, meaningfulness, and meaning. Treatment of these by the philosopher has perhaps been limited by the traditional problematic concerns and modes of analysis of epistemology. The linguist, to the best of my knowledge, has, at least until very recently, pretty much side-stepped these problems. The field called "psycholinguistics" in recent years *has* considered them, but in a mode predetermined by orienting attitudes and specialized theories of behaviorism. What I think necessary, at least as a preliminary, is relatively simple-minded *empirical* analysis of the conditions of communication and of actual definitional practice in the natural languages. If one believes, further, that scientific languages differentiate out of the natural language — and I do not see how this can be doubted — the conclusions could also be of interest from the point of view of science.

I have recently made a stab in such a direction and am impressed by what a bit of preliminary thinking seems to reveal. If we look at the problem of definition *psychologically,* we immediately see that a definition, if apprehended by a recipient, must result in a process of perceptual learning and that what is learned is the discrimination of the properties, relations, or system thereof that the definer wishes to designate by the term. This clearly means that definition, at bottom, is a *perceptual training process* and that everything that we know about the *conditions* of perceptual training and learning must apply to the analysis of definition. Adding to this a few obvious circumstances concerning the genesis and status of words of natural languages — circumstances that can be inferred from the study of sources no more esoteric than dictionaries — quite a few matters take on a new light. It emerges, for instance, that contrary to what we were once told by logical positivists and others, no natural language and no scientific one of any richness can be regarded as organized into logical levels such that all terms are reducible to, or definable upon, a common definition base (and indeed, as the usual story goes, an extremely restricted one, as e.g., the "observable predicates" of the "thing language"; cf. Carnap [1936–1937]). On the contrary, if we want to pinpoint with a term any reasonably subtle, embedded, or delicately "contoured" relation or property, we must often, if using verbal means of definition, build up our defining expression from words that are *just as,* or even more, "rarefied" (remote from the presumptive definition base) as the one at issue. Moreover, for defining abstract or subtle concepts or concepts based on "new" discriminations, we will have to go outside language and relate the term to a carefully controlled "perceptual display" (as it were) far more often than any logical positivist, especially of an older day, would care to admit.

Such findings, if they are that, are related to others at considerable variance with our lore and strictures concerning our *own* definitions in psychological discourse. Thus, one thing that eventuates is the utter irrationality of expecting that all terms will be understood and used with equal nicety by all people in a scientific field (even with a "competent investigator" clause thrown in), depending only on the adequacy of the "operational" definitions.

For instance, a recently published glossary of terms used in the "objective science of behavior" (Verplanck 1957) says of "operational" definitions: "They demand agreement; and they make it possible for anyone who is able to read to reconstruct the observations to which the terms apply." At another place, in a characterization of the "data language," the relevance of "training" is acknowledged, but in this way: "words . . . in the data language . . . must be defined so that anyone after a minimum of training can use them consistently." Now *a minimum of training* necessary for the consistent use of a word—particularly if that word denotes a highly embedded property or relation of events—may necessitate a *very great deal* of training. Yet in the psychological literature re empirical definition, it is quite clear that the force of such expressions is more like "minimal training" (absolutely) than the minimum of training *necessary* for discriminating "so-and-so."

It is strange that the very individuals who have espoused or accepted such a conception of the observation base often acknowledge in other connections that the application-conditions for observation terms, and terms close to the observation base, can only be learned and "discriminated" with sensitivity by working face-to-face with individuals who are masters of certain experimental crafts. Thus, there is a large group of individuals much interested in delicate and dramatic "shapings" of behavior who are ready, even eager, to admit that the true subtleties of the art can be assimilated only by prolonged laboratory contact with one of its acknowledged masters. They are right! But they have failed to generalize upon this truly profound knowledge. Language is at best a feeble instrument, even among members of a highly trained language community having quite limited problematic interests. None of the currently institutionalized sciences form single, homogeneous language communities. Physicists in one empirical area do not necessarily fully understand physicists in another; pathologists do not necessarily understand electrophysiologists, etc. And within each scientific area, even when cut rather finely, there may be distinguished disorderly *hierarchies* of language communities. In the extreme case, there may be quite definite and unique observable properties and relations which only two men, perhaps working in the same laboratory, may be able to perceive and denote by some linguistic expression. Moreover, it should be stressed that the stratification of language communities within a science may reflect variations in *sensitivity* of observers just as much as differential levels or foci of *training*. There was a time when Einstein was apprised of certain invariant properties of the universe, yet could communicate these "discriminations" to few men.

Now a language community must obviously be specified on a *psychological* criterion—a complex one demanding a certain criterial overlap of learned discriminations and specialized discriminative capacities (sensitivities) among members. Say that this criterion defines a "discrimination pool." I think there are strong grounds to believe that the discrimination pool demanded for adequate communication in *any* area of science is far richer, more differentiated, and subtle than ordinarily supposed. One may, for instance, think of a "pointer-reading" as some ultimate verifying operation (or reductive symptom). But the pointer is hooked up, both materially and inferentially, to a complex system of events, and the physicist must be attuned to relationships of great subtlety in that system if he is to interpret the pointer-reading in a truly significant way.[3] If one thinks, say, in terms of a presumably "simple" reduction sentence, the "test-result" (pointer position) may be specified via a relatively crass discrimination; the "test-condition" part may involve a most elaborate system of events which are *assumed to realize* an elaborate lattice of theoretical relationships, and the job of the physicist is to "discriminate" whether this is so. *That* is not a crass discrimination. Yet, be all this as it may, there is little question that the discrimination pools presupposed for communication in physical science as a whole may be fewer in number and, in each case, less differentiated and "rich" than the discrimination pools presupposed in biological science as a whole and especially psychology. In other words, the domain

3. Karl Zener makes a similar point in the context of an important analysis of "The Significance of Experience of the Individual for the Science of Psychology" (1958; cf. pp. 358 ff. therein).

of physical science is such as to necessitate fewer language communities than do the domains of biology or psychology. Moreover, physical science language communities may well be more stable and perhaps more readily enlarged.

There are many reasons for these differences. I shall mention only one. In psychology, problems concerning *any* range of human endeavor or experience can be the object of study. No definition of our science — however restrictive its heuristic effect may have been on problem selection — has ever called into question this awesome peculiarity of our subject matter. In recent decades we have sought security by addressing only small and rather unadventurous segments of our subject matter. But problems — *psychological* problems — of art and morality, of scientific creativity, of human sensibility in all manifestations, of language, problem solution, and, of course, society, personality, etc., *do* stand before us almost untouched. If psychology is to study the conditions of the phenomena in any of these areas, it must premise its research on "discrimination pools," each of which overlaps to some definite extent with the discrimination pools of all of those widely ranged human areas. That is not to say that, for example, the psychological student of art must be an artist. (It would not hurt!) But it is grotesque to suppose that someone totally devoid of the special discriminations and sensitivities of the artist could make contributions to the psychology of art — just as grotesque as to expect, say, that an illiterate could contribute to the psychology of language.

All this is shamefully obvious, but the consequences — if the history of psychology be evidence — are not. In psychology we must have many language communities: many sub-groups of individuals equipped with diverse stocks of discriminations and differently specialized sensitivities. *By definition,* we must have a greater number of language communities in psychology than perhaps in any other field of inquiry currently institutionalized. We must also expect more variability, both in sensitivity and in achieved discriminations, than within other scientific language communities. Indeed, the present position suggests that the *minimal* acceptable size of a language community for psychology must be a community of no more than two persons. Any formulation of the meaning criterion demanding a wider consensus group for *admission* of a term as meaningful would eliminate much meaning either from our universe of approachable data, or from that of the scientifically sayable. Worse than the *amount* of meaning lost would be its altitude — for science is such that at any given time its best ideas are likely to reside in only a few of its towering sensibilities.

In the most general terms, the behaviorist has sought to ensure inter-subjectivity by fixed definitional linkages to simple "objective indicators." But such an analysis as the one just vaguely summarized makes it plain that much communication which in fact takes place could not be mediated by definition based on such a paradigm. Often the application of a term (and of course the initial learning of its sense) will depend on the perception of highly subtle or embedded relational constancies in event manifolds that are fleeting, that vary from occasion to occasion, that evade ostension in its primordial "finger-pointing" sense, etc. Such meanings cannot be conveyed with any sharpness by a stipulated linkage to the elements of a "definition base" (as usually conceived), by an enumeration of stable and crassly discriminable "observable properties" or "symptoms," or indeed, by any conjunction or disjunction of these, whatever their number. The behaviorist who wishes to universalize the language community by such definitional practice will either be thwarted or end up with an extraordinarily crass language community, an extraordinarily crass set of descriptive and/or systemic concepts, and an extraordinarily degraded formulation of the psychological questions of potential interest to human beings. If this be democracy, it is not the kind that has characterized the sciences that the behaviorist is most eager to emulate.

The behaviorist who can acknowledge these things (if such there be) will inevitably fall back upon the demand for definition in such a way as to ensure *public* applicability of terms (two or more observers must be able to perceive the identical referent), and *public* verifiability of statements containing them. But once the inadequacies of the older reductionist paradigms of definition are seen, insistence on such "publicity" becomes an exceedingly arbitrary form of obstinacy. For if it be granted that the language community cannot always be *universalized* with respect to *all* significant terms, the question of whether the referent be located in direct experience or in the "public" world becomes a relatively minor matter. In both cases, the fact of communication (thus "checkability") will be contingent on relevant observer sensitivities—which latter are, in principle at least, open to specification. In both cases, communication will often not be all or none, but rather a matter of degree. For both cases, the history of mankind and of science gives overwhelming evidence that high degrees of inter-observer agreement are attainable. Moreover, terms having both "types" of referent *can and do* enter into stable predictive relationships. What can be at the basis of persisting behavioristic negativism in the face of such considerations other than a deep metaphysical bias?

3. Pragmatic Consequences of Behaviorism: Effect on Problem Selection and Treatment

Here we resume a thread developed toward the end of the historical outline. There three points concerning effects of behaviorism on problem selection were stressed: (1) After expressing a resolve in 1913 to "put away for a time" the "threadbare" topics (as, e.g., the higher thought processes) of subjectivist psychology, Watson immediately proceeded to break that resolve and paced a trend in the classical interval for verbalistic "solutions" of the germane problems. (2) Neobehaviorism reacted to this largely by side-stepping the "higher processes" in the hope that laws concerning these would be forthcoming as secondary derivations from primary principles of simple learning and (in some cases) motivation. (3) Such derivations not coming markedly into evidence in the interval 1930–50, neo-neobehaviorism returns to a concern with perception and central process toward the end of this interval.

In general, perhaps the most decisive indictment of the behaviorist position is its long-term restrictive impact on problem selection and (what in effect can amount to the same thing) on problem treatment. If Watson and other classical behaviorists gave attention to "complex" phenomena discriminated by the older psychologies and by human beings generally, it was certainly not to study them but to liquidate them by fiat. The attitude of neobehaviorism is perhaps a cleaner one; but, in its concern with *general* laws of behavior based on intensive analysis of animal learning in a few standard situations, it fled the subtler fluxions (not to mention certain obvious hard facts of human function) so vigorously that these matters were all but forgotten. A policy initially of "gradualism" soon congealed into one of evading, even denying, subject matter. For most of the past thirty years, psychologists have allowed the rat to preempt the human, have shied away from investigations even of "behavior" when it is under the control of complex or labile internal factors, have concentrated on dependent variable indicators of a type dictated more by methodological caution than problematic relevance, etc. These facts are patent.

But in the present period of neo-neobehaviorism it *looks* as if S-R analysis is finally addressing the long-neglected matters of human import, righting the historic balance. About this, I hate to be cynical. I certainly welcome the renewed interests in perception, cognition, language, etc. These interests are a reassuring sign that ultimately subject matter will assert itself, that the world will not be totally subdued by a solipsism, however aggressive. But I think that these newer interests are best interpreted as a fading of the behaviorist blinders rather than as a proof of the viability of the position. For if problematic concerns now seem less constricted, the character of the treatment given to formerly bypassed problems suggests that these are not really being joined: they are again — as in Watson's day — being exorcized. True, they are being exorcized in a more sophisticated way — but the sophistication derives from the disposition of neo-neobehaviorists to take the findings of other groups of psychologists more seriously than did Watson.

If I had time, I think I could make the following kind of case: Much of the current behaviorist concern with perception and central process is given to S-R explications and paraphrases of phenomena and lawful relations discriminated by Gestalt and other non-behavioristic perception psychologists, by non-behavioristic students of cognition, by developmental psychologists like Piaget, by physiological psychologists and neurophysiologists. An examination of such "liberalized" positions as that of Neal Miller will give many illustrations of this sort of thing (e.g., Miller 1959). Here he orders his "functionally defined" notions of central stimulus and response (along with the subsidiary hypothesis that laws discovered at the periphery may hold within the center) to phenomena discovered by Ivo Kohler and Wolfgang Köhler, to analyses made by Norbert Wiener, to discoveries made within brain physiology. Miller has an S-R explanation of everything.

With respect to analyses of this sort, which, though sometimes ingenious, involve a cosmically flexible use of S and R, I should think a critical question would be this: What is the probability that the *empirical discoveries* now finally being given a loose paraphrase in S-R terms would have ever been made via research efforts guided by an S-R terminology or, more properly, a scientific sensibility wholly grooved in that idiom? What do such S-R explications and translations prove with respect to the heuristic fruitfulness of S-R concepts and the associated orienting attitudes? The point may be driven home by an example. Another contributor to *Psychology: A Study of a Science,* Fred Attneave — an information theorist of neo-neobehaviorist cast — shows in his contribution a remarkable grasp of current developments in perception, neurophysiology, informational analysis, etc. (Attneave 1962). He is sympathetic to current attempts to extrapolate neobehavioristic periphery laws to the center and to the use of S-R language for phrasing central process. I think him above that sort of thing and said as much to him in a letter. His reply was that he considered the use of such a vocabulary helpful and that, though he himself took such usage lightly, he condoned neo-neobehavioristic practice in this regard. But he did not answer a more specific question that I had raised. His own analysis had made use of many particulate findings of recent neurophysiology like, for instance, Hernandez-Peon's discovery of central feedback to the receptors. What I wanted to have was his estimate of the probability that such a fact would have been *discovered* in the first instance by individuals who perceived the organismic universe through a homogeneously S-R screen.

More generally, I think there is something frightening about the way neo-neobehaviorism is treating the newly reclaimed subject matters. It is not merely that proffered problem solutions are trivial and limited in significant research consequences. That is bad enough. But the *attitudes* toward subject matter and toward the nature of knowledge at once betokened by such "solutions" and spawned in the wake of their acceptance seem to me as perverse as in the day of Watson. Scientific knowledge is, of course, "selective"—but when ontology is distorted, denied, or evaded past a certain point, one is no longer in the context of serious scholarship.

This lack of respect for ontology, let us face it, has remained pretty much constant throughout the history of behaviorism. I think people have largely forgotten that the notions of S and R originally had something to do with specific end-organ activities. Throughout the history of behaviorism, these words have been extended in reference in ways not even held together by the thinnest kind of metaphor. By a point quite early in the progress of *classical* behaviorism, every mentalist category distinguished in the history of thought, including, I think, the medieval cholers, had been phrased either as a stimulus or a response or as both. These tendencies were not diminished but, instead, burgeoned during the phase of neobehaviorism—especially in the hands of theorists committed to the study of man-pertinent processes but committed also, as we all perforce are, to the maintenance of professional respectability. Neo-neobehaviorism is now upon us, and the situation grows worse. In pursuit of the strategy of extending periphery laws to the center, the brain must now be furbished with stimuli and responses. The mildly refractory ontological circumstance that the brain contains no sense organs or muscles is easily handled by "functional definitions" of S and R.

Thus we get the present family of analyses which phrase central events in terms of one or another so-called S-R mechanism (all of them quite similar). The general idea is that a second S-R system, or, more properly, an R-S system, is interpolated between the peripheral stimulus and the response. The interpolated response corresponds to a neural event, or a molar-perceptual or cognitive process which is some function of neural events. This is controlled by the peripheral stimulus and in turn controls the final overt response. Since present neurophysiology makes it clear that neural impulses in the central nervous system get implicated in complex interactive and reverberatory circuits, the R's generously imputed to the gray matter are supposed also to give rise to correlated S's (on the analogy to response-produced stimulation), while these S's, of course, can lead to further R's. When, after making a typical analysis of this sort, Miller (1959, 242) points out that his notion of central response leaves him free "to exploit" such matters as "images . . . perceptual responses," etc., it would seem that he uses the word "exploit" advisedly.

4. S-R Scholasticism

A feature of the behaviorist framework which by now is perhaps apparent in painful detail is the almost incredibly undifferentiated and crass character of its major analytical tools — its exclusive *end terms* of analysis and, in some formulations, the only terms of analysis: S and R. Karl Zener has recently pointed out that:

> in no other science is there a single, unqualified noun referring to the totality of events studied by that science, comparable to the term *behavior*. There are optical, mechanical, magnetic, intra-atomic events, all of which are physical events; there are a variety of biological events — metabolism, growth, reproduction, contraction, secretion; but no single, unqualified term exists in either science comprehending all of the events which constitute its subject matter. Furthermore, there are no biological laws comparable in *generality* to stimulus-response laws — no such physical or chemical laws. No other science handicaps itself with the incubus of a term which so discourages analysis and encourages overgenerality of interpretation of obtained functional relationships.
>
> The overabstract character of the concept of behavior (and that of stimulus) tends finally to produce the illusion that a *conceptually homogeneous set of lawful relationships* has been achieved or is achievable in psychology. (Zener and Gaffron 1962, 541)

I heartily agree. I also agree with Zener's further contention that psychology cannot avoid the use of a conceptually heterogeneous language. I would add that it was the philosophical presuppositions of the Age of Theory that prompted the absurdities of this quest for conceptual homogeneity and unbridled generality.

What we have, in effect, is a form of scholasticism in which what passes for "theorizing" involves arbitrary combinations and permutations among a few simple conceptual counters. It is as if physics proceeded in terms of three concepts: "cause," "effect," and, say, the notion of an "associative connection" between the first two. (Some physicists might wish to discriminate also a special event, "delta," the presence of which produces a finite increment in the strength of the "associative connection.") What the S-R theorists have ended up with is not a set of genuine analytic concepts—these to have any "bite" must be sufficiently differentiated to register at least a few of the observable subject matter distinctions—but a kind of primitive thought mold necessarily presupposed in all "causal," or if one prefers, "functional" thinking. In effect they have given to us as the primary analytic concepts for the most ambitious science ever conceived a mildly camouflaged paradigm for Hume's analysis of causality.

III. Phenomenology

I had hoped to consider certain of the problems and prospects that arise when experience is unembarrassedly acknowledged as a part of the psychological universe and addressed as an object of study. But my assigned task in this symposium was to consider behaviorism. That I have done—even if I have not exactly "represented" behaviorism. Others will no doubt fulfil this last function, and Drs. MacLeod and Rogers will give positive consideration to problems of experiential analysis. I feel impelled, however, to close with a few general points concerning what is called "phenomenology," if only to ensure that the incidence of my analysis of behaviorism not be misinterpreted.

I want to make it plain that I think there to be an intense current need for particular analyses of many issues connected with the use of experiential variables in psychology. Experientialism—if I may substitute that word for the term "phenomenology," which I dislike—was driven underground in American psychology for almost forty years. Even those committed to the acknowledgment of experiential events and to the use of experiential variables in their systematic work tended, because of the climate prevailing in that interval, to avoid direct discussion of the many methodico-creative problems that must be joined for effective development of a psychology that takes experience seriously. The paucity of direct considerations of such issues, say in the writings of the classical Gestalt psychologists or of Lewin (at least the writings of these men while in America), is in a way astounding. There are, after all, open and important questions having to do with the relations between experience and "report," optimal techniques for experiential observation, prospects for methods of observer training which might increase the sharpness and reliability of experience-language (this in turn depending on more general issues in the psychology of language), the formulation of adequate independent and dependent (experiential) variable categories, optimal modes for integrating behavioral and experiential data, and many others. These are no simple problems; they are not "methodological" in the idle, role-playing sense: the fate of psychology must be very much bound up with progress toward their resolution.

Because of the weakening hegemony of behaviorism, experientialists are currently somewhat less furtive. And such people as Gibson, Zener and Gaffron, Rogers and his group, Murray, are making significant strides, both substantive and methodic. Yet many long-neglected problems of the sort just mentioned are, of course, *still* wide open. A significant psychology, that long-heralded entity, is contingent on massive and responsible attack on such problems.

Yet many of the new dissidents, instead of attacking the questions raised by their readiness to confront experience in terms adjusted to the indigenous requirements of psychology, turn to fashionable forms of philosophical obscurantism — notably existentialism. I consider this trend regrettable. At the risk of ending up without any friends at all, I should like to say why.

The current turn to existentialism has the earmarks of the least fruitful kind of escape from a set of traditional constraints — an escape to an *Answer* rather than to a *problem*. Behaviorism won its initial acceptance because of severe shortcomings in the methodic proposals and research practices of early "phenomenologistic" programs in psychology. And it continued to thrive because of the absence in our science of muscular efforts toward reconsideration of those issues in the strategy of experiential analysis which earlier experientialism had handled in such artificial and limited ways.

Nothing could more jeopardize the prospects of the current counter-behaviorist revolution than the embracing of ready-made "answers" to these questions framed within the tradition of a philosophic school which — however charitably one tries to be disposed — can only reveal itself to have a high tolerance, if not a positive appetite, for the opaque. To unearth whatever might be suggestive for scientific modes of analysis in existentialism would, to put it modestly, require a level of scholarship, self-determining critical insight, and analytic prowess that no current psychologist is likely to have. This is no insult to psychologists, for existentialism, perhaps more than any other trend in modern thought, requires, for any degree of comprehension that might transcend the content of a few identifying slogans, first-hand and long immersion in one of the nuclear language communities in which existentialist philosophy is practiced. And even were that condition satisfied, the outcome would perforce remain in doubt. Merleau-Ponty, who is regarded as one of the most technically competent philosophers among the French existentialists, opens his book on the *Phenomenology of Perception* (1962) in this way:

> What is phenomenology? It may seem strange that this question has still to be asked half a century after the first works of Husserl. The fact remains that it has by no means been answered. (vii)

An analogy may be useful. *Effective* scientific development of psychoanalytic theory would, in the opinion of many, require insightful and rigorous re-analysis of a vast body of doctrine that has been generated in *that* field. Yet — despite the fact that the communicative problem in the psychoanalytic literature (great though it be) is minuscule in comparison with that presented by existentialist writing — not a few decades have gone by without such a task having been accomplished.

In light of such considerations, one is somewhat worried by the style of the current interest in existentialism in American psychology. There are woolly revivalist overtones — a disposition to accept in advance an intellectual object the properties of which have hardly been cognized. And there are indications that existentialism is tending to be viewed, in some global sense, as an *external source of authority* for whatever ideas the viewer already owns that he feels to be unconventional. There is a marked parallelism here with the tendency of the neobehaviorists to seek support for attitudes which *they* had already embraced by a similarly global appeal to a prestigeful philosophical movement: in that instance, logical positivism. All of these tendencies are painfully apparent in a widely known symposium published under the title *Existential Psychology* (May 1961) (it may be of interest that one of the contributions is entitled "Existential Psychology — What's in It for Us?") and in the introduction to a widely influential anthology entitled *Existence* (May, Angel, and Ellenberger 1958).

If existential philosophy is to be of concrete significance for the problems of a psychology of experience, this remains to be *established*. The slogans per se (e.g., "existence precedes essence") are not especially illuminating, whatever comfort they may give. My guess, though limited by very slight contact with existentialist literature, is that even if the conditions for *responsible* exploitation were met, there might not be a great contribution to psychology forthcoming.

There is, I tend to think, a kind of kink in the communicative practices of existentialists which requires close study—however libertarian one tends to be about the conditions of meaningful communication. *Headlong assaults on the ineffable are commendable, but they are not preguaranteed to succeed.* One finds in reading, say, Sartre, a fluidity of discourse, a tendency to be only partially and variably constrained by the terms of posed problems, a love of paradox and of cryptic yet somehow pregnant slogans, and (especially in Sartre's case) a tendency toward public relations opportunism—all of which do not exactly make for pellucid discourse or a homogeneous distribution of profundity. These things must be faced: *scientists* especially cannot afford to ignore them. Some of these tendencies may not be incompatible with the purposes of literary discourse—though this can be questioned, and I, for one, would—but they certainly are incompatible with the purposes of scientific discourse.

Turning to certain more homely considerations, I have tended to note with true dismay that students with existentialist identifications (and one sees not a few these days), though often sensitive people with the best possible impulses, seem possessed of the same habit of thought and of communication that I have tried to reconstruct re Sartre. They simply are off in some realm of epigrammatic nuance, of ardent association-chasing, before a problem even gets stated, whether by themselves or others. They do not seem to think like scientists, however Dionysian one's conception thereof, nor do they, in my estimation, think like effective or able humanists. I think this unfortunate: they are often talented young men who hold values of the sort desperately needed in psychology.

I will spare this patient audience a summary. I merely wish to emphasize that, though it may not have seemed so at all points, we have been discussing grave matters. Modern society has provision for an ample margin of waste, especially of ideas. But nowhere can such "give" in the system lead to less happy consequences than in psychology. For if psychology does not influence man's image of himself, what branch of the scholarly community does? That modern psychology has projected an image of man which is as demeaning as it is simplistic, few intelligent and sensitive non-psychologists would deny. To such men—whether they be scientist, humanist, or citizen—psychology has increasingly become an object of derision. *They* are safe, even when most despairing. But for the rest, the mass dehumanization process which characterizes our time—the simplification of sensibility, homogenization of taste, attenuation of the capacity for experience—continues apace. Of all fields in the community of scholarship, it should be psychology which combats this trend. Instead, we have played no small role in augmenting and supporting it. It should be a matter of embarrassment that the few who are effectively working against the deterioration of culture are the physicists, biologists, philosophers, historians, humanists, even administrators, participating in the redefinition of knowledge to which I referred in my opening paragraphs, but *not ourselves.* Is it not time that we raise the courage to relent?

3

The Age of the "Paradigm"

Foreword

In the psychology of the early 1960s, the imagery of "theory" (and the transitional imagery of "models" which had roughly the significance of "theory" asserted at a lower level of confidence than formerly, and with more explicit recognition of nomological lacunae) began to give way to the imagery of the Kuhnian "paradigm." The chief form of commerce in fundamental psychology shifted from "theory-construction" to "paradigm-promotion." This chapter considers the circumstances, meaning, and certain consequences of that shift.

It is argued that Kuhn was badly misread by psychologists. The result was even greater obfuscation concerning the nature of significant inquiry than prevailed at the height of the Age of Theory. Very much the same objectives as those formerly promised by "rigorous" hypothetico-deductive formulation and verification of theories were then seen as attainable via a quasi-political process much like "running" a candidate paradigm for election. The chapter concludes with an argument that *no* formulation or paradigm in the psychological studies can ever prove preemptive.

The core of the chapter derives from section 2 of "Language Communities, Search Cells, and the Psychological Studies" (Koch 1976a). The chapter also draws from an unpublished contribution to a symposium concerning current paradigms in psychology presented at the 1974 annual convention of the American Psychological Association.

«

It is fashionable these days to speak of a "crisis" of alternate "paradigms" in psychology. But the metaphor of "crisis" has been applicable to psychology—and indeed applied—on each of the 36,500 days in its century-long history qua "science." Crisis—whether of methods, schools, theories, or, as we now tend to say, paradigms—is endemic to psychology. It is the inevitable fruit of the very idea of a single, conceptually coherent enterprise whose objective is the positive study of "all" consciousness, experience, conduct, action, or behavior. On *such* a conception, it must always be thus—just as surely as it must remain forever impossible to render an unspecified universe into a universe of discourse. Perhaps that is all I have to say.

Competitive conceptual crises within knowledge-seeking groups may, of course, vary in severity in a variety of ways. The number of alternate conceptual templates competing at a given time is one of them. The frequency distribution of users (or advocates) of the respective templates is another. The crisis condition of psychology has, over its history, varied considerably in these respects. For instance, during a period which I have called the "Age of Theory" (between, roughly, 1930 and the early fifties), the gross-structure of our profession was such that the bulk of American psychologists fell into only three conceptual camps: the neobehavioristic (vastly in the ascendancy), the Gestalt or field-theoretical, and—though a small and marginal camp—the psychoanalytic. (The fine-structure was considerably more intricate!) And the quality of crisis in this interval was relatively "benign" in another sense. Though the members of each group wished their own theories to achieve universal sway, the wish was tempered by at least a dim perception of the utility (from the standpoint of their group) of having a few clearly defined sets of "enemies." It was thus possible, by means of the early ritualization of a set of intergroup polemical policies, to achieve a kind of happy symbiosis. The members of each group could evade the onerous challenge of fleshing out the details of their own primitive and lacunae-ridden theoretical programs by fixing upon a few stable research contexts in which putative disagreements could be fought out. Moreover, since certain epistemological and methodic agreements transcended the theory groups, it was possible to believe that such polemical "research" was *constructive:* a policy of empirical testing of differential consequences of contending points of view would surely move the field toward conceptual unification.

That period of relatively bland "crisis" began to break down in the early to mid-fifties under the impact of a complex of "rational" and extrarational factors far too intricate to unravel at this place. The theories — most of which had claimed an unbridled range of application to "all" psychological phenomena — began to be perceived for the largely vacuous, indeterminate meta-programs that they were; it was also becoming apparent that the various programs had not moved toward any greater determinacy for periods of up to twenty years, and that the polemical research had settled virtually nothing. And some people began to sense that even if these theory-like formulations *had* been theories, the terms of most were such as to have little or no bearing on ranges of phenomena worthy of human interest. Finally, it slowly became apparent (if only dimly and partially) that the epistemic and formal procedural patterns — deriving mainly from the "rational reconstructions" of logical positivism and from operationism — which had guided the development of the more influential "theories" wereutterly inappropriate to the requirements of a psychological subject matter and, indeed, based on highly inadequate generalizations of the practice of physics.

Along with the disaffection just sketched, crisis, of course, burgeoned. Beginning in the early fifties, and at an accelerating rate ever since, many new conceptual and research options were asserted, and many old ones resuscitated. "Theoretical" grandiosity contracted (regarding intended scope, claimed cognitive accomplishment, anticipated predictive specificity), and both conceptual and methodic strategies were diversified. Though many psychologists continued to promote their favored conceptual templates in the messianic spirit of converting the entire psychological research community (and, indeed, the world), it was possible, for a decade or so, to discern a new problem-centered modesty on the part of many.

Then came Thomas Kuhn. I am far from suggesting a devil theory of Thomas Kuhn. If there is anything devilish in the circumstances I am about to mention, this must be attributed to the strangely dysfunctional interaction between psychology and philosophy that has been evident during this century. It is a paradox that a "science" which for a hundred years has taken vast pride in its hard-won independence from philosophy has, over much of that interval, continued to seek out its marching orders from that queen of many edicts. That the queen is a notoriously fickle one no one can deny, but the crux of the difficulty is that most psychologists are not outstandingly precise readers, especially when it comes to philosophy. (If it be argued that Kuhn is a historian and not a philosopher, my response is that his 1962 book had philosophical objectives.) Be all this as it may, Kuhn is a strangely difficult writer. He combines a tendency to be overly pat in the main outlines of his thinking with an allusive and fluidly accretive mode of defining the conceptual elements of his framework. *The Structure of Scientific Revolutions* (1962) is, in essence, a definition *in usu* of three correlative notions: "paradigms," "normal science," and "revolutionary (or extraordinary) science." All three — and especially the central notion of paradigm — emerge as vague, though suggestive, concepts with exceedingly open meaning-horizons. It is the kind of writing that is open to easy misinterpretation by the initiate in the fields addressed by the book and to wild misinterpretation by the uninitiate.

Many psychologists took the message to be that a Kuhnian paradigm is an *X* (a conceptual frame, a way of "seeing," a vocabulary, a single "idea," an experimental method or situation, a mensurational device) which is somehow enormously easier to achieve than what they had thought a "theory" to be — and that a paradigm (in effect, any old paradigm), once universalized within a scientific community, would *guarantee* progress toward increasingly differentiated knowledge. Further, Kuhn seemed to be telling them, all that was necessary for "normal science" and for the easy ecstasy of "puzzle-solving" to supervene was agreement on a paradigm by the members of the community. And agreement was to be attained by "persuasion" — or quite possibly a well-intentioned unanimous vote in the interest of the social weal. (How could a guy with reservations stand in the way?) Never had the price of attaining the status of integral and progressive science appeared so cheap!

The rest of the story hardly requires summarization. At some point preceding the mid-sixties, the imagery (and associated programmatic cant) of paradigms began rapidly to replace the imagery and cant of theories and models. Paradigm promotion became the new form of psychological commerce. Every day sees the propulsion of a brand new paradigm, and every month marks a seminar or convention symposium designed to select a victorious paradigm that will render psychology one and progressive for a tidy stretch of time, if not forever. Psychology is back on the "unity" track with a vengeance — and with the ludicrous consequence that never has the field been comparably obfuscated by the babble of so vast and contentious a plurality of parochial voices.

To take but one illustration of the tradition of paradigm-promoting just described, one might refer to the carefully planned 1975 *Nebraska Symposium on Motivation* (Arnold 1976), which that year was devoted to "Conceptual Foundations of Psychology." The first half of that symposium was given to the views of a number of nonmainstream systematic thinkers. The voices were those of serious and able scholars (Professors Giorgi, Day, Riegel, and Rychlak) who have thought long and responsibly about their positions. Moreover, these are courageous men of unusually self-determining cast, who challenge mainstream thinking at impressive depths. Most of the newer paradigms are, after all, merely local ripples on the surface of a tide of hoary scientistic stratagems. Nevertheless, in the two days of the first session of the symposium, a single audience was courted by the competing claims of a phenomenological paradigm, a "contemporary behaviorism" paradigm, a paradigm advocating "developmental dialecticism," and a paradigm urging a "telic explanation of human behavior," to be implemented within the "objective" verificational resources of traditional "logic of science." Each of these paradigm proposals solicits acceptance by the *entire* psychological community. Each urges, that is, the universalization of its own conceptual template, its own language, within the psychological community.

For many years, I have been urging that it is feckless and illusive to anticipate or search for a single paradigm for psychology, and have been inviting recognition of this by the proposal that "scientific" psychology be reconceived as *the psychological studies*. Psychology, in my view, *cannot* be a coherent discipline, howsoever "coherence" be defined. I shall develop my grounds for this view in chapter 4, but in the present one it will be instructive to examine the phenomenon of "Kuhn in psychology." The bulk of the chapter consists of an analysis of the senses in which misreadings of Thomas Kuhn have given psychologists a false optimism concerning the prospects for an integral discipline—not neglecting an attempt to identify certain of the first-order vaguenesses in Kuhn himself. It concludes with a consideration of an issue which is as much fraught with moral as with cognitive import: Can paradigms, whether of large or limited scope, be *preemptive?*

The most substantial part of the presentation will be the analysis of Kuhn's ideas, both in terms of their intrinsic content and their misreading by psychologists and social scientists. The intentions are explicative; I will hold criticisms of Kuhn to a minimum in that certain of these will emerge either by implication or directly in later chapters.

1. The Kuhnian Paradigm and the New Optimism Concerning a Unified Psychology

Before entering this topic, it may be well to note for the benefit of psychologists addicted to the notion of paradigms that there are currently in the literature two Kuhns offering two very different analyses of the character of paradigms. Some would say that there are more than two. Indeed, one of Kuhn's critics, Margaret Masterman (1970), distinguished twenty-one senses in which the word *paradigm* had been used in the 1962 (original) version of *The Structure of Scientific Revolutions*. Subsequent to this and many other criticisms of the original position by philosophers of science, Kuhn published several emendations of the position (e.g., 1970a, 1970b, 1970c, 1974). Of these, the one which should probably be regarded as official is contained in a "postscript" to the second edition of his book (1970c). The notion of paradigm is now developed in a radically different way from the original treatment. If Kuhn has not achieved ultimate clarity, he at least has altered the treatment in such a way that many of the wilder construals and expectations engendered in psychologists and social scientists by his initial account would *now* be less likely to be drawn. We will confront aspects of the new Kuhn later, but it is the old Kuhn who has had the far-reaching—and, in my opinion, unfortunate—impact on psychologists still in evidence.

The Kuhn of 1962

Despite the vaguenesses that Kuhn now acknowledges, there is much evidence to suggest that the old Kuhn was being read as superficially as was Bridgman in another day (cf. chapter 14). Kuhn's book, *The Structure of Scientific Revolutions,* fell into a cluster of efforts directed toward reassessment of the dominating positivistic views of science of this century—a movement which, by the early sixties, when Kuhn published, had already become so widespread and advanced as itself to justify the adjective *revolutionary*. In my Rice Symposium paper of 1963 (Koch 1964 [chapter 2]), I was already able to identify that new look at the nature of knowledge and cite an extensive bibliography. The force of this rescrutiny relative to *scientific* knowledge was to challenge both the sense and the utility of so-called rational reconstructions of the nature of science, and to move toward a view of the scientific enterprise more fully cognizant of the empirical particularities of inquiry. The working scientist, the historian of science, and (at least in principle) the psychological and sociological observer of science were seen to have perspectives which invited fundamental readjustment of images of science that had been arrived at through purely philosophic or logical means.

Among the important convergences already developing within this movement were the following: the scientific process was being seen as at all stages underdetermined by rule; theory was being seen as relatively independent from any strict induction base on the one side or confirmation domain on the other, while its genesis, elaboration, productiveness, reception, and fate were seen to be far more dependent on inherent aesthetic and other value-engendering properties than formerly. Perhaps the most profound member of this group was Michael Polanyi (1958), who powerfully challenged the modern tendency to *identify* the knowable and the sayable. He makes, in effect, the concept of *skill* central in his argument and analyzes in extensive detail the senses in which "knowing" must be regarded a skilled performance of a type reducible to no algorithm, resistant in principle to full specification, and governable only in loose and underdetermined ways (if at all) by "rules." For Polanyi, language use is always dependent on conjoint extra-articulate or "tacit" processes, and thus full formalization or explication of any cognitive achievement represents an impossible ideal.

Kuhn's work was a useful addition — in some ways subtle, in other ways overly pat, and in still others vague — to this incipient tradition of thought. Its special force lies in his disposition to take the history of science as criterial with respect to many of the issues concerning inquiry formerly thought to lie within the special province of the philosopher or epistemologist of science. His unifying notion of the paradigm and his bipolar typology of normal versus revolutionary science are gross but suggestive tools in this endeavor. The special quality of his contribution is his ardent and knowledgeable use of particulate examples from the history of science in such a way as to wear down the contours of traditional hyperrationalistic models of the scientific enterprise. His central notion of paradigms is thinly specified and flexibly used, to some extent deliberately so. The following is as close to an explicit definition of paradigm as he gets during the course of an entire book:

> [A paradigm is an] achievement . . . sufficiently unprecedented to attract an enduring group of adherents away from competing modes of scientific activity. Simultaneously, it [is] sufficiently open-ended to leave all sorts of problems for the redefined group of practitioners to resolve.
>
> Achievements that share these two characteristics I shall henceforth refer to as "paradigms," a term that relates closely to "normal science." By choosing it, I mean to suggest that some accepted examples of actual scientific practice — examples which include law, theory, application, and instrumentation to-

97

gether — provide models from which spring particular coherent traditions of scientific research. These are the traditions which the historian describes under such rubrics as "Ptolemaic astronomy" (or "Copernican"), "Aristotelian dynamics" (or "Newtonian"), "corpuscular optics" (or "wave optics"), and so on. The study of paradigms, including many that are far more specialized than those named illustratively above, is what mainly prepares the student for membership in the particular scientific community with which he will later practice. Because he there joins men who learned the bases of their field from the same concrete models, his subsequent practice will seldom evoke overt disagreement over fundamentals. Men whose research is based on shared paradigms are committed to the same rules and standards for scientific practice. That commitment and the apparent consensus it produces are prerequisites for normal science, i.e., for the genesis and continuation of a particular research tradition. (Kuhn 1962, 10–11)

Over and above this relatively explicit (though, as one can see, open-ended) definition, the meaning of the term continuously but asystematically burgeons by its application in particular contexts throughout Kuhn's book. Any *full* definition *in usu* would reveal the concept to be a vague one with an exceedingly open horizon. A paradigm is always localized in an *achievement* of some complexity but it may vary markedly in relation to scope or centering (e.g., it may center primarily on a theory, a law, an instrumental method, a pregnant system of classification or measurement, etc.). In most applications, it is clear, though, that at the core of a paradigm is a substantive idea about nature (usually conceived by Kuhn, on a perceptual-cognitive model, as a mode of seeing, a Gestalt, "a conceptual network through which scientists view the world") which is somehow highly revealing, which permits a more precise solution of older problems discriminated within an area and opens up new ones, and which commands wide assent. Though the paradigm must have broad generality relative to the area of science for which it holds, the area itself may be quite narrow.

It cannot be emphasized too strongly that Kuhn's notion of "paradigm" is not any and every construal of the standard natural language word *paradigm* ("pattern, exemplar, example," in the OED sense) but a rather special concept which seeks to disembed from the history of science a kind of theory of its special dynamic and genius. It takes Kuhn the entirety of his densely packed (if short) book (1962) to *suggest* his sense of "paradigm." *The Kuhnian paradigm is minimally a substantive cognitive achievement of sufficient differentiation and power to permit within an area corresponding to its range of application a period of "normal science." And the mark of such a period is that the entire scientific community is enabled to address a range of significant and determinate "puzzles" which are suggested by (and the solution of which facilitated by) the terms of the paradigm.*

The outlines of Kuhn's notions of "normal science" as a paradigm-dominated interval marked by "puzzle-solving," and of "revolutionary science" as an interval during which anomalies encountered by an old paradigm trigger controversial efforts toward the creation and acceptance of a new paradigm, are well known. It is not my intention here to review Kuhn's work in detail, but it is necessary to hold certain other features of his position in mind. Thus, for instance, competing paradigms bearing on the same or overlapping domains are held to be "incommensurable" in ways analogous to the differential perceptual organizations induced by a fluctuating figure. Paradigm shift is seen to be a matter neither of strict verification nor falsification (on any of the formal criteria suggested by logicians of science) but, rather, a matter of gradual perception by the scientific community that the new paradigm is not only capable of removing the anomalies that invited its creation but is in other ways a more efficient and richer problem-solving instrument. Though the new paradigm is typically able to handle most of the problems dealt with by its predecessor (and often with greater precision and adequacy), it *may* be unequipped to handle certain of the problems (both solved and unsolved) within the range of the old paradigm. Because of this feature and incommensurability in other respects, a science cannot be said to progress in any *linear* way.

From all of these considerations, it follows that adoption of a new paradigm is mediated not by strict *proof* but, rather, by *persuasion*. Though Kuhn does not exempt the operation of adventitious and extrarational factors from this process of persuasion, he does recognize that the process is mainly grounded on rational considerations such as success at solving old problems and at generating and solving new ones. And he acknowledges the role of factors which correlate with such problem-solving criteria, such as the aesthetic appeal of the new paradigm. Indeed, his analysis of the conditions of paradigm shift lead him to the conclusion that *any* new paradigm that wins universal adoption in a scientific community is *necessarily* a more efficient problem-solving instrument than the one it supplants.

Finally, it should be noted that Kuhn, in his eagerness to redirect analytical attention toward the particularities of scientific inquiry rather than the generalizations and models which epistemologists have abstracted out of inquiry, makes a self-conscious point of sidestepping the notion of truth in its relation to science until almost the very end of his book. Two-and-a-half pages before his concluding line, he pridefully reports: "It is now time to notice that until the last very few pages the term 'truth' had entered this essay only in a quotation from Francis Bacon" (1962, 169). At this point, he embarks on a rather clumsy and irresolute coda in defense of the thesis that "we may . . . have to relinquish the notion . . . that changes of paradigm carry scientists and those who learn from them closer and closer to the truth" (169). In this very same context, though, he reasserts his belief in the inevitability of progress (in the sense previously defined) in science, and acknowledges that the "developmental process described in this essay [is] . . . a process whose successive stages are characterized by an increasingly detailed and refined understanding of nature" (169). Nevertheless, he rejects the view that science "draws constantly nearer to some goal set by nature in advance" (170). He prefers to phrase science as an "evolution from" rather than an "evolution toward."

Unobjectionable as these points may be, they will be seen to represent a surprisingly partial and inept consideration of the intricate problem-cluster associated with the analysis of scientific truth (or of related notions such as probability). Instead of joining these issues in any differentiated way, he addresses a monolithic conception of truth (truth with a capital T) of a sort that could not, at this phase in the history of culture, be taken seriously by anyone save a participant in a fraternity seminar. Despite this, we find Kuhn saying, in the last paragraph of his book, the following:

> Anyone who has followed the argument this far will nevertheless feel the need to ask why the evolutionary process should work. What must nature, including man, be like in order that science be possible at all? Why should scientific communities be able to reach a firm consensus unattainable in other fields? Why should consensus endure across one paradigm change after another? And why should paradigm change invariably produce an instrument more perfect in any sense than those known before? From one point of view those questions, excepting the first, have already been answered. But from another they are as open as they were when this essay began. It is not only the scientific community that must be special. The world of which that community is a part must also possess quite spe-

cial characteristics, and we are no closer than we were at the start to knowing what these must be. (1962, 172)

It should be utterly clear, then, that the 1962 Kuhn is by no means a conventionalist, a consensualist, or immune from ontological commitments. Indeed, these words and many others in the body of the essay show that his analysis invites and requires a theory of truth, and that though it is consonant with a *range* of answers, it limits that range.

I first read *The Structure of Scientific Revolutions* just a few months after it was published, at a time when I was feverishly working on a range of problems closely related to the ones it addressed. There was an apparent commonality in the drift of Kuhn's and my thinking, but I was nevertheless strangely depressed. Kuhn is not an opaque writer but his mode of exposition — the apparent black-or-whiteness of his concepts despite the gray penumbras which emerge only on close reading — is such that he can be easily misinterpreted. I predicted that his impact on psychology could be appallingly counterproductive, and I fear that I have been confirmed. Let me indicate a few of the misuses of Kuhn that I then foresaw.

1. Because of the natural language connotations of the word *paradigm* that any reader is likely to bring with him, and because of the accretive method of definition that Kuhn employs in developing the concept, it seemed to me that psychologists would be likely to perceive a Kuhnian paradigm as much more easily achievable than, say, an articulated theory. After all, Kuhn nowhere reconstructs in their full complexity any of the paradigms he discusses. Indeed, the force of his position is that paradigms resist full specification in principle; they are largely embedded in exceedingly intricate practices or, as Polanyi might say, tacit skills, within scientific communities. Yet so variably and fragmentarily are they addressed by Kuhn (for one illustrative purpose or another) that it is possible to believe a paradigm to be almost anything bearing an ordering relation to inquiry: a conceptual frame, a dimensional system, a descriptive grammar, a set of tentatively identified "variables," an iconic model at one or another level of specification, a classificatory system.

It should be recalled that by the early sixties psychologists had lived through a fifteen-year process of attenuation of their systematic expectations: the hope for immediate hypothetico-deductive theories adequate to all psychology had given way to the pursuit of "miniature" theories still of hypothetico-deductive cast; the latter had given way to the search for iconic or mathematical "models" of one or another degree of generality (and best characterized, relative to the performance of the modelers, as hypothetico-deductive formulations having more highly visible nomological holes than those put forward as of yore and asserted at lower levels of confidence). But here was Kuhn *apparently* saying that even physics is merely a matter of paradigms and that a paradigm can be almost anything. Thus was ushered in the strange phase of psychological history in which we now live: the thirst for generality can be easily slaked; psychology can become unitary, and inexorably progress throughout all future time via universal acceptance of a vocabulary, an "image of man," a method for the experimental analysis of behavior which can implement the lawful relations among three endlessly pregnant concepts or by the convenient and eminently rational adoption of a "general system theory."

2. The heady prospect of easy integration opened up by this misreading of Kuhn's primary concept of paradigm can be (and has been) shored up by many secondary misreadings. The conventionalism and nominalism once fostered by versions of logical positivism can now return in truly virulent form on the authority of a misread Kuhn. If persuasion, not proof, is the condition of paradigm change, why can't "persuasion" be read as "propaganda" or "attitude change"? *Psychologists* know a thing or two about such matters! If cognitive advance is inevitable under conditions of normal science, and normal science happens when a paradigm is universalized within a scientific community, and, moreover, if the condition of that happy state of affairs is merely "consensus," then why can't psychologists get together and merely agree on a paradigm: any old paradigm? And, finally, if science has nothing to do with truth, then it matters little which paradigm we agree on; it is the agreement that is important, not the content of the paradigm.

In presenting these misinterpretations in short compass I have been forced toward the verge of caricature. But many paradigms pushed by the paradigm-pushing psychologists of the past decade are proof of such misreadings of Kuhn. In this abuse of his authority, Kuhn himself is not blameless. But he does not quite deserve his psychological following.

The "New" Kuhn

Coming now to the *new* Kuhn—as evinced in the second edition of his book (1970c) and in two contributions (1970a, 1970b) to a symposium volume on his views—it should immediately be noted that he takes pains to scotch the central misinterpretation that I have tried to lay bare in the preceding analysis. Apparently, Kuhn had become nervous about the rapid proliferation of paradigm proposals—each containing a built-in promise of "normal" or progressive scientific status—which had become evident in fields like psychology and the social sciences. Thus we find him saying in "Reflections on My Critics" (1970b):

> In any case, there are many fields—I shall call them proto-sciences—in which practice does generate testable conclusions but which nonetheless resemble philosophy and the arts rather than the established sciences in their developmental patterns. I think, for example, of fields like chemistry and electricity before the mid-eighteenth century . . . or of many of the social sciences today. In these fields, too . . . incessant criticism and continual striving for a fresh start are primary forces, and need to be. No more than in philosophy and the arts, however, do they result in clear-cut progress.
>
> I conclude, in short, that the proto-sciences, like the arts and philosophy, lack some element which, in the mature sciences, permits the more obvious forms of progress. *It is not, however, anything that a methodological prescription can provide.* . . . I claim no therapy to assist the transformation of a proto-science to a science, nor do I suppose that anything of the sort is to be had. *If . . . some social scientists take from me the view that they can improve the status of their field by first legislating agreement on fundamentals and then turning to puzzle solving, they are badly misconstruing my point.* (1970b, 244–45; italics added)

I hasten to note that later in the same paragraph Kuhn does say a few words which could seriously fuzz the above message in the minds of autistic proto-scientific readers:

> A sentence I once used when discussing the special efficacy of mathematical theories applies equally here: "As in individual development, so in the scientific group, maturity comes most surely to those who know how to wait." Fortunately, though no prescription will force it, the transition to maturity does come to many fields, and it is well worth waiting and struggling to attain. (1970b, 245)

Lest this addendum precipitate another wild orgy of paradigm promoting, I should add that the extended context of Kuhn's discussion at this place makes it quite clear that Kuhn is making no promises but, rather, is trying to establish, for the edification of his critics, that his analysis applies only "after" the occurrence of "progress" (for the achievement of which state his theory offers no formula) "become[s] an obvious characteristic of a field." And I would presume it equally clear that even if Kuhn were meaning to reassure psychologists or some other proto-scientific group, his *intent* could have little to do with the outcome of any strategy of "waiting" or even "struggling."

Kuhn addresses the same issue (does any old paradigm bring tranquility and progress?) in the "postscript" to the second edition of *The Structure of Scientific Revolutions*. We here find him renouncing his 1962 distinction between the "pre-paradigm" and "post-paradigm" periods in the development of a scientific field, and saying:

> The nature of that transition to maturity deserves fuller discussion than it has received in this book [meaning the original 1962 text], particularly from those concerned with the development of the contemporary social sciences. To that end it may help to point out that the transition need not (I now think should not) be associated with the first acquisition of a paradigm. The members of all scientific communities, including the schools of the "pre-paradigm" period, share the sorts of elements which I have collectively labeled "a paradigm." What changes with the transition to maturity is not the presence of a paradigm but rather its nature. *Only after the change is normal puzzle-solving research possible. Many of the attributes of a developed science which I have above associated with the acquisition of a paradigm I would therefore now discuss as consequences of the acquisition of the sort of paradigm that identifies challenging puzzles, supplies clues to their solution, and guarantees that the truly clever practitioner will succeed.* (Kuhn 1970c, 178–79; italics added)

These clarifications, important though they be, represent negligible elements in the overall pattern of changes in Kuhn's current position. It is impossible to convey the entire pattern in brief compass but it is well that psychologists be apprised that the changes are far-reaching. And certain of them have a bearing on the themes of this chapter. In the eight years between the two editions of Kuhn's book, philosophers and others had subjected the position to vigorous criticism. For instance: some saw the distinction between normal and revolutionary science as too stark and schematic, and some saw it as no distinction at all; some saw the notion of "puzzle-solving" as a thin and inadequate registration of what competent scientists do in periods of theoretical stability; Kuhn was criticized for "psychologism" and for oversociologizing the conception of science; there was strong criticism on many fronts concerning inadequacies of his analysis of theory choice or appraisal and of conceptual change in general (he was often accused of "irrationalism" and "subjectivity" in relation to these matters); there were many objections to Kuhn's views concerning the "incommensurability" of competing "paradigms" or theories and thus to his assessment of communicative barriers separating paradigm groups during scientific crises; overarching all these challenges and others was a barrage of complaints about the ambiguity of his presentation, especially in relation to the central notion of paradigms. The current Kuhn position is in part an accommodation to challenges of this order, in part a rejoinder to them, and, one can assume, in part a self-initiated effort to refine and develop the earlier thinking.

The notion of "paradigm" is now *dramatically* different: its sprawling reference field has been pulled back to the much more limited (though, as we shall see, still rangy) denotation of what Kuhn chooses to call "exemplars." To bring this about necessitated a complex maneuver involving the realignment of certain old ideas and the introduction of new conceptual elements. In brief, Kuhn now feels that it is circular to define a scientific community via the sharing of a paradigm. If he rewrote his book, "it would therefore open with a discussion of the community structure of science" and communities would be identified "without prior recourse to paradigms." Though the sociological methods for isolating such groups are not all "in hand," a community consists "of the practitioners of a scientific specialty. To an extent unparalleled in most other fields, they have undergone similar educations and professional initiations; in the process they have absorbed the same technical literature and drawn many of the same lessons from it" (1970c, 177). Again, "the members of a scientific community see themselves and are seen by others as the men uniquely responsible for the pursuit of a set of shared goals, including the training of their successors. Within such groups communication is relatively full and professional judgment relatively unanimous" (177). Communities exist "at numerous levels," ranging from "the community of all natural scientists" and, at descending "levels," whole sciences and their various subfields. One arrives at something like an ultimate level with communities "of perhaps one hundred members, occasionally significantly fewer," having shared problematic interests of a delimited sort (Kuhn takes "the phage group prior to its public acclaim" as an example), and identifiable via "formal and informal communication networks" and citation patterns. Kuhn notes also that usually "individual scientists . . . will belong to several such groups." And he concludes: "communities of this sort are the units that this book has presented as the producers and validators of scientific knowledge. Paradigms are something shared by the members of such groups" (177–78)

But *what* are paradigms? The answer is intricate! One *first* isolates communities as just described. If one should then ask what "do its members share that accounts for the relative fullness of their professional communication and the relative unanimity of their professional judgments," Kuhn would answer (and does), "to that question my original text licenses the answer, a paradigm or set of paradigms" (182). He *now* feels the term "inappropriate" for so general a use. Though scientists might suggest "they share a theory or set of theories," Kuhn feels that "'theory' connotes a structure far more limited . . . than the one required here." Instead he suggests *disciplinary matrix* as the "common possession" of the community. And the matrix comprehends "all or most of the objects of group commitment that my original text makes paradigms, parts of paradigms, or paradigmatic." But *now* they are "no longer to be discussed as though they were all of a piece" (182).

The disciplinary matrix is then said to comprise four sorts of component. Rapidly now:

1. *Symbolic generalizations.* These are the "formal" components of the disciplinary matrix, and Kuhn uses the logical form of a universal generalization as illustrative prototype.

2. *Beliefs in particular models.* These might include substantive theoretical models or heuristic ones. *They* supply "preferred or permissible analogies and metaphors." Kuhn points out that he would formerly have called such components "metaphysical paradigms" or "the metaphysical parts of paradigms."

3. *Values.* These are "more widely shared among different communities than either symbolic generalizations or models" (184). Values have a peculiar importance, for Kuhn makes it clear that he will now lodge his account of the very sensitive issues of "crisis" identification and theory choice in the application of the group values by its members. What he says in this connection is worthy of quotation, for we are here dealing with the basis of Kuhn's theory of rational decision in science:

> Probably the most deeply held values concern predictions: they should be accurate; quantitative predictions are preferable to qualitative ones; whatever the margin of permissible error, it should be consistently satisfied in a given field; and so on.

There are also, however, values to be used in judging whole theories: *they must, first and foremost, permit puzzle-formulation and solution;* where possible they should be simple, self-consistent, and plausible, compatible, that is, with other theories currently deployed. (185; italics added)

4. *Exemplars.* This final "element" in the disciplinary matrix brings us to what now remains of the notion of paradigm! "For it the term 'paradigm' would be entirely appropriate" (186). Indeed, which of the two terms Kuhn proposes to use from this point on is not quite clear; in the "postscript," his preference in the matter oscillates, though paradigm is ultimately given the edge. And again we must quote:

By it [exemplars] I mean, initially, the concrete problem-solutions that students encounter from the start of their scientific education, whether in laboratories, on examinations, or at the ends of chapters in science texts. To these shared examples should, however, be added at least some of the technical problem-solutions found in the periodical literature that scientists encounter during their post-educational research careers and that also show them by example how their job is to be done. More than other sorts of components of the disciplinary matrix, differences between sets of exemplars provide the community fine-structure of science. All physicists, for example, begin by learning the same exemplars: problems such as the inclined plane, the conical pendulum, and Keplerian orbits; instruments such as the vernier, the calorimeter, and the Wheatstone bridge. As their training develops, however, the symbolic generalizations they share are increasingly illustrated by different exemplars. Though both solid-state and field-theoretic physicists share the Schrödinger equation, only its more elementary applications are common to both groups. (187)

It should be noted, of course, that we have merely broached the outline of Kuhn's new position. In the "postscript" (and other recent writing) Kuhn proceeds to develop and exploit this apparatus in the context of analyses of issues raised by his critics and, no doubt, by his own sense of the requirements for strengthening the theory. The crux of his interest in these discussions is in explicating the detailed properties of exemplars which—because of the "tacit," non-rule-subsumable perceptual information they convey—he regards as the source of whatever uniquely differentiates his position from "rational-reconstructionist" views of science. And, in debates over theory choice, he makes a stab at spelling out in a more differentiated way what he means by "incommensurability." Throughout his pursuit of such issues, Kuhn has tended to presuppose something very much like a *perceptual* theory of definition. For instance, he tries to show that the ability to apply a scientific generalization (law or "law-schema") significantly depends on "learning from problems to see situations as like each other," and therefore: "That sort of learning is not acquired by exclusively verbal means. Rather it comes as one is given words together with concrete examples of how they function in use; nature and words are learned together. To borrow once more Michael Polanyi's useful phrase, what results from this process is 'tacit knowledge' which is learned by doing science rather than by acquiring rules for doing it" (1970c, 190–91).

In a number of passages (1970c, 187–206; 1970b, 266–77) he develops such ideas suggestively and, at one point, issues the following invitation: "[P]hilosophers of science will need to follow other contemporary philosophers in examining, to a previously unprecedented depth, the manner in which language fits the world, asking how terms attach to nature, how those attachments are learned, and how they are transmitted from one generation to another by the members of a language community" (1970b, 235). Neither Kuhn, however, nor philosophers of science (nor indeed any other kinds of philosophers) are likely to do this in a way especially illuminating for the *detailed* problems and prospects of psychology. Almost forty years ago, I began to raise precisely the complex of questions mentioned in Kuhn's invitation (in an unpublished, but frequently presented, 1959 paper entitled "Towards an Indigenous Methodology" [Koch 1959c]), and though I have tapped these ideas briefly in a few publications over the years (Koch 1961b, 1964, 1973b), I have never published on this work in extenso. The explicit notion of specialized "language communities" (whether scientific or natural) was a central part of my analysis, and my approach may be seen as providing a particulate rationale for the conditions and consequences of communicative mismatches and incommensurabilities. But, more importantly, the analysis was trained upon specific communicative problems of *psychology* and provides, I think, an "in principle" basis for the rejection of any belief that psychology can become a homogeneous or coherent discipline. A policy of "waiting" for this "protoscience" to become "mature" will be met by no other outcome than frustration, and as for "struggling," that policy may well contaminate the stream of our thinking for the next thousand years.

I have tried to convey the thinking of the "two Kuhns" in sufficient detail to exorcize the current assumption that the paradigm is a one-word solution to all problems of psychology. However wistful the hope of success in that objective, there has also been an ulterior one of some importance to the purpose of this book. For the contour of Kuhn's views will provide a useful foil and comparison basis for issues subsequently to be discussed (especially chapter 5).

But I should not like to conclude this section before giving at least a thumbnail summary of my attitudes towards Kuhn's contributions. Though I have held back from criticism of Kuhn in my effort to trace the impact of widespread misinterpretations of his position by psychologists and social scientists, it should not thereby be taken that I am a votary of the position in either of its forms.

To me, the only unarguable element in the Kuhn picture is the recognition of the *role* of "tacit knowledge" and of how this must qualify rule-saturated versions of the scientific enterprise. But, as I point out elsewhere, the originator of that notion, Michael Polanyi (1958), has charted its ramifications in a mode incomparably more revealing, profound, compelling, incisive, and eloquent than has Kuhn. Polanyi stands to Kuhn as does Beethoven to Bacharach!

My many demurs to Kuhn can only be summarized here. He has, I think, a limited appreciation of the role of differential observer sensitivities in science; a limited understanding of the complexity of language use and thus of the presence of differentially competent language appliers and subcommunities of such within the same scientific language community; a naïve and outmoded sense of perceptual process, which he phrases in a lay version of a nineteenth-century language of "stimuli," "sensations," "awareness of sensations," "interpretations" upon sensations, etc. (cf. 1970c, 191–98). He has a deathly fear of ontologizing and is evasive at many junctures concerning definite realist implications of his analyses. Some of these matters I address in extenso, though implicatively, elsewhere in the book; here I wish to make my attitudes explicit.

More importantly, Kuhn's three primary metaphors (other than paradigm or exemplar)—normal science, revolutionary science, and puzzle-solving—are all, I think, seriously overschematic and misleading. I agree with Toulmin (1970, 1972) that the distinction between normal and revolutionary science is much too sharp—and perhaps totally unilluminating. The crux of the difficulty may be seen in the metaphor of puzzle-solving—a crass and indeed insulting characterization of what in fact goes on in the highly creative inquiry often required for the significant extension, re-finement, or corroboration of frameworks. Once we give up a rule-regulated conception of science (one which assumes that scientific method is automatically self-corrective, etc.), we must perceive—and acknowl-edge—the intensely creative character of *any* genuine scientific advance, however local and small by comparison with the creation of a new and powerful theory. To take the matter of experiment per se, it is important to acknowledge that a well-conducted experiment is a work of art, often of a very high order. No theory uniquely determines the terms of an experi-ment in the sense that a puzzle, even a difficult one, uniquely determines the terms of solution. Quite aside from the essentially connoisseurlike as-sessment determining the choice of a significant "consequence" for test, there is the largely open-ended creative task of arriving at a relevant, sensi-tively discriminating, and rigorous design, and the still more artistic task of shaping, out of the world flux, a material context which "truly" realizes the theoretical variables selected for study and their appropriate ensemble of initial conditions. And so on and on!

Finally, it may be instructive to ask why—in the early 1960s when psy-chology's Age of Theory ideology was ripe for liberalization—did psychol-ogists single out from among all the individuals then participating in the critique of the regnant positivistic conception of the nature of knowledge Thomas Kuhn? Why not Michael Polanyi—who, in the opinion of many (including, apparently, Kuhn), had elaborated in his 1958 masterwork, *Personal Knowledge,* the richest and most persuasive critique of the positivist attitude complex (scientism) not only in the then recent wave of reassess-ment but in the entire century? As we have suggested, the central virtues of Kuhn's analysis (as, e.g., his stress upon the fact that the meanings and application contexts of scientific formalisms are conveyed via "exemplars" which perceptually exhibit but cannot, in principle, specify by *rule* the use of the formalisms) are but shallow and devitalized semblances of Polanyi's thinking. I do not suggest for an instant that Kuhn has *translated* Polanyi into his own idiom. Yet, at the same time, it is regrettable to note that his principal reference to Polanyi is to his "useful phrase . . . 'tacit knowledge'" (Kuhn 1970c, 191).

Why, then, is Kuhn a household deity to psychologists, the seer who has led them into a presumably new era? Why not Polanyi? For one thing, Polanyi's wide span of informed interest and eloquent prose requires from the reader both intellectual effort and a high order of literacy! But—far more importantly—Polanyi's deeper and more differentiated analyses, and his effort to erect a frame in which scientific knowledge can be seen in meaningful relation to sentience in general and to the encompassing human enterprise, is *too* liberating: even when misapprehended, it seems to call for too great a departure from the cozy role-playing practices, and rationales, of an established pseudo-scientific discipline. Kuhn, by comparison, is a turgid writer who seems to be clear! Despite the fuzziness of his conceptual elements, they are deployed in a bold pattern: taken together, they can appear to have figural salience (and thus facilitate easy recall), however remote the figure may be from the meanings intended. "Paradigms," "normal science," "revolutionary science," "puzzle solving"—these words can even be taught to Psychology I students. Kuhn—in other words—can be *confidently* misread, and *that* he certainly has been, as we have seen.

In sum, then, the Kuhnian "liberalization" *confirmed* rather than challenged the diffuse positivistic attitudes inhabiting the minds of most psychologists. And indeed, even a *correct* reading of Kuhn's position will show it to constitute only a limited and superficial challenge to positivistic orthodoxy. His position is in some ways a transfer of the positivistic mentality from a "rational reconstructionist" view of the scientific enterprise to a sociological one.

2. Can Paradigms in Psychology Be Preemptive?

There is an interesting theme in Kuhn which bears on the stability of paradigms (in his full sense of the term) in periods of "normal science." In such periods, the paradigm is *constitutive of the world* of the scientists who work under its sway. It operates within them as a kind of perceptual-cognitive filter or grid of extremely compelling character. This is so for many reasons deriving ultimately from its massive history of success in solving problems and the institutionalization of the associated research practices within the educative mechanisms of the scientific community. Within *normal* science (when the paradigm is, by definition, universal to the scientific community) the paradigm may thus be said to have preemptive force as against the entertainment of alternate modes of structuring the world-segment addressed by the community. Even for normal science, however, this kind of preemptiveness is not in Kuhn's view absolute. Alternate paradigm candidates can be proposed by creative individuals at any time, though this tends to take place mainly in response to significant and persisting anomalies. And indeed, under such "crisis" conditions, an appreciable number of paradigm candidates may be formed.

Whatever the shortcomings of Kuhn's general account, such emphases on the perspectival and sensibility-dependent character of scientific knowledge as are implicit in the points that I have just summarized are of the first importance. One might have wished that psychology's Age of the Paradigm could have gotten straight at least *this* part of Kuhn's message. Instead, we are confronted with the paradox of a greater profusion of systematic (i.e., "paradigmatic") options competing for allegiance than ever before in the history of psychology qua science, *coexisting* with an order of self-righteous conviction (on the part of their votaries) in the preemptiveness of each paradigm that has rarely before been rivaled.

There is no harm in seeking as much generality as one may think desirable or feasible in the development of "paradigms" (so called). I happen to think it feckless and wasteful to seek to bring everything that psychologists do (or even everything significant or interesting that they do) under one conceptual or methodic or "dimensional" or analytic apparatus, but who can have the right to censure those who wish to try? I think it feckless *and false*, however, for such a paradigm explorer to view his or her effort as conceivably preemptive. By now we know enough not only about the nature of knowledge and the limits upon linguistic specification but about the inexhaustible complexity of a human subject matter to conclude that any paradigm bearing on the human reality must be perspectival, sensibility-dependent (relative to the inquirer), and further, that even paradigms bearing on the same limited human or organismic domain will rarely turn out to be commensurable, fusible, or in some sense, integratable. To neglect such considerations is to run the risk of revitalizing the role-playing conception of inquiry which for so long has dominated our field.

There are too many grotesque historical demonstrations of the overzealous promotion of paradigm proposals by promoters who lack the perspective to appreciate the perspectival character of their offerings. When we in the psychological studies discover our dignity, we will, for example, no longer tolerate pseudo-argument forms in defense of a paradigm which seek to dismiss all possible alternate views merely by disqualifying the class of all possible alternate viewers or critics within the "causal" or diagnostic categories of the paradigm itself. When, say, every objection to a reinforcement view of the human universe is attributed to a peculiarity or defect in the "reinforcement history" of the critic, we are in the presence of an extraordinary constriction of perspective, to say the least. In the Freud-Jung correspondence (Freud and Jung 1974), it is melancholy to find Jung (on the threshold of separation from his master) reminding Freud of his tendency to assess associates, and especially deviating ones, in terms of their neurotic resistances and distortions. The tendency among Freud's *followers* over much of the history of psychoanalysis to view dissidents and critics in symptomatic terms is, of course, news to no one; I must say, though, that I myself had not before been apprised of how poignantly pellucid was the precedent set by the master himself.

The bulk of my professional effort for the past forty years has been given to the patient demonstration of the *cognitive* disutilities that have stemmed from autistic, naïve, or meretricious efforts to court generality (in many specifiable senses of that term). It is *now* well to note that this tendency raises a *moral* question in a central sense. In the psychological studies, the attribution to any quasi-paradigm of a preemptive finality has the force of telling human beings precisely what they are, of fixing their essence, defining their ultimate worth, potential, meaning; cauterizing away that quality of ambiguity, mystery, search, that makes progress through a biography an adventure. Even were the claim to such a paradigm valid, the right to disseminate it would be a moral issue of the deepest sort. Were the claim specious — which all such claims necessarily are — propagation of the paradigm in the guise of a preemptive truth could only be thought monstrous.

After a one-hundred-year latency period, psychology has recently — and with notable celerity — developed a refined ethical sense concerning the human impact of such psychotechnologies as behavior modification and psychosurgery, such procedural proclivities as lying to experimental "subjects," and such forms of psychic voyeuring as are implicit in the enforced application of huge batteries of "personality" and other "mental" tests to the happy denizens of business and governmental organizations. No matter that these exalted sensitivities were elicited by Act of Congress, grant-making criteria of Federal funding agencies, and public outcry, rather than tortured self-scrutiny: every psychologist is now a Kierkegaard! But the ranks of Congress are not noted for the presence of epistemologists who might discern the deeper brutality of informing humankind that it must fit the mold of some thin scientistic schema containing a built-in rhetoric of being the sole and whole and final story.

Coda

The one-hundred-year search for a principle of coherence (whether theoretical, paradigmatic, or, indeed, metaphysical) adequate to all psychology is, in effect, the restless search of psychologists for *morale*. In some degree, every psychologist has suspected that his career may be addressed to a discipline that does not exist: that he has embarked upon a hollow commitment which will render his effort expendable, even ludicrous, in the eyes of history. I am an old dog, but have not yet had a colleague or professional acquaintance who has not manifested such a concern during those quiet evenings, parties or bar tête-à-têtes that conduce towards honest loquacity. And some, like William James, have publicly celebrated an inner hell of such doubts in every third paragraph.

But these anxious qualms spring from a thin nineteenth-century conception of the "disciplines" — especially those of scientific cast — from which psychologists seem somehow unable to detach themselves. If a man sees some part of human or organismic reality in a fresh and revealing way, and can communicate some part of that vision to one other person, *he* is no failure. That other person need not assimilate (or even apprehend) the vision (system, theory, paradigm) in full and literal detail, or even be able to specify precisely or localize what precisely he has learned. The criterion of significant influence need only be that the "donor's" vision enable the recipient to glimpse aspects of reality which he otherwise would not have noted. And the taker, in turn, will build *his* vision, at least in part, upon the ladder of the donor's vision.

Perspectives *cascade,* one from the other, but unlike the cascading of water, they may rise as well as fall. Such a relation guarantees that the cumulation of knowledge — in psychology as in other forms of inquiry — will be as inevitable as the certainty that no two inquirers will bring the same sensibility to their viewing of the world.

The calling of psychologist may seem a lonelier one than that of natural scientist, but a man is not cut off from his fellows by the absence of a *lingua franca*. Indeed, the absence of a *lingua franca* may move him towards richer and more subtle modes of communication. It is perhaps true that the practice of psychology calls for greater heart and independence in its inquirers than does that of many other disciplines. By this token, the psychologist may find his morale through the belated recognition of his own courage.

4

Psychology versus the Psychological Studies

Foreword

This chapter is an expansion and justification of my position, anticipated in chapter 1, concerning the *essential* perspectivism, particularism, and problem-dependent contextualism of psychological study. It is a modified and shortened version of my article "Reflections on the State of Psychology" (Koch 1971). I had been holding some such point of view since the early 1960s (cf. "Psychological Science versus the Science-Humanism Antinomy," Koch 1961b), but did not trace its consequences in quite so bold a way as I do in this chapter until 1969, in a short piece written for *Psychology Today* ("Psychology Cannot Be a Coherent Science," Koch 1969c).

The issue of *Social Research* containing the article on which this chapter is based was entitled "Critical Perspectives on the Social Sciences," and contained invited contributions from a number of social scientists who were known to have a jaundiced view of mainstream presuppositions of their specialties. It is because of this context that my introduction to this article sought to set the plight of psychology in relation to that of the social sciences in general. I am glad that I felt impelled to do this—for many of my views concerning endemic problems and limits of the psychological enterprise hold—often with greater force—for others of the social "sciences." I presume this in much of my writing but often do not make it explicit in that both my focus and my audience are those of psychology.

Nothing that has happened—either in psychology or the social studies—since 1971 would require an alteration of the position taken in this chapter. The fractionation of psychology into insulated areas of study and/or professional interest has continued at an accelerating pace.

It may be relevant to add that between circa 1970 and 1982 both the U.S. and the world population of "certified" psychologists approximately doubled; the world population doubled yet again in the following decade (Koch 1992b). This arithmetic circumstance itself enlarges the opportunity for increasing speciation of substantive and professional interests. It is my impression that in *other* social sciences pluralization of viewpoint and problematic commitment has also proceeded apace — and, moreover, that much of the *conceptual* speciation associated with such trends has involved an attrition upon "value-free" and scientistic presuppositions in those fields far in excess of analogous "discontent" in psychology. This last judgment may, however, need qualification by virtue of the massive realignment of interests of the psychological workforce — already under way considerably before 1971, but subsequently proceeding at a frenetic rate — as between "fundamental" and applied psychology. Fundamental psychologists comprise, by this date, a small and still shrinking part of the psychological workforce (cf. Koch 1992a, 31, where I quote figures which suggest that the 1978 ratio of "fundamental" to all other psychologists as about one in eight; over the next decade or so the ratio had shifted to perhaps one in ten; cf. Koch 1992b). Since clinical psychologists (by far the largest "specialty" of all), and even such academic sub-groupings as social psychologists, have tended in recent years not to take their intellectual marching orders from the "fundamental" grouping as abjectly as they once did, there is a possibility that "scientific" psychologists will dwindle into a small — and perhaps supererogatory — elite.

In light of all the above, I would say that post-1971 developments in psychology and social science would require no change in the message of this chapter other than a turning up of its volume.

1. Introduction

Discontent is endemic to the social sciences. The social scientist carries within him a debilitating inner stress — a form of stress perhaps best symbolized by the duality in Comte who, after founding the *science* of sociology on a strict positivistic basis, proceeded, some time later, to found what was possibly the most obsessively rule-saturated *religion* in all history (cf. Mill 1865). The social scientist must bravely sustain an appalling set of secret antinomies: He is a determinist who will remake society, a member of a thriving scientific field who can point to no determinate body of received knowledge or even opinion, a bandier-about of stipulations concerning how to construct impeccable science who is seriously compromised when asked to cite three nontrivial yet generally accepted laws in his given field.

A calamitous illustration of his plight is provided by the widely publicized study by Deutsch, Platt, and Senghaas (1971) which sought to isolate and determine the conditions favoring major "breakthroughs" in social science during this century. Some sixty-two breakthroughs are deployed over a vast chart and they turn out to involve such matters as Russell's and Whitehead's reduction of mathematics to logic, "logical empiricism and the unity of science," and "operational definitions" (*social* science, mind you!); also, Lenin's theory of revolution, Mao's doctrines of "peasant and guerilla organization," and Gandhi's principles of "non-violent political action" (social *science,* mind you!). (In relation to Gandhi's breakthrough, the informative table gravely notes, under its "Based on Whose Work" column, the dependence of his views upon those of the eminent social scientists, H. D. Thoreau and L. N. Tolstoy.) Not surprisingly, much of the table is made up of methodological breakthroughs—including many (like statistical decision theory, cybernetics, general systems theory, and so on) which in no sense can be attributed to social scientists, whatever their impact on the volume of social scientific busywork and quasi-theoretical patter; more surprisingly, the table includes "computers" as one of its formal *social* scientific breakthroughs.

When the table touches on substantive breakthroughs, it typically nominates loose clusters of effort—e.g., sociology of knowledge, "quantitative political science and basic theory," "functionalist anthropology and sociology," "culture and personality," "quantitative mathematical studies of war" (the latter of which is seen to be based on the social scientific labors of Dr. Thucydides). It is as if anything which succeeded in commanding moderately stable interest among social scientists—or could qualify as a course-listing in a decent number of departments—is a *breakthrough.* Here and there, this generous inventory can also be caught embracing two or more inconsonant viewpoints of such character that their *joint* breakthrough value would have to be construed as in the neighborhood of nullity: e.g., "behavioral psychology," "learning theory," and "conditioned reflexes" on the one hand, and "Gestalt psychology" on the other. Finally, although the grotesquerie of this list needs no belaboring, I cannot resist noting that certain of the "breakthroughs" (as, for example, the logistic view of mathematics) are not only irrelevant but—according to the current consensus of competent students in the field of origin—wrong. Perhaps the survival of the social sciences has been premised on the canny mental hygiene maintained by most social scientists in *not* conducting such inventories of progress as we have just examined.

It is probably impossible for a social scientist to evade the suspicion that the history of social science is the history of an illusion. It may be more difficult to suspect that the future one *invites* for a social science is the future of an illusion, yet this unwelcome suspicion has been entertained with impressive (and increasing) frequency over the past decade or so.

The history of social science has been a crisis history. Each theorist in each social science begins by discovering a fatal flaw in someone else's fundamental conception of the discipline. The discipline is *really* another kind of affair: It requires a different analytical unit; an alternate dimensional framework; a changed approach to "construct-formation" and measurement; a concentration upon a different range of the data-universe; a set of new explanatory concepts; a revised notion of the admissible forms of law-like statements; a weakened or strengthened or sharpened or loosened analysis of "prediction" or "causality" or "functional dependence" or "system." This metatheoretical chapter having been written, the theorist proceeds—to *more* metatheory, or meta-metatheory, or a slightly particularized disguise of the metatheory which he calls *the* "theory," or to a "model" purporting to satisfy the metatheoretical stipulations (but sensitive to no other constraints, least of all empirical ones). The theorist may even proceed to research "in line with" the metatheory or theory or model—but in line as well with an indeterminate and possibly infinite class of alternate rationales (including, as a special case, the null one of no rationale whatsoever).

We have thus been given—for more than one hundred years—a vast and varied set of prolegomena to action. But very little action. Only one element has remained broadly constant in this rich tradition of Babel: the practice of decorating (and justifying) each formulation with the iconology of science. Even *Geisteswissenschaftliche* social scientists, in the end, somehow turn out to be more *scientific* than their *Naturwissenschaftliche* opponents!

But a new kind of turmoil has supervened within the social sciences—a kind which may presage the end of a curious chapter in intellectual history. There is in every field a disposition to challenge the root metaphor of a social *science*. Though still a minority tendency, it is certainly a conspicuous one. It is manifested in ways so various as to render illustration arbitrary. Discontent over behaviorism (or what the political scientists oddly call "behavioralism") is of course patent, as is the corollary resurgence of phenomenological and experientialist viewpoints in sociology, political science, and psychology. Positivistic philosophies of science—and cognate methodological stipulations (like operationism) that have so severely inhibited the social studies—are now under heavy attrition, after having been exposed only to slow erosion for ten or fifteen years. Humanist approaches to history and even linguistics are finding a hearing, after the long interregnum of a scientistic orthodoxy. "Theory-construction" and "model-making" have lost something of their grandeur; "applied" concerns and even activist commitments are no longer seen as the sordid options of mental cripples.

Not all conceptual and methodological liberalization currently evident is tantamount to a rejection of the scientistic presuppositions of the social studies—some of the flexing is more like dodging. The significant fact, though, is that hardly any social scientists are not *at least* dodging. Perhaps more significant is why this is so: In a word, the customer (i.e., student) is no longer buying the dear, musty, turgid scientistic rhetoric. For good or for ill—and probably for both—world sensibility has been going through a sea change and recent generations of students have been at the forefront of those making the waves. To my cynical mind, the last two sentences taken together *imply* the inevitable demise of orthodox social science.

It is only in a climate like the present one that I, a middle-aged and obsessive scholar, would make such sweeping claims so confidently. The trends I have noted are so obvious that they require neither discernment nor courage for their statement. From this point on, I would like to do something slightly more specific—to delineate my grounds for discontent with my own field. Social scientists tend to regard psychology as the foundation discipline of the social sciences; most psychologists would agree, but would claim as well a status for their discipline within the biological and/or natural sciences. No other field associated with the social sciences has achieved so high a level of saturation with the imagery and putative game-forms of "science"; moreover, it is to psychology that other social sciences look for their methodological marching orders. Honest diagnosis of the state of psychology relative to its scientific pretensions could thus have critical consequences for our understanding of the condition of other social sciences.

Honest diagnosis tends to enlist a personal mode of expression. Despite this, perhaps my findings can augment the *general* pool of discontent—for I speak as one who has given a fifty-year career to exploring the prospects and conditions for psychology's becoming a significant enterprise. I will sketch the contours of my discontent with psychology as currently institutionalized, first, by discussing the condition of fundamental psychology, and then by considering aspects of psychology generally presumed appropriate to humanist analyses of man.

2. The Condition of Fundamental Psychology

Whether as a "science," or as *any* kind of coherent discipline devoted to the empirical study of man, psychology has been misconceived. Although a massive one-hundred-year effort to erect a discipline given to the positive study of man has here and there turned up a germane fact, or thrown off a spark of insight, these "victories" have had an adventitious relation to the programs believed to inspire them, and their sum total over time is overwhelmingly counterbalanced by the harvest of pseudoknowledge that has by now been reaped. The idolatry of Science that is characteristic of our age has ensured that this spurious knowledge, whether in whole or in part, be taken *seriously* by people everywhere—even by sensitive, creative, or sophisticated people. Such "knowledge," when assimilated by a person, is no neutral addition to his furniture of confusions: It has an awesome capacity to bias the deepest attitudes of man toward Man, to polarize sensibility. After all, the formulations of the positive study of man pretend to define human reality, to delimit the ends and mechanisms of conduct, the configurations and dynamics of personality, the optimal conditions of development and of learning, and, indeed, of individual and communal life.

This kind of pseudoknowledge can make a difference, an appalling difference. Everyone knows that modern psychology is stocked with a large inventory of "images of man." Everyone also knows which is the right image: There are broad but not absolute agreements at given eras. Indeed, the pooled pseudoknowledge that is much of psychology can be seen as a congeries of alternate—and exceedingly simple—"images," around each of which one finds a dense, scholastic cluster of supportive research, "theorizing" and methodological rhetoric. If one is drawn by unassailable scientific argument to the conclusion that man is a cockroach, rat, or dog, *that* makes a difference. It also makes a difference when one achieves ultimate certitude that man is a telephone exchange; a servomechanism; a binary digital computer; a reward-seeking vector; a hyphen between an S and R process; a stimulation-maximizer; a food, sex, or libido energy-converter; a "utilities" maximizing game-player; a status-seeker; a mutual ego-titillator; a mutual emotional (or actual) masturbator; or a hollow cocoon seeking ecstasy through the liquidation of its boundaries in the company of other cocoons similarly seeking ecstasy.

The violence of my apostasy may suggest to some that I wish to transfer to the humanities. I do not! In our century, the role of the *humanities* in the teaching of the humanities has not been especially more hygienic than the role of psychology. Indeed, the humanities have been sick in much the same way that psychology and the social sciences — and even the natural and biological sciences in certain of their excursions — have been sick. This has been due partly to direct contagion from the sciences: Too many humanists have contracted anywhere from a creeping to a rabid scientism from their abhorred colleagues in the sciences. Considering a philistine *philistine* protects one from philistinism no better than considering a leper leprous protects from leprosy. It is usually not hard to show that even humanists who surround their Dionysian labors with a thunderously anti-scientific rhetoric are in fact remarkably science-determined in their conception of method, their sense of the scholarly process, their theories — explicit or implicit — of human nature. But, to repeat, *contagion* from the sciences is only partly to blame; more fundamental are pervasive circumstances in culture and history which have inflicted the same pathology upon all fields of inquiry, although the symptoms may vary in the milieus of the different fields.

I do not hope to justify, or in some way prove, these general and contumelious statements within the confines of this chapter. But I do hope to suggest enough of the context that has persuaded me of their justice to establish that my claims have not been idle. If I cannot persuade the reader, I will settle for making him uneasy.

I shall have to limit myself to a collage of rather dogmatic analyses and impressions. Overarching the elements of this collage will be a single notion, the meaning and referential field of which I have been exploring for many years. It is that much modern scholarship exhibits a syndrome that may be called "ameaningful thinking" (the prefix has the same force as the *a-* in words like *amoral*). It is a central purpose of part 3 of this book to explore the nature, the broad distribution in modern intellectual life, and the historico-cultural etiology of ameaningful thinking. Indeed, chapters 2 and 3 have already illustrated the play of ameaningful thinking in psychology to a harrowing extent!

Here, let me merely identify "ameaningful thinking" as the type of method-dominated cognition that transfers the responsibility of the agent of inquiry to one or another set of sacrosanct methodic stratagems or heuristic rule-systems: an escape from the uncertainties and challenges of ardent problematic effort via the cozy presupposition that the rules somehow *contain* the answers. It is tantamount to a kind of generalized Laplaceanism, such that all answers to all questions are pre-ordained by the methodic codex of one's preference. On another metaphor, it is an implicit "doctrine" of cognitive preformation, such that given patient teamwork in the implementation of the rules, all theoretical knowledge, material technology, aesthetic artifacts, etc. requisite to the movement of the human race towards a state of secular perfection will inevitably forthcome on a schedule conditioned only by the magnitude of the necessary funding, and the efficiency of the requisite administrative apparatus.

Despite the extravagance of these metaphors, I regard ameaningful thinking as a *genuine* process-syndrome, a form of cognitive activity qualitatively different from "meaningful" thinking, one that is contingent on a rather different mode of biological and neural processing. But such issues are more appropriately developed later in the book (cf. especially chapter 7). For me, the notion of ameaning gives a certain consonance to the elements of the following collage, but I hope that each element will prove a proper *objet trouvé*, the integrity of which does not depend on its principle of selection. Cultural criticism is no lonely enterprise in our day, and each mournful entrepreneur purveys a different dirge.

Perhaps a few people of my ancient generation may recall a book by Grace Adams, entitled *Psychology: Science or Superstition?* (1931). I read it shortly after having been appalled and insulted by my first few undergraduate courses in psychology, and found in it both amusement and solace. The idea that psychology was a congeries of weird insularities was already a cliché, but the author developed this cliché in so sprightly and compelling a fashion that the field came through to me as in some perverse way inviting. So massive an absurdity cried out for redress. Besides—an absurdity so massive could hardly hold its own against a little clear thinking.

I did not then know that Clark Hull felt pretty much the same way about this book. Toward the beginning of one of his early theoretical papers, "The Conflicting Psychologies of Learning: A Way Out" (1935a), he refers to it in these words:

> The obvious implication of this general situation [the wide disagreement among psychologists] has recently called out a timely little book by Grace Adams entitled *Psychology: Science or Superstition?* In this work she points out what we all know only

too well — that among psychologists there is not only a bewilderingly large diversity of opinion, but that we are divided into sects, too many of which show emotional and other signs of religious fervor. This emotionalism and this inability to progress materially toward agreement obviously do not square with the ideals of objectivity and certainty which we associate with scientific investigation; they are, on the other hand, more than a little characteristic of metaphysical and theological controversy. Such a situation leads to the suspicion that we have not yet cast off the unfortunate influences of our early associations with metaphysicians. Somehow we have permitted ourselves to fall into essentially unscientific practices. Surely all psychologists truly interested in the welfare of psychology as a science, whatever their theoretical bias may be, should cooperate actively to correct this.

But before we can mend a condition we must discover the basis of the difficulty. A clue to this is furnished by the reassuring fact that persisting disagreements among us do not concern to any considerable extent the results of experiment, but are confined almost entirely to matters of theory. It is the thesis of this paper that such a paradoxical disparity between scientific experiment and scientific theory not only ought not to exist but that it need not and actually will not exist if the theory is truly scientific. It will be convenient in approaching this problem first to secure a little perspective by recalling the essential characteristics of some typical scientific procedures. (492)

After these remarks, Hull proceeds to a brief and schoolmasterly discussion of the "essentials of sound scientific theory" which, of course, recapitulates the schema of a hypothetico-deductive system. Such a résumé of hypothetico-deductive procedure appears in virtually every one of Hull's earlier theoretical articles; it is always conjoined with an invitation to contending theorists that they axiomatize their nebulous thoughts and that, in the event that determinate derivations diverging from Hull's own ensued, the difference be arbitrated in the laboratory.

It is sixty years later, and the theory that Hull so diligently contrived as his answer to the massive absurdity of the "psychologies" is becoming a dim memory even to the few who still work within its tradition. And every judgment, expectation, hope, and presupposition registered in the two paragraphs just quoted has been cruelly — indeed, extravagantly — thwarted by history. We are still divided into sects, "many of which show emotional and other signs of religious fervor," but perhaps thrice as many. Far from having yet "cast off the unfortunate influences of our early associations with metaphysicians," the emergence of a large American Psychological Association Division of "Philosophical Psychology," and of a large group of discipline-hopping philosophers specializing in philosophy of mind, has reinstalled the enemy at the very center of the citadel. Moreover, those who have most zealously practiced the rites of exorcism seem somehow to have drawn to themselves the heaviest succubi.

The judgment that "persisting disagreements . . . do not concern to any considerable extent the results of experiment" has certainly been gainsaid by the six decades of intervening history. It is rare that an experiment claimed to support a given theory is seen in that light by advocates of an alternate theory; it is rarer still that an experiment "generated" by a given theory, or merely performed in its ambiance, is seen by the outgroup as defining a valid or nontrivial empirical relationship. And, more generally, the entire conception of theory and of scientific method presupposed in this passage from Hull (and explicitly developed in succeeding paragraphs in the same source) has been all but given up in those areas of scholarship from which it was imported and has been markedly attenuated even in psychology.

Somewhat before Hull wrote the quoted passage, another thinker had expressed himself in rather similar vein. I take the liberty of changing one word in the quoted passages:

> The backward state of the psychological sciences can only be remedied by applying to them the methods of physical science, duly extended and generalized. . . .
> If there are some subjects on which the results obtained have finally received the unanimous assent of all who have attended to the proof, and others on which mankind have not yet been equally successful; on which the most sagacious minds have occupied themselves from the earliest date, and have never succeeded in establishing any considerable body of truths, so as to be beyond denial or doubt; it is by generalizing the methods successfully followed in the former inquiries, and adapting them to the latter, that we may hope to remove this blot on the face of science.

The writer was John Stuart Mill (1862, 546), and these words were written almost a century before the words quoted from Hull. My one liberty in quoting Mill was to substitute "psychological sciences" for "moral sciences" in the initial sentence—a permissible substitution in that he makes it quite clear that by "moral sciences" he means the social sciences, inclusive of psychology.

Mill was no lone or pristine voice; similar strategies were advanced before him and, indeed, implemented by his master Comte and by many of the French and English philosophers of the Enlightenment. Formal institutionalization of psychology as a *science* waited upon Wundt in 1879, but by this time an endeavor called "scientific psychology" was an inevitability, if not indeed a fact.

It is worth stressing that, prior to the late nineteenth century, there are no precedents in the history of ideas for the constitution of great new fields of knowledge by edict. The institutionalization of each new field of science in the early modern period was a *fait accompli* of an emerging substructure in the tissue of scientific knowledge. Sciences won their way to independence, and ultimately institutional status, by achieving enough knowledge to become sciences. Physics (in the modern sense), for instance, was practiced for several hundred years by independent gentlemen scholars before it even found a niche in the universities. By the late nineteenth century, these justly discriminated fields of science had given such food to man's cognitive and material hungers that his appetite had become insatiable. And, by this time, multiple lines of inquiry into the nature and trend of science itself began to focus into an apparently wholesome Victorian vision. It was a vision of a totally orderly universe, totally open to the methods of science, and a totally orderly science, totally open to the stratagems — and wants — of humankind. It was against such a sanguine, zealous background that psychology was stipulated into life.

At the time of its inception, psychology was unique in the extent to which its institutionalization preceded its content and its methods preceded its problems. If there are keys to history, this statement is surely a key to the history of modern psychology. Never had a group of thinkers been given so sharply specified an invitation to create. Never had inquirers been so harried by social wish, cultural optimism, extrinsic prescription, and by the advance scheduling of ways and means.

On the face of it, the nineteenth-century program for a science of psychology seems rational enough. It asks the human race to entertain a huge and wholly open hypothesis: precisely the hypothesis I have just quoted from Mill. Can the methods of natural science, "duly extended and generalized," be "adapted" to the "backward" studies of persons and society (humanity's experiences, actions, artifacts, values, institutions, history, future)? To entertain such a hypothesis responsibly is no light matter. Madhouses have been populated by responses to lighter intellectual burdens. No wonder that many inheritors of this awesome challenge have protected themselves from its ravages by reinterpreting the hypothesis as an a priori truth.

For more than a century now, many psychologists have seemed to suppose that the methods of natural science are totally specifiable and specified; that the applicability of these to social and human events is not only an established fact, but that no knowledge based on inquiries not saturated with the iconology of science is worth taking seriously. From the earliest days of the experimental pioneers, their stipulation that psychology be adequate to *science* outweighed their commitment that it be adequate to a human subject matter. From the beginning, some pooled schematic image of the *form* of science was dominant; respectability held more glamour than insight, caution than curiosity, feasibility than fidelity.

The history of psychology, then, is very much a history of changing views, doctrines, images about *what* to emulate in the natural sciences—especially physics. In the nineteenth century, this meant the *extension* of experimental method to subjective phenomena on a pattern in which specifiable elements of consciousness were to be related to physically manipulable and definable input variables ("stimuli"). For early behaviorism (1913–1930), it meant the *use* of experimental method exactly as in physics (i.e., "objectively")—experiential variables of any sort being regarded as unamenable to publicly verifiable specification, and thus beyond the pale of true science. The task of psychology thereby becomes one of determining correlations or "associative connections" between *stimuli* and *responses,* and the organism or person becomes an empty area at which myriad S and R processes intersect.

By the late 1920s, there was much objective experimentation but few bodies of clearly stated predictive principles comparable to the crowning achievements of physics: its theories. Instead, experimentation sometimes seemed aimless, "theoretical" hypotheses but loosely related to data, and debate idle. Thus, beginning around 1930, we get the emulation of natural science's *theoretical method* or, at least, the emulation of an image of that method which was then being projected upon the world by the philosophy of science and gaining broad acceptance. Thus commenced the phase of *neobehaviorism* which presumed (in practice, when not in principle) that the entire, awesome domain of psychological reality could be comprehended under sets of arbitrary and lacunae-ridden postulates, based in the main on the experimental analysis of rat behavior—and not rat behavior in anything like its full richness but limited to one or another presumably prototypical response such as choice-point behavior or lever-pressing. It required close to twenty years of frenetic pursuit of such a strategy for the hypothesis to emerge that it was perhaps a bit overoptimistic.

The next stage (from about 1948 on) in the enaction of a psychological science was to presume that the synoptic theoretical conceptions of classical neobehaviorism were overambitious, and that the corrective was to curtail the scope of the objectives while pursuing precisely the same empirical and analytical tactics. This ushered in a phase of miniature theories and "models" (the period might be called "deflated neobehaviorism"), usually developed against a background of stated or unstated belief to the effect that these formulations would automatically coalesce into a supertheory of cosmic scope.

But soon many began to doubt that the analysis of arbitrarily fixed-upon aspects of animal learning was an adequate induction basis for laws bearing on all organismic achievement and process. This disabusement, gaining appreciable spread at some point in the 1950s, led to a remarkable liberalization of behaviorist "methodology." It was now permissible to restore to the psychological universe a variety of intradermal processes and events of a sort which had been extradited by the peripheralistic necessities of earlier behaviorism. Fields like perception, cognition, and psychology of language could now be readdressed, but with the quaint proviso that the internal processes and events demarcated by these fields be treated exactly as if they were at the periphery of the organism, and thus externally observable. This *tour de force* was effected by the inspired discovery that brain events could be *called* central responses, and sometimes even stimuli, and thus that S-R laws discovered at the surface of the organism would almost surely hold at central levels. Thus was unleashed a period that my nomenclature would allow to be called either *neo-neobehaviorism* or "post-deflated-neobehaviorism" or, if one prefers, "inflated neobehaviorism."

But the readmission of fields like perception, cognition, and language proved a dangerous maneuver. Some behavioral scientists were emboldened to conjecture that there may be a psychological subject as well as a subject matter. They became quite free, even racy, in their language. There was even talk of plans, ideas, thought, will, minds — sometimes bereft of quotation marks. To be sure, some of these bold people mitigated their verbal transgressions by calling themselves *subjective behaviorists* (cf. Miller, Galanter, and Pribram 1960). Others did not. But all of them, being scientists, with the resurrected psychological *subject* upon them, saw the need to effect a more radical change of scientific strategy than any initiated by the successive phases of behaviorism. The strategy now becomes that of turning to the revered natural sciences, especially the engineering disciplines, not merely for prefabricated methods but prefabricated answers as well. Thus we get the models based on computer simulation (in some of which the computer *is* the psychological subject) or on transpositions to the events generated by actual human subjects of a variety of developments in applied mathematics, ranging from information theory to the theory of games. In this way the *science* of psychology maintains consistency with its history—by headlong retreat from the psychological subject immediately upon the long delayed moment of reconfrontation.

I hasten to emphasize that this brief exercise in history is biased, abstract, and selective to the point of caricature. But I believe it both biased *and* true, selective *and* illustrative, and, as caricature, revealing. It certainly does not comprehend *all* consequences of the entertainment, over time, of the Millian hypothesis and it does not intend to suggest that nothing has been learned.

The idea that psychology is a cumulative or progressive discipline—in the sense that psychologists had thought characteristic of the natural sciences they were seeking to emulate—is hardly borne out by its history. Indeed, there could be a way of writing the history of modern psychology which would have to acknowledge that most of the well verified and solid "advances" of any generality are registered by clusters of findings that help reveal the utter inadequacy of long flourishing analytical frameworks or so-called "theories." The hard knowledge that accrues in one generation typically disenfranchises the theoretical fictions of the previous one—and any new theoretical framework this hard knowledge is believed to suggest or support typically survives only until the next. If psychology is science, it is "science" of a strange kind. Its larger generalizations are not specified and refined through time and effort; they are merely replaced. Throughout its history as "science," the *hard* knowledge which it has deposited has usually been *negative* knowledge!

Examples are legion. In 1920 Lashley begins a research program designed to provide the physiological underpinnings of Watsonian conditioning theory and soon—to his astonishment—runs into findings utterly at variance with Watsonian or any other then imaginable version of associationism. After an unrelenting and often brilliant thirty-year pursuit of the problems suggested by these early findings, we find Lashley (1950) concluding:

> This series has yielded a good bit of information about what and where the memory trace is not. It has discovered nothing of the real nature of the engram. I sometimes feel, in reviewing the evidence on the localization of the memory trace, that the necessary conclusion is that learning just is not possible. (477–78)

To extend the story, it can be said that the truly impressive developments in subsequent biological psychology (after 1950), made possible by the powerful electrophysiological and other techniques then becoming available, have thus far had a similar force. As a result of dense piling up of much particulate evidence concerning such matters as graded excitation processes, central feedback to the receptors, "vertical" organization of brain process, and so on, the entire earlier history of psychophysiological theorizing can be seen as hopelessly simplistic. But, again, the main *general* contribution is negative knowledge. Indeed, one reading of this knowledge is that the established complexity of C.N.S. process is such as to make the prospect of biological explanation of psychological process even more remote than Lashley tended to suggest.[1] Furthermore, the complexity *now* apparent in neural function suggests orders of complexity in human action and experience that had been grossly slighted in the conceptualizations of behavioral and "psychological" psychology.

The experiments initiated by Gestalt psychology circa 1911 had a truly decisive significance—though this was long disputed—relative to the critique of Wundtian experimental psychology, structuralism, and later on, behaviorism. And no one can deny that many particular findings concerning simple aspects of perceptual organization have by now been contributed. I believe these discoveries to constitute one of the few islands of solid accomplishment in this century. But it must be noted that the *positive* proposals put forward toward psychological and neurophysiological "field"-theories—whether in general terms or as subtheories of restricted range such as that of "figural aftereffects"—now appear highly inadequate.

The examples from biological psychology and the special case of Gestalt

---

1. And indeed, as many philosophers of mind have increasingly stressed, the "intentional" character (and other properties) of psychological concepts, and their relations, renders senseless in principle any literal program of psychoneurological *reduction*.

theory are far from the strongest illustrations of the negativity of psychological knowledge. For in these cases there are at least grounds for believing that particular findings of permanent value—even if not ultimate adequacy—have eventuated. But these findings give us no purchase on any "truly" science-like general analysis of the events in their domain. They give us only a means for destroying older and misconceived analyses.

Other examples of "negative knowledge" of a rather more curious and depressing sort could be given—too many of them. These are the "discoveries" that a preexisting framework will not do, on the basis of "findings" which, however meticulously produced, tell us nothing intrinsically illuminating. Such findings may be negative ones on *two* counts: They gainsay a given nonframework on the basis of research that, taken by itself, must be a nondiscovery. Usually they bear only a polemical and role-playing relationship to a formulation which, on other grounds, is beginning to be acknowledged for the senseless thing that it is. The twists and turns in the dominance of or differential allegiances commanded by the diverse behavioristic theories of learning provide relevant examples—as may easily be inferred from our earlier comments on the behaviorisms. Other illustrations might be drawn from the somewhat more complex history of conceptual realignments, and changing influence patterns, among general depth-psychological or personality theories or among the subdoctrines bearing on the psychotherapies.

A history of psychology, which sought to derive the lessons for the empirical (i.e., sociological and psychological) understanding of inquiry implicit in the *negativity* of psychological "advance," would be a truly significant enterprise. But this is not the place for such an effort.

The Millian hypothesis has been under test for over a hundred years. It has been tested in billions of man-hours of research and of ardent theoretical thinking, scholarship, writing, planning, and administration. It has been tested in hundreds of laboratories by many thousands of investigators. There are now seventy thousand members of the American Psychological Association alone.[2] This massive test has generated a vast literature, a vast publication apparatus, a vast organizational structure. The test has received increasingly generous support from society. The test has not been a sleazy one.

In my estimation, the Millian hypothesis has been fulsomely discon-

---

2. The number was 25,000 in 1971, when the article on which this chapter is based was written.

firmed. I think it by this time utterly and finally clear that psychology cannot be a coherent science, or indeed a coherent field of scholarship, in any specifiable sense of coherence that can bear upon a field of inquiry. It can certainly not expect to become *theoretically* coherent; it is already clear that no large subdivision of inquiry, including physics, can. But neither is it realistic (or desirable) to strive toward coherence whether it be of method, linguistic and other communicative practices, size and degree of extensibility of consensus communities, or personal characteristics and training of investigators. As for the *subject* matter of psychology, it is difficult to see how it could ever have been thought to be a coherent one under any definition of the presumptive "science," whether in terms of mind, consciousness, experience, behavior, or, indeed, molecule aggregates or transistor circuits. Nothing as awesome as the total domain comprised by the functioning of all organisms can be thought the subject matter of a coherent discipline; such a belief would be tantamount to inviting into existence a *Doppelgänger* for every branch of knowledge — formal or informal, actual or potential — in the entire scattered and disorderly realm of human cognitive concerns, and expecting somehow that the *Doppelgängers* would mesh while their originals would continue to languish in chaos, each at its own station. Indeed, the picture requires that a special *Doppelgänger* be assigned to psychology itself. Urgently.

So much for coherence. But how about *"science"*? Are the bits and pieces into which psychology falls, in this account, sciences or something else? Even though the answer be a matter of definition, the construal and application of words can have momentous consequences.

"Science" is perhaps the most charged, the most glittering and — despite thermonuclear weaponry — the most reassuring word in the modern vocabulary. In the modern period, this innocent lexical unit has soaked up a meaning throughout four hundred years of use in primary association with the natural sciences. During that association, the core meaning of the word[3] — and culturally its most highly prized connotation — has become connected with a special analytical pattern emerging first in classical modern astronomy, achieving more distinct fruition in Newtonian mechanics, and undergoing further differentiation in postclassical physics.

---

3. It is often (and correctly) pointed out that rather different analytical or rational patterns can be discerned in the characteristic achievements of different areas of science: for instance, that parts of biology are purely taxonomic or are qualitative and still "genuine" science; that meteorology is a strangely mixed science, involving an assemblage of derivative subtheories but including large nonrationalized components. The "core meaning" I here at-

That analytical pattern, though it has been the object of great interest, has not yet been successfully explicated. No one doubts that it has been implicit in the skills of great physicists. There is reason to believe that the pattern is applicable in aspects of the biological sciences. I am not deluded that I can bring this pattern much closer to explication than has, say, Michael Polanyi—and I agree with him that to set the goal of full explication of such a matter is absurd. I think it possible to bring it into finer resolution than has yet been achieved but not, as it were, in passing. What can be said here, however, is that this pattern requires: (a) the disembedding from a domain of phenomena of a small family of "variables" which demarcate important aspects of the domain's structure, when that domain is considered as an idealized, momentary static system; and (b) that this family of variables be such, by virtue of appropriate internal relations, that it can be ordered to a mathematical or formal system capable of correctly describing changes in selected aspects of the state of the system as a function of time and/or system changes describable as alterations of the "values" of specified variables. To achieve (i.e., disembed) a family of variables having such properties is no mean feat, even in reference to rather "simple" natural systems (e.g., those constituting pressure-volume relations of a gas) having a highly "closed" character. It required a prolonged development of ancillary knowledge, culminating in an act of genius, to disembed the laws of such simple systems as those defined by the pendulum, the inclined plane, or the motions of falling bodies. Though there is currently much appreciation of the wide variability of natural systems on some such dimension as "closedness-openness" or "weakness-strength" of boundary conditions (thus, experimental isolability), insufficient concern has been given to the strong chance that at some critical point of system-openness, boundary-weakness, or mere internal complexity, the definitive analytic pattern may no longer apply. Von Bertalanffy has done an important service in spelling out certain implications for biology which stem from the "openness" of the systems characteristically addressed by that science, but he and other "systems theorists" in his tradition have not considered the question here

tribute to "science" is not intended as an ultimately correct and full demarcation criterion but, rather, as the text suggests, as "culturally" the "most highly prized connotation" of the word. Moreover, I think it *historically* the case that something like the "analytic pattern" I here try to describe is what most psychologists have in mind (if only inchoately) when they claim psychology to be a science, or seek to make it one.

The question of "demarcation" between science and other forms of inquiry is rejoined, from another incidence, in chapter 5 on "A Theory of Definition."

at issue. Rather, they tend to generate a rhetoric of confidence to the effect that the Empyrean must surely contain mathematical or logical methods suitable for the analysis of systems of any degree of openness or complexity.

I do not think even the Empyrean is that well stocked. If one considers, say, the familiar estimate that the human brain contains some ten billion neurological units, each with ramifications which may lead to as many as twenty-five thousand others — and bears in mind the complexity, density, lability, and mutual interdependencies of the processes at every point, and considers further that this extraordinarily differentiated piece of cyto-architecture is stuffed into a very small container — it is possible to believe that there are very tight limits within which our definitive analytic pattern may be applicable. Past some limiting point of analysis, even the finest microelectrode conceivable is likely to pick up mere noise. I think that in certain areas of biological psychology that point is being approached.

But biological psychology is perhaps the one area in which some approximation of the analytic pattern of science can be fruitfully applied, notwithstanding such limiting circumstances as have been mentioned. The one-hundred-year history of what is called "scientific psychology" has established beyond doubt that most other domains that psychologists have sought to order, in the name of "science" and via simulations of the analytical pattern definitive of science, do not and cannot meet the conditions for meaningful application of this pattern. If this conclusion seems arbitrary, one can only submit that a hypersufficiency of grounds for it are implicit in the preceding historical rundown of the behaviorisms. Consider that the central empirical area, which was the target of all that theoretical effort, was learning. Consider the hundreds of theoretical formulations, rational equations, and mathematical models of the learning process that have accrued; the thousands of research studies. And *now* consider that there is still no wide agreement, even at the crassest descriptive level, on the empirical conditions under which learning takes place, or even on the definition of learning or its empirical and rational relations to other psychological processes or phenomena. Consider also that after all this scientistic effort our actual *insight* into the learning process — as reflected in every humanly important context to which learning is relevant — has not improved one jot. An educator need not look far past his nose to perceive that point more clearly than he might wish.

Many legitimate and important domains of psychological *study*, then, cannot be called "science" in any significant sense, and continued application of this misleading metaphor can only vitiate, distort or pervert research effort. When I say this, it is important that what I am *not* saying be understood. I am *not* saying that the psychological studies should not be empirical, should not strive toward the rational classification of observed events, should not essay shrewd, tough-minded, particulate, and differentiated analyses of the interdependencies among significant events. I am not saying that statistical and mathematical methods are everywhere inapplicable. I am not saying that there are no subfields of psychology, as historically constituted, that can be regarded as parts of science—although it can be argued that the most clearly discernible of these, such as what is called "sensory psychology" and "biological psychology," might just as well (and perhaps more fruitfully) be regarded as parts of *biological* science. I *am* saying that—in fields as close to the heart of psychological studies as perception, cognition, motivation, and learning, and certainly social psychology, psychopathology, and personology, and, of course, aesthetics, the study of "creativity," and the empirical study of phenomena relevant to the domains of the extant humanities—in all these areas, such concepts as "law," "experiment," "measurement," "variable," "control," "theory," do not behave sufficiently like their homonyms in the established sciences to justify the extension to them of the term "science." To persist in the use of this highly charged metaphor is to shackle these fields of study with exceedingly unrealistic expectations concerning generality limits of the anticipated findings, predictive specificity and confidence levels, feasible research and data processing strategies, and modes of conceptual ordering. The inevitable heuristic effect is the enaction of imitation science rather than the generation of significant knowledge. Pursuit of imitation science, though a highly sophisticated skill, can only lead to the evasion and demeaning of subject matter and to a constriction of problematic interests. It is a deadly form of role-playing if one acknowledges that the psychological universe has something to do with persons. This kind of spurious knowledge can result in a corrupt human technology and spew forth upon man a stream of ever more degrading images of himself.

I am under no illusion that huge subcartels of the knowledge industry can be made to reorganize by rational suasion. I nevertheless propose that the essential noncohesiveness of the activities denoted by the term "psychology" be acknowledged by replacing it with some such locution as "the psychological studies." Students should no longer be tricked by a terminological rhetoric into the belief that they are studying a single discipline or any set of specialties rendered coherent by any actual or potential principle of coherence. The current "departments of psychology" should be called "departments of psychological studies." The change of name should mark a corresponding change in pedagogical rationale. The psychological studies, if they are really to address the historically constituted objectives of psychological thought, must range over an immense and disorderly spectrum of human activity and experience. If significant knowledge is the desideratum, problems must be approached with humility, methods must be contextual and flexible, and anticipations of synoptic breakthroughs held in check. At the very least, students should not be encouraged to believe it their responsibility to put together the pieces of a jigsaw puzzle that their professors long ago gave up trying to solve — a puzzle which is insoluble in principle, and which has the strange property of becoming less solvable with each attempt to assemble the fragments.

There are stronger proposals that might be made, but even my weak ones will not be heeded. William McDougall firmly believed that psychological study required such resources of maturity, sensitivity, and knowledge as to make it inappropriate at the undergraduate level. In 1942, Heinrich Klüver was already looking forward with enthusiasm to what he called "the impending dismemberment of psychology." The centrifugal trends already apparent to him have continued, but most of the many specialties and cliques that have emerged have not spun away into other disciplines. I myself tend to think that most of what is solid in the psychological studies could best be pursued in association with the scientific and humanistic areas to which they are germane. Biological psychology could only profit by incorporation within biology. Psycholinguistics should certainly be happening within linguistics.

But these questions of formal association are of minor importance. What is much more vital is that broad ranges of the psychological studies (e.g., the empirical analysis of art, psychological aspects of history and philosophy, empirical analysis of inquiry) are as relevant to the humanities as they are to the psychological studies. Many of these problems are almost completely bypassed by psychology as it currently exists, and are pursued — if at all — only in the humanities.

In psychology, for almost a hundred years, we have been vigorously erecting a discipline on a pattern unique in the history of scholarship. The hallmarks of our scholarly style have been: "advance by asseveration," "progress by proclamation," "proof by pronunciamento," "truth by trivialization," "experiment by exculpation," "rigor by role-playing." If this be discipline, it is a discipline of deceit. The few areas in which genuine insights or hard discoveries have been possible under these circumstances are seen as pockets of sedition — or, better, just not seen. A discipline of this character must rely upon an obsessive orthodoxy which exacts a terrible price from the self-determining or spontaneous of any age, and especially from the young.

I do not think that what goes on in orthodox graduate and undergraduate education can continue much longer. Our students are asked to read and memorize a literature consisting of an endless set of advertisements for the emptiest concepts, the most inflated theories, the most trivial "findings," and the most fetishistic yet heuristically self-defeating methods in scholarly history — and all of it conveyed in the dreariest and most turgid prose that ever met the printed page. For these riches, they must exchange whatever curiosity about the human condition may have carried them into the field; whatever awe or humility they may feel before the human and organismic universe; whatever resources of imagination or observational sensitivity they may bring to the study of that complex universe; whatever openness to experience — their own or that of others — they might have. Fine or ardent sensibilities should no longer be subjected to such debasement. A half-century of experience with students who have approached me for solace over difficulties occasioned by their resistance to the mainstream imperatives encountered in their psychological training convinces me that we lose some of the best potential contributors to the psychological studies. And this in two ways: they either "transfer" to another field or — what is far worse — decide on a tentative compromise with the prevailing value system, which almost inevitably congeals into a permanent one.

3. Humanistic Psychologies

Some will think that my analysis of the condition of psychology in terms of the behaviorisms has not done justice to other historic strands — especially those which reject or bypass the behaviorisms in the interest of maintaining more sensitive and adequate contact with a human subject matter. They will think, in the first instance, of the depth psychologies, especially those originating in Freud and in Jung. They will think of the connections in which a growing disaffection with behaviorism has been evident in the psychology of the last three decades — the return on the part of many to some form of experientialism, the embracement of phenomenological or existential alternatives to a behaviorist epistemology, even the emergence of a large grouping called "humanistic psychology." They will think of the corollary redistribution of research interest in the direction of man-pertinent problems: the massive concern with "creativity," the resurgence of interest in perception, cognition, and "complex" central process generally, the resumption of concern with developmental problems, the increase of interest and diversification of strategy in fields like educational psychology, and especially psychotherapy.

I am aware that the "behaviorisms" are but a part of the historical picture—and a diminishing (though still large) part. As for the recent, hopeful trends: the arduous "self-study" of psychology at midcentury which I directed, identified and to some extent furthered them. I saluted these trends as they became evident, and continued to do so over the years. But now, after three decades, it is not fatigue alone that makes my arm heavy.

It becomes increasingly apparent that the past is not easily sloughed off! Any field of inquiry which has enforced misphrasings and even denials of subject matter for seventy years will have so corrupted most concepts in the public domain, the thought-schemas of those who teach the young, and thus the sensibilities of the young that the past can somehow survive every proclamation of its demise. When the current questioner of that past does "embrace" experience and takes his sighting on the "great problems," what happens? Too often a kind of middlebrow simplism takes over, the ruling presuppositions of which are such that problems are defined grossly and still approached within the gamut of respectable, cant methods. In consequence, "solutions" may remain as trivial or beside the point as formerly. The thinking, in other words, remains of much the same grain as that manifested in restrictive forms of behaviorism. Often the net difference is that instead of getting "rigorous" imitation science we get fuzzy imitation science. Even those whose dissidence is such that they are prepared to throw away the methodological rulebook seem still to hold so callow and thin a conception of the human condition that they emerge with more monstrous "findings" than the methodological purists.

Behaviorism, I fear, must remain the prototype-case, if we are to understand the condition of psychology. The depth psychologies, to be sure, arose from a different tradition than did academic psychology and they present special properties and problems of their own. But they are responses to a similar configuration of forces in nineteenth-century culture and contain, in their very conception, assumptions as ameaningful as those at the basis of academic psychology. The increasing interactions and accommodations between the "depth" and the "academic" psychologies since the 1930s, when they first began to acknowledge each other, have enlarged the area of overlap among their ameaningful foundation-assumptions.

Since it is the depth psychologies to which humanists characteristically turn when in search of psychological guidance — whether the objective be a trusty methodic armamentarium or an insight that will solve the riddle of Hamlet or of Henry James's sexuality — I shall offer a few reckless judgments on the fruitfulness of that source of guidance. After that, I should like briefly to assess what manner of aid humanists may expect from the now wildly growing movement known as "humanistic psychology."[4]

The depth psychologies. It takes a fool's courage to address psychoanalysis in a few paragraphs.

Freud's work raises the problem of *how to read* with special insistence. His gifts were essentially the gifts of a humanist. He can be read as great essayist, trying desperately, erratically, and brilliantly to perceive order — or to order the disorder — in man's inner world. In this guise, he is a passionate yet humble and self-critical observer, often expressing his findings with beauty and even dramatic integrity. In this guise, he has the humanist's wisdom about the essential mystery of the human condition, and the vast and ultimately unbreachable limits upon the capacity of language to bring any aspect of the human reality under precise or final specification. He can also be read as the Father of a Science, the Founder of a Movement. In this guise, he is dogmatic — more finalistic than he has any right to be at each moment of his constantly changing theorizing — simplistic, not devoid of a managerial and public relations mentality, scientistic, and — yes — ameaningful. His greatness lies in his remarkable powers qua humanist. Yet he is almost always read qua scientist, and the successive hordes of his secondary, tertiary, and *n*-level commentators and disciples have progressively obscured the force and quality of his contribution by encouraging, indeed institutionalizing, the second reading.

Taking him in his better sense, he has left behind a set of insights which are landmarks in the slow, painful history of man's effort to bring his inner world under specification. His observations concerning repression, the

4. I retain this paragraph as written *in 1971*. That was close to the peak period when the central preoccupation of "Humanistic Psychology" was the "Encounter Movement" — indeed, a time when encounter groups (and their variants) were more in the eye of the public than any other product of the psychological enterprise. Although the movement ceased "wildly" to grow at some point in the mid-1970s, it is by no means extinct, and both its rationale and its methods have been soaked up within an enormous gamut of educational, counseling, healing, and "self-realization" technologies which continue to prosper and to multiply. It is thus worth pondering the significance of the fact that the ideology and technology of "encounter" has been perhaps the most conspicuous and far-reaching "contribution" to the public weal made by American psychology in this century. We will so ponder: briefly in this chapter, and more extensively in chapter 10.

mechanisms of defense, the motivated character of the dream, the psycho-pathology of everyday life, the intrapsychic ramifications of anxiety, the developmental weight of early experience, the role of fantasy, the tendency of mental events to cluster into relatively stable process-syndromes, the determinants of adult character structure — and, indeed, many others — are of permanent value. But they are of *differential* value: They map human reality in quite different degrees of precision and salience; they establish "cuts" within their phenomenal domain at a level of analysis appropriate to Freud's special objectives but one which does not preempt other levels of analysis, other angles of vision. And they certainly can be ordered to no family of variables which — by any stretch of the imagination — could conform, or be rendered conformable, to the requirements of what I have called the analytic pattern of science. Indeed, Freud is at his very worst in his theoretical and "meta-psychological" moments. Even the more limited of the subtheories, as for example, the theory of libidinal organization or of the etiology of the neuroses, are of *less* than limited value. It can be said that Freud's drive toward system was as ameaningfully motivated as that of the most role-playing type of behaviorist and, indeed, rather more in-eptly executed.

The ameaningful components in Freud's thought have burgeoned im-mensely in the hands of his disciples, his clarifiers, his rectifiers, and his developers. Latter-day attempts, both by psychoanalysts and psychologists, to "tighten up" psychoanalytic theory have only made it more of an amean-ingful mishmash. Efforts toward the experimental testing of psycho-analytic principles betray a misconception both of psychoanalysis and the nature of experiment. The widely shared idea that psychoanalysis is a "sci-ence" which can cumulate and progress by a logic of verification similar to that of physics or even biology is absurd. As a result of all these generous efforts, a jungle of phony discourse has grown up in this area which would be unique in its capacity to obfuscate the enthusiasts who assent to it, were it not for the superior virtuosity of certain existentialist philosophers. Worse than that, many simple people — and perhaps as regrettably, many complex ones — see some version of the psychoanalytic system language as definitive of the very warp and woof of the psychic universe. For them, the psychoanalytic concepts are the final and exhaustive building blocks of psychic ontology. They would not have themselves be human in any other way.

Humanists have not been notable for their capacity to thread their way through this jungle of discourse and penetrate through to the viable and illuminating ideas so effectively masked by the trees. I am not prepared to say that no humanist has profited in his labors by his contact with psychoanalysis, but I feel strongly that in general the humanities have been more hindered than helped by recourse to this tradition. For one thing, Freud's theory of art, even as unmodified by his clarifiers, is atrocious. The idea of artistic performance as a sublimation of a neurosis, even when true in a particular application, is trivial. It gives so little insight into the meaning and intrinsic laws of the art object or, more properly, the experience which it governs, that it is almost beside the point. And, more generally, the overall impact of psychoanalysis on the sympathetic critic or aesthetician has been to divert him or her to an undue concern with the biographico-genetic determination of art objects at the expense of explicative and analytic attention to the intrinsic value properties which they engender. And even as tools for genetic analysis, the ideas are limited and simplistic in the extreme!

It is Jung's virtue that he has made a somewhat similar critique of the inadequacy of Freudian psychoanalysis for the understanding of art or, indeed, any other type of autonomous cultural expression. It would be reassuring if his constantly growing influence upon humanists were based primarily on this critique. But what seem mainly to inspire humanists are the positive insights they glean from his theory of the symbol, and thus of the collective unconscious, and from his distinction between psychological and visionary art. My assessments of Jungian psychology—at least to the extent I have allowed myself to know his formulations—are rather more complex (and conflicted) than are my attitudes toward Freudian psychology. Certainly, there is less scientism in Jung and his followers, and the latter have had less success than the Freudians at screening out their master's work by the interposition of their own. But Jung's theoretical metaphors are too loose-grained for my taste, his definitional practice too casual, and his sense of expository logic is too gappy. His idea that one can construct a more comprehensive and adequate system for the understanding of mental life—by the expedient of accepting the Freudian account relative to the so-called "natural system" and supplementing this with a theory for the "cultural system"—presupposes a naïve and makeshift conception of systematic analysis, even in the humanist's sense of system. His distinction between psychological and visionary art makes little sense in its own terms, and less when applied to concrete works of art. It is conceivable that humanists may derive some important leads from Jung's ideas concerning archetypes and the significance of myths, but it requires great perspicaciousness and a strong sense of the nature and logic of evidence for the application of these ideas in any way that can be illuminating. With Jungians as with Freudians, however, there is a great temptation to see the master's concepts as fixed and finalistic elements of the psychic ontology rather than as modest posits of variable adequacy, the best of which may map aspects of mental ontology only loosely and from a special perspective that cannot be preemptive.

"Humanistic psychology." As I have already suggested, an appreciable number of psychologists had become restive over behaviorism by the mid-1950s. It is not surprising that most of them were clinical psychologists or others whose pursuits forced them into contact with a human subject matter. Perhaps it is a law that the early stages of a period of dissidence are the better ones. Be this as it may, the bases of the protests were varied, and at least a limited diversity of routes was chosen by the protestors in their search for a more significant professional commitment. At about this time (the mid-1950s), Abraham Maslow, a psychologist who had long complained about the "means-centeredness" and scientism of psychology and who was then by way of discovering the promise of existentialism, called for a "third force" in psychology. Fairly soon, such a group — calling themselves "humanistic psychologists" — began to emerge. Initially, it seemed a motley group with heterogeneous interests. At a symposium in the early 1960s (cf. chapter 2) I remember characterizing it as not a "force" at all but, rather, "a large number of individuals who would have . . . difficulty communicating with each other and who stand for nothing focal, other than a feeling of disaffection from the emphases of recent American psychology." The group did not interest me especially, and I must confess to a weak disposition toward reading its journal or following its course. I might add that in 1964 I joined the Ford Foundation, and for three years found myself following the course of very little in psychology.

During this period, the fervor of the humanistic movement became channeled mainly into one pursuit (though it took an infinity of forms): the release of individual "human potential" via contrived modes of group interaction. This so-called Group Movement comprehended such variants as "Encounter Groups," "Marathon Groups," "T-Groups," "Sensitivity Groups," "Emergence Therapy," "Be-Ins," "Attack-Ins," and so on.[5] The variants were many; one of the prophets of the movement, Dr. William C. Schutz of Esalen (he prefers to be called Bill), explained why this is so:

5. The Group Movement in humanistic psychology is treated in more detail in chapter 10. *Eds.*

The fact that no one method works well for everyone creates a need for a multiplicity of methods. By having a wide variety of approaches, it is more likely that each person can find one or more techniques that he can work with profitably. Also, each person is at a different point in his psychological development. For one person one technique might be just what he needs to enter into a new, better phase of life. For another, it might just start a series of events which then need to be followed up by more similar experiences. (Schutz 1967, 12)

But all these methods were based on *one* fundamental assumption: the therapeutic and growth-releasing potential of total psychic transparency, total self-exposure. More generally, they presupposed an ultimate theory of man as *socius:* man as an undifferentiated and diffused region in a social space inhabited concurrently by all other men thus diffused. Every technique, every manipulative gimmick, cherished and wielded by the lovable, shaggy workers in this field, was selected relative to its efficacy for such an end. In his popular do-it-yourself manual on these methods (entitled *Joy*), Dr. Schutz was quite explicit about the "philosophy" of the movement:

The underlying philosophy behind the human-potential thrust is that of openness and honesty. A man must be willing to let himself be known to himself and to others. He must express and explore his feelings and open up areas long dormant and possibly painful, with the faith that in the long run the pain will give way to a release of vast potential for creativity and joy. This is an exhilarating and frightening prospect, one which is often accompanied by agony, but which usually leads to ecstasy. (16–17)

The tone of this book, I might add, is a magnificent testimonial to the vulgarity—the treacly, kitschy, crass sensibility—of Man Diffused. The book abounds with inspiring quotations from *Man of La Mancha*. It is continually informing the reader that the group therapy situation is one in which he can "use people with profit"; it is crammed with tonic proclamations like "the pursuit of joy is exciting"; and it evinces high mastery of the art of tautology—e.g., "Artistic activity is a more complex activity, requiring the simultaneous interplay of many organ systems." Were there space, this work would merit extensive quotation.

It would be an insult to spell out to a literate audience the threat to human dignity implicit in this entire far-flung "human potential" movement. It challenges any conception of the person that would make life worth living, to a degree far in excess of behaviorism. Yet in some ways its message is surprisingly akin to that of behaviorism. The human potential movement obliterates the content and boundaries of the self by transporting it out of the organism — not merely to its periphery but right out into public, social space. The force of behaviorism is merely to legislate the inner life out of existence for *science*, while allowing the citizen to entertain the illusion, perhaps even the reality, of having one. Skinner gallantly acknowledges a world of "private stimulation"; Schutz is saying, in effect, that a world of *private* stimulation is unhealthy. As for the issue of scientism, it is true that the "human-potentialists" pride themselves on their utter freedom from the constraints of any official theoretical or experimental methodology. They generate a militant rhetoric of anti-rigor, and are derisive about the "up-tight," whether in scholarship or life. But as fix-it men to the uphung, they have a passion for the unending collection and elaboration of group engineering *methods*. They have a barrel of them for every type of hang-up. Have hope!

The moral and logic of this vignette are too obvious. "Humanistic psychology" started as a revolt against ameaning — against the fifty-year constraint of an ontology-defiling epistemology and the near-century-long constraint of a prejudged Millian hypothesis. In almost no time at all it achieved a conception of human nature so gross as to make behaviorism seem a form of Victorian sentimentality — which perhaps it was. We have come farther than full circle. The resources of ameaning are formidable!

I wish I could offer a constructive and merry coda. I cannot. I am boxed by my own version of the truth.

2

STEPS TOWARD
RECONSTRUCTION

5

A Theory of Definition: Implications for Psychology, Science, and the Humanities

Foreword

This chapter deals with the problem of definition of psychological terms but also has implications for the general theory of definition. The analysis is directed in the first instance towards problems of "empirical" or "factual" definition (in the once fashionable sense of such terms among positivists and cognate groups) but bears on certain problems of theoretical or conceptual definition as well, in that no sharp dividing line is seen to exist between the two cases. The point of view may be characterized as a *psychological* theory of definition, in that it regards the problem of defining terms as, at bottom, one of perceptual guidance. The approach is offered as an alternative to (among other things) the doctrine of "operational definition" and related, but more technical, criteria of a sort at one time put forward by logical positivism—in other words, an alternative to that body of definitional lore which still powerfully influences conceptualization, systematic practice, and even problem formulation in psychology. It should be noted in passing that, though in *philosophy* positivist meaning criteria have long languished in dereliction, strong echoes of such stipulations continue to constrain and distort inquiry in *psychology*. The detailed arguments of this chapter seek to effectuate a coup de grace that should have been accomplished fifty years ago. But it is hoped that the force of the analysis is as much reconstructive as liberating: not only is a recentering of psychology's conception of "theory" suggested, but the essential relevance of psychological study to complex human performances of a sort which it had long bypassed, or relegated to the humanities, is made manifest.

The chapter combines part of my chapter on "Definition" from the manuscript for *Psychology and the Human Agent* with materials from my article "Language Communities, Search Cells, and the Psychological Studies" (Koch 1976a). The core of my position concerning definition was developed in the late 1950s; its first coherent statement was in an unpublished 1959 paper, "Towards an Indigenous Methodology" (Koch 1959c).

Introduction and Background

Beliefs concerning the magical potency of a device called "operational definition" have been the most stable of the inheritances from that paradigm of science which began to regulate psychological inquiry in the early thirties, and which I have held definitive of psychology's "Age of Theory." Virtually every element of that rule-saturated model of virtuous scientific conduct has come under widespread questioning or been abandoned. Such changes were massively documented in *Psychology: A Study of a Science* by the very men who were responsible for the importation of this model into psychology from the philosophy of science of circa 1930. And more extensive documentation of this changing atmosphere can be found throughout the recent psychological literature.

The scientism still widely prevalent in psychology is now shored up primarily by one residual element of the old methodological scaffold: the doctrine associated with operational definition. This deeply ingrained lore exerts no trivial impact on inquiry. For any set of rules which stipulate how concepts *must* be *introduced* into a field of inquiry—which stipulate, in fact, how concepts and thus the systematic relations built upon them must be linked to the empirical world—must delimit the admissible subject matter of that field. The recent and, in my opinion, healthy liberalization of psychology's conception of its proper domain proves the happy fact that no rule, no methodological directive, can wholly determine inquiring action. But action can be hampered and constrained by rule.

"Operationism" is a strangely ambitious doctrine. It purports to show psychologists (actually scientists in general, but our concern is with the doctrine as it has functioned in psychology) how to avoid the generation of nonsense, and how to protect themselves, should it nevertheless be perpetrated by the innocent or the malicious. It is a doctrine believed to have the power of anchoring theory in empirical fact, and ensuring that technical discourse be clear, determinate, unambiguously testable. It is a doctrine which has been invoked as infallible asepsis for the purification of "traditional" psychological discourse, and infallible prophylaxis for all future discourse. It has been seen as the eternal guarantor of an objectivist epistemology. To some it has even appealed as a formula for the task of psychology, while to others it has comprised a large part of the formulary essential to theoretical action.

What is *curious* about this doctrine is that no single instance of meaningful discourse in history has ever satisfied its requirements. Any "statement" which *did* literally satisfy its requirements would not be worth making. Every *meaningful* use of every concept for which a psychologist has given a definition in terms purported to be in conformity with the doctrine has violated that doctrine. Every definition cast in the terms of the doctrine has been *intelligible* only to the extent that it has deviated from the paradigm(s) recommended by the doctrine; the same may be said with respect to the precision and nicety of the definition.

Despite the preceding circumstances, the body of doctrine in question has for almost a half-century been closer to the sacrosanct than anything in the gamut of psychological "methodology." Though, during the early years of its reign in psychology, it elicited some analytic protest, I can think of few explicit demurs that have been registered in the psychological literature of the past forty years.

We should not confuse what is here meant by operational definition with the contexts of its use in the compass of Bridgman's writings, or any given one of them. Bridgman's early writings were freely and variably interpreted by the original protagonists of operational definition in psychology. The burgeoning methodological literature of the late thirties increased the variability. From the late thirties onwards, this dilute Bridgmanian doctrine in the psychological literature began to coalesce with equally variable, adventitiously selective, and free interpretations of definitional doctrines based on the literature of logical positivism. Even the originating "movements" of logical positivism and operationism were not, in general, clearly distinguished by psychologists, and thus the term, "operational definition," came to be applied to a mélange of definitional folklores, the remote ancestry of which may be allocated to Bridgman and certain logical positivist formulations. By the present phase, this amorphous set of beliefs may be said to have very little in common other than the name "operational definition" and the paradoxical properties just summarized.

In this chapter, I shall present the outlines of a theory of definition having consequences for psychology which must be adjudged radical relative to long-regnant methodological stereotype. Strangely, however, this theory will turn out to be based on simpleminded *psychological* considerations. The theory is available to anyone who *looks* with reasonable sharpness of focus at phenomena of human communication as it takes place within the familiar resources of natural language. All that is required of the viewer is some significant degree of literacy, the suspension of whatever baggage of belief he or she has inherited concerning the strictures on communication in *scientific* contexts, and empirical openness.

As an exercise in the pathology of knowledge (which has become my favorite field), a little of the relevant history may be amusing. When, in the early thirties, the Age of Theory began its search for a set of decision procedures, it could have turned to the large number of criteria for the cognitive significance of statements which logical positivism and neopragmatism had already made available. Instead, partly by historical accident, psychology focused on the early formulations of Bridgman's "operational criterion" of meaning which, by phrasing the meaning of a scientific concept in terms of corresponding *experimental* and (ultimately) observational operations, offered attractive imagery to a science at once self-conscious of its newly won experimental status and eager to get experiment into tighter relation with theory. If psychologists had done their reading in slightly different order, they might have focused on the proposals of Schlick, or of early mid-Carnap, or of the neopragmatist C. I. Lewis, or, in fact, on a variety of other criteria having an intent similar to Bridgman's.[1] In such a case, the clang of the psychological literature regarding definition would today be different.

The lore concerning operational definition soon began to fuse with the lore concerning logical positivism. In 1936–37, Carnap published, in "Testability and Meaning," what was quickly to become the most influential analysis of meaningfulness in the history of logical positivism. Although no presentation in the psychological literature has done justice to the technical detail of Carnap's treatment, his notions of the "disposition concept," the "reduction sentence," and "chains" thereof (and, most especially, the "observable predicates" of the "thing language" as the reduction basis for the language of science) soon entered the jargon of psychological commerce. Since 1937, there has been the lushest proliferation of philosophical discussions of meaning in history. Not only have Carnap and

---

1. "Bridgman in psychology" could form a peculiarly revealing chapter in the history of ideas! Surely no author in the history of "methodology" can have been "used" more and read less. For an account of how Bridgman's views were (and continue to be) distorted by psychologists, see chapter 14.

other positivists liberalized their meaning criteria out of all recognition, but analytic philosophers and others have uncovered new vistas of subtlety. Yet, to this very day, little of this has penetrated into psychology.

Those who *have* followed recent discussions of meaning and language in the extrapsychological literature will perhaps respond to my analysis more with a feeling of *déjà vu* than of shock. In the decades since beginning to think on these lines, I have been encouraged—though sometimes grudgingly so—to note that developments in philosophic meaning theory (over a broad gamut of "positions") and, to some extent, in linguistics have moved in a similar direction. Having published so little on my views, I can at least assert an option open to all procrastinators by claiming pre-science.

There are strong affinities between aspects of my position and emphases of some analytic philosophers. In its concern with the role of metaphor in natural language and in science, the present position falls into a growing cluster of analyses exemplified by Max Black (1954, 1962) and Mary Hesse (1954, 1966). Some of the thinking in the ambience of Chomsky's approach to linguistics—for example, Lenneberg's (1967) speculations on "reference"—is also consonant with the present views. Polanyi's (1958) analysis of word use as essentially a *skill* dependent on tacit processes which cannot, in principle, be rendered fully effable, has also a family resemblance to the present analysis. Yet all these similarities are rather more evident in certain termini of the analyses than in the routes over which they proceed. I think my route an especially instructive one for *psychology*, in that at no point does it stray far from psychological terrain.

Sketch of a Psychological Theory of Definition

To make the bearing of my analysis on the concrete problems of psychological theorists evident at the very outset, it is well that I commence with one of the principal findings of the project that eventuated in the six volumes of *Psychology: A Study of a Science* (Koch 1959b, 1962b, 1963). One of my main objectives in directing that study was to invite from a large number of psychological theorists a comparison between the particularities of their conceptual and systematic practice and what the more or less "official" epistemology of the profession in those days—which was essentially a logical positivist epistemology—said they *ought* to be doing. One of the largest and most conspicuous convergences among the thirty-six systematists who participated in the first half of the study (Study I, vols. 1–3) was the difficulty they reported or evinced in bringing their definitional practice into line with "operational" and cognate doctrine. This trend and others are extensively discussed in the epilogue to Study I (Koch 1959a).

The "difficulty" (really a vast and varied panoply of individual cognitive pains) might be summarized in this way: Men — whether they were learning theorists talking about intervening variables like "reaction potential" or "need-cathexis," or even specific applications of S and R; or personality theorists talking about "themas," "ego structure," "the self," or "presses"; or social psychologists talking about "constraint," "conformity," "systems of strain," "object-instrumental attitudes," or "group cohesion" — all seem to have the impression that in some sense they are talking *meaningfully*. Yet when Tolman (1959, 147–48) confesses that he cannot pin down the meaning of his intervening variables to the particularities of defining experiments or empirical "pointer readings" (his final conclusion was that for him they seem to be a useful "psychologic"); or when Guthrie (1959, 164–66) insists that applications of S and R depend on perceptual sensitivities of observers and must in the case of S presuppose inferences about "meaning" to the organism; or when personality and social theorists indicate in the most varied ways that their concepts are at an astronomic distance from the defining base as conventionally conceived — all are saying that the official conception of the observation base, together with the stipulated form of its linkage to scientific concepts, will not permit them to talk meaningfully. *These men feel that, at least in restricted language communities, they can communicate. Yet the official epistemology will not permit them to believe that they can communicate meaningfully.*

Such an impasse should certainly license the daring to raise questions about the *conditions* of human communication. There are, of course, many answers to such questions in a variety of disciplines — but they are in most cases precommitted answers which presuppose a special theory of language. At least initially, we should be absolute empiricists and raise questions about what goes on when words — single lexical units — are used meaningfully in ordinary discourse. How are words in the natural languages defined? What governs their meaning-transformations and accretions over time? What makes some words clear and others fuzzy, some abstract and some less so? What is involved in penetrating, revealing, or creative uses of language as against flat, obfuscating, or rote uses? What in particular are at least some of the preconditions for persons understanding each other? And so on. It cannot be overemphasized that *at the beginning* such questions should be asked in commonsense terms — that is, in the idiom of natural language itself. Even within this idiom, the questions are large questions to which we can expect only small, slow answers.[2]

It will perhaps be objected that one does not consult the slovenly natural languages for canons of linguistic procedure in *science*. Granted! To whatever extent possible, scientific language (by definition) is to be so forged as to give more terse, precise, salient, and unambiguous descriptions of events, and generalizations upon them, than natural language. And the cognitive and predictive aims of science will entail the dropping out of certain features and functions for which natural language has been specialized, and the appearance of other features special to the ends of science.

It should, however, be emphasized that the psychological processes which mediate communication cannot be *absolutely* different as between scientific and natural languages; whatever processes are constitutive of meaning must be the same, even if scientific languages are so constructed as to restrict their functioning in certain ways. And a second consideration must have truly decisive importance for psychology, namely: *the subject matter of psychology is such that every significant meaning that can be conveyed in a natural language must, in principle, constitute potential data for our discipline.* I do not mean merely the words (or signs) that convey these meanings, but the signs as meaningful, or even the meanings as psychological processes per se. Any theory of definition for the *psychological language* which identifies the observation base—and the rules for "constructing" terms upon it—in a way that does not meet this requirement is arbitrarily limiting the subject matter of our discipline to a corresponding degree. A psy-

---

2. The questions I raise here and address in the sequel will seem to the reader either stale or obvious: Stale in the sense that linguists (especially psycholinguists) and philosophers must surely have "dispatched" these primitive questions concerning the semantic behavior and nature of single lexical units. Have we not seen an explosion of interest in language, especially in the flurry of sophisticated activity sparked by the Chomskian era? Obvious in the sense that the circumstances of word use are surely among the most intimate and ubiquitous phenomena available to any literate person. It is my contention, however, that the detailed "behavior" of lexical units is so stupendously complex that students of language have tended, both wittingly and unwittingly, to make strong simplifying assumptions concerning "rudimentary" semantic matters as a precondition to pursuit of their often fulsome theoretical objectives. As for the matter of "obviousness," may I make the obvious point that incessant saturation in a field of phenomena is one of the strongest conceivable barriers to precise specification or analysis of those phenomena. (The elusiveness of complex psychological, and especially linguistic, events to their owners is perhaps *too* obvious a point to add!) My chief communicative difficulty in the following analyses will stem from the *familiarity* to the reader of the processes I try to explicate. I can only invite the reader to look over my shoulder and focus with me on what he and I already know; my expository task would be a breeze if the topic were utterly strange to him—and perhaps to me!

chology unafraid to face its proper universe of questions must, then, have a language sufficiently rich and free to render in some way, or admit, any meaningful discrimination that can be made in a natural language.

As a move of minimal size toward such an analysis of definition, let us consider the case of a single English word. I choose the word *dignity* partly because it has a "psychological" reference in the natural language, partly because most persons would agree that this word can be used meaningfully, and partly because it is at a level of epistemic complexity roughly comparable to such concepts of the personality theorist as trait-names.[3]

Let us first ask where we would get if we tried to "reduce" this concept to an observation base similar to that stipulated by operational or physical-thing language criteria. Does dignity mean a posture with a certain stiffness coefficient—or, more generously, "erect bearing"? Does it mean a "quiet voice"? Can it—still more generously—be applied to a professor such that when he has an obstreperous student in class, he freezes him with a cold glance? Or must it be a professor such that he never has obstreperous students? Note that the "reductive" or "operational symptoms" even in their initial formulation are already fairly far from an "ultimate" physical-thing observation base. We would need at least an angular criterion for "erect bearing," and a decibel cutoff point for "quiet voice." "Cold glance" and "obstreperous student" would give us still more trouble, unless we were so afflicted with physicalism as to believe that a thermometer and some such device as a windsock would solve the problem.

But these latter objections are nothing to the point. Everyone would rapidly agree that no single symptom of the type mentioned would be a reliable "index" of dignity (application rule for the term) and, moreover, that no *conjunction* or *disjunction* of such symptoms, whatever the size of the class, could give an adequate definition. People would immediately say: "Erect bearing, yes, but not stiff or haughty." "Quiet voice, probably, but not always—there are times when the essence of dignity is passionate, even explosive utterance." As a matter of fact, rather subtle qualifications would now emerge. Some persons would begin to require that the erect, nonstiff, nonhaughty bearing would perhaps also be characterized by the quality of "grace." And that the quality of "grace" extend to demeanor, movement,

---

3. There is also a special joy in acknowledging that it is a word which B. F. Skinner (1971) found dangerously obfuscatory. It is amusing to note that forty years ago I fixed upon dignity as a prototype word for exhibiting the complexity and the remarkable richness of the "meanings" of common lexical units in a natural language. Unfortunately, I could not then know how naughty and deluded I was in so doing.

vocalization, how one holds an object, nods, etc., etc. Matters have by now become quite complex, and "symptoms" of dignity are beginning to get specified within a subtle relational network, the terms of which are themselves epistemically no less complex than the term under definition. Soon, however, it would be perceived that no given number (whether conjunctive or disjunctive) of even such qualified and complex *symptoms* of dignity would give a really "good" (i.e., sensitively discriminating) definition.

Take, for instance, the matter of "quiet voice"—even in the qualified form which admits circumstances under which "nonquiet" voice must be interpreted as "evidence" of dignity. One easily goes further than an enumeration, so to say, of "test condition–test result" *exceptions*. One quickly perceives that "quiet voice" is *a vagrant and un-nicely bounded quality of dignity, even as a symptomatic quality having some kind of probability relationship to the trait.* One perhaps says: "Not quiet but, rather, a tone adjusted to a balanced, fitting, yet self-contained assessment of a situation." Matters are now indeed complicated. Language is directing the perception of the observer to an exceedingly subtle relational aspect of a situation, and doing this via other concepts, each of which discriminates comparably subtle relational qualities to the one being defined. Yet airy as is this relational lattice, there are unquestionably many observers who can and do agree in diagnoses of such *symptoms* of dignity as tone of voice in this way.

But note that in trying to get into proper focus and shading *symptomatic* manifestations of dignity like voice tone, we seem unwittingly to have drawn on a *quite general specification* of dignity as a relational quality of human events—*a quality the presence or absence of which would determine the symptomatic relevance of a given instance of voice quality or, indeed, a wide range of other possible symptoms.* Indeed, we begin to see that there is in some sense a "theory" of dignity in the natural language, one of extraordinary subtlety and wide involvements—and, no doubt, differentially accessible to different users and definers of language.

Even at *this* point, we discover with some shock that we have barely begun to isolate the "defining properties" of dignity. Is dignity merely (one could almost say, "really") a tendency toward balanced, fitting, self-contained actions in situations? Much further and finer specification may be required for ultimate nicety. Thus dignity may involve fittingness or appropriateness, but certainly not in the sense of observing, or conforming to, *propriety.* Rather, what seems involved is a flexible appropriateness "above" propriety, in which individuality is consistently defined, yet subtly, rather than conspicuously or flamboyantly. Matters are now horribly involved, but I am certain that individuals who apply this word sensitively (relative to the use-context at issue) presuppose a criterion no less complex and, moreover, one which, whatever the words of *their* definition — indeed, even if they can give no definition — discriminates a subtle relational quality much like the one I have sought to specify in the above formulations.

And sensitive appliers of the term would recognize many other things. For instance, there are many personal styles of dignity. And there are many partially overlapping concepts to which dignity is related in the lattice of language — for example, nobility, stateliness, gravity, worth, excellence, honorableness — which could also provide certain of the terms for an "isolation" of relevant relational characters. It should be noted, too, that a full reconstruction from usage would probably result in the discrimination of *several* relational characters — each as (so to say) specialized as the "definition" just attempted. And *these,* in actual usage, would form disjuncts so that the term might properly be used in different contexts to denote quite different relational characters.[4]

Other matters should be noted. It is probable that dignity — in the sense under analysis — had reference originally to a "molar" attribute of persons. But, of course, it has been extended to properties of personal actions, qual-

---

4. The above discussion of dignity has concentrated on a differentially attributive sense of the word, in which it attaches to properties of individuals in relation to their actions or to particular individual actions. Intricate as this individually attributive usage turns out to be, it may be less so than certain other meaning-disjuncts of the term.

For instance, there is a generic usage — as in such phrases as "the dignity of man" — which is so complex in reference as to prompt many tough-minded persons (or, what often comes to the same thing, simple-minded ones) to shrug off the usage as vacuous. What seems involved in this usage is a generalized ontological sense of dignity — a conception of man as the most complex and highly organized being in the known universe and, by virtue of that status, an entity of inherent *worth.* Moreover, since the constitutive condition of this worth or value is that of membership in a genus as such, all men share equally in this worth (i.e., "worth" in the sense here at issue): each individual, as human, is entitled to the respect of his fellows and to particular varieties of consideration appropriate to his or her humanity. Such modalities of consideration are often localized as "rights" or "entitlements" within the ethical and legal categories of the West.

A finer analysis of this generic sense of dignity would disclose many subtheories clustering in an asystematic way about the notion and attempting more particulate specification of ontological properties deemed unique to man on grounds of which he merits one or another entitlement, form of consideration, or respect. Thus man may be seen as a being uniquely conscious of his mortality, uniquely baffled by the circumstances of his origin and *raison d'être,* uniquely terrified by the awesome extent and impenetrability of the universe, uniquely apprised of the certainty of his suffering. Hence the special kind of courage and gallantry implicit in his occupancy of the human condition, his admirable resourcefulness in wresting order from chaos, his justifiable pride in his accomplishments, however small, erratic, and

ities of thought and sentiment, and characteristics of aesthetic objects (as, say, when we talk about the dignity of form, color, line, or of literary style, or, indeed, the dignity of the structures, representational or no, conveyed by a work of art). And we can talk meaningfully about the dignity of animals, and of aspects of animals such as personality, behavior, form, and physiognomy. It is vital to recognize that many of the so-called extensions of dignity are not *merely arbitrary* but are based, to one or another degree, on a type of *metaphor—that is, the perception in new settings of relational characters which in fact overlap with (or are similar to) the characters already tagged by an "old" term.* Such a mechanism of metaphor is fundamental to the growth—including meaning extensions, differentiations, and refinements—of natural languages.

Of course, not all extensions of word meanings are based on metaphor. Many *are* arbitrary. Some, though based on metaphor, discriminate only vaguely overlapping, or less differentiated, relational qualities of events and may thus be fairly said to constitute debased usages of the word. In truly *creative* uses of language, the meaning of a word may be sharpened and enriched by attaching it to contexts of events in which the original relational characters tagged by the term are more purely or richly exhibited, *or* by explicating a term (through "definition" or use) in a new linguistic context in such a way as to achieve the same result. Actually, the "correct" (at

---

infrequent. Again, there is the fact of man's "double agency": his unique reflexivity or self-consciousness; his capacity therefore for self-criticism, for assessing and revising the course and consequences of his own activities. Again, man is the only being of which tragic actions or a tragic trajectory of action may be predicated and, of course, the only natural being capable of apprehending the precise and subtle configuration of circumstances definitive of tragedy. Indeed, one possible definition of man is that he is the only *tragic being* in nature.

This limited précis of the generic theory of human dignity, of course, only scratches the surface—and hardly begins to suggest the complexity of this particular meaning-disjunct. There is indeed a vast and differentiated "literature of dignity" in the history of the humanities and in many other contexts within the history of natural and technical language. It is far from being an empty literature and, wherever meaningful, it has nothing—absolutely *nothing*—to do with the "conspicuousness [or inconspicuousness] of the causes of behavior," as one of the litterateurs of "dignity" (Skinner 1971, 50) would have it.

As an addendum to demonstrate further the richness of the concept of dignity, it may be noted that there is *another,* nonequalitarian sense of dignity-as-worth. The sense of "worth" here at issue registers a differential quality of achievement, of personhood. I hold back from more sustained analysis of this disjunct except to note that it is related in complex ways to both of the senses already analyzed: possession or manifestation of dignity in the sense analyzed in the text may be one of the conditions constitutive of worth in this sense; worth in the present "differential" sense seems in part metaphorically related to worth in the generic sense, and is probably the historically prior "base" for the metaphor.

any level) *momentary* use of language by an individual presupposes a process very like metaphor, because the perceptual conditions for application of a term are never identical on different occasions. The limiting case of metaphor, *psychologically* speaking, would be some kind of quite habitual transposition process from one dated instance of the conditions of application to another. More discriminating uses of metaphor, as when language is used in fresh or creative ways, may involve effortful perceptual search in new contexts for subtle relational qualities which overlap with more standard meanings of words.

An important corollary of the present analysis must now be noted. Not everyone can use the words of a natural language with equal nicety or precision. Not even all literate people. There are various levels of "goodness" with which language can be applied, defined, understood. The precision and subtlety of what an individual does with a word depends on the precision, delicacy, differentiation, etc. of the perceptual discrimination which *for him* has been tagged by that word. It depends also on other factors such as his ability to make further fine discriminations of certain types — thus, his capacity for inventive metaphor. Can everyone discriminate the referent of *dignity* with equal nicety? Of course not. Some will use the word incorrectly in all circumstances. Others will use it with varying degrees of imprecision by relatively rote application to "symptomatic" contexts, at one or another of the levels that we illustrated. Subtle forms of dignity will elude them, and they will often see or assert "dignity" where it is not.

Other factors equal, the persons capable of using the term most precisely and creatively are those who, in fact, are most dignified. The truly dignified person is constantly discovering or creating new forms of dignity. He is continually solving "dignity problems." He is an artist of dignity. The relational properties controlling his behavior may not be accessible to *him* for verbalization. But if they are to be accessible for linguistic coding by *anyone,* the coder must be "sensitized" to comparable or overlapping relational properties.

It follows that *there is no single language community* for the understanding, use, or explication of *dignity*. There is a multiplicity of language communities, each at different levels of the relevant sensitivity. To insist on fixing the definition of a term by reduction, via a standard linkage relation, to some tightly restricted observation base — say, the first or second level of symptomatic statements of our illustration — would be to sacrifice the possibility of precise or subtle communication. Far worse, *it would eliminate much meaning and knowledge from the universe.* Moreover, any observation base built at the level of the "symptomatic statements" of our examples would *still* be very remote from a physical-thing or operational language, as usually conceived.

The minimum admissible size of a language community for the natural language "theory" of dignity should properly be a group of two — preferably the two people who are at once the most experientially sensitive and linguistically adept, in respect of the relevant phenomena, in the world. The only stipulation would be that these men be able to communicate reliably about their special forte.[5] All other language communities regarding dignity, by definition, say less when they use the word and know less about the distribution of dignity in the universe. The only way in which the richest and most differentiated conceptions of (or knowledge about) dignity could be spread more widely would be if the language community "at the summit" could devise means for communicating their knowledge to language communities at lower levels. *This, in general, could be done only by perceptual training techniques which might in the most determinate possible way guide members of less sensitive communities toward discrimination of the relevant relational characters.* In this way, the language community at the summit could be enlarged, but it is absurd to expect that it could be universalized.

Most of the suggestions I would make about a theory of definition adequate to the demands of psychology are implicit in the discussion of *dignity*. That discussion was a slovenly mode for their introduction, but per-

---

5. A language community of so restricted a size as is here at issue raises, with especial insistence, the possibility of use-consistencies by imposture, by overlapping hallucinations, or even by mutual self-deception. These specters may, of course, arise in language communities of *any* size, but it is a rational presumption that the larger the community the less likely the chances of such "false reliabilities." Even so, there is a worldwide "flying saucer" community of impressive magnitude. At bottom, then, the criterion of communicative reliability that we all presuppose demands that the agreers be *competent* in a way relevant to the use-domain in question. My position in effect spells out certain literal consequences of taking *competence* (relevant discriminative sensitivity) seriously as a requirement of language communities. When we suspect "summit" or small language communities, we characteristically (a) ask for the credentials of the members (if the two agreers are Einstein and von Neumann, rather than two sophomore science students, we are more likely to accredit the esoteric communication in question); (b) hopefully await evidence of successful efforts of the summit community to enlarge its membership. Neither of these "procedures" contains any *final* guarantee against nonsense. That hazard we must all accept: to promulgate the myth that nonsense can be averted *in principle* is only to augment its supply! May I suggest that presumably mature and tough-minded men in several fields of scholarship have long spent too much worry over the hazard of nonsense; they should have more confidence in their capacity to hold their own against an occasional crackpot.

haps quicker and more intelligible than abstract statement. I will now try to extract the bearing of that strange analysis on some problems of the theory of definition.

Definition in Natural Language

The lexical elements of a language have two aspects, a conventional one and a nonconventional. The nonconventional aspect is in fact the discriminations — perceivable "things," properties, and relations, whether simple or complex, crass or delicate, obvious or subtle — to which signs are *allocated*. It is only the allocation that is conventional — that is, the choice of sign and stipulation that it "stand for" such-and-such a thing, property, or relation. The "corresponding" discriminable qualities are in the strictest sense the "meanings" conveyed by words. In any dated instance of the meaningful use of a word, the meaning, as a *psychological process*, is the *perception* of some one or more of the correlated things, properties, or relations. In a loose sense it can be said that words index and, within limits, stabilize *discriminal experiences*. Natural language preserves and records the history of human sensibility (discriminal experiences) at all levels — from simple, practical discriminations among properties and relations of objects, to the most subtle and "rarefied" and creative oscillations of sensibility in which high-order relational qualities may be perceived as common to a wide range of diverse perceptual contexts.

The natural language is thus heterogeneous, and an uneven communicative tool. It may contain both "good" and "poor" concepts (in special senses of these terms). A "good" concept may involve the fixing by a conventional sign of some discriminal experience (say, of a "complex" relational quality) which is in fact common to many event matrices and that does reveal and demarcate something highly significant about the world. A "poor" concept may involve the assignment of a name to a "fuzzy" discriminal experience, one which in fact isolates trivial, vagrant, or "local" aspects of events — one which does not have the generality imputed to it, is contingent, accidental, illusory, etc. And one might distinguish also "good" and "poor" *definitions* (independent of the goodness of the concept). A glance at dictionaries of different quality will show this to be the case. Some definitions are in terms of relatively rote and symptomatic "examples"; others bound the salient properties or relations in a delicate and well-specified way.

Examination of definitional practice in natural language will show that terms are defined in three basic modes:

1. By an equivalence rule connecting the term with a *synonym*. This presupposes, of course, that the application conditions (i.e., discriminable properties or relations) for the defining term are already known by the person to whom the definition is addressed (call him the addressee). There are, incidentally, far fewer true synonyms in natural languages than usually supposed; meaning shadings are such that partial synonymy is more often the case. A "sensitive" discussion of this point is to be found in Samuel Johnson's preface to his *Dictionary of the English Language* (1755).

2. By *metaphor*, in the sense already described. Dictionary definition by metaphor seeks to direct or guide perception to the relevant properties or relations (or system thereof) by eliciting a similar or overlapping discrimination via a configuration of words for each of which the addressee is presumed already to have the appropriate discriminations. Note that such definition in terms of the familiar does not necessarily reduce the concept to a more crass set of discriminations. The defining terms may designate equally subtle or even more subtle properties and/or relations than the term under definition.

3. By *example*—the dictionary case being the "textual quotations" exhibiting the use of the term in various contexts. This is a mixed case in that some of the textual citations are definitions via metaphor, others specify the term *symptomatically*. It is interesting to note that the great lexicographers (like Johnson, and the authors of the *Oxford English Dictionary*) seek their examples from the works of the "best" authors and, I believe, rather favor metaphorical to symptomatic citations.

Note, finally, that no dictionary of natural language reduces its words to a standard definition base — no matter how generously defined. Dictionaries which try so far as possible to give definitions in terms of crasser discriminations, presumed to be "familiar" to the largest number of addressees, are likely to give poor definitions. Systems like "basic English," which do propose something like "reduction" to a definition base, vastly reduce the range and nicety of meanings (not *merely* "emotive," but *cognitive*) that the language can convey. Shakespeare in basic English is not basic Shakespeare — it is impoverished and garbled Shakespeare!

Dictionary practice is instructive, but locked within language. It is of more general significance to ask about definition as it takes place in the learning or teaching of language or in the adjudication of questions of usage for which dictionaries are inadequate. Here again, the three forms of definition already mentioned are used. In our discussion of *dignity*, the main types were illustrated. But there is a great difference under these circumstances. One may direct perception *outside* of language by pointing, or what has been called "ostensive definition." But if pointing be interpreted as a sightline along a finger, we will reduce language to a barren thing. Finger pointing is not a sufficiently specific identifying operation for the discrimination of embedded, subtle, or abstract relations or qualities. But the present formulation would imply that pointing, interpreted far more broadly as *perceptual guidance,* is at the basis of all definition. In this special sense, all modes of definition are ostensive.

The problem of definition is a special form of the problem of perceptual training. And any definition is at bottom an attempt to guide the addressee toward making a relevant perceptual discrimination. Thus, all methods and devices which can conceivably lead to perceptual learning are relevant to the problems of definition. In the ideal case, we reproduce the conditions which cause the relevant properties or relations to appear in the purest possible form, and the "pointing operation" is the stipulation that the experience which occurs under these conditions is a dated instance of the "meaning" of the term. Psychologists too well know that it is not easy to approximate the ideal case, even for crass discriminations. It should now be emphasized that purely verbal definition is a process of *surrogate pointing.* The defining expression can only *guide* the addressee toward contexts that "embody" the relevant property or relation (actually, a similar one), which may then be noted or not noted. *Verbal definition* per se is a most limited and imperfect medium for conveying empirical meanings.

Implications for the Observation Base of Psychology

The implications of the preceding analyses for the observation base (so-called) are obvious. *The observation base must be a far more extensive domain than is ordinarily thought. This is almost unquestionably the case for all science, but conspicuously so for psychology. Indeed, the entire conception of an observation base linked by orderly relations to concepts of higher order is called into question.* It becomes literally meaningless to talk about an observation base to or from which definitions of higher-order terms are "reduced" or "constructed." No logical combinatorial process will give us the intricately determined and highly specific "relational qualities" designated by *dignity,* from symptomatic indices even as complex as "quiet voice," no matter how varied and numerous. Nor can such relational qualities be *reduced* (in, e.g., the sense of Carnap's "reduction sentence" analysis) to symptomatic indices of this order—no matter how many reduction sentences are written. *Dignity* is no technical psychological concept, but the orders of abstraction and relational specificity which psychology must discriminate in *its* concepts are at least as great and, with respect to important or interesting problems, much greater. Moreover, whatever determinate meanings are conveyed by concepts like *dignity* represent aspects of the universe which psychology cannot fairly rule out, and which it must be willing to accept and use as *data*.

The universe of what used to be called "direct observables" must be vastly expanded. Many "theoretical" and presumably higher-order terms must be seen to discriminate definite, if perceptually highly embedded, properties and relations of events and things — to designate them in a direct way. There is a sense in which certain designations of a word like *dignity* are just as directly observable as, say, the referent of the term *red*. From this point of view, there is no distinction, in principle, between terms of the sort thought to be observation terms and those of a sort thought to be theory terms. One may talk very roughly in terms of differential degrees of abstractness, generality, subtlety, embeddedness, etc. of the properties and relations denoted by terms, but such distinctions do not fall into any systematic arrangement of "levels." If this position implies something akin to a realism, then be it said that it is one based on empirical analysis of human communication, not on metaphysical grounds.

Careful survey of definitional *practice* (as distinguished from claimed rationale) in psychology will show that it corresponds in detail to the analysis here put forward. This is so, whether at ethereal levels of personality theory or stonier levels of learning formulations. People do not construct or reduce their definitions upon an observation base, because no general meaning could be communicated in this way. When they do provide so-called operational definitions for higher-order terms, they are either not being consistent with what they really have in mind or they are providing *examples* which may, by *metaphor* or *symptom*, convey application conditions in some degree. The difficulties raised regarding definition by contributors to *Psychology: A Study of a Science* are ample evidence of this.

Examination of definitional practice shows that the definer typically attempts to direct perception toward certain discriminations by a combination of *metaphor* and a *range of examples*.[6] Communication will take place only if the addressee is equipped with the stock of discriminations called upon by the defining terms of the definition. This is a necessary, not a sufficient condition for communication. The definer must mobilize the

---

6. Max Black (1954, 24–45) talks of "range definitions" in an analysis which is consonant, in some ways, with the present account.

presumptive stock of discriminations with sufficient skill to maximize the chance that perception of the intended property or relation will occur. But no amount of skill can *guarantee* that the addressee—even if he *does* have the relevant discriminations—will perceive the intended referent. The addressee is beset by contingencies of much the same order as those posed by "hidden-figure" puzzles. There is an element of luck in all successful communication.

This general analysis, it should be emphasized, unites the problem of concept formation with that of concept definition and application. The theorist who has achieved an "insight" with respect to important "causal" determinants of experience or behavior has made a perception of some constant relational attribute of mental functioning, behavior, etc., which in general has not been made. The problem of definition then becomes the problem of teaching persons how to perceive that constant relational attribute. If the attribute is a highly embedded, subtle, or delicately contoured one, such a process of teaching may be very difficult indeed. The discriminations coded in extant language, technical or natural, may be entirely inadequate. The means for reproducing instances which embody the relation may not be within the control of the definer. The event matrices constitutive of instances of the relation may be provided by the world too infrequently or fleetingly for differentiated "pointing." When such event matrices do occur, the significant relation may be masked by many others more conspicuous.

In other words, we get very much the picture which the epilogue to Study I (Koch 1959a) gave of the definitional difficulties experienced with special insistence by the personality and social theorists in *Psychology: A Study of a Science.* Needless to say, the fact that such difficulties may be experienced constitutes no presumption that the relation discriminated by the theorist represents some profound regularity in the universe. *But, by the same token, the occurrence of such communicative difficulties justifies no presumption that the concept is empty or nonsensical.* It must be anticipated also that in cases of exceedingly tenuous and subtle concepts, the language community sufficiently sensitive to make or approximate the necessary discrimination may be extremely small.[7] Indeed, at this point it is well that the question of psychological language communities engage our attention.

7. Karl Zener (1958) conducts an illuminating exploration of issues concerning the qualifications of language communities relative to specific ranges of psychological phenomena in his essay "The Significance of Experience of the Individual for the Science of Psychology."

Psychological Language Communities

On any theory of meaning, the criterion of "intersubjectivity" is, of course, basic. But the critical question is: intersubjectivity among whom? Who are the people who must be able to agree on the application conditions for a term or statement? It is not necessarily the business of philosophical analysis to pursue this question in detail. But the "imagery" of the more fashionable philosophical formulations has tended to suggest extraordinarily weak credentials for membership in the language community. To be sure, there is often some clause restricting membership to "competent investigators" or "adequately trained" persons. Interpretation of statements at any level "above" the ultimate definition base is usually seen as dependent upon such "training." But the usual illustrations of statements *within the definition base* are so chosen as to give to many the impression that membership in the language community may be met by the capacity to perceive pointer-scale coincidences, to see red, and perhaps to read. Of course, this was never *intended* by the philosophical analysts. But certainly their theories of definition, as imported into psychology and modified by the prevailing intellectual atmosphere, tend to represent the language community as a most accessible club.

For instance, a published "glossary" of terms used in the "objective science of behavior" (Verplanck 1957) says of "operational definitions," "They demand agreement, and they make it possible for anyone who is able to read to reconstruct the observations to which the terms apply" (iii). At another place, in characterization of the "data language" (definition or observation base, as we have been speaking), the relevance of "training" is acknowledged, but in this way: "words . . . in the data-language . . . must be defined so that anyone after a minimum of training can use them consistently" (iii). Now a *minimum of training* necessary for the consistent use of a word—particularly if that word denote a highly embedded property or relation of events—may necessitate a *very great deal of training* indeed. Yet, in the psychological literature regarding empirical definition, it is quite clear that the force of such expressions is more like "absolute minimum of training" than the minimum of training necessary for discriminating "so-and-so."

It is strange that the very individuals who espouse or accept such a conception of the observation base often acknowledge, in other connections, that the application conditions for observation terms, and terms close to the observation base, can only be learned and "discriminated" with sensitivity by working face-to-face with individuals who are masters of certain experimental crafts. Thus there is a large group of individuals, much interested in delicate and dramatic "shapings" of animal behavior, who are ready, even eager, to admit that the true subtleties of the art can be assimilated only by prolonged laboratory contact with one of its acknowledged masters.[8] They are right! But they have failed to generalize upon this truly profound knowledge. Language is at best a feeble instrument even among members of a highly trained language community having quite limited problematic interests.

None of the currently institutionalized sciences form single, homogeneous language communities. Physicists in one empirical area do not necessarily fully "understand" physicists in another; pathologists do not necessarily understand electrophysiologists, and so on. And within each scientific area, even when cut rather finely, one may distinguish disorderly "hierarchies" of language communities: in the extreme case, there may be quite definite and unique observable properties and relations which only two men, perhaps working in the same laboratory, may be able to perceive, and denote by some linguistic expression. Moreover, it should be stressed that the stratification of language communities within a science may reflect variations in *sensitivity* of observers just as much as differential levels or foci of *training*. There was a time when Einstein was apprised of certain invariant properties of the universe, yet could communicate these "discriminations" to few men.[9] If it be objected that Einstein did not directly "observe" these properties (which on my view he in some sense did), then take the context, say, of medical diagnosis for ready illustrations of a similar principle.

Now a language community must obviously be specified on a *psychological* criterion—a complex one demanding a certain criterial overlap of learned *discriminations* and specialized *discriminative capacities* (sensitivities)

---

8. For instance, the very same author quoted above in the capacity of behavior-science lexicographer has pointed out in an illuminating analysis of the early phase of Skinner's "system," "Those who have observed work with animal behavior in different laboratories are often struck by the remarkable degree of control which the experimental technique of Skinner and his students enables them to exert over rats, pigeons, pigs and people. . . . While it may be argued that the group has avoided problems or situations yielding poorer control, it must be pointed out that many who have tried to duplicate the procedures cannot always do so until they have had an opportunity to observe them in action" (Verplanck 1954, 272).

9. Stephen Toulmin (1972) has pointed out that at an early phase of what became known as the theory of relativity, Einstein had considered naming the theory "invariant theory."

among members. Say that this criterion defines a "discrimination pool." I think there are strong grounds to believe that the discrimination pool demanded for adequate communication in *any* area of science is far richer, more differentiated, and subtle than ordinarily supposed. One may, for instance, think of a "pointer reading" as some ultimate verifying operation (or reductive symptom). But the pointer is hooked up, both materially and inferentially, to a complex system of events, and the physicist must be attuned to relationships of great subtlety in that system if he is to interpret the pointer reading in a truly significant way. If one thinks, say, in terms of a presumably "simple" reduction sentence, the "test-result" (pointer position) may be specified via a relatively crass discrimination; the "test-condition" part may involve a most elaborate system of events which are *assumed to realize* an elaborate lattice of theoretical relationships, and the job of the physicist is to "discriminate" whether this is so. *That* is not a crass discrimination.

Yet, be all this as it may, there is little question that the discrimination pools presupposed for communication in physical science as a whole may be fewer in number and, in each case, less differentiated and "rich" than the discrimination pools presupposed in biological science as a whole, while the discrimination pools required by biology are probably less varied and (often) less internally differentiated than those ideally required by psychology. The domain of physical science is not only such as to necessitate fewer language communities than do the domains of biology or psychology, but it may well be that physical science language communities are more stable and perhaps more readily enlarged.

There are many reasons for these differences. I shall consider only one. *In psychology, problems concerning any range of human endeavor or experience can be the object of study.* No definition of our discipline — however restrictive its heuristic effect may have been on problem selection — has ever called into question this awesome peculiarity of our subject matter. In recent decades we have sought security by addressing only small and rather unadventurous segments of our subject matter. But problems — psychological problems — of art and morality, of scientific creativity, of human sensibility in all manifestations, of language, problem-solution, and, of course, society, personality, etc., stand before us almost untouched. If psychology is to study the conditions of the phenomena in any of these areas, it must premise its research on discrimination pools each of which overlaps to some definite extent with the "first-order" discrimination pools operative within all of those widely ranged human areas. This is not to say that, for example, the student of the psychology of science must be a creative inquirer in the given science, the psychology of which he studies. (It would not hurt!) Nor is it reasonable to demand that all psychological students of art be artists. But it is grotesque to suppose that someone totally devoid of the special discriminations and sensitivities of the natural scientist, or the artist, could make contributions to the psychology of either field—just as grotesque as to expect, say, that an illiterate could contribute to the psychology of language.

All this is shamefully obvious, but the consequences—if the history of psychology be evidence—are not. In psychology we must have many language communities, many subgroups of individuals equipped with diverse stocks of discriminations and differently specialized sensitivities. *By definition*, we must have a greater number of language communities in psychology than in any other field of inquiry currently institutionalized. We must also expect more variability, both in sensitivity and in achieved discriminations, than within other scientific language communities. As Karl Zener pointed out, psychology has long lived with a conception of its observation base such that, if a sophomore student cannot perceive a phenomenon, it is not there. And if that phenomenon be the referent of a term, the term is meaningless. The present position, however, suggests—just as has already been illustrated in the discussion of *dignity*—that the minimal acceptable size of a language community for psychology must be a community of two persons. Any formulation of a "meaning criterion" demanding a wider consensus group for *admission* of a term as meaningful would eliminate much meaning either from our universe of approachable data or from that of the scientifically (or humanly) sayable. Worse than the *amount* of meaning lost would be its altitude—for any discipline (whether scientific or other) is such that at any given time its best ideas are likely to reside in only a few of its towering sensibilities.

Relations of the Present Analysis to Some Cognate Trends in Philosophy

The force of the present position can be further clarified by comparisons with certain recent trends in the philosophical treatment of language and meaning. I restrict discussion to brief comparisons with certain emphases of analytic philosophy and with the views of Michael Polanyi.

Analytic philosophy. It will already be evident that there is a distinct consonance between certain trends of *analytic philosophy* and the point of view I have sketched. I shall suggest a few of the differences.

Until recently, most analytic philosophers have tended to regard something like *standard* "use" as adjudicative with respect to philosophic, and sometimes other, issues. They have often been criticized, and I think fairly so, for regarding "use" — as established by some combination of the *Oxford English Dictionary* and the given philosopher's linguistic sensibility (in varying proportion) — as a final court of appeal. Related to this has been an equally widespread tendency to eschew extralinguistic "considerations" in philosophic discussion: to choose to stay within language if not in fact be held within its circle by the "lingua-centric predicament."

In contradistinction, the present view would urge that anything like "standard" use would often give us a far less differentiated, subtle, delicately contoured, or nice definition of a concept than might be required for the analytic or investigative purposes at hand. If we refer back to the analysis of *dignity* — and to our comments concerning the multiplicity of language communities, each at different levels of sensitivity and/or achieved fineness of discrimination with respect to the application conditions for a term — then clearly even the best extant dictionary definition could have a leveling or "normalizing" influence, if taken as criterial in preference, say, to the definition of a "summit," or near-summit, community. Even with respect to the "ordinary language" per se, processes of inventive metaphor that can be presumed frequently to take place in the functioning of the more highly sensitive members of the overall language group can be expected to result in individual usages of greater nicety and, in some sense, fuller cognitive content than the best *dictionary* definitions.

Our perceptually oriented view of meaning directs attention to the fact that language *change* (which can, of course, be either retrograde or toward sharpening and enrichment) is, in the more fortunate cases, mediated by discovery. Users of language are *appliers* of language, and when the perceptual disposition governing a word is enriched or refined by the noting of what we have called an overlapping relational property in a new (and perhaps less masked) world context, then *knowledge* has been extended. When definition is seen in a perceptual frame, one expects meanings ever to be refined in the crucibles of at least some sensibilities, and such "refinements" are but another name for new knowledge about the universe. Thus, to the very same extent that the concept of "standard use" exerts a normalizing pressure on definition, it tends to draw attention away from the fact that much definition, and certainly the species called "empirical," is as much definition "of" the world as it is of a term. Though definition be *within language,* our "perceptual" frame constantly reminds us that language is about something—however embedded, intricately contoured, or fluidly deployed that something may be.

Most of the above divergences from what I have taken to be the tendency of analytic philosophy are no doubt related to the initial difference of problematic incidence between the approach of that "movement" and my own. I am concerned with *empirical* analysis of the *conditions* of communication, as these bear on the problem of definition; analytic philosophers are concerned with explicating the meanings of "given" communications, and exploring the rule or "use" structures of natural languages, with a view toward the resolution of philosophic perplexities. My premises bespeak the naïve faith in the facts that persons perceptually interact with an external world, that aspects of that world causally related to such interactions are specifiable as stimulating energies—inclusive of distributions, gradients, and higher-order derivatives thereof, à la Gibson (1959, 1966)—of the sort open to an empirical scientist. Philosophers, however, would bring about their own technological unemployment with cataclysmic immediacy if they *began* with such premises. If philosophy is the disease of which it is the cure, it is well that it proceed slowly.

Michael Polanyi. This great man is rarely acknowledged by philosophers of science—even by those who have been moving in the direction of his thinking. When mentioned at all, the acknowledgment is often grudging. For instance, Kuhn, whose views in large areas can be seen as a pallid and crude semblance of Polanyi's, cites him only in connection with his (Kuhn's) borrowing of the "useful phrase," "tacit knowledge." For such reasons—and also because he is often little more than a name to psychologists—I commence with a brief and absurdly inadequate précis of his viewpoint.

This philosopher has powerfully challenged the modern tendency to *identify* the knowable and the sayable. He has developed the most sustained and powerful argument in the history of thought to the effect that "there are things that we know but cannot tell" (1962, 601). He has made, in effect, the concept of *skill* central in his argument, and has analyzed in extensive and fascinating detail the senses in which "knowing" must be regarded a skilled performance of a type reducible to no algorithm, resistant in principle to full specification, governable only in loose and underdetermined ways (if at all) by "rules," and warrantable ultimately by no verificatory method other than "personal" and responsible accreditation by the knower. Such, in brief, is Polanyi's conception of *tacit knowing* on which *explicit knowledge* is always, if in varying degree, founded.

The role and "structure" of tacit knowing, in its varying interplay with the explicit, form one of the main strands of Polanyi's work, one which he pursues with remarkable energy over much of the face of inquiry. In course of this exploration, many stereotypes concerning the nature and methods of science fall by the wayside: for example, that the scientist is a neutral and "detached" observer and applier of rules; that there is a fixed and inviolable logic of verification or evidence which, either in principle or in fact, regulates the fate of scientific ideas; that the differential adequacy of theories in the same domain is a matter merely of convenience, economy, or a kind of "fruitfulness" not grounded in truth; that presumably crucial or decisive experimental disconfirmations of a theory (e.g., the Michaelson-Morley experiment) can, per se, *enforce* a creative theoretical change; that the Laplacean paradigm is a sensible ideal for human knowledge; that "formalization" can be complete; that mathematical and logical systems are based on arbitrary assumptions and are developed via a wholly mechanical process of manipulating rules. The preceding is but a random representation of a few of the topics examined with originality, and often depth, at various places in *Personal Knowledge* (1958) and in others of Polanyi's writings (1959, 1966).

Not a few of the stereotypes questioned by Polanyi have, of course, come under fairly general criticism during the past two or three decades. But Polanyi — largely by exploiting the particularities of his long and distinguished experience in science — has generated the most comprehensive and telling critique of modern scientism thus far put forward. To this task, he has brought a generous range of competences over and above his purely scientific ones: his critique of scientism is therefore linked with the elaboration of a new, "post-critical" philosophical vision. The constructive and analytic ingredients in Polanyi's thinking are, within limits, separable; it is the latter (and, in my opinion, more important) component which primarily concerns us here.

Even from the above general account, it will immediately be detected that there are strong consonances between the present theory of definition and central emphases of Polanyi. Thus, for instance, the present approach, in its own way, has all along been underlining the *limits* of purely linguistic specification. And it has emphasized the dependence of communication on extralinguistic (perceptive) processes which, by their very nature, can never be rendered fully effable. Insofar as I have suggested that the sharpness and/or delicacy of the "meaning-contour" tagged by a term for an individual will depend on such matters as his ability at "disembedding" — and have emphasized, in addition, that precision, subtlety, and richness of language use will depend upon capacity for inventive metaphor — I, too, have been presuming the capacity to use even a single lexical unit meaningfully to be tantamount to a *skill.*

There are many coincidences of more specific character than the above, as between the two accounts. Thus, for instance, Polanyi's observations concerning the role of tradition, connoisseurship, and apprenticeship in scientific communication and training (1958, chapters 4, 6, 7) are paralleled — more prosaically — in my account by its emphasis on what might be called "differentiated laboratory ostension" (via "perceptual displays") as something like a criterial paradigm for effective empirical definition within scientific language communities. Polanyi sees effective definition and meaningful use of language generally as giving knowledge about the world — and so, of course, does the present account. Polanyi sees a scientific theory as in some sense definitive of reality (e.g., 1958, 3–17); the present account, in suggesting that the terms of a theory may be seen as designating "directly" highly embedded features of the universe, suggests a basis for such a position.

The Perceptual Theory of Definition: Summary

The present formulation tries to make intelligible why many terms in the natural language and in science can have general, yet *specific,* meaning in terms of the perceptual conditions of their learning and the nature of language as a psychological process. It suggests that *verification* can often be much more direct than is ordinarily supposed. It implies that a term can "tag" and preserve perceptual discriminations often of great specificity, yet highly abstract and general in the sense of being invariant for a large range of events. It supposes (at least in the typical case of *verbal* definition) that such terms are defined via other linguistic counters which have been attached to discriminations already in the repertoire of the addressee, and that definition so mobilizes these as to direct perception to the *relevant* thing, property, or relation. It supposes, further, that the ideal and often criterial case of definition is a differentiated form of "ostension" which would seek to direct perception to the relevant referent via a perceptual display that might "exhibit" the referent in its most conspicuous, sharply contoured, and pure form.

The present position presupposes that the processes of communication, as they have gone on for thousands of years in the natural languages, will have built up intricate, layered, often vastly ramified systems of *meaning* (via word interrelationships). These, though they often will be found to specify external and internal events with precision, will often require extension and differentiation in accordance with new human knowledge. The position assumes that the task of science (and of scholarship) is to devise means for making those meanings more precise, systematic, and univocal, to whatever extent its varied ranges of subject matter may permit, and thereby to isolate and discover new meanings in the universe. It proposes that the only "criterion" of *meaningfulness* be an *empirical* determination of whether two or more human beings can communicate consistently with the given *term* or *language*. It warns that requiring any number greater than two as the *minimal* size of an admissible language community is to run the risk of losing much valuable meaning and knowledge. It acknowledges that the communicative objective in science is the *maximization* of a language community, but *not* via definitional schemas that would reduce meaningful discourse to babbling, and arrogate babbling to "technically" meaningful status. It assures the practicing psychologist that he needs no permission from *any source whatsoever* to be as imaginative, penetrating, and insightful as he is able, and as contextual in his methods as his specific problems may require. Finally, it leaves many problems untouched and all of them open.

Science, the Humanities, and the Psychological Studies

The preceding account of definition should give us a purchase on the relations between the sciences and the humanities, and this, in turn, will facilitate a better understanding of endemic characteristics of the psychological studies.

The Sciences and the Humanities

It is already fairly obvious that our analysis of "empirical" definition tends to destroy certain of the traditional bases for any sharp separation between the sciences and the humanities. The distinction often presupposes that scientific and humanistic uses of language must differ in principle. It is sometimes believed that, whereas one can expect — even demand — homogeneity of use and interpretation of terms (thus "universality" of agreement) in a *science,* one must expect the very opposite in a "humanity." It is sometimes argued that, whereas many conceptualizations in the humanities require a unique integrative type of "understanding" (a species of "wholistic grasping"), the scientist may coast along on simple discriminations of a limited number of elemental "data language" referents.

A certain kind of "tough-minded" psychologist will perhaps be disturbed that distinctions of the order above illustrated are blunted by the present analysis. Amusingly, psychology is one of the few fields in the community of scholarship in which it could still seem heretical to suggest that a germ-proof curtain cannot be erected between science and the humanities. The appalling threat upon intellectual hygiene thereby created has been weathered quite heroically by the physicists, mathematicians, biologists, historians of science, and philosophers (among others) who are participating in a massive reassessment of the positivistic picture of inquiry which has now been going on for over four decades. That the methods and ends of science are continuous with those of human inquiry in any of its forms—whether in practical contexts or so-called humanistic ones—is an *empirical* generalization from which few competent students of science would any longer dissent. It is perhaps worth reminding scientistic purists in psychology that a tough-minded pragmatist like John Dewey urged precisely such a generalization upon the world over many decades of his long career (e.g., Dewey 1910, 1917, 1938), and that he came to this generalization largely on *psychological* grounds. Like much else in Dewey, this point long went unheeded. It is now widely heeded, or at least a similar one is acknowledged, but it is a "point" which calls for continuing (indeed, permanent) development, especially along psychological lines. In recent years, some development it has received, but very little via psychological modes of analysis, and very little of *that* by psychologists. My psychologically based sketch of definition can be seen as one small step in such a tradition of analysis as is invited by Dewey's emphasis on the commonalities among all forms of human inquiry.

Even psychologists, then, will have to accept it that scientists in their best moments do not merely manipulate symbols or apparatus: they perceive *meanings*, subtle relational unities, contrasts, transitions, and recurrences, in their experience. So do poets. And artists. And creative administrators. And the methods of artistic problem-solution, of poetic problem-solution, of "practical" problem-solution can be shown to parallel in large ways those of scientific problem-solution.

What, then, are the differences? They are in fact harder to specify than the similarities. There is no single dividing line, however delicate and wavery, between *the* sciences and *the* humanities, but only wavery and delicate differences between given sciences, given areas of practical activity, given humanities. Science differs from practical problem-solution in different ways than from, say, poetry. Indeed, science "in general" may be more like poetry than it is, say, like "business." But, then again, we must face the fact that some sciences, at some phases of development, are more like business.

A possible set of differences of some generality between much of science and much work in the humanities may flow from the widely recognized interest of science in *control* of phenomena (by no means its *only* interest). This leads to the perception of different types of relations (thus meanings) in the universe than the poet or artist is likely to isolate, and results ultimately in different *modes* of communication. The scientist becomes interested in the consensus of his language community in not quite the same way that the artist is interested in consensus. The scientist seeks to maximize his language community to *whatever extent possible*. That is a necessary condition to the maximization of prediction and control. The artist (unless he is second-rate or an opportunist), being interested in the maximization of *meaning* with no practical end in view, seeks only a consensus from those equipped to see, even if it be *only* himself. Science to be efficient must be continuous, cumulative. Art to be great must be discontinuous. But even these two familiar generalizations are half-truths which emphasize the waveryness of *any* boundary. For science to be *great*, it must be discontinuous. And there are *types* of continuity and even cumulation that can be discerned in art. But the differential "aims" of science and art to which we are here pointing will at least ensure differential incidences of discontinuity.

It is this *interest in maximizing* the language community which has led to the belief that science must have a simple, almost universally comprehensible, definition base. But, as we have seen, realistic consideration of practice shows that this is not the case. *The language community of a science cannot be broadened by reducing delicate and subtle discriminations to "crasser" ones, but only by using crasser discriminations as means for directing perception toward the relevant "finer" relations and properties.* This last corollary of a perceptual theory of definition contains, I think, the key to an understanding of the empirical — and very possibly the formal — methods of science.

The characteristic methods of science — partialing out of variables, experimentation, etc. — are "devices" which can enable perception of delicate relational aspects of events (causal unities, etc.) by causing them to occur repeatedly in the purest (least embedded) possible event context. The utility of pointer readings, simple indices, etc., where possible, is essentially that these dependably mobilize crasser discriminations in such a way as to favor "perception" of the relevant, "finer" property or relation. The special extensions of language associated with science provide differentiated signs for tagging and "preserving" the new "meanings" that are discovered.

Technical scientific languages develop in the first instance as differentiations of the natural language.

Theoretical terms are tags for perceptual cuts upon, or "disembeddings" from, the world-flux. There is no separate realm of "observation terms" to which they must be linked for the mediation of either application or communication. When a term is called "theoretical," there is a presumption that it enters into a network of relations with other terms having a salient bearing on some world domain. An experiment—whatever else it may be—is a device for directing the perceptual-cognitive apparatus toward the detection of the relation between two or more such concepts. *An experiment is one of many nonverbal forms of definition.*

Not having delusions of grandeur, I do not pretend to be in a position to give any final interpretation of the role of what were recently held to be the artificial languages of science, namely, logic and mathematics. So far as I can see, my position concerning "meaning" is compatible with any of the philosophical views—rationalistic *or* empiristic—which grant logic and mathematics ontological content. In my idiom, the formal disciplines are based in the first instance on perceptual disembeddings of structural and relational characters of the world. But so are empirical-scientific concepts, especially of the sort called "theoretical." In ontologistic views of logic or mathematics, it is usual to see the formal concepts as discriminating markedly more general characters of the world than do the concepts of empirical science. In congruent fashion, the present analysis would base logical and mathematical concepts on perceptual disembeddings of *extremely general* structural and relational invariants of experience. The disembeddings may be thought of as second- or *n*th-order segregations of invariants of our own "processings" of world-inputs, or as operating "directly" upon those inputs, or—what is more likely—as (in differing contexts) *either* of the preceding. Obviously, such a statement goes no further than suggesting the possibility of the translation of a range of extant alternate views into a perceptual vocabulary. But I think that differentiated thinking and research in a perception-oriented frame about logic, mathematics, and, indeed, "natural" grammar could be fruitful.

Despite the above, some psychologists will no doubt *still* be appalled by the implication that psychology in certain of its reaches (and, indeed, as regards some of its core areas like perception, cognition, motivation, learning, social psychology, psychopathology, personology, aesthetics, the analysis of creativity) must turn out to involve modes of inquiry rather more like those of the humanities than the sciences. Perhaps they will feel that humanistic knowledge is "soft" knowledge, based on soft intellectual disciplines, while scientific knowledge and research discipline is hard. But musicology is hard (in several senses), as are classics, comparative philology, biblical archeology, and responsible forms of literary criticism. And philosophy—even logic and the philosophy of science—is typically assigned to the humanities.

Return to the question of "cumulativeness"—an issue which still requires more perspicacious analysis than it has yet received in the history of thought, and one which I certainly do not hope to dispatch in passing. But it should be emphasized that no epistemologist or historian of science any longer believes that scientific knowledge moves in a linear and continuous progression, and it is doubtful that any competent student of science in this century ever did. It did not wait upon Thomas Kuhn to stress the discontinuities and divigations in the temporal trajectory of science; such of his masters as Alexandre Koyré, George Sarton, and, of course, Conant were sharply apprised of such matters. Cumulation means literally a "heaping up," and the heaping up of knowledge is as characteristic of the so-called humanities as it is of the sciences. It may be thought that in science this heaping up has a special force: that of a progressive refinement, differentiation, and specificity of knowledge (at least in the long run), and indeed, this may be one of the differentia between science in the strict sense and the humanities. But it must be carefully asked whether this happy property of scientific knowledge is conferred upon it by the magic of scientific methods per se or by characteristics of the world domains addressed by the established sciences which render these methods (like the "analytic pattern" of physics as discerned in chapter 4) applicable and fertile.

Only in the pages of *Popular Mechanics* (if there) do we any longer see vestiges of a "cosmic-eye" view of science as a *durch-und-durch* impersonal and objective enterprise. Scientific inquiry and its outcome are now seen to be sensibility-dependent and perspectival in much the sense heretofore seen as definitive of humanistic modes of knowing. There are subtle differences, as we have seen, in the degree of transmissibility of the knowledge achievable in the sciences as against the humanities, the sharpness and scope of the formulations that can be attained, and, perhaps, the multiplicity of significant perspectives from which the characteristic phenomena of each may be approached at any given time. But there *is* cumulation in the humanities, and it is easy to explicate the sense in which this is so.

Take, for example, the polymorphous, tenuous, ramified, and "open-horizon" concept of love, human love. The history of the humanities presents us with not a few savorers and explicators of this rather intricate context of human phenomenology, each approaching that context with his or her own special angle of vision, sensibility, and range of sensitivity. Plato has told us something about love; so have Shakespeare, Joyce, and Laurence Durrell, to pick out three other inquirers almost at random. No one would consider their perspectives as nondifferential and nonpreclusive in important respects. These four explorers have left behind four sets of spectacles through which differential modalities, contours, textures, and involvements of love may be viewed. The opportunity each of us now has to view love through each of these sets of spectacles does not mean that—by some magic of conceptual optics—they can be combined into one set of integrating spectacles, but it certainly does mean that the availability of the *four*, as against any given one, creates a potential for enriching our sense, our understanding of love. *This* is a form of cumulation, and a precious one.

Certain other circumstances should be noted. Shakespeare's theory of love does not refine the Platonic theory. Nor does Joyce refine or in some sense improve upon these two illustrious predecessors, and, most assuredly, Durrell does not represent some kind of advance upon the findings of his three predecessors. It is just that these four explorers perceive their bounded, yet inexhaustible, domain *differently*. Does it therefore follow that each is uninfluenced by his predecessors or that the perspectives and "findings" of each are genetically independent of those of his predecessors? I do not think so. The sensibility of each explorer has been enriched by the discriminations registered in the artifacts bearing the imprint of his predecessors; he can thus be enabled to arrive at his angle of search, of vision, at least in part with the help of the discriminations achieved by his intellectual forebears. That, too, is cumulation—and in a more subtle sense than mere "heaping up."

It is my contention that much of psychological inquiry and knowledge must permanently and in principle have characteristics rather more akin to such features of humanistic scholarship as I have just tried to convey than to scientific research, even when the conception of scientific research is liberalized—as it has been by Polanyi, Bronowski, and others—in such a way as to punctuate its continuities with humanistic and all other forms of knowledge seeking.

Search Cells and Language Incommensurabilities

Historically, contemporaneously, and, I submit, in principle, the psychological studies represent an assemblage of specialized language communities, research groups, or, if you will, cliques, claques, application groups, action groups, interest groups, and the like. I will call such associations of inquirers pursuing roughly common problems from a common point of view, and thus sharing a specialized language, *search cells*. Each of us has been or is a member of one or more such cells. In relation to our primary or most intimate cell, one of the most poignant phenomena with which we are all at some level familiar is that we seem to know more when communicating with our fellow community members than when trying to communicate across community boundaries. And naturally, the insights provided by the conceptual net of our given community are so striking to us that we are impelled to see what its reticulations bring forth in other waters. And we almost always "lose perspective" in this process: we generously emerge with a single "paradigm" for all psychology.

Using the word *psychology* in the collective sense, it is important to see that the growth of the field involves not so much the broadening of research interests from an established base as the *multiplication* of research interests. The case is not wholly different in the natural sciences. But the polymorphous character of the phenomena that we address and their extraordinary variety, tenuousness, and subtlety are such that the assertion of significant research options increasingly forces us into not only more and more specialized search cells (thus language communities), but ones increasingly insulated by virtue of incommensurabilities of their respective discrimination pools.

Now, each of these community languages is a differentiation out of the natural language, and each "language" is only loosely systematic and of mixed composition. It is therefore not surprising that single minds can "speak" and understand several (sometimes many) such languages, in some degree. That does not mean that the speaker has integrated or can integrate these asystematically different languages. When "speaking" each (at any level) there is a change of perspective. A perspective is not the kind of thing that can fuse. Perspectival knowledge *multiplies,* but the nature of a human universe and our resources for ordering that universe are such that attempts toward large integrations or fusions can make no sense. When intentions of this sort are nevertheless asserted, we get knowledge-forms, not knowledge.

This question of the incommensurability of the discrimination pools (thus the "languages") of the nuclear search cells requires careful examination. Naturally, as between any two search cells, the incommensurability is not necessarily total. The incommensurabilities may be slight or marked, tractable or "vicious." But in a domain of such awesome range as that discriminated by the extant definitions of psychology—and one characterized by phenomena so complex and labile—many of the incommensurabilities between the languages of different search cells will be vicious ones. If the domain-segments approached by two different search cells are, in some sense, distant ones, viciousness is pretty well guaranteed. Cross-cell communication, say, between an appropriately composed (in respect to discrimination pool) cell concerned with the psychology of musical composition and a cell of rote learning investigators (or, perhaps, microelectrode analysts of brain function) is likely to be seriously muffled, if only for the fact that few members of the latter groups are likely to have any technical understanding of or refined sensitivity to music. Indeed, the musical composition cell may have difficulty communicating with, say, a cell concentrating on the psychology of visual art, and vice versa. Of course, there would be nothing counterproductive about the language incommensurabilities of such groups if they did not imperialistically presume that their respective languages were extensible to each other's domain—or, perhaps, the entire domain of "psychology." In that event, we would simply have groups of investigators pursuing different *psychological studies*.

Now consider the case of cells addressing similar or overlapping subdomains but via different languages, conceptual templates, nets, frameworks. In general, two such groups will have made different disembeddings from, different perceptual cuts upon, the world-flux. If psychological events had a kind of logical layer-cake structure, or some kind of orderly crystal-like faceting (and if the human mind were something like a camera), we could perhaps conclude that the languages might be ultimately summable, combinable into some kind of logical structure or fusible into some more general "containing" language. But psychological events tend not to be like that. Characteristically, they are multiply determined, ambiguous in their human meaning, polymorphous, contextually "environed" or embedded in complex and vaguely bounded ways, evanescent and labile in the extreme. Relative to their different analytical purposes, predictive aims, practical ends in view, metaphor-forming capacities, perceptual sensitivities, preexisting discrimination repertoires, different *theorists* (and ultimately the search cells forming about them) will make asystematically different perceptual cuts upon the same domain. They will identify "variables" of markedly different grain and meaning-contour, selected and linked on different principles of grouping. The cuts, variables, concepts, that is, will in all likelihood establish different universes of discourse, even if loose ones.

Constraints upon Intracell Communication

Turn now to another characteristic of search cells. Insofar as a cell is a language community in my sense of the term, the community will have a "vertical" structure: it will consist of a quasi-hierarchical assemblage of subcommunities, the members of each of which "speak" and apply the language with differential competence. The fullness and precision of *intragroup* communication will thus be limited by this differential competence in the language use. Applying such considerations at the level of the individual inquirer, it can be said that there must necessarily be an idiosyncratic component in the use of the language. Such individual idiosyncrasy (and subgroup variability) is clearly by no means peculiar to *psychological* language communities. The same point may be made in relation to physics or any other natural science (or, indeed, natural language communities). But the hallmark of a science like physics is that its successful algorithmic resources and relatively univocal and precise "perceptual displays" are such as to contain communicative idiosyncrasy within narrow limits. Since — as I have tried to argue from many incidences — comparably determinate definitional devices are not available to most psychological language communities, we can expect muffled, cross-purposeful, or ambiguous *intragroup* communication within many of our search cells.

The point here at issue carries some severe entailments for the psychological studies, and some interesting ones even for the natural sciences. It is surprising, for instance, how little attention philosophers and historians of science have given to tracing out the ramifications of *leadership* in scientific communities. Be this as it may, psychological search cells are characteristically followerships (in some cases, *claques* might be the better word) in the ambience of a *leader*. The leader has forged the language and uses it with "summit" (not necessarily consummate) skill and richness. Bearing in mind the degrees of embeddedness and perceptual masking that we have seen, in the analysis of definition, to be characteristic of the referents of psychological concepts, it is clear that there must be tight limits — especially if the language be a rich one — to the leader's success at teaching or conveying the language to his followers. Even the most capable of them will internalize a rather different conceptual template than the leader's. As for the less capable, they may internalize words, slogans, but use them in rote or meaningless ways.

Such communicative difficulties will, of course, vary in severity in the different psychological studies and sometimes as between different search cells within a given one of the psychological studies. But in certain fields of psychology — as, for instance, psychopathology and social psychology — the consequences of such communicative mismatches may be far-reaching. I suspect, for instance, that not only do no two psychoanalysts *do* psychoanalysis in the same way (a fact granted by virtually everyone), but that no two of them "speak" psychoanalysis in sufficiently similar ways to warrant the conclusion that they hold the "same" theory. Yet, though Freud's formulations may be criticizable on many grounds, it is unfair to criticize him on this one. Whatever the limitations, certain of the concepts and concept relations have cut more deeply (and brought more back) than perhaps any concepts that have been formed in the history of psychology. Nevertheless, by virtue of the inevitable communicative difficulties I have tried to discriminate, it would be absurd to expect that such a theory could be *collaboratively* developed, refined in anything resembling a "progressive" way, or tested in any sense comprehended in conventional canons of research design or "formal" evidence. But this is not to say that whatever of it the followership has internalized has not enriched their professional sensibilities or in some way fed, sharpened, and guided their particular therapeutic skills.[10]

10. In stressing the inevitability of language incommensurabilities and communicative mismatches — as I have in this essay — my intent has been to delineate certain of the principled constraints upon the psychological studies which are seldom acknowledged in a sufficiently sharp way. A certain parochialism and fragmentation of search cells is necessitated by the terms of my analysis, but I do not wish to be interpreted as reveling in these circumstances or in any way discouraging efforts toward communicating *across* search cells. Nor do I advocate that the interests of all cells be trained upon domains of narrow scope. The relevant issues are intricate in the extreme, and I cannot address all of them in a single chapter. But — peremptorily — the following things can be noted:

(1) Attempts to "converse" across cells should be ardently pursued — and possible knowledge overlaps, conceptual homologies, areas of translatability, potential contexts of useful borrowing (whether substantive or methodic), mutual complementations or supplementations should be identified. The force of my argument is that in most such cross-cell collating it will be unrealistic (and indeed counterproductive) to anticipate total or any "large" degree of integrability — whether via translation, efforts to establish detailed isomorphic relations, logical subsumability in the one direction or the other, joint deducibility from a more general language, or any other type of *systematic* alignment (as, e.g., the addition, by mere logical conjunction, of the two languages in the hope that what emerges will constitute a coherent universe of discourse).

(2) If *differentiated* knowledge be the desideratum, many search cells will have to concentrate on limited (and, it can be hoped, significant) contexts of human or organismic activity. But it is proper and desirable that some cells not confine their research and explanatory objectives to tightly circumscribed phenotypic domains. May I illustratively distinguish two of the types of such cells.

(a) The traditional *process* areas of psychology — as, for example, perception, cognition,

The Question of Community-Language or "Theory" Appraisal

It is my contention that most others of the psychological studies which address ranges of experience or action worthy of human interest face communicative problems similar to (if often less severe than) those of psychoanalysis. Though some may think this a despairing conclusion, I hasten to note that I think it liberating. Nevertheless, the great question that remains is how does one appraise a psychological "language," theory, conceptual template? And, of course, how does one choose between contending languages when they both have (or claim to have) an overlap in their range of application? Does the present theory of perceptual definition assume that all languages, theories, templates, nets, frames, or perspectives bearing on a psychological subject matter are, if not equally adequate, at least ade-

---

learning, motivation—are, of course, concerned with general principles of human (or organismic) functioning, whether at "psychological" or biological levels, conceived as cutting across all "phenotypic" domains. The multiple search cells in each such process area may legitimately seek knowledge of great generality. Nevertheless, the arguments in the text strongly suggest the likelihood, relative to any subject matter so complex as that discriminated by a process area, that at any time in history there will be a plurality of languages in a given area such that no single one will rationally merit preemptive allegiance. Indeed, it is already evident—cf. Koch 1962a—that there is no ultimately rational or perspective-independent basis even for demarcating or *defining* a process area.

Another epistemic peculiarity of the process areas is best shown with the aid of Kuhn's distinction (1970c, 188–89) between a law schema and a law. He points out that Newton's second law, for instance, generally written as $f = ma$, is not in *that form* directly subject to "logical and mathematical manipulation." Rather, it is a schema or sketch, of which the less general (but manipulable) instantiations vary markedly in different problem situations. "For the case of free fall, $f = ma$ becomes $mg = m(d^2s/dt^2)$; for the simple pendulum it is transformed to $mg \sin \theta = -ml(d^2\theta/dt^2)$; for a pair of interacting harmonic oscillators it becomes two equations, the first of which may be written $m_1(d^2s_1/dt^2) + k_1s_1 = k_2(s_2 - s_1 + d)$; and for more complex situations, such as the gyroscope, it takes still other forms, the family resemblance of which to $f = ma$ is still harder to discover." "Laws" of the type sought in the process areas are almost inevitably of a degree of schematism in excess of this Newtonian example selected by Kuhn. If the "law" is held to be applicable across the entire domain of psychological events, the distance between its generalized, schematic form and many of its contexts of application can only be adjudged immense. If we want *differentiated* knowledge, such schemas, per se, could have but limited guidance value. Indeed, for a long time to come, it may prove more fruitful to work toward the law-schema from particular, bounded domains than to proceed in the reverse direction. But this caution certainly does not counterindicate the value of working in the direction from process-law to phenotype. Both directions should be pursued.

(b) Another type of search cell—of which there should be many at any given time—are those concerned, in one way or another, with "the large picture." My position certainly does not denigrate or discourage comprehensive thinking within the psychological studies—endeavors which, in the light of technical-psychological and/or all other relevant sources of knowledge, seek visions, images, portraits, philosophies ("theories," if you will) of psycholog-

quate in some degree? Must the "rational" attitude be that of complete libertarianism?

I do not think so. Nor do I think the answer an easy one. For it is not my position alone that raises such questions. Ever since the breakdown of what might be called "rational reconstructionism" in the philosophy of science, the entire issue of "rational grounds" for theory appraisal or selection has been conspicuously up in the air. The historico-sociologically oriented students of science have by no means given an ultimately "satisfying" answer. Kuhn's is, at least on the surface, question-begging. He says in effect that a theory will be selected because of its "puzzle-solving" power, and that scientific communities prize this property (it is perhaps their superordinate "value"), but he is vague in his specification of any independent criteria for the initial identification of the property.

It may be that there is no ultimately *satisfying* answer: the lack of closure that we feel when confronted with such apparently circular answers may in fact be the gap that has been left by the disappearance of the delusion—fortified for several thousand years by the history of philosophy—that human rationality can be rendered inviolable by a set of rules. My own delusional system is not such as to give me confidence that I can fill in this gap. But it suggests the following outline of an "answer."

My position poses fewer difficulties than most in respect to theory (or framework or concept) "appraisal." There is a sense in which both a theory of truth and a theory of error are built into the analysis of definition I have put forward. As we have seen: "Though definition be *within language,* our

---

ical man, of the human condition, of human nature, of mind. In the terms given by convention, some of this endeavor will take the form of "personality theory"; some of it "philosophy of mind"; some of it "speculative psychology"; some of it "religion"; some of it the kind of textbook writing which seeks a strong organization within a wide range of material. Not a few of the seminal thinkers in the history of psychology (e.g., Aristotle, Freud, William James) fall into this category of comprehensive thinkers or visionaries.

What my position strongly urges, however, is that this mixed category of effort be seen in more accurate terms than formerly. These comprehensive explorers of man and mind do not offer us the kind of differentiated knowledge that we associate with either the mature sciences or the analytical and explicative humanities in their more rigorous forms. If what they offer can be called "theory," it is certainly not theory in the sense most prized in science—the mark of which is the capacity to mediate highly specified knowledge, whether predictive or elucidatory, of concrete phenomena. That the knowledge offered us by these explorers of comprehensive intent will be strongly perspectival and sensibility-dependent goes, of course, without saying. And it is precisely the kinds of search cells forming about such thinkers that will manifest in their more severe forms the *intragroup* communicative difficulties delineated in the text.

'perceptual' frame constantly reminds us that language is about something—however embedded, intricately contoured, or fluidly deployed that something may be" (pp. 169–170). Though, as we have also seen (pp. 160–162), there are "good" concepts and "poor" concepts coded within the natural language—and indeed, concepts which stabilize not only "fuzzy" discriminal experiences, but trivial, vagrant, local, or even illusory ones—the natural language may be seen as "containing" a vast, sprawling, and variably adequate ontology of the human universe. And of course, language can be *used* at varying levels of nicety, precision, or penetration—not excluding a zero level. Given terms can be applied in rote fashion (via "symptom") or in richly meaningful ways (via "creative metaphor").

Further, since language emanates from human beings, it can play the whole assemblage of deceptive games typified by "lying," it can be skewed in its bearing on reality by motive, wish, or autism; its application can be distorted or deflected by the conditions which produce perceptual illusion; or its relation to the world dimmed and realigned through psychopathological or neurological "disturbance." There are other grievous ontology-distorting factors of which psychologists are aware, and to which they might well give more investigative attention. I am, for instance, very much impressed with the endemic human need for crawling into cozy conceptual boxes—*any box,* so long as it gives promise of relieving the pains of cognitive uncertainty or easing problematic tension. This poignant human need, at any cost, for a frame, an abacus, a system, map, or set of rules which can seem to offer the wisp of a hope for resolving uncertainty makes all of us vulnerable—in one degree or another—to the claims of simplistic, reductive, hypergeneral, or in other ways ontology-distorting frames, so long as they have the appearance of "systematicity." There are many epistemic consequences of this fear-driven human propensity to seek bondage within such frames which require deep study.

There has been increasing acknowledgment in recent decades of a curious contrast between psychology and the established sciences. There is a strong sense in which psychology was already "established" before it *commenced,* whether as science or any other kind of institutionalized technical enterprise. At my appearance at the Nebraska Symposium on Motivation in 1956 I found myself saying:

> It is often not sufficiently held in mind that psychology does not start with neutral and unmanipulated data, but that the conditions of human life are such as to force us to entertain

185

theories of ourselves. These "theories of ourselves" — the syntax of which we seldom explore — are often, to the extent that they are acknowledged, allocated to "common sense" or "practical life" or some such limbo and then forgotten. What is not acknowledged is that such theory *itself* constitutes a most abstract and epistemologically complex ordering of the data of experience and behavior. What is truly remarkable is the degree of success that has attended such naïve theoretical effort, despite evident imperfections. Nevertheless, one aim of psychological science must, by definition, be at least ultimately to supplant such "theory" with better theory (Koch 1956, 60)

Philosophers of mind have done a superb job in recent decades in asserting and implementing considerations of the above order (and through no invitation from me!). They have indeed begun to explore the "syntax" and lexicon of the "theories of ourselves" which are embedded in the ordinary language. They have traced with sensitivity the ramified meaning-contours of such mental (and intricately context-dependent) terms as *intention, emotion* (and its subspecifications), *motive, wish,* and the like. They have made progress at disembedding from the natural language the complex use structures governing the assignment of "reasons" versus "causes," and such fundamental distinctions as that between "action" and "movement." Their work has indeed begun to suggest the subtlety, complexity, and differentiation of the psychological knowledge coded within natural language. But their admirable analytic purposes are special ones, and it should not be forgotten that the subtle knowledge embedded in the natural language has been explored, clarified, and extended by every competent humanist in the history of thought and, of course, by others. I mean no disrespect to my colleagues who pursue philosophy of mind when I say that I would rather go to Shakespeare or even Durrell for an analysis of "love" than to an analytic philosopher.

Once we appreciate the vast resources of psychological knowledge coded in the natural language, and internalized in the sensibilities of those who use it well, it should become a paramount matter of intellectual responsibility for those who explore the human condition to ensure that this knowledge is not degraded, distorted, or obliterated in their technical conceptualizations. I am at one with philosophers of mind in seeing this maxim as a central *rational* decision basis for the appraisal of theories, frameworks, or concepts in the human "sciences." That it is not the *only* decision basis will emerge in a moment.

If the knowledge coded in natural language and internalized in human sensibility gives us a kind of ontology of the human universe, it then becomes possible roughly to distinguish three kinds of theories or conceptual frameworks within the human studies: some that are *ontology-distorting*, some that are *ontology-respecting*, and some that are *ontology-revealing*. My theory of definition permits me to call *ontology-distorting* any technical framework which obliterates or does not permit us in some way to "recapture" the network of epistemically rich (or, in my special sense, "good") concepts in the range of natural language bearing on its domain. A frame which merely "respects" such distinctions but does not (by processes of metaphor as I have described them, etc.) permit the sharpening, extension, supplementation, or enrichment of the natural-language knowledge is *ontology-respecting*. A frame which *does* permit such sharpening, supplementation, or enrichment of the natural-language knowledge is *ontology-revealing*. At any given time it is, I think, possible to find, within the gamut of the psychological studies, conspicuous instances of frameworks within each of these categories. At any given time, it will also be possible to find frameworks which—because of early developmental status or other considerations—must be adjudged of *indeterminate classification*. Because of the specialized character of the languages of psychological search cells that I have taken pains to exhibit, I readily acknowledge that rational policy in respect to assigning frameworks to this *last* class obliges one to be rather generous. On the same basis, I acknowledge also that there may be instances such that *no* extant person may be truly qualified (by virtue of joint resources of relevant natural-language sensibility and mastery of the search-cell language) to make any assignment other than into the "indeterminate" category. *That* type of hazard is not confined to the psychological studies; it is present in *every* field of scholarship. However, the hazard is a terrifying one in psychology because of its oft-claimed mission to illuminate, regulate, control, or "improve" the human condition.

It may be well, at this phase, to give a few illustrations of frameworks within the psychological studies which I believe to fall into the respective categories.

Ontology-distorting frameworks. I think the Skinnerian framework a superb example of the ontology-distorting variety. I certainly do not hope to make this judgment plausible in a few sentences to those who reside within this framework. But consider the poverty of a conceptual abacus that would phrase the entire psychological ontology within three or four enormously general and contextually rubbery concepts (e.g., "operant behavior," "reinforcement," "contingencies of reinforcement," and "stimuli," inclusive of "private" stimuli). Yet this framework claims comprehensive applicability to the *entire* domain of significant human events by the simple strategy of obliterating most of the psychological distinctions coded in the natural language, or "translating" them into the hyperflexible schematism of the framework concepts. A set of experimental generalizations based on the analysis of the "rates" of arbitrarily selected repetitive behaviors of rats and pigeons is extrapolated—with no allowance for (or even consideration of) the local and contextual conditions of the findings—to "all" behavior. The remarkable detail in which the "schedules of reinforcement" were worked out for rate fluctuations of the bar-pressing and key-pecking behaviors studied in the foundational experiments is used to mask the astronomical analogical distances between the "laws" and their context of application. A certain plausibility is loaned to this autistic analogical leaping (in contradistinction to the leaps of other S-R theorists), in that a quasi-"purposive" connotation is built into the notion of an operant by virtue of its instrumental character serving as the defining criterion. As Skinner says:

> Possibly no charge is more often leveled against behaviorism or a science of behavior than that it cannot deal with purpose or intention. A stimulus-response formula has no answer, but operant behavior is the very field of purpose and intention. By its nature it is directed toward the future: a person acts *in order that* something will happen, and the order is temporal. (1974, 55)

Ontology-respecting frameworks. Tolman's theory, in my estimation, was in many ways an ontology-respecting formulation. His insistence, as evinced in the many successively revised formulations put forward throughout his career, that even rat behavior could not be meaningfully addressed other than through the discrimination of a large number of particulate perceptual and cognitive "variables" betokened a considerable respect for the way things are in both the rat and the human universe. His attempt to *define* such concepts objectively, in terms of "pointer-reading" experiments, he adjudged, at the very end of his career, to be a failure (1959). But all through his career, he engagingly admitted that he was at heart a "crypto-phenomenologist." It is arguable as to whether his theorizing was *ontology-revealing*. But he did shore up the dignity of rats and men during the long period when this was under severe attrition in psychology.

Ontology-revealing frameworks. I will cite three examples that fall into this category.

Gibson's (1950, 1959, 1966) perceptual theorizing has pointed to the possibility that there may be many dimensions of physical stimulus specification — the "higher-order variables" of stimulation — which have not been touched by classical sensory psychology. And he makes this possibility concrete and convincing by experimentally identifying certain variables "of adjacent and successive order" which seem related in orderly ways to variables of phenomenal experience and reporting behavior. To the extent that a program of this sort is successful, it supplements and refines the previously achieved discriminations of the human race bearing upon the domain not only of psychology but of physics.

Less well known than Gibson's framework — but bearing a family resemblance to it — is that of *Zener and Gaffron* (1962) which led to the isolation of "novel" dimensions of visual experience via the dedicated and patient comparison of art objects, photographs, and natural objects in their normal aspect as against their mirror-image reversals, inversions, and partial rotations. The subtle phenomenal properties which the investigators and their subjects were able to discern through such comparisons represent important extensions of human discrimination. Moreover, it was possible to show the dependence of different clusterings or organizations of these properties on variations in looking or survey behavior, quadrant of the visual field under survey, indices of hemisphere dominance, and other factors — and to make plausible inferences from these discoveries as to the character of the central processes that could mediate them. It is instructive to note that the qualifications for membership or even responsible interest in the Zener-Gaffron search cell are rather special ones: a capacity for precise analysis of visual experience, knowledge of the history of visual art and a sensitivity to its artifacts, detailed familiarity with twentieth-century perception psychology, and a considerable background in neuroanatomy and neurophysiology. It is no surprise that this particular language community is a rather small one!

Moving to a conceptual framework of markedly different cast, *Henry Murray's* (1959) remarkably differentiated anatomizing of experience and action via a range of finely discriminated concepts like *press, cathexis, dyadic system, thema, serials, ordination,* etc., provides a frame which, if "used" by an appropriately sensitive viewer, can be *ontology-revealing.*

Frameworks of indeterminate classification. To me, a conspicuous class of examples would be the frameworks associated with the computer modeling of mind and artificial intelligence. Obviously, the appraisal of such programs will depend upon the specific case. There is, however, a grave danger here of simplistic ontological distortion. The critical question, always, is how sensitive was the initial "job analysis" of the human process under simulation or "modeling." It is my impression that in most of the cases given us by history there is a marked oversimplification and distortion of the target process (or outcome). The history of machine-translation efforts may, perhaps, be taken as a prototypical case (cf. Bar-Hillel 1964). Yet, in comparison to the efforts to recompose complex psychological processes from arbitrarily stipulated S-R postulates, there is in the computer theorizing at least an *intent to respect ontology*. My tendency is to come out with an answer somewhere between *ontology-distorting* and *-respecting* for this class of effort. I doubt that anything *ontology-revealing* has yet been achieved. But with respect to the still nascent efforts, the rational and fair policy is to suspend classification. It need hardly be added—in light of all I have said concerning the texture of the psychological studies—that I am *not* looking forward to a comprehensive computer theory of mind.

And *now* it will be asked *where* are the "rational" safeguards against deception, meretriciousness, obscurantism, distortion, error? Where are the rational criteria, the decision rules that *guarantee* forward movement? But, of course, there *are* none. We are *on our own*—as we always have been. Yet mankind has managed to learn a thing or two.[11]

11. Knowing something about the apperceptive equipment of psychologists, I am sure that in reading these paragraphs on framework (or theory) appraisal many of them will get the impression that I am disenfranchising all of the traditional lore concerning the corroboration of knowledge claims by experimental test, canons of evidence, and the associated statistical, mathematical, and instrumentative "methodology." I am not! I beg the reader to note my effort (pp. 175–176) to define the rationale and function of experimentation and other "characteristic methods of science" in terms of a perceptual theory of definition; my comments (chapter 4, pp. 131–134) concerning the applicability of the "analytic pattern of science" to fields like sensory and biological psychology; my hospitality to the use of mathematical and statistical method (and design) where significantly applicable (chapter 4, p. 134); and my constant emphasis on the need to gear the psychological studies to the seeking of particulate and *differentiated* knowledge, not fuzzy sloganizing, global word magic, or hypergeneral and ersatz law delivering.

I reject no methods—however humble or however grand—the rationality of which has been established by their productiveness in mediating illuminating or useful knowledge in any context. I merely demand that method be used in appropriate and non-role-playing ways relative to the problems at issue, and that problems be chosen not wholly in terms of their amenability to particular methods considered honorific. And I emphatically argue, concerning hypothesis or theory appraisal, that even the most rigorous methods of science *enforce* no verdicts, no conclusions: it is *we*, the inquirers, who conclude or make verdicts; "verificational" methodology *suggests,* gives us *clues,* and the more rigorous and contextually apposite the method, the more dependable the clues. But the *conclusion,* the *appraisal* is a *decision* which must disembed an underlying pattern in an intricate "environment" of meanings, only one strand of which is the naked empirical finding or distribution of such, however "well verified."

My theory of definition is a theory of our capacity to define the real; it is also a theory of our capacity to detect (and indeed commit) error. We have no recourse but to follow Michael Polanyi when he says:

> I believe that we should accredit in ourselves the capacity for appraising our own articulation. Indeed, all our strivings towards precision imply our reliance on such a capacity. To deny or even doubt our possession of it would discredit any effort to express ourselves correctly, and the very conception of words as consistently used utterances would dissolve if we failed to accredit this capacity. This does not imply that this capacity is infallible, but merely that we are competent to exercise it and must ultimately rely on our exercise of it. This we must admit if we are to speak at all, which I believe to be incumbent on us to do. (1958, 91)

What safeguards we have, then, against irrationality, imprecision, error must be situated within ourselves. History and any individual biography will show these safeguards to be grotesquely fragile and tenuous, but they are there. It is a late date in history to report that even well-intentioned knowledge-seeking enterprises can pose a threat, can temporarily or permanently fail, can—even when partly successful—create grave hazards for the race. Because of its bearing on man's conception of himself, psychology *especially* is fraught with danger. The well-intentioned effort to emulate "successful" features of other knowledge-seeking enterprises which address quite different domains has backfired and produced much pseudoknowledge. And such pseudoknowledge now threatens to obliterate much that mankind already knows.

A view of the sort developed in this chapter can do little to rectify this state of affairs. But it can do something. Should the false authority claimed by psychology in its constant flaunting of the banner of Science be stripped away, the plight of the human race might be slightly alleviated. Even non-specialist human beings would then become less prone to relinquish to the claims of false authority what they already know or can discover. And if they learn to *trust* their capacities for intellectual appraisal, then even non-specialists may find themselves able to detect, at least in some degree, the more flagrant *ontology-distorting* claims of psychological "scientists" or savants—not always and not everyone, just sometimes and some. And if *investigators* in the psychological studies could adopt some such modest outlook as the one I have tried to convey, then man's bane might well become man's hope.

6

The Concept of "Value Properties" in Relation to Motivation, Perception, and the Axiological Disciplines

Foreword

This chapter seeks to develop a concept that has a bearing on several fundamental areas of psychology — and which can illumine central features of the several disciplines that have traditionally addressed value phenomena. It may be hoped also that the notion of "value properties" can lend clarity to the consideration of the relations between science and value. The analysis supplements certain of the "reconstructive" implications of the preceding chapter by showing that major psychological problems cannot be addressed except at levels of experiential sensitivity cultivated in the past only in the humanities. If a presumption can be created for the "existence" of values in the sense developed in this chapter, then a basis will have been laid for work of joint interest to the humanities (whether historical, explicative, or creative), to philosophy, and to psychology. By the same token, a potential for collaboration will have opened across the gamut of these disciplines.

The notion of "value properties" was first proposed in Koch 1956, a contribution to the 1956 *Nebraska Symposium on Motivation*. That article was one of the first focally to address the neglected phenomena of what I called "intrinsic motivation" — a topic which subsequently became an institutionalized interest-rubric within fundamental and applied psychology. A subsequent article reflecting my continued thinking concerning "value properties" was Koch 1969d, published in *The Anatomy of Knowledge*, edited by M. Grene. The most highly elaborated treatment to date is contained in the manuscript for *Psychology and the Human Agent;* the present chapter is a blend of that material and Koch 1969d.

Incidentally, I have spoken often on aspects of this work over the years. Psychologists *rarely* get the point! Artists *invariably* do! Philosophers *usually* do. Among the psychologists who expressed especial interest in one or another version of this thinking were Wolfgang Köhler, E. C. Tolman, and J. J. Gibson. In a long letter, Tolman (a very generous man) conveyed his opinion that the acknowledgment of value properties should have a "revolutionary" impact on the field of motivation—but added that it probably would *not,* under the conditions then prevailing, unless I supplemented my conceptual analysis with a few confirmatory rat studies. (I have long thought the "rats as rhetoric" theory of scientific communication—implicit in this half-serious and half-cynical recommendation of Tolman's—to be an especially vivid registration of the "Age of Theory" atmosphere.)

«

Psychology *must* play a critical, if not a central, role in any detailed and intellectually responsible exploration of science-humanities relations and, more generally, in efforts to throw into finer resolution the texture of human inquiry and knowledge. But "must" is a modality word, and philosophers have had trouble with the modalities for centuries. Most intelligent non-psychologists would see no trace of "necessity" in the role here attributed to psychology: they would, in fact, have excellent grounds for thinking psychology the *least likely* of any discipline in the gamut of scholarship to contribute to the clarification of such issues. Yet understanding of the organization of human knowledge—and especially such understanding as might result in more effective conditions for its pursuit—must surely depend on an understanding of the processes of which such knowledge is a product. And psychology is *the* discipline in the family of scholarship which, by virtue of its *purported* domain, must lay claim to the empirical study of such processes as a central concern. For, if psychology be the field which studies the functioning of intact organisms, including human ones, its relevance to those aspects of function which result in knowledge can hardly be gainsaid—and this, whether the "definition" of the discipline be couched in terms of mind, experience, behavior, or, indeed, neuron assemblages, transistor circuits, or protons.

If psychology is truly to implement its relevance to phenomena of the humanities, certain brute facts must be faced—and then transcended. By this point in the present book, they will not be unfamiliar to the reader. Ever since declaring itself an independent science, psychology has been far more concerned with being precisely that—a "science"—than with self-determining confrontation of its historically constituted subject matter. Its history has been largely a matter of emulating the methods, forms, symbols, of the established sciences. In so doing, there has been an inevitable tendency to retreat from broad and intensely significant ranges of its subject matter, and to form rationales for so doing which could only invite further retreat. There has been, at least until recently, an ever-widening estrangement between the scientific makers of human science and the humanistic explorers of the content of man. Indeed, in its search for scientific respectability, psychology has erected a widely shared epistemology and a conceptual language which render virtually impossible the exploration of the content of man in a differentiated way. So deeply engrained are these in the sensibilities of inquirers that even the deviant few who seek to study subtle or complex human phenomena are badly handicapped. And, of the few who sally into these unfamiliar regions, most seem more bent on conquest than exploration.

The most extensive and differentiated "theory" of the psychology of creative activity of the *century* was published in 1964. Significantly, its author—Mr. Arthur Koestler—was not a psychologist. What is more significant is that he felt compelled to devote some 250 pages of his massive *Act of Creation* to an excoriating critique of modern psychology. I am tempted to add that where he surmounted his hostility to the extent of borrowing certain psychological ideas, he was, more often than not, hoist on the petard of his own generosity. Though the "creative process" began to be discovered—with a shock more of amazement than of recognition—by American psychologists some forty years ago, it is still the case (several thousand research articles later) that when these students of "creativity" wish to characterize the "process" in a phenomenally relevant way, they tend to fall back on a single lecture, more than eighty years old, of Poincaré's (1913), or a small book by another mathematician (Hadamard 1945), or an anthology of excerpted descriptions (by writers and others) of the creative process, collected by a professor of English (Ghiselin 1952). When they search for more exalted guidance in forming paradigms for "problem-solving," etc., they are apt to turn to the work of a third mathematician (Polya 1945, 1954) on "heuristics" and related matters.

More generally, the non-psychologists who are participating in the ongoing "redefinition of knowledge" are sharply apprised of the relevance of psychological modes of analysis to their enterprise. People like Polanyi, Kuhn, and Hanson, have, in different ways, stressed the dependence of problems in epistemology and the so-called "logic of science" on psychology. But when they look for the relevant psychological knowledge, it proves to be either non-existent, inadequate, or trivial. Sometimes—as in Koestler's case—there is fairly early recognition that the availabilities in extant psychology are hopeless. Sometimes—as in the instance of Polanyi—there is a disposition to exploit extant psychology for its possible bearing on the investigation of inquiry to the limit and, in my opinion, even a little past that point. What is clear, though, in Polanyi's work, as it is in Koestler's or that of the mathematicians cited above, is that the truly significant psychology that makes its appearance comes out of the men in question and not from the field bearing that name.

It would, of course, be too cynical to suggest that extant psychology has *nothing* to offer to such inquiries into inquiry or analyses of "creative" phenomena as are here at issue. Hanson (1958, 9–15) for instance, finds considerable aid and comfort (and relevantly so) in exploring the bearing of reversible and hidden-figure "illusions" on the analysis of scientific observation! There is, in fact, much in the psychology of perception (not excluding classical psychophysics), and certainly something in fields like learning and memory, and more than a little in developmental psychology, biological psychology, and in the "depth" psychologies and psychiatric disciplines which has *potential* relevance to the "subtler fluxions" of inquiring and creative process. But this potential—whatever its shape and size—will not be actualized until there are decent numbers of psychologists capable of doing the work. It is not easy to state the requirements for such work. But if it is to pertain to inquiry, invention, discovery, connoisseurship, evaluation, in any one of the humanities, scholarly or creative, any one of the sciences as *significantly* practiced, even any context of practical activity— then the *existence* of the phenomena in the given area must be granted and respected. That seems like a weak requirement, but it has not generally been met. And a further, equally obvious, requirement has been even less generally met: he who would inquire into the psychology of any area of human endeavor must be, in some significant sense, at home in that area. As we made plain in the discussion of definition, the student of the psychology of art or literature or music or science must have an adequate supply of the perceptual skills and achieved discriminations appropriate to the given field.

The first, and weaker, of the above requirements points to a condition in psychology with which we have been grappling all through the last chapter. It is, in short, the tendency—most obviously exemplified by behaviorism—to obliterate vast ranges of psychology's proper subject matter (and, indeed, the "fine structure" of all subject matter) enforced by a simplistic conception of definition, and thus of psychology's "observation base." This defective analysis of the conditions for technical communication in psychology has for long years shored up descriptive practice which, in effect, legislate most of the phenomena of the humanities out of "technical" psychological existence. Indeed (as we have seen), if one makes a fully literal interpretation of the long dominant paradigms of definition, all meaningful human phenomena must be proscribed from the psychological language, but I am happy to acknowledge that our discipline has allowed itself a sort of twilight existence by the simple expedient of inconsistency with its claimed rationale. Naturally, the game demands that the inconsistencies be of controlled amplitude, so that grievous distortions, effacements, and exclusions of phenomena are nevertheless successfully perpetrated.

It is to an examination of one of the more subtle contexts in which the reality-defiling simplisms of psychology's past live on that the present chapter is devoted. The field of motivation has seen much ferment and, indeed, genuine progress, since the early fifties. Despite this, one is impressed at how much even those who most genuinely wish to embrace human phenomena are hampered by the restrictions of an inadequate conceptualization. Daily that conceptualization is rendered more unnatural and misleading by the research progress just noted. Yet it persists. The most abstract features of the conceptualization to which I allude have, incidentally, not been unique to behaviorism. Certain of them were evident before behaviorism, and seem to have been come by independently during this century by other schools of thought. Yet, during the behaviorist era, the details of this conceptualization were developed and rigidified to such an extent that it now seems an immutable thought-mold of all inquirers, whatever the inconsonance of the evidence that they themselves generate.

To the extent that we can dig out from the influence of behaviorism, to that extent we clear the way for work in psychology that might have a chance of making differentiated contact with human phenomena. But the aim of our analysis will be more specific than that, and in several senses. The analysis will demonstrate, I think, that major psychological problems cannot be addressed except at levels of experiential sensitivity commonly cultivated in the past only in the humanities. It shows, further, that when such a requirement is given heed, psychology can begin to say things which are relevant to the humanities and, indeed, can reveal itself to the humanist as an ally.

More specifically, the analysis will show that any phrasing of phenomena called "motivational" which does not blight them demands recognition of an utter interpenetration between what philosophers have been wont to call the "realms" of "fact" and of "value." The resulting concept of "value properties" will, I think, make it difficult to doubt that differentiated value-events occur as objective characters of experience, are related in lawful ways to the biological and, ultimately, "stimulus" processes of which experience is a function, and that such value-events are, in perhaps the typical instance, *not* need-dependent, as would be demanded by most motivational theories in psychology or by "interest theories" of value in philosophy.

If a presumption can be created for the "existence" of values in this sense, and if plausible grounds can be developed for the prospects of subjecting them to empirical study, then a basis will have been laid for work of joint interest to every discriminable area of the humanities, both scholarly and creative, to philosophy, and to psychology. By the same token, a potential — indeed, a need — for collaboration will have been opened across the entire gamut of these disciplines. Ability to specify (however crudely) objective value processes and their determinants, and to understand the relations of such processes to other isolable phenomena within the disciplines mentioned would, of course, have critical importance, not only in respect to each of those domains, but for any analysis of inquiry or of knowledge which might do justice at once to their general features and their field-specific particularities. In other words, the analysis of value properties as here essayed will serve as an illustration of the type of work towards exploring the texture of inquiry and of knowledge that I have urged at various points in this book.

The above promises would indeed be as febrile as they may sound if I were proposing to go any appreciable distance towards their fulfillment. I propose nothing of the sort, but merely to point to the feasibility of an important line of inquiry, one that can never be completed. And even this last verges on overstatement, for the line of inquiry at issue will prove to be one which every human being has already commenced.

Value Properties and Motivation

Twentieth-century theories of motivation have generated a gigantic mass of words. But most of these words presuppose and elaborate a single, simple conceptual schematism. This schematism — which I shall here call the "extrinsic model," sometimes "extrinsic grammar" — seems to be deeply embedded, at least in the West, in certain of the interpretive categories of "common sense," and this for a sizable stretch of history.

In the commonsense epistemology of the West, there has long been a tendency to phrase all behavior and sequences thereof in goal-directed terms: to refer behavior in all instances to ends, or end states, which are believed to restore some lack, deficiency, or deprivation in the organism. I have called this presumption a kind of rough-and-ready "instrumentalism" which forever and always places action into an "in order to" context. In this commonsense theory, behavior is uniformly assumed predictable and intelligible when the form "X does Y in order to . . ." is completed. In many instances in practical life it is possible to fill in this form in a predictively useful way. Often, however, a readily identifiable referent for the end term is not available. In such cases we assume that the form must hold, and so we hypothesize or invent an end term which may or may not turn out to be predictively trivial and empty. For instance: X does Y in order to be happy, punish himself, be peaceful, potent, respected, excited, playful, or wise.

Precisely this commonsense framework — or syntax, if you will — has been carried over into the *technical* theories of motivation of the modern period. In the technical theories, the central assumption is that action is always initiated, directed, or sustained by an inferred internal state called variously a motive, drive, need, tension system, or what-not, and terminated by attainment of a situation which removes, diminishes, "satisfies," or in any other fashion alleviates that state. The model is essentially one of disequilibrium-equilibrium restoral, and each of the many "theories of motivation" proposes a different imagery for thinking and talking about the model and the criterial circumstances or end state under which such disequilibria are reduced or removed. Matters are rendered pat and tidy in the various theories by the assumption that all action can be apportioned to (a) a limited number of biologically given, end-determining systems (considered denumerable, but rarely specified past the point of a few "e.g.'s" like hunger and sex), and (b) learned modifications and derivatives of these systems variously called second-order or acquired motives, drives, etc.

My proposal, I think, is a quite simple one. In essence, it points up the limitations of referring *all* action to extrinsic, end-determining systems, as just specified; it challenges the fidelity to fact and the fruitfulness of so doing. At the most primitive level, it says: if you look about you, even in the most superficial way, you will see that all behavior is *not* goal directed, does not fall into an "in order to" context. In this connection, I have presented (Koch 1956; also chapter 7) a fairly detailed descriptive phenomenology of a characteristic sequence of "creative" behavior, which shows that if this state of high productive motivation be seen by the person as related to an extrinsic end (e.g., approval, material reward, etc.) the state becomes disrupted to an extent corresponding to the activity of so seeing. If, on the other hand, some blanket motive of the sort that certain theories reserve for such circumstances, like anxiety, is hypothesized, one can only say that the presence of anxiety in any reportable sense seems only to disrupt this creative state, and in precise proportion to the degree of anxiety.

If such states seem rare and tenuous, suppose we think of a single daily round and ask ourselves whether *everything* that we do falls into some clear-cut "in-order-to" context. Will we not discover a rather surprising fraction of the day to be spent in such ways as "doodling," tapping out rhythms, being the owners of perseverating melodies, nonsense rhymes, "irrelevant" memory episodes; noting the attractiveness of a woman, the fetching quality of a small child, the charm of a shadow-pattern on the wall, the loveliness of a familiar object in a particular distribution of light; looking at the picture over our desk, or out of the window; feeling disturbed at someone's tie, repelled by a face, entranced by a voice; telling jokes, idly conversing, reading a novel, playing the piano, adjusting the wrong position of a picture or a vase, gardening, playing chess, driving a responsive open car, fishing, gazing at a log-fire. Yet *goal-directedness* is presumably the *fact* on which virtually all of modern motivational theory is based.

The answer of the motivational theorist is immediate. He has of course himself noticed certain facts of the same order. Indeed, much of motivational theory is given to the elaboration of detailed hypothetical rationales for such facts, and these the theorists will have neatly prepackaged for immediate delivery. There will be a package containing the principle of "irrelevant drive"; others, "displacement" and other substitutional relations. An extraordinarily large package will contain freely postulated end states, as, e.g., "exploratory drive" and its satiation, "curiosity drive" and its satisfaction, perceptual drives, aesthetic drives, play drives, not to mention that vast complement of needs for achievement, self-realization, growth, and even "pleasurable tension." Another parcel will contain the principle of secondary reinforcement or some variant thereof like subgoal learning, secondary cathexis, etc. Another will provide a convenient set of learning principles which can be unwrapped whenever one wishes to make plausible the possibility that some acquired drive (e.g., anxiety, social approval) which one arbitrarily assigns to a bit of seemingly unmotivated behavior, *could* have been learned. Another contains the principle of functional autonomy. There are indeed a sufficient number of packages to make possible the handling of any presumed negative instance in *several* ways. Why skimp?

The answer to all this is certainly obvious. The very multiplication of these packages as more and more facts of the "in-and-for itself" variety are acknowledged, makes the original analysis, which was prized for its economy and generality, increasingly cumbersome. But more importantly, it becomes clear that the *search* for generality consisted in slicing behavior to a very arbitrary scheme: the result was a mock generality which started with inadequate categories and then sought rectification through more and more *ad hoc* specifications. In the end, even the apparent economy is lost and so, largely, is sense.

A great deal of what we do falls, then, into no obvious "in-order-to" context, unless, in some variable degree, we force matters by exploiting the ever-available flexibility of everyday or theoretical language. Some may find comfort in completing "in-order-to" forms for such behaviors with constructions like "have fun," "get stimulated," "derive pleasure," "relax," "satisfy play or aesthetic needs," but the significance of an assertion is indifferent to the comfort of the asserter.

It cannot be denied, of course, that conventional motivational grammar can make sense in certain of these cases, depending on the concrete circumstances in which specific instances of such behaviors occur. For instance: I *can be* fishing "in-order-to" carry out the doctor's orders, i.e., in order to get well. I can be "suffering" the memorial re-enactment of some idiotic film "in order to" crowd out, i.e., reduce, anxiety, or "in order to" fall asleep. I *can* be driving in an open car "in order to" get to the grocer's "in order to" satisfy hunger. Note, of course, that statements of this sort convey nothing whatsoever with respect to the *intrinsic character* of "fishing" (or any dated fishing episode for X), about "memorial re-enactments" of presented imaginative materials (in this case, films), or any dated episode thereof for X, or about the actual process of driving a responsive open car on a fine day.

Statements of the sort illustrated condense, so to say, a rich, differentiated, "action-experience" syndrome into the referent of an abstract denotative counter. What little information they convey (when "true") is neither meaningless nor necessarily trivial, but *what* they convey are enormously abstract, loose-grained, binary-termed interconnections in a biography.

(When such propositions are transformed into universal ones, the reference is, of course, to an infinite class of the germane biographic events.) Such statements can indeed be useful in mediating practical predictions; it is no doubt by virtue of a long history of such predictive success that the extrinsic motivational grammar has congealed in the natural language. But let us note in the same breath that each one of the many "activities" so far chosen for illustration is of the sort that typically occurs, as is sometimes said, "*in and for itself*." Though users of the natural language often feel compelled to throw instances of "in and for itself" activity into fallacious "instrumental" or "purposive" contexts, the natural language *also* has facilities, though often loosely used ones, for acknowledging activities that are not in fact directed towards extrinsic goals (e.g., the very ascription "in and for itself," forms like "X does Y only because he likes Y," etc.). And, over and above such rudimentary resources for acknowledging "in and for itself" activity, the natural language has a lexical machinery for fine-grained and subtle *analysis* of such "activities" as the history of creative literature, plus that of several of the explicative humanities, should make obvious.

In the light of the preceding considerations, it is almost astounding that psychology, at least motivational psychology, has been so selective. It has extracted the "extrinsic grammar" from the natural language, but has almost completely overlooked the resources for acknowledging and describing "in and for itself" activity syndromes. In overlooking these resources, it has, of course, bypassed the phenomena to which they attest, no small omission when one considers that to extirpate this particular "class" of phenomena is to denude action and experience of everything that may be said to be "intrinsically valuable." If the hope of the motivational theorist is that he will repair this minor oversight by ultimately "recomposing" the omitted phenomena from the laws of "extrinsic motivation" when these are sufficiently "known," one can only admire his appetite for frustration. One meets such feckless optimism all over the face of psychology! The fact that science is selective does not mean that *any* principle or conceptualization that one selects will do. Still less does it mean that if what one "selects" initially orders but the merest "fraction" of a domain that it will, by some hypothetico-deductive magic, secrete consequences that flow into all the vast reaches of empty space corresponding to the systematist's initial oversights.

The relation between extrinsic and intrinsic determinants of action constitutes a most difficult problem for any metatheory of motivation (or indeed, of any other psychological "process-area"). But it is a problem that can hardly be grappled with until one begins to get features of the intrinsic grammar into some kind of focus. The lead that we will follow will be to scrutinize more closely what seems involved in activity which is phenomenally of an "in and for itself" variety, as opposed to clear-cut instances of the "in order to" sort of thing.

Let us begin with some informal observations concerning "play." I would resent being told that at any time I had a generalized need for *play* per se. I do not like to think of myself as that diffuse. I never liked cards. Nor even chess. And I rarely entertain urges towards the idle agitation of my musculature. My play "needs," or activity "needs," etc., have been such that, if described with any precision at all, we soon find ourselves outside the *idiom* of "needs." I have been *drawn towards* certain specific activities which—because they fall into no obvious context of gainful employ, biological necessity, or jockeying for social reward, etc.—could be *called* play. But I have been drawn to these activities, and not others, because (among other reasons) they "contain," "afford," "generate" specific properties or relations in my experience towards which I am adient. *I like these particular activities because they are the particular kinds of activities they are*—not because they reduce my "play drive," or are conducive towards my well-being (often they are not), or my status (some of them make me look quite ludicrous), or my virility pride.

Do I like them, then, by virtue of nothing? *On the contrary*, I like them by virtue of something far more *definite*, "real," if you will, than anything that could be phrased in the extrinsic mode. Each one I like because of *specific* properties or relations immanent, intrinsic, within the given action. Or better, the properties and relations *are* the "liking" (that, too, is a terribly promiscuous word). The *determinants* of such properties and relations in any ongoing activity can plausibly be thought to be dated instances of aspects of neural process which occur each over a family of conditions. Similar properties or relations would be produced (other factors constant) the next time I engaged in the given activity. And no doubt there are families of activities which share similar properties and relations of the sort I am trying to describe. Thus there may be a certain consonance (by no means an absolute one) about the *kinds* of "play" activities that I like. But, more importantly, properties or relations of the same or similar sorts may be generated within activity contexts that would be classified in ways quite other than play: eating, aesthetic experience, sexual activities, problem-solving, etc.

I call such properties or relations *"value properties,"* and the (hypothetical) aspects of neural process which generate them, *"value-determining properties."* Value, or value-determining properties, to which an organism is adient, I call "positive"; those to which the organism is abient, "negative." Adience and abience of organisms are controlled by value-determining properties (or by extension, value properties) of different signs.

It can be instructive to consider from the point of view just adumbrated any of the types of "in and for itself" activity to which it is common gratuitously to impute extrinsic, end-determining systems with their corresponding end states. Thus, for instance, one can only wince at the tendency to talk about such things as "curiosity drives," "exploratory drives," "sensory drives," "perceptual drives," etc., as if the "activities" which are held to "satisfy" each of these "drives" (if indeed they are distinct) were just so much undifferentiated neutral pap that came by the yard. I am inclined to think that even the experimental monkeys who learn discrimination problems for the sole reward of being allowed visual access to their environments from their otherwise enclosed quarters, are being maligned when it is suggested that what their "drive" leads them to seek is "visual stimulation." Could it not be that even for the monkeys there are sights they might prefer not to see? Be this as it may, when explanations of this order are extended, say, to visually mediated aesthetic activities in man, the reduction to a paplike basis of those particulate experiences to which many human beings attribute intense (and differentiated) values, can only be held grotesque.

To make such points graphic and further to clarify the notion of value properties, it may be well to take a second, slightly more formal, example. I take the hypothetical instance of a person looking at a painting:

X looks at a painting for five minutes, and we ask, "Why?" The grammar of extrinsic determination will generate a lush supply of answers. X looks in order to satisfy a need for "aesthetic experience." X looks in order to derive pleasure. X looks because the picture happens to contain Napoleon and because he has a strong drive to dominate. X looks because "paintings" are learned reducers of anxiety. X looks in order to satisfy a need based on the association of the color of his mother's dress with the ground-color of the painting. Answers of this order have only two common properties: They all refer the behavior to an extrinsic, end-determining system, *and* they contain very little, if any, information. Anyone who has looked at paintings as paintings knows that if X is *really* responding to the painting, then any of the above statements which may happen to be true are trivial.

A psychologically naïve person who *can* respond to paintings would say that an important part of the story—the essential part—has been omitted. There is a sense in which X could be looking at the painting only because of something intrinsic in the act of looking at this particular painting. Such a person would say that *if* the conditions of our example presuppose that X is really looking at the painting *as* a painting, the painting will produce a differentiated process in X which is correlated with the act of viewing. The fact that X continues to view the painting or shows "adience" towards it in other ways, is equivalent to the fact that this process occurs. X may report on this process only in very general terms ("interesting," "lovely," "pleasurable"), or he *may* be able to specify certain qualities of the experience by virtue of which he is "held" by the painting.

Suppose we assume that there are certain immanent qualities and relations within the process which are specifically responsible for any evidence of "adience" which X displays. Call these "value-determining properties." We can then, with full tautological sanction, say that X looks at the painting for five minutes because it produces a process characterized by certain value-determining properties. This statement, of course, is an empty form—but note immediately that it is not necessarily more empty than calling behavior, say, "drive-reducing." It now becomes an empirical question as to *what* such value-determining properties, intrinsic to the viewing of paintings, may be, either for X or for populations of viewers.

Though it is extraordinarily difficult to answer such questions, it is by no means impossible. The degree of agreement in aesthetic responsiveness and valuation among individuals of widely varied environmental background but of comparable sensitivity and intelligence is very remarkable indeed. Articulate and perceptive art historians, practicing artists, critics, and teachers have also proved it possible to develop a sufficiently differentiated vocabulary about painting-produced intradermal processes to communicate, at least within limits, intersubjectively. I say this with full appreciation of the high incidence of gibberish generated by many such individuals. Perhaps the incidence would ultimately decrease if fewer psychologists legislated painting-produced processes out of existence.

Looking at a painting can, of course, be the terminal segment of a sequence of "directed" activity. If I take a cab in order to go to the museum to see a Klee exhibit, there is a valid sense in which I can say that the behavior is directed towards an anticipated process having "positive" value-determining properties. I can build up expectation chains which terminate in anticipated processes with value properties. The occurrence of a process with "positive" value-determining property may be functionally related to behavior modification in certain of the ways currently attributed to the reduction or satisfaction of extrinsic motives, except that for the occurrence of processes having positive value, *the postulation of no extrinsic motive is required.*

Before going further, it will be helpful to discriminate some of the things that we do *not* imply when we phrase directed behavior in terms of intrinsic-value properties. We are *not*, for instance, suggesting something tantamount to a "hedonism." I must flatly say that "positive value properties," as immanent within the processes that determine action, are *not* "pleasure," and "negative value properties" (as the basis of "abience") are not "pain." There are circumstances under which feedback from the act of tearing off one's ear might be said to engender positive value properties. More importantly, it must be stressed that, to the extent that hedonistic language is not formulated in the extrinsic mode (i.e., to the extent that hedonism acknowledges intrinsic regulation), it makes a very general and homogeneous identification of the nature and range of intrinsic value properties (viz., "pleasure and pain"). It introduces, as it were, an enormous prejudgment or simplification of the nature and range of possible value-determining properties, and thus of the conditions by virtue of which the adience (or abience) of behavior may be governed. It gives up the ghost before the scientific task is started.

It becomes important now to note that even in cases where the extrinsic" model seems distinctly to fit (e.g., the "biogenic" drives), it may still yield an extraordinarily crass specification of the activities involved, and either overlook their subtle (and often more consequential) aspects, or phrase them in a highly misleading way. The case of the "hunger drive" may be worth brief consideration from this point of view.

The fact that humans eat and show adience towards and within "eating behavior" has been interpreted both by common sense and by science as evidence for the postulation of the "intervening variable," hunger. Ordinary people *and* scientists (physiologists, nutritionists, psychologists) have raised many questions about the properties of this end-determining state in the *extrinsic mode,* and have accumulated a large and, within limits, solid body of facts about the relation of this state to antecedent environmental conditions, to physiological and biochemical processes, and to consequent behavior. Such information mediates practically useful predictions and is certainly scientifically meaningful. If X is observed eating, one possible answer to the question, "Why does X eat?" is clearly that he is *hungry* in the sense specified by this knowledge.

However, most people know that there are conditions under which the above explanation is false (X eats but is not hungry) and conditions under which it is trivial (X eats and is hungry but will drop an insufficiently rare steak on the floor). Most of us know, that is, that there is a sense in which eating behavior takes place in and for itself, a sense in which it must be some function of an immediate, specific, ongoing, internal process having other and more differentiated properties than those assigned to hunger as a *general* variable of the sort defined by "extrinsic" analysis. And, if X is adient towards this plate of food, it is entirely legitimate to apply our tautological rule and say that the behavior persists and varies through time in a certain way by virtue of certain value-determining properties intrinsic to the eating process.

Is there any evidence that our blank form may be filled in—evidence that such value properties are isolable? One need only recall that in civilized cultures cooking is an art form and that the discriminating ingestion of food is a form of connoisseurship. There is no reason in principle why value properties (or classes of such) of the sort intrinsic to eating processes may not yield to increasingly accurate identification. It is already possible for most of us to comment on a meal in a more particulate way than some such exclamation as "Delicious!" Great chefs, summit, or near-summit, members of gourmet communities, professional wine and tea tasters, have in fact achieved a gastronomic-experience language of impressive differentiation and specificity. (It would, incidentally, be of more than casual interest to study such groups with respect to important questions that bear on the extension of experience language for purposes of psychological report.) It is worth noting, further, that it is entirely possible that certain of the value properties intrinsic to eating processes may be of the same order as, or in some way analogous to, value properties involved, say, in visual art-produced processes.

Because the notion of "value properties" is often found difficult,[1] let us

---

1. In the years since first beginning to think about matters germane to "value properties," I have had great difficulty in communicating about them with most psychologists, but none at all with artists, art teachers and students, and the one art historian with whom I have discussed the topic. Communication has also been quite feasible with most people of literary background. I found it fairly easy to get the notion across to a large group of undergraduates on the occasion of a Symposium on Science-Humanities Relations at a good small college. Only occasionally have I run into a graduate student (in psychology) who seems able to understand these simple ideas. The reader may interpret the present bit of biography as he will. If he detects a somewhat frenzied repetitiveness with respect to certain points in this chapter, perhaps it will help him to understand.

take the case of another activity-class which can be acceptably, but only very loosely, phrased in a language of extrinsic determination: sexual activity. On this topic, the twentieth century has seen a vast liberation of curiosity, scientific and otherwise. Yet the textbook picture of sex, human sex, as a tension relievable by orgasm—a kind of tickle mounting to a pain which is then cataclysmically alleviated—is hardly ever questioned at theoretical levels (at least in academic psychology). When it is, it is likely to be in some such way as to consider the remarkable possibility that some forms of "excitement" (e.g., mounting preclimactic "tension") may themselves be pleasurable, and this may be cited, say, as a difficulty for the drive reduction theory, but not for some other drive theory, say some form of neohedonism like "affective arousal," which recognizes that the transition from some pleasure to more pleasure may be reinforcing. But our view would stress that sexual activity is a complex sequence with a rich potential for value properties; for ordered, creatively discoverable combinations, patterns, structures of value properties, which are immanent in the detailed quiddities of sexual action. Sexual experience, like certain other experiential contexts, offers a potential for art and artifice not unnoticed in the history of literature, fictional and confessional, but rarely even distantly mirrored in the technical *conceptualizations*. (The technical *data language* is another matter, but even here the "fineness" of the units of analysis involved in much empirical work is aptly symbolized by Kinsey's chief dependent variable, namely the "outlet" and frequencies thereof.) The vast involvement with this theme at private, literary, and technical levels, has produced little towards a precise specification of experiential value properties, certainly none particularly useful at scientific levels.

Sex, eating behavior, activities written off to curiosity, play, perceptual drives, creative behavior, etc., are contexts each with a vast potential for the "discovery" and creative reassemblage of *symphonies* of value properties. Doubtless each such context offers a potential for differential ranges of value properties, but it is highly likely that there is marked overlap among such ranges. Indeed, formal or relational similarities in experiences that "belong" to quite different contexts of this sort suggest that nature sets a fairly modest limitation on the number of "fundamental" value properties implicated in activity. There is much reason to believe, from the protocols of experientially sensitive and articulate people, as well as from the observation of action, that certain of the value properties intrinsic to such varied contexts of events as the "perception" of (and directed behavior towards) a picture, a poem, a "problem" (whether scientific, mathematical, or personal), a "puzzle" in and for itself, are of an analogous order and in some sense overlap. And, as we have just tried to show, it is reasonable to believe that the so-called consummatory aspects of hunger or of sex "contain" relational qualities not dissimilar to some of the value properties immanent in "complex" activities like those listed in the last sentence.

Once the detailed phenomena of directed behavior are rephrased in terms of intrinsic value properties, it becomes possible to reinspect the extrinsic language of drives and the like, and determine what utility it might actually contain. For *some* behaviors clearly are brought to an end or are otherwise altered by consummations, and organisms clearly show both restless *and* directed activities in the absence of the relevant consummatory objects. Questions about the relations between what one might call *extrinsic* and *intrinsic grammar* for the optimal phrasing of motivational phenomena are among the most important for the future of motivational theory.

Whatever is viable in the drive language is, of course, based in the first instance on "organizations" of activity sequences which converge on a common end-state. Each such organization, if veridical, would permit differential (but overlapping) ranges of value properties to "come into play." No doubt *primary* organizations of this sort, when veridical, are related to deviations of internal physiological states, the readjustments of which play a role in the adaptive economy. When such deviations are present, it is probable that certain value properties, or ranges thereof, are given especial salience and effectiveness with respect to the detailed moment-to-moment control of directed behavior. That all activities, however, must be contingent on such deviation-states, seems on the face of it absurd. Behavior will often be directed by value properties which have nothing to do with gross organizations of this sort, and which may in fact conflict with the adjustment of the concurrent deviation. Much of what is called "learned motivation" will consist not in "modifications of primary drives" — whatever that can mean — but rather in the building up of expectations and expectation-chains which terminate in anticipated processes with value properties. "Learned drives," whatever that means, would be built up as systems of anticipation of value property constellations and sequences.

Some Consequences for Aesthetics

Some such conception as "value properties" is perhaps more likely to obtrude upon an inquirer while surveying phenomena called "motivational" than other conventionally discriminated fields of psychology. For one is here compelled to think about factors which determine the "directedness" of experience and action: the characters of events which organisms tend to strive towards, maximize, prolong, savor, prize, cherish, etc., and those which in specific ways the organism tends to flee, take precaution against, avoid, terminate, dislike, loathe, pass on from, minimize, reject. Even if one begins analysis in the extrinsic mode, one is soon forced into contact with those characters which, by criteria of the directionality of action and experience, may be said to be in some sense "good" and in some sense "bad." And as soon as one can discern that organisms are oriented not in reference to "good" and "bad" as global, generalized states of affairs, but rather in reference to a plurality of particulate "goods" and "bads," having differentially specifiable effects, one is fairly close to a conception like "value properties."

Once in possession of the notion of value properties, however, it is clear that they are not specifically "motivational" (whatever that can mean), but rather that such relational features of experience and action as are discriminated by that concept will be ubiquitous in psychological functioning. Any analysis of experience or action, then, which does not slight or, for some practical reason, "suppress" its fine structure must take cognizance at some level of value properties. If one thinks in terms of functionally isolable psychological processes of the sort loosely bounded by major "fields" of psychology, it will immediately be obvious that, for instance, concrete value-property distributions will be the warp and woof of all *perceptual* processes. Every percept will contain relational characters "corresponding" to value properties; indeed, immanent within percepts of differing degrees of articulation and complexity will be correspondingly different value-property structures. Obviously, the intention is not to assimilate *all* "terms" and relations of a percept to a constellation of value properties: rather, the relation of analytically discriminable "parts" of a percept to whatever value properties are immanent is a "many-one" relation.

Any conceivable percept, then, — whether a simple "abstract" contour or an exquisitely articulated and richly meaningful painting, whether an isolated noise or tone or a symphony, whether a punctiform patch of white pigment on a dark ground or a delicately expressive and mobile human face — will project a particulate distribution of value properties. Consider also something already implicit in certain of the preceding examples: that if one thinks of the psychological processes of *meaning* in *perceptual* terms (as was suggested in the last chapter), then any dated occurrence of a meaning — whether of a word or phrase or other linguistic unit, whether of a work of art, a gesture, a social "response," a historical event—will also "contain" a unique value property distribution. Again, perceptual "feedback" from one's *own* activities, and inner processes and states, must also be thought to "contain" value properties. And certain classes of value properties may he thought to emerge from interactive relations as among "multidimensional" organizations of formal, meaningful, and actional suborganizations (to the extent these may be discriminable for analytic purposes).

Differentiated value events, then, are omnipresent in psychological function. If fact and value are ontologically disparate or in some sense separated "realms" or aspects of the universe, I do not know what the psychological evidence could be. I do not in fact see how one can conceive of any such monster as an axiologically neutral fact, or, for that matter, a factually neutral value.

Perhaps we have come to the preceding conclusion too rapidly, but I do not see how it can be resisted—nor indeed that much further argument is required once the concept of value properties emerges. Those, however, who may initially find such a conclusion too great a wrench upon their previous beliefs, may find that it gains plausibility as we consider certain of its consequences. Since brief exploration is all that can be undertaken at this place, I shall move rapidly and more or less at random over a scattering of themes.

The reader will no doubt wish that his first payment on the promissory note issued by the preceding analyses will be concrete illustrations of the "value properties" which have been talked about with such indirection. The reader's wish is unfair! Much as I would like to oblige, I cannot accomplish in passing what several thousand years of human, humanistic, and scientific analysis has failed to do. In the case of visual art–produced experience, the typical kinds of things that the aestheticians, articulate artists, and art critics have been able to come up with in millennia of analysis have been such global discriminations as harmony, symmetry, order, "significant form," "dynamic tension," "unity in variety," the "ratio of order to complexity," etc. By "value properties" I have in mind far more specific relational attributes of experience. They could, to borrow a cue from Gibson, be contingent upon subtle relational invariants in arrays of stimulation, as distributed over space and cumulated over time. They are almost certainly related to what Gibson would call "high order variables of stimulation" and are themselves high order relational variables within experience. The isolation of such value properties will not be accomplished within any specifiable time limit, will require learning to use language in new ways, and will require most of all the efforts of many individuals of exceptional and specialized sensitivity in significant areas of experience.

Certain of the difficulties that one faces in any attempt, even in a loose first-approximation way, to circumscribe value properties may perhaps be suggested by an informal example. For several years I have been impressed with an elusive common property of many perceptual "manifolds" in highly diverse contexts — a property which seems one of the marks of "elegance" or a certain kind of "sophistication" (in some special, "valuable" sense of the term). I suspect the quality in question — which is quite specific and can be only loosely suggested by any word currently in the natural language — to be intrinsic, in some fairly rudimentary sense, to simple perceptual contours having certain canonical properties. But how specify these canonical (value) properties? It is not easy!

The most effective presently available method (at least for me) would be by "differentiated ostension" via a large range of perceptual materials "possessing" the type of contour which I believe to have the canonical properties in question. If the addressee could then independently pick out further appropriate examples — perhaps localizing the contours with the canonical properties by finger tracing, or some such differentiated ostension — the presumption would be that he had in some degree at least disembedded the intended referent, and thus that communication had in some measure been achieved. Naturally, whether the addressee found the property or property-complex in question to enter into similar relations within *his* experience to those I find in mine, whether he too found the property in some sense "attractive," etc., would be open to determination. Naturally, also, we could agree on a name for the property, either by selecting an available one from the natural language or by invention. Such a procedure would give some knowledge of this hypothetical value property, but not much.

Finer knowledge would be achieved if, say, a skilled artist could disembed the relational invariants constitutive of the percept properties in question sufficiently well to "create" instantiating contours, so to say ad libitum. The artist, of course, might not be able, especially initially, to *specify* the relational invariants which "guide" his drawings. Should he (or anyone else) succeed at any level in making these effable, a still finer level of knowledge would be achieved. A further level of fineness might be achieved if now it became possible to relate this preceding specification of the "critical" invariants to such a mathematico-physical metric for specifying "higher-order variables" of stimulation, as has been conceived (very programmatically) by Gibson (1959, 1966). Bearing in mind the limits of knowledge, analysis, language — not to mention the embeddedness of the phenomena at issue — it should be clear that even our ultimate encroachments upon "value properties" must be thought to be loosely approximative. But it should also be clear that the limiting precision cannot be established a priori, and that even small increments of precision are worthwhile.

If I were at this moment asked to specify verbally my "bounding" of the percept properties constitutive of what I have loosely called "elegance," I would have to be extremely vague. (Contour-drawings might help, but I do not wish the example to be taken quite that seriously!) Consider imaginatively characteristic examples of "high fashion" costumes, aristocratic faces, fine *gran turismo* motor cars, "sophisticated" furniture (of any era), a range of highly stylized genres or "schools" of art (e.g., Mannerism, Art Nouveau). Contrast these — to keep things simple, in terms of contour — with characteristic instances of grossly "non-sophisticated" forms of the relevant categories. For me, one fairly conspicuous difference is that in the "elegant," or "sophisticated" case, the forms tend organically to encompass, yet transcend and subdue, a certain specific "awkwardness," "ungainliness," "disruptive-tension," "distortion." A certain specific *range* of such "awkwardnesses," etc., of course, each given instance being unique and "appropriate" to the contour in which it is encompassed. The awkwardness, however, must have a special and in some sense meaningful relation to the form in which it is housed. The whole must conquer it, be victorious over the tension set up by the awkwardness. But the awkwardness must be such that the whole is enriched and given style, quiddity, bite, wit, life, dash, depth (not necessarily in the spatial sense), interest, by its presence.

Now this description leaves me highly thwarted: it misses what I have in mind by a light-year. But if the reader can accept that what I have in mind is not entirely illusory, we can forget, for purposes of the *example,* whether even minimal justice has been done to the "value property" at issue. We can nevertheless note a number of interesting things:

Note first that in talking about this fairly specialized value property, the description presupposes that the "elegant" or "sophisticated" forms are more "complex," contain more "tension" or "conflict," have a different "ratio of order to complexity," and a more "significant form" than the negative cases. But all of these time-worn counters of aesthetic-perceptual analysis are so utterly general that no matter how sensitively or discriminatingly applied, they could tell us next to nothing about the specialized "property" that we are after. Though not one of these counters is non-significant, they could be applied and reapplied for several millennia (and some have) with no refinement or even cumulative increase of analytic knowledge. It is my contention that not only aesthetics and the humanities, but for reasons which I hope by now to be obvious, psychology, will remain in a very bad way indeed if we cannot do better.

Another thing worth noting is that once the search for such a relatively specific X as the one at issue has begun, possible interconnections with a very broad range of other psychological phenomena begin, if only vaguely, to suggest themselves. If, say, we begin with some such loose mapping of our X as "overcoming an awkwardness," it is clear that the nature and sub-species of the "awkwardness" would invite (and indeed require) analysis, as would the *mode* of "overcoming." Interpreting the "awkwardness" as a somewhat "repugnant" element which enriches the whole that conquers it, one can immediately think, say, of certain perfumes, the subtlety of which is much dependent on specific interplays against "unpleasant" olfactory components, certain exquisite examples of culinary art which depend on such subduals of the inappropriate or slightly repugnant (e.g., a certain Central European pastry blends a many-layered sweet crust with an intensely salted filling of cabbage). One thinks, further, (and perhaps more loosely) of a large class of contexts which involve the "overcoming" of recalcitrant, gross, rough, crudely textured, or otherwise "inappropriate" *materials* ("content") by a specific over-all *form:* e.g., use of folk-dialect or slang, or even an arbitrarily restricted language like that of symbolist po-etry—in literature; use of "trash" and bric-a-brac in modern sculpture, "paintings," and collages. Keeping in mind the over-all range of these ex-amples, it is already obvious that no single "value property" abstraction would give an equally apt description of every "case" (or indeed any two cases). But it is equally clear that some degree of kinship which is yet more specific than whatever might be described by the traditional aesthetic counters (e.g., tension) is in principle achievable. More importantly, what seems to be suggested is that value properties will fall into similarity-classes, the comparative investigation of which may in fact throw light on differentiations which would have never emerged if not for the superordi-nate similarities. One can thus look towards an anatomizing of the vari-ables implicated in perceptual, motivational, and related psychological pro-cess of a sort that might give truly differentiated, yet general, insight into the fine structure of experience and action.

It will perhaps seem natural to think of value properties as being relevant to the "formal" aspect of art, as divorced from representational "content," "meaning" etc. But such an impulse can only stem from certain of the traditional vagaries concerning the significance of "content." For, as has already been briefly noted, if one follows the proposal of this book that we think of "meaning" in a perceptual mode, then a distribution of value properties will be as much a "parameter" of the *meaning* of an aesthetic (or any perceptual) object as of its "form." This, incidentally, is implicitly recognized in much traditional aesthetic analysis in the tendency to apply global value-property categories of the order already illustrated (e.g., "unity in variety"; "tension," "conflict," and their dynamic resolution; "harmony") indifferently to phenomena of formal or contentual character: e.g., "conflict" in relation, say, to the interplay of formal elements in an abstract design, or in relation to the clash of motive in the drama; "complexity" in relation to the differentiation of form in visual art, music, or literature, as against complexity of any "representational content" that may be said to be conveyed by specific objects in any of those areas.

In the terms of the present conception, then, to the extent that "form" and "content" are analytically separated, there can be said to be separate value-property distributions corresponding to each. The total effect of the aesthetic (or other perceptual) object, insofar as mediated by value properties, can then be said to be a joint function of (1) value properties of the form, (2) value properties of the content, and (3) (very importantly) value properties which can be conceptualized as relationally determined by interactions of the formal and contentual ones. These latter "resultant" value properties would, of course, be implicated in the entire range of phenomena that aestheticians and critics consider in relation to such matters as "appropriateness" of formal to contentual aspects of the art object, and to the many controlled effects in the arts which are based on stresses or other modes of interaction, often ones which dynamically change over time (e.g., in poetry), as between formal and contentual "elements."

One general consequence for aesthetic theory of such points as have just been urged might be mentioned in passing. A familiar topic of aesthetic and critical speculation bears on the differential potentialities of the different primary "art forms" (e.g., painting, sculpture, music, architecture, poetry, the novel, etc.) and the various sub-specifications of these into sub-forms of increasing particularity, depending upon "medium," genre, "intent-category," some such dimension as "scope," "style" (in some collective sense), etc. A more or less standing premise of criticism is that the work of art be assessed relative to criteria appropriate to the genus (*cum differentia*) to which the work is allocated. When, however, the characteristics of the different art categories are considered or, say, when some question arises as to the absolute evaluation of a work of art, independently of its "category," analysis tends to become highly indeterminate and often to proceed in terms of some such diffuse notions as the differential "complexity," "richness," "depth," "scope," permitted by the different art forms.

Assuredly the present pre-theoretical speculations offer no pat or immediate solutions to such problems. But they do suggest these problems to be open to continuing and increasingly determinate analysis. For in the present terms, the differential characteristics of the various art forms, media, styles, etc., which will determine the potentialities of each for aesthetic experience, will depend upon the differential ranges of value properties which may be engendered within the resources of each. It is certainly reasonable to expect that the specialized value properties mobilizable by, say, painting vs. architecture, by oil painting vs. water color, by epic poetry vs. lyrical, by differing prosodic forms in general, by poetry vs. the novel, the novel in its different forms, the twelve-tone scale vs. the normal scale, and so on and on, differ markedly in range, though no doubt there is much overlapping. It should be possible ultimately to specify such differences not merely in a neutral jargon of "complexity" and the like, but in a far more illuminating way.

Such knowledge would obviously have important consequences not only for the theory and practice of criticism, but for more general questions. Among the latter is an issue which has long been treated rather superficially: that of whether art (in contradistinction to science) is "noncumulative." This "issue" is, of course, shorthand for a disorderly family of questions, none of them resolvable in passing. But the present line of thinking does suggest there to be one fairly determinate sense in which art may be said to be cumulative: i.e., artists of different sensibility and objective will inevitably "explore" (whether by intention or no) the potentialities of the "form," "medium," etc., within which they work; the very "uniqueness" attributed by all to the artist's "methods" and achievements will thus ensure within the history of any given "form" that much will be learned about its distinctive potential for the mobilization of value properties. Critics to some extent acknowledge this state of affairs by their frequent (and often glib) diagnoses of the demise through "exhaustion" of one or another form, tendency, genre. From the present point of view, then, there is a definite, if limited, sense in which it is "more" than metaphorical to talk about "experimentation" in reference to art and even to expect that "findings" (though most will remain implicit) cumulate. The great and self-conscious emphasis on "experimentalism" evidenced in most of the arts during the twentieth century can thus be seen to be founded on something more substantial than merely a chic image—even though, as we will have occasion to note in the next two chapters, some of the passion behind the use of this image has an extra-aesthetic origin.

Though I believe that many more consequences of programmatic importance for aesthetics tend to follow from any such notion as "value properties," it is no part of my intention to continue a story which lacks all of its central characters. The immediate purpose of the above brief references to aesthetics was further to explicate the hypothetical notion of "value properties." But in so doing, we are thrust up against considerations which clarify the force of a point which thus far has been made only in passing. Recognition of the importance of increasingly fine specification of value properties not only opens a bridge between psychology and the humanities—more particularly, it points to a special and necessary kind of dependence of psychology on certain research resources that can only be made available by the humanities. The chief research "instrument" for disembedding value properties can only be human discrimination—and not just the kind of discrimination practiced by the most readily accessible sophomore but, rather, discrimination as informed by finely textured and relevantly specialized *sensibility*. In this of all areas, psychology must finally abjure its long cherished belief that "observer-characteristics" are of minor importance (if indeed observers are granted *any* relevance to observation whatsoever!). To make significant progress towards the isolation of value properties will require the observational efforts not merely of individuals who are equipped by training with stocks of discriminations appropriate to the area in which value phenomena are sought, but individuals of outstanding discriminal and even creative capacity in those areas. Collaboration should be sought, then, from individuals who are at "summit" or near-summit levels in the humanities and the arts. And it should be added that individuals from every discriminable field within the scholarly and critical humanities, the creative and performing arts, would be appropriate for the type of research here being envisaged.

It might well be asked what the *psychologist* would have to offer to such research! At best, not much, but what little he *could* offer is none the less vital. Research oriented towards value properties could, of course, not even be posed, let alone go forward, if not informed and in some sense regulated by the available knowledge, method, and technical lore of perception psychology. Experimental technique deriving from psychophysical method in the broadest sense would have to be tapped, as would knowledge and method concerning sensory mechanisms, neurophysiology of perception, perceptual learning, etc. Any such research must, of course, not only be guided by background knowledge from these areas, but must be premised on creative capacities for applying and extending this knowledge to concrete problems of stimulus control, data analysis, methods for extension and refinement of experience language, and so on. It goes without saying that the psychologist must be an individual having a sufficient overlap of knowledge and sensitivity with the humanist in the latter's own field; else collaboration is futile. It goes without saying, also, that the humanist be an individual with a respect for empirical modes of analysis and a controllable set of intolerances towards such matters as the interest of science in generalization. Finally, it should be emphasized that the optimal form of collaboration in such research would be something like full partnership: it is not desirable that the humanist's role be restricted to that of "observer," nor that the psychologist's role preclude ardent first-person observational effort.

When all is said and done, the main thing that psychology can offer in specific liaisons with humanists (or to humanists in general) is in fact most of what has been authentic in its accomplishments to date. The great advances within psychology thus far — and these are not to be underestimated by the humanist or anyone else — have been in the domain of discovering the pitfalls inherent in any attempt to isolate functionally significant conditions of organismic action and experience, and in "methods" (however approximative) for coping with, compensating for, circumventing these pitfalls. If the humanist complains that many of the variables thus far isolated and studied by psychology seem to him insignificant, that is not entirely to the point. Some substantial core of experimental analysis, statistical compensation, environmental "input" control, and control or measurement of background variables within the organism, emerging from this work has quite general significance for the analysis of organismic systems, whatever the "units" of analysis, problems, or hypotheses that are entertained.

Near-History Relatives: The Gestaltists and Gibson

The conception of "value properties" is not without relatives in the near history of psychology. In contrasting the present conception with a few of the latter, one may hope not only to bring into focus a little of the historical context, but perhaps further to clarify the notion of value properties.

A fairly obvious overlap, though one difficult to bound sharply, may be discerned between what I intend by value properties and certain of the usages of the notion of "tertiary qualities" by such Gestalt psychologists as Wertheimer and Köhler. The usage range in question tends to identify "tertiary qualities" with *objectively localized* percept qualities of a sort thought to correspond to relational field effects of a relatively high order. The notion typically carries the further suggestion that the field invariance to which the quality is ordered is in some degree of isomorphy with a relational attribute, often a subtle one, of the stimulus configuration. If this cumbrous reconstruction from the Gestalt usage (I have not been able to find an explicit definition) is correct, it would of course constitute "tertiary qualities" as so general a class as to make clearcut separation from that of the *Gestaltqualitäten* impossible. Indeed, this latter may be the intention, for the source containing the most extensive range of illustrations of what Köhler, in *other* writings, calls "tertiary qualities" eschews that designation in favor of "*Ehrenfels* qualities." Typical examples given by Köhler are "power" as localized in "lightning and in thunder," "tenderness in a spring day," "sadness in a rainy afternoon" (1938, 16); "the 'major' or the 'minor' character of a melody" (1937, 276). The following interesting paragraph provides further examples:

> It would not be difficult to show that all percepts have such qualities. When things are called "tall" or "bulky," persons "slender" or "stout," movements "clumsy" or "graceful," reference is made to definite Von Ehrenfels–qualities. When we describe events as "sudden" or "smooth," "jerky" or "continuous" we refer to the same class. Esthetically they are doubtless of paramount importance, but they are hardly less so, I think, in biological contexts. The color of the hair, the pitch of the voice may have much to do with the strong impression which specific persons of one sex make upon specific persons of the other. Still, properties of shape, of gesture, and of general movement are generally found to be at least as dangerous — and these are Von Ehrenfels–qualities. (Köhler 1937, 276)

From the preceding culling, it should already be clear that the qualities vary in several respects, not the least of which is degree of relevance to factors determinative of the "directionality" of action (thus, "value"). Nevertheless, most of the above "qualities" are so relevant in some degree, and the quoted paragraph reveals a further affinity to the present notion of "value properties" by explicit acknowledgment of the importance of the qualities at issue, both "*aesthetically*" and in "*biological contexts.*" The affinity is further underlined by the fact that in *The Place of Value in a World of Facts* (1938) Köhler, on several occasions, refers to specific examples that he cites of "tertiary qualities" as "value-qualities" and in at least one place (78) as "value-properties."[2]

The overlap between Köhler's conception of "tertiary qualities" (and "value qualities") and the present ideas is substantial. But the differences are substantial, too — though difficult to state. Köhler's (and other Gestalt) illustrations will be seen to point to qualities which are relatively "close to the surface" (i.e., not "deeply" or complexly embedded) of the perceptual manifolds in which they "inhere," which, though general, have a generality not in excess of most pattern-dependent words in a natural language; and which indeed are rarely ordered to any *phenomenal* description or bounding much in excess of the allocation of a single natural language word. The more or less standard Gestalt tendency re tertiary and value qualities, then, is merely to identify certain relational attributes of the perceptual ecology which are "expressive" of perceptual qualities (e.g., of mood, emotion, physiognomy) at about the level already discriminated by descriptive words of the natural language. Such identifications of tertiary qualities in the Gestalt writing is usually in the service of an argument (valid, in my estimation) meant to show that these are "genuinely" *objective* percept attributes and not the results of Einfühlung, association or any other variety of "enrichment." The characteristic motive, then, tends to be polemical rather than analytical.

In contradistinction, the present concept of value properties would seek to *begin* analysis at approximately the point at which the typical Gestalt "location" of tertiary qualities leaves off. The hope (admittedly *only* a hope) is to achieve a delicately specified isolation of relational structures associated with the "value" aspects of experience and action of considerably greater *generality* than those demarcated by "tertiary qualities" in the typical Gestalt application. Indeed, the hope would be to explore the possibil-

2. I detected this detailed correspondence of terminology upon referring to *The Place of Value in a World of Facts*, after not having returned to that book since reading it in 1939. The context in which "value properties" occurs is of some interest. It occurs in reference to the following examples (78) of "tertiary qualities": "That face looks mean — and I abhor it. Dignity I hear in those words which I have just heard Mr. X. speaking — and I respect him. Her gait is clumsy — and I prefer to look away."

ity of ultimately "modeling" all value properties on a limited number of fundamental, if systematically complex, dimensions. Whatever the limits on this last desideratum, it is unlikely that they preclude the chances of a fairly far-reaching conceptual sharpening and realignment of the extant gross and unsystematic natural language value-property "categories." Moreover, as we have seen from our discussion of motivation and the brief comments on issues of aesthetics, there is reason to believe that important value properties of a sort implicated in significant ranges of human experience and action have thus far wholly eluded identification within the natural language.

The difference, then, between what I have taken to be the Gestalt *modus* concerning tertiary qualities and the present proposals re value properties are very great, despite marked consonances. That the difference is one mainly of heuristic import does not make it any the smaller. For if my reading of the situation of psychology be correct, heuristic considerations can be all important! The fact is that the present position calls for commencement of a tradition of committed, expert, endlessly painstaking phenomenal analysis, one which accepts it that thus far the perceptual ecology has been far from completely explored and thus one which looks towards discovery of new phenomenal distinctions. But classical Gestalt psychology, after its well known initial wave of phenomenological discoveries, was long content to rest on these. The congeries of neo-Gestalt efforts left in the wake of the classical "movement" has not notably — despite important new departures — reactivated the long-lapsed phenomenological enterprise.

We have noted several times in this chapter a consonance between Gibson's conception of a "perceptual psychophysics" (e.g., 1950, 1959, 1966) and aspects of the present speculations. He has done psychology a service in presenting convincing conceptual and experimental arguments for the radical extension of classical psychophysics that comes about by taking note of the actual complexity and richness of the world of stimulating energies, even as physically conceived. He has stressed that there are dimensions of stimulus specification which have not been touched by classical sensory psychology: in particular, "higher-order variables" of relational character which emerge by taking into account macroscopic properties of the spatially and/or temporally extended "stimulus arrays" which in fact impinge upon the receptor surfaces of organisms. As Gibson has put it: "The important [variables] for perception and behavior are variables of the adjacent and successive order of frequencies and intensities, that is, variables of the stimulus *array* and of the stimulus *flow*. There are gradients, derivatives, ratios, and rates in this flowing array of energy, and these are the higher order variables of stimulation which the theory postulates" (1959, 464). This recognition of the potential richness of the stimulating-environment having been asserted, Gibson can proceed to the definitive "hypothesis" of his program—that of "psychophysical correspondence." In *Psychology: A Study of a Science,* Gibson states it in these words: "for every aspect or property of the phenomenal world of an individual in contact with his environment, however subtle, there is a variable of the energy flux at his receptors, however complex, with which the phenomenal property would correspond if a psychophysical experiment could be performed" (1959, 465).

It is clear that the concept of "value properties" presupposes a complexity of the stimulating environment (and a likelihood for the efficacy of relational invariants in stimulation) of an order comparable to Gibson's conception. In the discussion not only of value properties but (in the last chapter) of meaning, I have been stressing and, where not stressing, strongly assuming that much of perceptual experience will be contingent upon relational characters of stimulation, many of them extremely subtle (and certainly neglected in classical psychophysics), and many of "high order," even in the literal sense of requiring conceptualization as relations themselves built upon relational "terms" or a hierarchy thereof.

Earlier in this chapter, I distinguished between "value properties" as relational characters of experience and "value-determining properties" as relational characters of the neural (or, more generally, biological) process of which the former is a function. May I now violate a resolution not to over-garnish the present speculations with terminology by introducing the term, "value-generating properties" to correspond to characters of stimulation (usually relational and of "high order") of which value-determining properties and, ultimately, value properties are some function. But in the present conception, it is distinctly not the case that *all* "value properties" will be "bound" to external stimulation (or even internal, in any literal sense of "stimulation"), nor do we hold that in the extensive range of instances in which value properties *are* "stimulus-bound" that they are *uniquely* a function of the stimulus, or that stimulus-specification is the *only* important or instructive problem that confronts causal analysis. For, in general, value properties (or any other phenomenal characters) can arise only as a result of the organism's *processing,* whether concurrent or after a time-lapse, of the external input. Moreover, if one accepts any leads at all, either from commonsense guesswork or current neurophysiology, one must conceive of the organism's processing operations as hierarchically organized in such a way that often what is registered phenomenally will be contingent upon the processing of lower-level "process-transforms." Finally, the present view presumes that value-*determining* properties are intrinsic to neural function; indeed, that they are in some sense criterial with respect to the "direction" of neural dynamics: thus it must be assumed that relatively "autonomous" operations (in the sense of minimal concurrent stimulus control) of the sort involved in thinking, etc., will be a not insignificant source of phenomenal value properties. In consequence, the present view expects nothing like the monolithic and relatively direct dependence of value properties, or any other aspect of perception, on stimulation suggested by Gibson's theoretical imagery. Even if the limiting precision of stimulus specification were attainable, our view would expect nothing like "complete" or detailed isomorphism with the "corresponding" value property in most instances.

Gibson's governing presuppositions and certain aspects of his method have been subjected to a far more demanding critique from an incidence similar to the above by Zener and Gaffron (1962) in their contribution to *Psychology: A Study of a Science*. In my estimation, the phase analysis of perception there proposed embeds the important and viable aspects of Gibson's program into a constructive framework of great power for the study of perception. Little could be gained by an attempt to reduce Zener and Gaffron's intricate scaffolding of proposals to a summary in these pages. But it would be in the ambience of some such view of perception as theirs that the present vague speculations about value properties—if they were to be carried further—would have to be implemented.

As an addendum to the preceding "pre-theoretical" survey, which may help towards the tying together of the concept of value properties and certain cognate distinctions frequently met in psychological literature, the following brief suggestions may be worth making.

"Preferences," "tastes," and Values, in that use which regards them as durable preference dispositions, can be thought of as the constitutionally *given* or learned salience in experience or action of given ranges or clusterings of value properties. An individual comes to "prize" certain value properties relatively more than others; in a rough way, one may reconstruct for a given person his characteristic hierarchic "structure" of "value-property-families" (Values).

Naturally, it can be no more incumbent on me than anyone else to give the final details of how such differential prizings are formed; nor am I better prepared than others to pre-delineate the relative "role," or detailed interpenetration, of constitutional cum maturational vs. learning factors. Two points, however, are to be sharply emphasized: First, whatever can be meant by "endowment," the "biologically given," "constitution," etc. (at any given level of maturation) must be thought to have greater weight and more differentiated influence on motivational and perceptual tendencies than has been acknowledged in much of recent psychological theory. Secondly, learning in its relations to motivational, perceptual, and cognitive organization must be seen to be very much a process of discrimination — discrimination both upon the external stimulus-input and upon the organism's own inner states and operations. But, as the last sentence suggests, I think it folly to maintain, as does Gibson, that learning is *entirely* a process of stimulus discrimination. Whether what Gibson leaves out[3] is best phrased as "enrichment" (cf. Gibson and Gibson 1955; Postman 1955), I do not know, but certainly discrimination will at any given time always be superposed upon, and partly determined by, the total organization of the "stored" schemas of past discrimination (however this be conceptualized), by motivational conditions, by other concurrent biological states, *and by* the intrinsically regulated input-processing systems of the organism (cf. Zener and Gaffron 1962) for which we have much gross commonsense, and increasing neurophysiological, evidence.

Coda: Philosophy, Science, and Value

Here we shall peer into this threatening jungle but briefly and hesitantly for fear that an actual entrance would result in a book within a book. The following few pages are offered only to punctuate the utter divergence between any analysis which sees the world so fulsomely inhabited with value phenomena as the present one and recently dominant views of the proper domain of axiological study, the relations between "value" and science, and thus more generally the place of value in the context of "knowledge." If the analyses of this chapter are in any measure correct, then fundamental reconstruction is called for in the sweeping connections just mentioned.

---

3. The "empty organism" aspect of Gibson's phrasing of the task of psychology stands as a mystery for the sociologist of science. One can appreciate the aseptic quality of such a conception for those who wish to deny or bypass the presence in the universe of *experiential* states of affairs, but for a *phenomenologist* to regard a few patches of receptor surface as the only embodiment of the organism standing between the stimulus array and its "perceptual world" is decidedly odd.

The dimension of the reconstructive task that would have to be joined can be revealed only by reference to a view, some form of which dominated axiological thinking from the late twenties until recently: the "emotivist theory." This was the more or less official view of logical positivism, but its imprint can be seen as well in some of the more sophisticated thinking of the analytic philosophers. It is easily summarized. Recall that the meaning-cosmology of classical logical positivism is exhausted by (1) formal tautologies, and (2) verifiable empirical statements. Question: Are value judgments tautologies? No — or at least *some* are not (and, be it noted, if "sin is evil" is a tautology, it is not a "good" one, not the kind that falls into the class of logical and mathematical propositions). Question: Are value judgments verifiable by observation? No: "conceit is sinful" seemed to these observers to have no clear-cut linkage to an "observable thing" definition base. Strictly, an ethical or aesthetic judgment is *meaningless*. Or it is at least "cognitively" meaningless. What then are ethical or aesthetic utterances? They are exclamations (or, if you prefer, ejaculations, imprecations, or some such emotional "expression"): they are expressions of approving or disapproving feeling, affect, emotion. Such a view was stated very sharply and simply by Ayer (1936) and has been elaborated in varying degrees of detail by others (rather fulsomely by Stevenson 1944). Let us assure ourselves as to what this view is really saying. As A. C. Graham, an analytic philosopher, has pointed out (1961, 13–14), the view in effect is saying that "[t]here can be no fruitful dispute over questions of value except in terms of tastes and goals which the disputants happen to share. Moses blew off his emotions about murder by saying 'thou shalt not kill'; and if a killer from Auschwitz happens to feel differently, *de gustibus non disputandum.*"

Within the ambiance of analytic philosophy, the emotivist view soon shaded over into (or was supplemented by) the "imperativist" view, which holds that value judgments, pronouncements, standards, etc., are in effect commands. Since analytic philosophers had stressed the multiplicity of "use"-functions in language, it was no longer to be maintained that value utterances are *meaningless*, but rather that being commands, they "behaved" in a very different way than did factual statements. As Graham puts it: "With this change of viewpoint it becomes possible to admit that moral and aesthetic standards do not say anything true or false about entities called 'goodness' and 'beauty' or about inclinations in taste, and yet to hold they are as meaningful as statements of fact" (14–15).

Analytic philosophy is currently extricating itself from the almost incredible simplism of such positions in the work of people like Hare (1963), Kerner (1966), and von Wright (1963). But it is too optimistic to believe that views of this order no longer have currency in philosophy. What is worse, they live on in large segments of the scientific community and of the culture at large, into both of which contexts such views sifted, against little resistance, a long time ago. Indeed, there is a sense in which such views existed in science and the general culture considerably before they were reborn as technical philosophical formulations. Of course, "emotivism" and "imperativism" must also be seen in the line of subjectivistic views of value in philosophy and, to some extent, psychology, of which they are perhaps the supreme vulgarization. Subjectivistic theories agree in seeing value "constituted" in isolation to the needs, motives, purposes, interests, wants, wishes, of individual persons or organisms: Values are thus regarded as ends or goals of systems of motivation to which they are extrinsic in the very sense described in our earlier analyses of the "extrinsic grammar."

Though sustained analysis in the philosophic mode is not here meet, a few remarks may perhaps clarify certain consequences of the present position. Suppose we start with some such sentence as "That picture is exquisite" or "That action is noble." It is hardly necessary to explain that from the present point of view these propositions are not equivalent (or fairly transformable) to "Picture, wheee!" or "Action, uhhuh!" (the "emotivist" interpretation) or to "Look at that picture!" (or "buy it" or "copy it"), or "Emulate that action!" From the present point of view, such statements are just as much "factual" as, say, "That picture is large" or "That action was rapid." In some sense more "factual" (if one be permitted degrees of "facticity") in that explication, even at relatively gross levels, of the "value properties" which "*in fact*" are governing discriminating application of "exquisite," say in some concrete instance of a complex painting, could in principle convey far more information than explication of the characters by virtue of which the picture may be said to be "large." If the rejoinder be "Yes, but there is still a difference in that virtually every user of a language could apply 'large' correctly (and explicate the basis of its use), whereas in the case of 'exquisite' we can expect much disagreement in application and in explication," then I must refer the questioner back to the entire analysis of definition and meaning of chapter 5. And I must add that the history of art and of taste provides overwhelming evidence that if we compose a hierarchy of language communities for "exquisite" against appropriate criteria of training and sensitivity, we will find impressive intra-community agreements with respect both to application and explication.

One can only conclude that the concept of "fact"—or its linguistic counterpart, as e.g., "factual" or "indicative" statement—is sorely in need of reanalysis. Facts must in some way be conceived as differentially charged with value, and whatever else a value may "be," it is a special kind of fact. Value statements in indicative form are not disguised exclamations or imperatives or, as other subjectivistic theories would have it, expressions of interest, wish, or need. Indeed, it is rather more fruitful to regard value utterances in "normative" or "imperative" form as disguised *indicative statements,* in that, at least when made responsibly, they emerge from a context of knowledge or "belief" within the speaker which could be unpacked into the "factual" or "indicative" statements on which the imperative is grounded.

The last point may be worth further examination. Let us concentrate on the case of a "command." When we give a command, we do this within a context of belief that it will lead to such-and-such consequences for the commander, the commandee, for a third person, for a given group, the "world," etc. Part of that context of belief is a judgment that the intended consequent, or chain thereof, or ultimate consequent is "good," "bad," "desirable," "undesirable" (often in *specific ways*) with respect to such-and-such or so-and-so. Such a judgment can in principle be unpacked into a sequence of meaningful ("factually" or "indicatively" meaningful, if one prefers) propositions re value properties. The mysterious "leap" from the "is" to the "ought" is no mystery. It is no great epistemological profundity that the rules of English do not permit one to say that a "command" is "verifiable." The fact that it is useful for a language to contain specialized forms which register to a hearer that an action, change of belief, or some such thing is being called for, tells us no profound fact about the universe. As we have suggested, the context of knowledge, belief, expectation, etc., from which a command "issues" can be described via a collectivity of "is" statements, a sub-class of which can be said to be indicative of *value properties.* That "is" often signalizes empirically "verifiable" attribution (or predication, etc.), and "ought" obligation (or an "imperative" intent, or imperiousness, sententiousness, arrogance, petulance, prudishness, or passion) is a useful feature of language, but not a regulative principle of the universe.

To repeat, then, the concept of "fact" needs radical revamping: "facts" are suffused with "value"; and "value" diffused in "fact." The last statement is a homespun prolegomenon to a metaphysics. But as a *psychologist,* I can see no other beginning.

Turning now to the relations between values and science — as seen now by the *scientist* — it can be said that the simplisms long accepted by many men of the white cloth exceed in vacuity even the philosophic ones which we have just examined. Thus, it is still something like standard belief that science is concerned exclusively with "neutral" factual relationships, that it seeks "objective" knowledge of invariable associations of observable events, or probably empirical regularities, that it can talk about instrumental relationships or "means-end" relationships, *but can say nothing about ends.* Insofar as the standard patter permits reference to "values," their relevance must be allocated, so to say, to the human or social context in which, for some obscene reason, science happens to be embedded. Thus it is permissible to suggest that the scientist, as a *citizen,* should be concerned with the relation between scientific knowledge and human welfare, that it is desirable that he take an interest in determining that scientific knowledge be applied to "good" social ends and not evil ones, etc. The *very* daring are even now beginning to go so far as to admit that certain moral traits of the *scientist* have a relevance to science — that it is desirable that he have a respect for the "truth," desirable that he not fudge his data.

Perhaps the reader will feel with some indignation that the preceding account is too cynical: has there not, after all, been a great clamor in scientific circles about such matters as the "responsibility of the scientist"? There in fact has, and I would be the last to think it an unhappy development. But *even* those concerned to bring about sharper recognition of the relevance of value factors to science tend to proceed as if the issues can be encapsulated and dispatched in two or three generalizations, or perhaps admonitions. A case in point may be found in C. P. Snow's article on "The Moral Unneutrality of Science" (1961) in which the story comes down pretty much to the fact that scientists respect the truth, and should; that they tend more than most other groups to care about people, inclusive of the poor, and should; that they lead relatively cleaner lives with less divorce than do, on average, members of certain other groups, and should. From another of Snow's contributions (1959), we learn that scientists have "the future in their bones." And should.

In rather marked contradistinction to the stereotypes concerning science-value relations, the present position suggests considerations of the following order: Value-property distributions will suffuse all perception, all meaning; such "parameters" of psychological process do not hygienically cancel out when the context becomes one of science. Scientific languages, no matter how restricted, will generate meanings suffused by value properties; indeed, the languages themselves considered as perceptual objects will also "generate" value properties.

Much of science is concerned with the understanding, explication, or causal analysis of value phenomena — or perhaps more properly, phenomena suffused to one or another extent with value properties. If one were to make a global generalization (requiring marked qualification in certain areas), it could be said that as one ascends the scale from the physical sciences through the biological sciences to the social sciences and finally the humanities, one confronts "subject matters" more and more richly permeated with value properties or, more precisely put, these various subject matters may be ordered in terms of differential concentration upon value-property aspects of each. If it be maintained that those who work at the *scientific* levels are *confined* to *factual* statements about the value "aspects" of their subject matter, then I reply that we have shown conventional usage of "fact" to be either incorrect or systematically ambiguous in the very sense that begs the question. Surely if a scientist discovers a polio vaccine, no semantic prohibition should prevent him from "leaping" from a well-formed and well-evidenced means-end statement to the "ought"-injunction that adds a directive-rider to the cognitive content. If it be maintained that the scientist is still merely making a conditional statement of the form "if you wish (for some damn fool reason) to remain well . . . , etc., etc.," then the uncouth answer might well be that the state of health is self-recommending by virtue of intrinsic value properties.

Consider now the *actual human context of science*. Or better, the human center. Put the scientist, the actor, back in the picture from which he has been for so long excluded. We have argued that value-determining properties are generated by the neural processes which are the substrate of action; that they must in some sense be thought criterial with respect to the moment-by-moment directionality of action. That we can as yet only speak a metaphoric and vague language about such matters has nothing to do with the force of the evidence that recommends such metaphors. In reaching towards understanding, lawful analysis, "control," if you will, of the phenomena which entice their interest, scientists are reaching towards meanings, towards the maximization of certain value properties immanent within those meanings, and throughout are guided by value-determining properties which are some function of the concurrent "input" and their own internal "processings." The latter will reflect, among other factors, those quasi-permanent "structures" that we also sometimes call "values" in the sense manifested by durable preference-dispositions, etc. Values in this sense are often roughly equated with "tastes," "prizings," "attitudes," sometimes with "needs," etc. However such enduring value systems be conceptualized, they may be seen as organizations which govern the moment-to-moment salience, potency, of differential "clusters" or ranges of "specialized" value properties.

Such durable value dispositions (call them Values) will be heavily implicated in the "options" that a scientist asserts in inquiry, the moment-to-moment decisions that he makes. Are such events rare? There is a way of describing inquiry which sees it, and validly so, as a sequence of human options, a flow of decisions. Yet even the obvious Value foci provided by the optional elements in science tend to be bypassed in standard discussions of science and value. Consider the contingency, at all times, of the scientific enterprise on the "aims" of the scientist, on his predilections with respect to choice of "method," both conceptual and empirical, his predilections with respect to mode of problem formulation, his sense of scientific "importance," his perception of the relation between his actions and the standards of his colleagues or the needs of society; his predilections concerning factors in light of which he adjusts his scientific beliefs or assertions to "evidence"; his preferences with respect to modes of theoretical processing, with respect to optimal modes of conduct in the polemical situations of science; and on and on. Hopefully, many of his options are fixed upon in terms of the "rational" productivity of their consequences in the choices of others, present and past. Hopefully, they remain contingent in some degree upon such consequences as experienced in his own biography. But such matters are *choices;* they are *decisions.* Nothing should conceal their determination by processes having marked value components (however these be phrased), nor should anything conceal the value aspects of the web of commitment and dedication which interpenetrates all the activities of scientists.

Paul Dirac has recently been widely quoted as having written, "It is more important to have beauty in one's equations than to have them fit experiment." Polanyi has placed strong and consistent emphasis on what he has called the "harmonious character" of a theoretical conception or set of ideas in guiding its creation, elaboration, productiveness, and fate. Virtually all major creative figures in the history of theoretical physics and of mathematics — and before these, the Pythagoreans — have said something of the same sort. Indeed, it is a *truism* of the "formal" disciplines generally—logic as well as mathematics—that "elegance" is a prime desideratum. And even logical positivists have included on occasion "elegance"—along with "economy" and the like—as a mark of the "fruitfulness" of theory. Can this vast range of agreement point to something purely adventitious? At this inordinately complex and important level too, then, value is criterial with respect to science.

The present analysis may have seemed at times to be absorbing *everything* in science, all of "fact," into value. Perhaps it has in some sense gone too far in this direction: it is not yet easy to talk about such problems. But judging from the circumstances just mentioned, the present account is in good company. What I should like to urge, though, is that, instructive though it be to acknowledge "beauty", "harmony," "elegance," as criterial with respect to scientific theory, to the processes of thinking which result in theory, this is but the beginning of instruction. "Beauty," "harmony," "elegance," land us back within the most global value-abstractions of aesthetics; they are on a par as well with "good" and "right" in ethics. The burden of this chapter has been to urge that the human race cannot forever rest content with so non-specific and gross a level of analysis of its most meaningful accomplishments, prized artifacts, significant phenomena. The concept of value properties may involve no more than an assertion of faith that finer degrees of specification are possible. Yet in our most fluent dialogues with ourselves and with our friends, when they are fluent, we have proved on countless occasions that finer knowledge is possible.

3

STUDIES IN THE PATHOLOGY
OF KNOWLEDGE

7

The Allures of Ameaning
in Modern Psychology

Foreword

This chapter develops the notion — central to all analyses of part 3 — of *ameaningful thinking*, and explores its manifestations in the recent history of psychology. The chapter derives from a Morrison Lecture presented at the Scripps Institute in 1961. It was published in an anthology of Morrison Lectures in 1965 (Koch 1965). It will be evident that I have used the notion of "ameaningful thinking" in many subsequent writings, but in those contexts have been able to develop it only in fragmentary ways. Indeed, the term seems to have been taken up by quite a few psychologists. But only in this initiating paper does it find detailed elucidation and application.

«

Several years ago, while speaking at a public conference at a certain university, I enunciated — in the course of a limp effort at academic wit — the need for progress in a field called "cognitive pathologistics." Within a few minutes an intense young lady from the audience, obviously in distress at having by-passed this area, was asking me for a bibliography. I have since thought of that woman from time to time with a growing realization that the joke was on me. For the few things I have written in the interim seem to be addressed precisely to the task of rescuing that bibliography from the null class. The present chapter continues that task and, in my humble opinion, takes the science of cognitive pathologistics into a new era. The grubby empirical groundwork is over; we are entering our constructive phase; we are at the threshold of a new world view.

Certain strange convictions force me to believe that there are junctures when it is most in the interests of a field of scholarship to bypass its cognitive products — methods, data, findings, concepts, theories — and focus on certain pervasive features of the cognitive *processes* which mediate those products. The first axiom of cognitive pathologistics is one which stresses the limits of *symptomatic* treatment. Should there be deficiencies in cognitive products, despite widespread variability in *certain* of their properties from man to man and era to era, it becomes rational therapeutic policy to look for possible causes in certain pervasive properties of the processes from which they result. It becomes rational, that is, to entertain questions about the habits and style of thinking in the field. If pathology can be located at *such* levels, this would at least put us by way of the terms for the cure.

I will suggest that there is such a pathology in psychology, and phrase it as a tendency towards *ameaningful modes of thinking.* I mean something *very specific* by "ameaningful thinking," but it is hard to delineate in words, to disembed from practice (either one's own or the collective practice of the discipline). It will be apparent that everything I say about ameaning has already been said in some form by others. But not in a form which is truly functional — which enables us to trace the immensity of its ramifications, which gives us the kind of topographic map that we can *feel*. Otherwise there would be less of the phenomenon! I cannot hope to go far towards *such* a delineation. The thing fights us; it refuses to be detected; it tricks us by infecting our weapons.

Because of its elusiveness, I shall be forced to rely on a method of metaphor. Here is an initial fusillade: when we think ameaningfully, there is a tendency to defend ourselves against the object of thought or inquiry, rather than to embrace it; to maintain from it a circumspect distance rather than to become host to it; to master the object of inquiry rather than to understand it; to engage in a transaction with it rather than in a love affair; to use it rather than to savor it. More particularly, ameaningful thought or inquiry regards knowledge as the result of "processing" rather than of discovery; it presumes that knowledge is an almost automatic result of a gimmickry, an assembly line, a "methodology"; it assumes that inquiring behavior is so rigidly and fully regulated by *rule* that in its conception of inquiry it sometimes allows the rules totally to displace their human users. Presuming as it does that knowledge is "generated" by processing, its conception of knowledge is fictionalistic, conventionalistic, "a-ontological." So strongly does it see knowledge under such aspects that it sometimes seems to suppose that the object of inquiry is an ungainly and annoying irrelevance, that knowledge can be created by fiat.

My main concern here is ameaning in *psychology*. But trends towards ameaningful thought can be seen throughout modern scholarly culture and, indeed, in practical life. These trends have deeply affected the sensibility of modern man, and are, I think, related to that de-differentiation of human experience to which a growing army of social critics refer, under such terms as "dehumanization." I think that psychology is a victim of the worldwide trend towards ameaning, and that the general trend had its roots in certain developments in the nineteenth century. Psychology (as well as social science), however, exhibits the trend in an extreme form, largely because of the circumstances of its institutionalization — circumstances to which I shall refer later.

The importance of exploring the ameaning syndrome in psychology is very great, for if ameaningful modes of thought are to be *contained* at world levels, they must, in my opinion, first be contained in psychology. The rationale for this belief seems to me incontrovertible. To "contain" ameaningful thinking means in the first instance to identify, to understand its particularities in an empirically sensitive way; and in the second, to isolate the conditions that can decrease its incidence. If these two problems are not psychological problems, I invite you to name an extant field of scholarship to which they can be relegated. Though there are no strong grounds for optimism about psychology's capacity to do these things, there are, I believe, in the recent atmosphere of our discipline a few signs that the situation could dramatically improve. Some of these I have tried to summarize in my *Epilogue* to Study I of *Psychology: A Study of a Science* (Koch 1959a).

I hope that the relevance of these observations to the problem of science-humanities relations is already clear. If the tendency for ameaningful to displace meaningful modes of thinking *is* a world phenomenon, such tendencies will be evident both in the sciences and in the humanities. It is no good to ask for a closure of the so-called "gap" between these two divisions of inquiry unless we recognize that we must go behind the conventional "ideologies," the codifications of the nature of inquiry, in each and identify their largely ameaningful bases. There is something wrong, something off-center, about modern man's conception of the nature of his own knowledge, and this cannot be put right until the contours of ameaning are localized. In this connection, too, psychology could play a profoundly important, if not the leading role.

235

Meaningful versus Ameaningful Thinking

Shockingly unfashionable though it be relative to the recent tenor of psychology, it is best that we start, in developing points outlined in my introductory remarks, with some simple experiential description. In describing differences between meaningful and ameaningful thinking, I cannot be systematic because we are dealing with phenomena that are too little understood, even at descriptive levels. I cannot be profound because most of us have lost, or have never acquired, the habit of differentiated analysis of our experience, and few have the capacity for analyzing it profoundly. That I cannot be complete is obvious, but I cannot even strive towards completeness because of the need for rapid movement.

These cautions having been observed, let us content ourselves with an extremely crude description of certain characteristics of *extreme* instances of meaningful and of ameaningful thinking.

I shall begin with some rather free descriptions I once made of the consequences for intellectual and creative activity of two very different human motivational states — states which I held to be qualitatively different in ways of the utmost importance to man, and yet recognition of which had been bypassed in conventional motivational theory.[1]

With respect to creative work or intellectual work of any degree of complexity, I cannot distinguish a single continuum of motivational "strength." All I can succeed in doing is roughly to distinguish two qualitatively different "states." This distinction may be "all or none," or it could conceivably be argued that there are two qualitatively different intensity continua, each of rather small compass. Call these states "A" and "B." Specific dated occurrences of these states may, of course, vary in activity content and in temporal spread. The temporal unit may be a matter of a few hours to a few weeks. In making the following observations, I have in mind selected characteristics of relatively long-range A and B states.

State A

I am distractible, flighty, self-prepossessed, rueful over the course of my life and the value choices it has entailed. I feel depressed, continually drowsy, guilty about my purposelessness and general ineffectiveness. The

---

1. The discussion of States A and B below is expanded somewhat from its presentation in the original paper, and is taken from Koch 1956, 65–69. *Eds.*

world is a flaccid structure of neutral tone and value. My responses towards people are bumbling, inert, ineffective, rejective. There is evidence to suggest that I am unpleasant to live with. My self-image constricts into a small desiccated thing: I am physically unattractive, devoid of color, wit, or style. An enormous distance seems to supervene between myself and my most prized values. I am aesthetically desensitized; my system of tastes becomes cheapened and more tolerant.

State A, though partially and casually described here, is a system predicated of and involving the entire person. And the "consequent" of the state which is now the object of interest — performance, with reference to a specified context of creative and intellectual work — is but another part of the same "system."

Under conditions of State A, creative or complex intellectual activity is first of all unlikely. Unfortunately, the conditions of life are such as frequently to demand that it occur. These "conditions" may be endogenously defined as, e.g., guilt, anxiety, or they may be pressures deriving from external agencies, e.g., deadlines, teaching obligations. Either of these classes of conditions can be characterized, if we follow conventional motivational logic, as defining *extrinsic* contexts for the performances that are called for. In other words, if such conditions are effective, *then* I will be working *in order to* relieve guilt, meet a deadline, get a promotion, please a friend. What is the performance like under these circumstances?

I rapidly pass over the fact that under such pressures one passes through innumerable resistances, escape detours, rationalizations, before getting into the problem situation. One may finally "get" or be impelled into the problem situation, but one never, as it were, "gets committed." Thinking is slow, rigid, disorganized, formless, and inelegant. Memory tends towards the "rote" and is saturated with spotty amnesia. Verbalization and writing is unfluent, stilted, imprecise, turgid — either overliteral or overallusive — devoid of wit or flavor. Reading is slow, with much backtracking. The absolute ceiling with respect to the apprehension of complex relationships, the perception of subtle similarities and differences and of meaning nuances, the ability to filter the thought sequence through a complex assemblage of constraints — becomes suffocatingly low.

The unhappy fact about State A, at least for me, is that no manipulation of "extrinsic" conditions, or augmentation in the strength thereof, seems to improve matters much. One remains a prisoner to State A until it runs its course.

State B

Like State A, State B also constitutes a quite specific syndrome. It can be partly characterized as exhibiting the opposite (in some sense) of many of the properties that we attributed to State A. To the extent that this is true, I shall omit the details.

The central and decisive "mark" of State B is domination of the person by the problem context, or, better, by a certain direction defined by the problem context — a "diffuse" but absolutely compelling direction. All systems of personality seem "polarized" into the behavior; thus the personality is either integrated or, in a special sense, simplified, as you will. In State B, you do not merely "work at" or "on" the task; you have *committed yourself* to the task, and in some sense you *are* the task or vice versa.

Perhaps one of the most remarkable properties of B is that thoughts relevant to the problem context seem to well up with no apparent effort. They merely present themselves. The spontaneity and fluency of ideation and the freedom from customary blockages seem similar to certain characteristics of the dream or certain states of near-dissociation. As in these latter conditions, it is often difficult to "fix," hold in mind, the thoughts which occur. In fact, in State B, most of the "effortfulness" or "strain" encountered has to do not with the generation of ideas relevant to the problem context but with their decoding, fixing, or verbalization, and their selection and assemblage with respect to socially standardized requirements of communication. Effortful as such operations may be, verbalization, writing, reading, and all functionally significant breakdowns thereof are at a qualitatively different level from the A state of affairs.

Careful and sensitive descriptive phenomenologies of B states are badly needed — especially from individuals whose B-state products, unlike mine, are *genuinely* "creative." For the present illustrative purpose, I shall merely list a few additional properties of B states, and in some cases contrast them with the dismal state of affairs in A.

1. The B state carries with it tremendous tolerance for fatigue. One can work eight, ten, fourteen hours continuously with no marked subjective fatigue and no evidence of impairment of performance. (In A, two or three hours can be unbearably tiring.) Curiously enough, there seem to be two occasions in the B sequence of a given day when the spontaneous emergence of ideas (the "it thinks" phenomenon) is at a maximum. One is shortly after awakening — even from a sleep produced by strong

sedation. (In A, on the other hand, not an engram begins to twitch until late in the afternoon.) The other occasion is towards the very end of the work sequence, either during its terminal phase, or while preparing for or falling asleep. I might add that the ideas which present themselves on these occasions tend to be, in some sense, the most organized, the most relevant to the problem context, of any in the entire pedestrian array of a given day.

2. It may be of some relevance to note that, in addition to suppression of fatigue, there is marked suppression of hunger and other so-called primary drive conditions. The need for alcohol also decreases markedly.

3. The primary affect-tone of State B is that of mild to strong euphoria. One feels energized but peaceful. Anxiety, in any reportable sense of the term, is minimal or non-existent. In fact, in my experience, one of the essential preconditions (onset conditions) of B is that anxiety be at a minimal level. Should some external or internal factor produce anxiety *during* B, then most characteristics of the state of the sort specified above become disrupted to an extent commensurate with the amount of anxiety.

4. During State B, *any* conditions, whether they arise from the environment or from the self, which define an *extrinsic* context to which the performance is seen as related, tend to produce disruption of B — a deviation of B towards the A state of affairs. Any factor, that is, that leads to an "in order to" consideration, that brackets the work on the task as instrumental to success or accomplishment or relaxation, will tend to throw the B state, in specifiable respects, towards A, and will disrupt or impair the performance. Any anticipation of, or speculation about, the *consequences* to which the finished work might lead — praise, reproof, understanding, misunderstanding, acceptance, rejection — will also vitiate the performance.

Needless to say, the type of intellectual activity described as characteristic of State A would be roughly illustrative of what we are calling *ameaningful* thinking, while the State B activity syndrome would be illustrative of *meaningful* thinking.

I claim nothing original for the preceding descriptions except their rough accuracy relative to my own experience. Most of the characteristics attributed to B activity can be found in virtually every description of the so-called "creative process" on record. It is in fact the commonality of such experiences to all mankind that I wish to stress.

To the preceding descriptions, I wish to add certain additional characteristics which might help discriminate between "high values" of meaningful and ameaningful thinking, respectively.

Meaningful thinking involves the *direct perception* of unveiled, vivid relations which seem to spring from the quiddities, particularities, of the objects of thought, the "problem situations" which form the occasions of thought. There is an intimate, an organic determination of the form and substance of thought by the properties of the object, the terms of the problem. Wertheimer (1945) has emphasized this determination of solution by clearly perceived structural properties of the problem in his analysis of "productive thinking," and has provisionally explored the possibilities of phrasing the movement of productive thinking in terms of certain Gestalt-organizing tendencies; Köhler (1938), in rather less detail, has recognized such phenomena and has considered them in terms of his analysis of "requiredness." The present intention is not to essay causal analysis of the phenomena, but merely to specify further, in what still must be a crude way, certain of their characteristics.

Perhaps the feature most important to stress is one which has already been suggested in various ways. In meaningful thinking, the mind "caresses," flows joyously into, over, around, the relational matrix defined by the problem, the object. Polanyi (1958) talks about the "indwelling" of understanding in the objects of inquiry. Certainly there is a merging of person and object, problem, task: one is *inside* the problem or object; better, one *is* the problem; better still, "*one*" is not — only the problem or object, its terms and relations, exist, and *these* are real in the fullest, most vivid, electric, irrefragable way. It is a fair *descriptive* generalization to say that meaningful thinking is in some primitive, accepting, artless, unselfconscious sense *ontologistic* in character. Whether the problem pertain to natural events, human experience, organismic action, to the artifacts (symbolic or otherwise) of individual or social human effort; whether the problem be analytic or creative, practical or theoretical, scientific, aesthetic, mathematical, or personal — meaningful thinking, while it is taking place, perceives its objects directly and spontaneously as inhabiting a universe; as existent facts, as having ontological status. Moreover, it perceives its objects as *valued entities,* or more precisely as having concrete and differentiated value properties which themselves are an objective and irrefragable part of the world.

Coming now to *ameaningful thinking,* its marks are suggested by such adjectives as extrinsically-occasioned or forced, rigid, nonfluent, relatively formless, undifferentiated, grossly instrumental, unspontaneous, rote, rule-bound, psychologically *a-ontologistic*. The movement of thought is slow, its purview relatively narrow; a great distance seems to supervene between the person and the object of knowledge. The terms and relations of the object of inquiry or the problem are seen, as it were, through an inverted telescope: detail, structure, quiddity, are obliterated; relative to the state of affairs in highly meaningful thinking, objects of knowledge become caricatures, if not faceless. Being caricatures, being faceless — they lose reality; they are not inhabited by the mind, not caressingly explored in that they have little interest or color. They are dealt with, conjured with, arranged into relatively gross means-end or antecedent-consequent relationships. The world becoming relatively flaccid, the object of knowledge becoming relatively indistinct, the world or any given part of it is not felt fully or passionately, is perceived as devoid of objective value. "Cognitive anesthesia" might be a clinical designation of this latter condition.

The two features of ameaningful thinking that I most wish to stress are its *"a-ontologism"* and its *rule-bound* character. Its *a-ontologism* we have just tried to convey. To the extent that the object of knowledge is apprehended in a faceless, undifferentiated way, its object-character dissipates. The object or problem is perceived as having little reality, little interest, little (or neutral) value. The *rule-bound* nature of ameaningful thinking follows from its forced, unfluent character. Since it is usually motivated by extrinsic pressure or practical exigency, it will carry analysis only to some minimum point compatible with the "handling" of the exigency in question. But even such analysis poses a challenge, demands effortful activity. Ameaningful thinking thus tends to rely obsessively on crutches: rules, codes, prescriptions, stable stratagems for the processing of knowledge, rigid methods. In extreme forms, ameaningful thinking tends to become obsessive and magical. Its rule-dependency calls for, and over time generates, rationales or ideologies, mystiques of "systematicity," of impeccable, clean, hygienic, presumably rational, irrefragable orderliness.

Meaningful thinking in its "highest" forms — I do not mean highest relative to a population, but relative to an individual ceiling — occurs with extreme rarity at best. As we know from the protocols even of highly gifted, creative individuals, its incidence can be maximized only by the most conscientious and delicate husbanding — by arrangements for work which often strive to realize a most intricate concatenation of environmental and personal variables. For *any* individual, the incidence of highly meaningful thought "episodes," though rare at best, can be modified. If it is valued, meaningful thinking can be "sought" by learning, and causing to be realized, the circumstances that bear some probability relation to its occurrence. Highly meaningful thought episodes, as we have described them, represent a kind of process syndrome; no doubt they can be triggered only under special biological and neural conditions of the organism, some (but *not* all) of which are accessible to control.

A corollary to the preceding statements is that the statistical incidence of highly meaningful thinking in populations, whether these be sub-parts of a society or culture, entire societies or cultures, or indeed, populations "defined" by historical epochs, is within limits variable. Lamentably, the nature of the phenomenon is such that its incidence can probably more easily be made to decrease than to increase. It is now possible to state one of the central theses of this chapter. For any population, the relative incidence of highly meaningful or ameaningful thinking will be determined to a large extent by the values which the group places upon either. Such values will, of course, be embedded in the ideologies or rationales of knowledge-seeking behavior dominant in the group, and will pervade all institutions and agencies which influence intellectual or scholarly style, habit, sensibility.

The besetting cognitive problems of a culture, a sub-culture, an era, can thus be very much a reflection of whatever factors lead to the relative valuation of meaningful and ameaningful thinking. One must even face the possibility that cultures can arise which place so limited a value upon meaningful thinking that many of its members are deprived absolutely of the possibility of achieving "high" orders of meaningful thought relative to their capacities, or of discriminating such states, should they occur, as in some sense valuable or even different from ameaningful thinking. It will be my contention that something very much like such a culture has arrived and that the culture in question is the world culture of the twentieth century.

Ameaning in Modern Psychology

Before documenting the portentous statement just made on the extravagant scale of generality demanded by its sweep, it is best that we consider the somewhat more modest problem of ameaning in *psychology*. For, as I have suggested, the case of psychology can give us a firmer purchase on ameaning than virtually any other subdivision of the scholarly community.

I intensely dislike saying what I now must, because it can so easily be misinterpreted. To chart in a few pages the contours of ameaning in psychology *responsibly*—which means not only in scholarly detail, but with charity, awareness of the historical inevitabilities that have formed the field from *without,* and discriminating recognition of the genuine advances which, despite all, have been made—is impossible.

It is dizzying to decide where to enter the syndrome of ameaning presented by modern psychology, and on which of the innumerable symptoms to train attention. I will choose indicators relevant to the two features of ameaningful thinking that have been most stressed—rule-dependency and a-ontologism.

Rule-Dependency

That modern psychology is dominated by a dependence on and concern for method, that this is rooted in deep security needs and betrays the desire for the respect accorded by society to the older natural sciences, is pretty well known on both sides of the science-humanities barricades. What is not known is the *magnitude* and ramifications of this dependence and certain particularities of its impact on the history of psychology.

Of profound importance to the story of psychology's method-dependence are the circumstances of its institutionalization as an independent science (as discussed in chapter 4, pp. 124–126). At the time of its inception, *psychology was unique in the extent to which its institutionalization preceded its content and its methods preceded its problems.* If there are keys to history, this statement is surely a key to the brief history of modern psychology. Never had a group of thinkers been given so sharply specified an invitation to create. Never had inquiring men been so harried by social need, cultural optimism, extrinsic prescription, by the advance scheduling of ways and means.

Now I do not want to be interpreted as saying that method per se—even one formed in advance of its locus of application—is a bad thing. Man's capacity to evaluate his own inquiring action, to form generalizations upon its worth, integrity, the efficacy of its relations to his ends in view, is one of his most inspiring capacities and powerful cognitive tools. Methodic thinking can of course be either meaningful or ameaningful. And the *application* of method to first-order inquiring action can be carried out either meaningfully or ameaningfully. What is truly sad, however, is that there are circumstances under which a meaningful method can be applied ameaningfully. And indeed, if the history of inquiry be any guide, any *rigid* and *undeviating* reliance on method, however meaningful in the first instance relative to the locus of its "discovery," can get the inquirer into trouble.

There is a kind of scientism which is the most rational and *meaningful* policy available to man. It is the kind that sees rules as *guides*, not recipes, for action. It is the kind that sees the application of a rule as more the story of the applier's action than of the rule. It is the kind that clearly recognizes that rules are templates through which action is somehow squeezed, while in this process of squeezing, the templates themselves are continually bent and twisted — sometimes in ways which make apparent the need for new ones. This kind of scientism deeply knows that in the development of a science the decisive question is the nicety of interplay between present extensions of the methodic past and present inventions of the methodic future.

Few who look fairly at the brief history of our science could agree that this balance between tradition and creative innovation — prescription and production, discipline and decision — has for any sizable interval been optimal. From the earliest days of the experimental pioneers, man's stipulation that psychology be adequate to *science* outweighed his commitment that it be adequate to man. From the beginning, some pooled schematic image of the *form* of science was dominant: respectability held more glamour than insight, caution than curiosity, feasibility than fidelity or fruitfulness. A telling consequence — even in the early days when such trends were qualified by youth — was the ever-widening estrangement between the scientific makers of human science and the humanistic explorers of the content of man. It is, for instance, significant that a Freud, when he arrived, did not emerge from the laboratories of nineteenth-century experimental psychology; nor was the ensuing tradition of work particularly hospitable to his ideas until rendered desperate by the human vacuum in its own content.

The history of psychology, then, is very much a history of changing views, doctrines, images, about *what to emulate in the natural sciences* — especially physics. In the nineteenth century, this meant the *extension* of experimental method to subjective phenomena; for early behaviorism it meant the *use* of experimental method exactly as in physics (objectively). By the late twenties, there was much objective experimentation, but few bodies of clearly stated predictive principles comparable to the crowning achievement of physics: its theories. Instead, experimentation sometimes seemed aimless, "theoretical" hypotheses but loosely related to data, and debate idle. We thus get, beginning around 1930, the emulation of natural science's *theoretical method*.

Our best insight into the method-fetishism of modern psychology can be derived from the period marked by the hegemony of behaviorism. At least in American psychology the period 1913 through 1930, though not without strife among contending schools, came quite rapidly to be dominated by behaviorism. The period 1930 until about 1960 saw the ascendancy of neobehaviorism. There is no need, I am sure, to summarize what behaviorism has stood for. Its framework commitments concerning exclusive reliance on "objective" data, on the behavior of the "other"; its anti-experientialism; its disposition to phrase all lawful relations of legitimate interest to psychology in terms of stimuli and responses; its reliance on exclusively peripheral hypotheses for the explanation of such complex "behavior" forms as thinking — all this is well known inside and even outside psychology. Such framework commitments were retained by the neobehaviorists, but elaborated into detailed "theoretical" structures in accordance with the dictates of a *theoretical methodology* presumed to represent, in the first instance, a generalization of the practice of physics. Naturally, psychology did not go directly to physics for this model, but turned instead for its directives to middlemen. These were, in the main, philosophers of science (especially logical positivists) and a number of physical science methodologists who had been codifying a synoptic view of the nature of science and who, by the early thirties, were actively exporting that view from within their specialties to the scholarly community at large. The view is based on a logical reconstruction of a few selected formulations in theoretical physics and puts forward a detailed model of the scientific enterprise which has come to be known as the "hypothetico-deductive method."

The hypothetico-deductive model represents science as *self-corrective*, and seems to offer itself as a more or less painless instrumentality for scientific advance. It was seized upon with passion by the dominating psychologists of the early thirties in the ardent desire to escape from the futile and rather stagnant controversies of the "schools" of an earlier era. Neobehaviorism can be said to have involved a marriage of behaviorist framework commitments with the hypothetico-deductive model. But psychologists of other conceptual predilections followed suit in accepting the hypothetico-deductive model and other aspects of logical-positivist doctrine in one or another degree. It can thus fairly be said that the methodic horizons, and indeed the more general scientific aims of systematic psychology, were set from the early thirties on by logical positivism and by such related groups of ideas as operationism and neo-pragmatism. I have called the interval from roughly 1930 to roughly 1960 the "Age of Theory," in that all activities were subordinated to the production of a "commodity" called "theory" *in a quite special sense defined by the age.* It is as if something called "theory" became an end in itself—a bauble, a trinket—of which it was neither appropriate nor fair, and certainly most naïve, to inquire into its human relevance. Indeed, most formulations of the era were based on animal data, and some haughtily claimed a restriction of reference to animal, usually rat, behavior. Many other procedural and epistemological agreements existed during this interval; these I leave to your knowledge, or your imagination if you be not a psychologist.

Latterly, the methodic agreements and certain of the substantive ideas of the Age of Theory have been under considerable attrition. This is evidenced by many developments in the psychological literature since the early fifties and emerges with especial force in *Psychology: A Study of a Science* (Koch 1959b, 1962b, 1963). Though a hopeful sign, the attrition for the most part is cautious and indirect, and consists rather more in a decrease of optimism with respect to the imminent and grandiose conquest of the major problems of the field, via the Age of Theory methods, than it does in a relinquishment of the method-fetishism that had sustained the earlier optimism. There has, for instance, been a change of imagery in the direction of modesty: an example would be the tendency to talk of "models" rather than "theories." Again, many no longer take hypothetico-deductive method in all of its detail seriously as a feasible guide for action. I most definitely do not wish to undervalue these changes and the many other more important ones which we here have no time to discuss. There is in the present period a wider dispersion of methodic and, what is more important, *substantive* ideas than perhaps ever before in our discipline. This *could* presage a significant change in the climate of the field, including a reduction of method-fetishism, but there is *also*—I speak on present evidence, not merely extrapolation from our past—a chance that new methodic orthodoxies will congeal. If there were ever a time at which sensitization to the problem of ameaning might have a salutary effect, it is now, at the present choice-point.

But all this sounds innocuous. How can we make method-fetishism graphic? I shall consider scattered Age of Theory examples. I only wish I could develop each in sufficient detail to give it life.

1. The hypothetico-deductive (and similar) models of scientific action are said to be *self-corrective* in the sense that the progressive interplay of postulates, derivations, and the experimental confirmation or disconfirmation of the latter should in the long run lead to a progressive refinement and sharpening of the postulate set. This is perfectly true as a statement of the abstract *ideal* properties of this procedural model. The model, bear in mind, is a *logical reconstruction*. But when the model is *applied* by a human user who essays a hypothetico-deductive theory, it is not the model that corrects the theory, but the user. I apologize for stating so obvious a fact. But it is hardly an exaggeration to say that during the heyday of hypothetico-deductive theory this rudimentary distinction was not preserved. The construction of a theory is an intensely creative task, and if its basic hypotheses do not demarcate significant (and hopefully, profound) regularities in the universe, there can be no hope whatsoever that the methods of its elaboration and testing, no matter how impeccable, will per se bring it any closer to adequacy. Yet, during the Age of Theory (and even still), there were many votaries of one or another of the dominant hypothetico-deductive "formulations" whose rejoinder to critics who questioned the empirical *plausibility* of their postulates was that such considerations were irrelevant. For, it would be pointed out with some hauteur, if the postulates were inadequate, this would ultimately be exposed and corrected by the inexorable processes of hypothetico-deductive machinery. Indeed, it was often maintained with passion that the principal requirement for a good theory was that it be *definite* and formally impeccable. The *meaning* of its assumptions was a secondary consideration, if at all relevant.

Such contentions hardly require an answer. But if there were time, it would be much fun to establish what should be a highly sobering fact: that a theory which begins with arbitrary, off-center, ameaningful, or artifactual assumptions can, when operated upon in ways from which rigorous men have not been exempt — can, with no apparent violation of the rules — progressively become more and more inadequate. Indeed, such a deteriorating state of affairs can be enthusiastically made to persist for years.

2. It should now be noted that during the entire interval of almost universal hypothetico-deductive frenzy, very few theories were actually put forward in a way approximating the literal details of hypothetico-deductive form. Moreover, of these *none* came close to passing the tests demanded by the logic of science for even minimal *formal* adequacy (let alone adequacy of substance). I once tried to show this in a lengthy analysis (Koch

1954) of the theory generally acknowledged to be the most formally advanced put forward in the history of psychology—Hull's theory of behavior. Defenders of this theory, and even some neutrals, took the position that no scientific theory could survive so demanding an analysis. Perhaps they were right, but Hull had set his objectives, modeled his theory, on precisely such demands, and the general presumption in the field was that the demands had been satisfied. Moreover, their point was rather general. Not a few of my demands were rather weak ones: for instance, I discovered that different parts of one of the major postulates contradicted each other, thus canceling out the possibility of *using* a postulate intended to function in every concrete prediction mediated by the system. But it is not my intention to pursue this matter here—Hull's system was a truly manful attempt to realize the hypothetico-deductive method in psychology, and it ultimately demonstrated once and for all that the hypothetico-deductive method in its classical form is not feasible for our discipline.

Hull's attempt had real grandeur; the main point I want to make at this juncture is on the grotesque side. It is that the hypothetico-deductive frenzy was mainly a frenzy for a terminology. The field's need for "system" was resolved in a verbal imagery-system. What occurred was a mass "as-if" phenomenon with an elision of the "as-if." People talked a crisp, reassuring game of postulates, derivations, theorems, rules of inference, explicit definitions, coordinating definitions, operational definitions, etc. Since the hope for *mathematical* systematization ran high, this was supplemented by incantatory use of terms like variable, constant, parameter, function, equation, often in absolutely metaphorical contexts.

3. Cross-cutting the hypothetico-deductive image system (but reconcilable with it) was a gimmickry which purported to show certain major features of any strategy for building a theory in psychology: the major classes of variables that were necessary, where they were to come from, how their "explicit" functional interrelations were to be determined. This schema went so far as to include a standard method for inferring postulates from experimental evidence. I refer to the *intervening variable paradigm* for the construction of psychological theory, put forward by Tolman in the mid-thirties and taken over by many of the influential theorists of the Age of Theory. Psychologists will know what I mean by the intervening variable paradigm; non-psychologists need not for the present purpose. The point is that the intervening variable was supposed to ensure great generality or economy of statement of postulates; it was supposed to ensure, also, a clear-cut and secure relationship between theoretical concepts and empir-

ical evidence such that the theory would always generate its predictions via explicit *rules* and not through the intuitive whim of the theorist or applier.

It should now be noted that most major theories of the era — of the Age of Theory — *did* put forward their assumptions in the form of intervening variable functions, sometimes quantitatively specified ones. These functions were often advanced as having unbridled generality, as holding for "all" organismic behavior. Actually, though, these assumptions were rarely based on more than one experiment, usually a rat experiment, in which the behavior studied had a necessarily local and situation-bound character (even for the species). It took approximately *twenty-five years* of this sort of thing for the suspicion to dawn (even then, only in a few people) that the postulates and intervening variables so obtained were very possibly not much less local than the data on which they were based. Actually, in 1959 Tolman himself, the originator of intervening variable doctrine, finally pointed to this drab prospect and indicated that intervening variables could be conceived as "merely an aid to thinking ('my thinking,' if you will)" (Tolman 1959, 148). And in the same volume, Neal Miller, another outstanding theorist, called sharply into question the empirically warranted *generality* of all intervening variable functions so far put forward by any theorist whomsoever, by making an acute analysis of the "[e]xperimental design required but seldom used to justify intervening variables" (Miller 1959, 276–80).

One could go on in this vein indefinitely, but psychologists will be able to fill out the picture to any extent that their comfort will allow, while non-psychologists will certainly have the general point, not to mention an accumulation of boredom, already in hand. These examples make fairly clear, I think, what I mean by method-fetishism in psychology. And I expect you will have noticed by now that these examples have also put us well on the way towards an understanding of a-ontologism in psychology.

A-ontologism

Rule-dependence, in the amplitude in which we have been observing it, can hardly be rendered intelligible if we do not assume it to be organically related to a-ontologism. To believe that knowledge can be conjured into existence by method *to this extent* presupposes a special set of attitudes towards the nature of knowledge. Only if one conceives the object of inquiry as a pallid, distant, faceless thing; only if our explanatory concepts are fictions which somehow, by fortune or fiat, enable us to order whatever experience we have; only if one phenomenon, problem, has approximately the same flaccid interest as another; only if we are locked within a world of language, the meanings of which are compounded from a few gross observable inputs — only then can we conceivably assume that method, given as little human help as already noted, can *create* knowledge. Method-fetishism in the degree to which it exists in psychology means, in short, that investigators have little respect for the objects of inquiry, the subject matter of their discipline.

There was a time in the history of the West when a naïve belief was widespread to the effect that there is a relation between knowledge and truth; that what we are after in intellectual pursuits is to discover, know, record, creatively express truth. The premise of a-ontologism is far more sophisticated: it assumes that truth is manufactured, and manufactured more by method than by man. To preserve this assumption, the line between autism and knowledge, subject and object, grows dim. Wherever a problem appears refractory to a revered method, the problem is denied. As time goes on, there occurs a massive retreat from subject matter. Problems begin to be selected and formulated against criteria which preguarantee the apparent success of the method. A progressive trivialization of research sets in. Ultimately, the touchstone of a method, of a theory bearing the hallmark of that method, is its capacity to "generate research" in some generalized, neutral-pap sense of the term. A quantitative research-productivity standard becomes established for evaluating the success of a theory, a method. The nature, significance, illumination-value, relevance to human problems of the research in question is not at issue; research is research. The workforce is large and eager.

A-ontologism, then, ultimately comes down to a strange kind of subjectivism, such that in the names of *objectivity,* Science, rigor, method, the most extreme autisms are brought into being. Subject matter is conquered by evasion, distortion, or denial; the trivial becomes the profound and vice-versa — all this under the impeccable aegis of method. Perhaps the a-ontologism of modern psychology may best be illustrated by two series of brief examples, one suggested by various problems raised by the history of behaviorism, the other based on the tendency of psychology to employ what we shall call "simplistic models."

A-ontologism in Behaviorism

The demonstration of a-ontologism as severe in psychology would hardly have to go further than the disenfranchisement of experience as a legitimate object of inquiry stipulated by Watson in 1913 and observed almost absolutely in American psychology until only a few years ago, when an appreciable, but still small number of dissidents began to question the doctrine. I do not wish to get caught up in a discussion of behaviorist epistemology at the present time, except to say that it was never tenable, never consistent, and was based on shifting rationales; that from it were adduced the most various prescriptions for inquiring action; and that at every point in history it was naïve relative to the philosophical analyses it leaned on for authority. The dogma was sustained by one thing and one thing only, and this is vividly suggested in the imagery chosen by Watson in his first presentation of the behaviorist position when he announced his intention to make psychology a "purely objective, experimental branch of natural science" (Watson 1913, 158). I am not saying that there were not aspects of the "school" psychology from which Watson was in revolt that rendered his attitudes rational in some degree, but that is not the issue here. What *is* the issue is that we have in this one doctrine the most stupendous instance of a-ontologism in the history of science, an example of cognitive denial so sweeping that one would have to look to primitive magic to find a precedent.

What also should concern us here—though this is so obvious as hardly to require statement—is what this dogma has meant with respect to the prospects for psychology's confronting phenomena of humanistic import. During behaviorism's forty-year hegemony, it was rare of course that any significant human problem was approached, at least in fundamental psychology. But a more pernicious effect has been this: any discipline that for forty years has shied away from experiential analysis must generate a conceptual language which renders virtually impossible a differentiated exploration of the content of man. The categories of thought, of analysis, of such a discipline must structuralize phenomena in such artificial, crass, and "grainy" terms as to be almost wholly inapplicable to a *meaningful* subject matter. In consequence, now that a growing number of people in our discipline have a disposition to embrace human, and even experiential problems, what happens? A kind of middlebrow simplism takes over, in which the ruling presuppositions, categories of analysis, and so on, are such that problems are defined grossly, "solutions" are often structural and rather hollow. Even super-dissidents, who wish more strongly than ever to dig out from behaviorism, find their thinking imprinted with the grain of its concepts, and their talk sounding the clang of its language.

The preceding points take us by natural transition to another example of the kind of a-ontologism motivating, embedded in, and fostered by behaviorism. As is well known, this hard-headed school, with its obsessive eagerness to be objective and to talk the language of physical science, has phrased all lawful relationships of psychology in terms of stimulus and response. As is also well known, there have been multiple and serious ambiguities in the definition and use of these terms for more than seventy years. Bear in mind that in *all* behavioristic systems — classical and neo-classical — these are the end-terms of analysis (the independent and dependent variables), while in most of the systems all other conceptual entities introduced (the intervening variables) are of the nature of sub-specifications of stimulus and response "processes." In other words, all these theories talk about stimuli and responses and little else. Yet throughout the history of such formulations there have been serious, and most of the time *neglected,* ambiguities in the definition of stimulus and response. The a-ontology here hardly needs spelling out.

Taking the matter a bit further, let us note in the simplest terms the basis of these persisting difficulties with S and R. The problem started with Watson. He gave two quite distinct and not easily collatable criteria of stimulus and two of response. The first criterion for stimulus is the way Watson would like to have it. This is the physical energy criterion, a measurable physical energy, or change thereof, which is known to have the capacity to excite specialized receptors of a sense organ. He would like to have it this way because this is objective, physical, quantitative, and manipulatable. The first criterion for response has precisely the same virtues: this is the physiological criterion of contraction of muscle spindles or secretion of glands. Yet, as Watson points out in another part of his argument, he wants his psychology to be able to predict such states of affairs as individuals taking food, building a house, swimming, writing a letter, building a skyscraper, drawing plans, having babies, writing books. (These are Watson's actual examples.) And he is apprised that to them he must relate such "complex" antecedent conditions as total (one would have to say "perceived") environmental contexts of one sort or another, e.g., "words and sentences of a language," "the printed score of a Beethoven symphony." He effects this by saying that when "the factors leading to reaction are more complex, as, for example, in the social world, we speak of *situation.*" Analogously, "we employ in psychology the physiological term 'response,' but again we must slightly extend its use." For the "complex responses" such as have been illustrated, the suggested term is "adjustment" (Watson 1919, 10–12). As is known to all, Watson simply assumed out of hand that his "situations" and "adjustments" were analyzable into, or composable from, his stimuli and responses and, of course, that laws based on the simple stimuli and responses will hold for the complex. The problems thereby raised ramified throughout the subsequent history of behaviorism.

Some writers rose to them by the ingenious device, already illustrated, of denial. During the period of neobehaviorism, there was a tendency to face these problems more stalwartly, but many of the answers remained Pickwickian, while usage remained inconstant. More recently, during a phase that might be called neo-neobehaviorism, modal practice has been to reject Watson's *first* and/or physiological criteria of S and R, and to stick with fair consistency to criteria similar to Watson's second pair, those constitutive of "situation" and "adjustment." Indeed, there is even a tendency to acknowledge that such molar and patterned events cannot in important instances be measured or recorded by a physical gimmickry, but depend for their identification on the perceptual sensitivities of human observers.

Attendant upon the use of stimulus, response, and derivatives as the almost exclusive language of psychological description and theoretical analysis, has been a well-known evolution of *word-fetishism,* having striking a-ontologistic nuances. Those hardy individuals who did approach human phenomena soon found the counters of behaviorist thought rather too restricted for their nefarious purposes. After all, even Watson's *second* pair of criteria did set up the notion of S and R in ways which bore *some* functional relation to end-organ activity. There thus commenced a lush tradition for extending the reference of S and R, often in ways involving stupendous distortions of ontology. By a point quite early in the game, every mentalist category distinguished in the history of thought, including, I think, the medieval cholers, had been phrased either as a stimulus or a response, or both. Of particular interest is a tendency which is at once a sign of a very promising "liberalization" among neo-neobehaviorists, and a fearsome indication of the persistence of a-ontologism.

Stimulus-response theory, in its early and neobehaviorist phase, had almost completely bypassed the study of perception and, more generally, central (brain-dependent) process. Beginning in the early fifties, certain S-R theorists began to will these fields back into existence, and by now there is a massive convergence of interest in such applications of the S-R approach. The strategy employed by these theorists (not unanticipated in earlier behaviorism, but never explored in detail) runs like this: if events outside the skin, known as "stimuli," in their associations with events at the periphery of the organism, known as "responses," have yielded certain stable "laws" of behavior, why cannot all this useful information be applied to the (externally unobservable) events *inside* the organism, including micro-events in the brain, and even certain correlated occurrences that had been called "experiential" by medievalists (and still bruited to be vaguely about in certain furtive "verbal reports"). The idea, then, is to test the hypothesis that the lawful S-R relationships discovered at the periphery of the organism also hold in the center.

My concern here is not with the logic of that hypothesis, the evaluation of which is a tricky affair. But to continue with that part of the story here relevant: if such a hypothesis is to be tested, then there must be stimuli and responses in the brain. Now, even an audience composed wholly of humanists will, I think, follow when I say there are no sense organs or muscles in the brain. This mildly refractory ontological circumstance has lessened the élan of these theorists not at all. What possible objection could the brain have to being furbished with stimuli and responses? Thus we get the family of analyses that phrase central events in terms of one or another so-called S-R mechanism (all of them quite similar). The general idea is that a second S-R system, or more properly, R-S system, is interpolated between the peripheral stimulus and the response. The interpolated response corresponds to a neural event, or a molar-perceptual or cognitive process which is some function of neural events. This is controlled by the peripheral stimulus and in turn controls the final overt response. Since present neurophysiology makes it clear that neural impulses in the central nervous system get implicated in complex interactive and reverberatory circuits, the R's generously imputed to the grey matter are supposed also to give rise to correlated S's (on the analogy to response-produced stimulation of the sort, say, involved in kinesthesis), while these S's, of course, can lead to further R's. A typical analysis of this sort is presented by Neal Miller. He makes it clear that his notion of "central response," so-called, leaves him free *"to exploit"* (note the language!) such matters as images, "perceptual responses," "the possibility that central responses can contribute to the focusing of attention," thinking, and many other matters (Miller 1959, 242).

Simplistic Models

The great successes of early modern science were associated with a pattern of analysis intended to reduce natural phenomena to their simplest possible terms, and then to answer questions concerning them by means of an artificial simplification of nature in which those terms were realized. Such an account is, of course, so incomplete as to be question-begging. For instance, what do we mean by "simple terms"? How do we arrive at them? Is any old set of terms or "variables" good enough so long as they are "simple"? Must there not be some kind of relevance of the analytic variables to the phenomena? Obviously, any adequate discussion of the modern analytico-experimental method considers such questions and many others. But, from the modern history of psychology, it would seem that psychologists had not.

Having early perceived that science proceeds via analytic simplification, psychology apparently decided that the content of an analytic model relative to the properties of the subject matter domain is irrelevant, and that all that counts is the degree of simplicity. It also apparently decided that it could find double indemnity by choosing subject matter domains, objects of inquiry, not much less simple than the projected analytic model. In consequence, the characteristic strategy of fundamental psychology has been to look for delimited research areas which seem to be yielding stable functional relationships. It was important that the variables involved in the experiments in these areas seem determinately and easily manipulatable or measurable, that the situations be such as to give promise of high degrees of control of extraneous factors, that quantitative or statistical technique seem readily applicable, and so on. The tactic would then be to attempt a theoretical simplification of such data by reducing them to a smaller number of presumably more fundamental variables and their relations (the analytic model). From these, it was hoped deductions could be made that would be relevant not only to new, and perhaps more specific, phenomena within the original induction base, but relevant also to quite other ranges of phenomena and, hopefully, all behavior. The history of the use of conditioned response research is an excellent example of this strategy.

An alternate, and in some ways more expeditious, strategy has been merely to forget about psychological phenomena completely and search outside the discipline for a pre-made analytical model in some prestigious field like physics, certain areas of mathematics, or latterly, engineering, and see whether it could be made to fit within psychology. Should a fit, even in the most tenuous degree, be established to any domain of data within psychology, the presumption is that a profound thing has happened and that the bridgehead must now be extended, wheresoever it may lead, if anywhere. A well-known set of examples is the models of the cybernetic family.

Some day, but not here, I would like to do an analysis of the questions raised by the "strategies" just loosely described. What I wish most to emphasize here is that no meaningful scientific simplification, on *any* criterion of the meaningful, has an *arbitrary* relation to *what* is being simplified. Moreover, the entire question of what is simple and what complex needs careful analysis. The abysmal presumption, prompted by the a-ontologism of our field, that one set of phenomena is as good as another for analytic attack, provided only that it is expeditiously researchable, must be examined. It is very possibly the case, for instance, that psychology will not be able to isolate significant variables (even for application to phenomena now considered "simple") in any other way than by serious and *meaningful* study of phenomena now considered complex. It is my hunch, for instance, that the analysis of human experience and behavior at such apparently complex levels as aesthetic and creative functioning may be an indispensable condition for the isolation of variables which might give *meaningful* knowledge about *simpler* functioning. And it goes without saying that the understanding of human performances *at* such levels as I have just mentioned can begin to come about *only* by the gallant expedient of granting their existence and studying them. It is highly dubious that we will ever discover worthwhile knowledge about man in his most valued and presumably complex performances, by trying in some sense to recompose them from laws based on what we *now* regard as simple phenomena. The reverse is far more likely, an argument which is developed in chapter 6 in the context of the field of motivation.

No model, no set of analytic variables intended to organize a domain, whatever it be, *meaningfully,* can be expected to bear fruit *merely* because it is simple. It must also be in some sense true (the properties of the model must be in some sort of isomorphism with the properties of the domain). This is most unlikely to come about by mere chance. The knower must think meaningfully, must try to disembed constant relational attributes of the phenomena in the domain and "see" their interdependencies. He must grant the existence of the domain, he must respect its reality, he must caress with his mind its relational contours. There is no gimmickry for this, no methodology, but I think it already possible to make such things less mysterious than might appear from the extravagance of my metaphors. Appropriately enough, an analysis of one of the most a-ontologistic contexts of recent psychological thought — the problem of how we "define" (that is, introduce and link to the empirical world) psychological concepts — already promises a start in this direction (cf. chapter 5).

As a final symptom of ameaning in my sampling, I point to one which in a way symbolizes all others. This is the appalling tendency, among individuals at all levels of training and sophistication in our discipline, in effect to identify our discipline with a set of sentences rather than a set of immensely exciting phenomena, objects of inquiry. I remember the first day I taught a class admonishing my students that we are "all walking psychological laboratories." For the revolting form of this figure of speech I now, fifty years after, ask your indulgence. As for its meaning, I still think it admirable, but I must confess that I had not notably lived by this injunction before it was delivered into my mouth, nor did I for an unconscionable time thereafter. It is almost incredible in a discipline as young as ours that we all seem to restrict thinking to what others have thought about, "found," "worked on," "reported," organized into "theoretical formulations," programmatic pronunciamentos, methodological stipulations, etc. Our occasional frightened sorties into the world of phenomena are more like visits to a stuffy and rather badly compiled museum. We see not living quiddities which invite wonder, commitment, and our best sensitivities, but *exhibits*, exhibits of phenomena too well studied by other men with too little passion.

Ameaning in World Culture

It would be ameaningful of me to apologize for the level of discourse now forced upon me. Breathlessly, then:

It has been creditable of C. P. Snow (1959) to dramatize the fact that in the modern world scientists and humanists form two largely insulated "cultures." And he has given a portrait of two mythic characters — heroes of the modern world — the philistine scientist and the woolly and scientifically illiterate humanist.

It is Snow's belief — and here there is almost a consensus among concerned people — that one settles the problem mainly by the production of double personalities. That is, one pumps humanistic knowledge into scientists and vice versa. This is handled either via appropriate curricular adjustments or — for victims of the older educational order — through remedial reading of the relevant category.

I have already pointed out elsewhere (Koch 1961b, 636–37) that I think this solution so limited as to be almost beside the point. Few people have gone *behind* the "two cultures" and inquired deeply into the basis of the antagonism. And more importantly, few have considered the possibility that there may be something wrong with the ideology, the sets of procedural rationales, the imagery-systems of *either* culture, or perhaps both. Such deficiencies of ideology could, of course, reflect deficiencies already present in creative or inquiring action, and at the same time could, by heuristic effect, easily promote a further deterioration of inquiry. Considerations like these make it profoundly important to reassess present and recent conceptions of the nature of knowledge in both the sciences and the humanities, and indeed, in practical life or anywhere else. Short of intense and creative commitment to such issues, no rational policy — if policy be possible — concerning man's cognitive future can be formed.

By this point it is hardly a secret that I hold the deficiencies in our conception of knowledge, and in the pursuit thereof, to be intimately linked with ameaningful modes of thinking. I have said that especially since the late nineteenth century the relative incidence of ameaningful thinking has increased. I have seen psychology as an accelerated instance of this trend, and thus have been able to use psychology as a kind of clinical exhibit of the resulting syndrome. In one or another degree, however, the same syndrome can be detected in every science and in every one of the humanities. That ameaningful thinking has been tending to displace meaningful throughout culture, I certainly do not hope here to document. But be you scientist, humanist, or citizen, I ask you to probe deeply into your own knowledge about knowledge, and consider the justice of the following impressionistic pattern.

In presenting these terminal paragraphs on the natural history of ameaning, I shall be forced to use the worst kind of shorthand reifications and to commit other scholarly sins. As feeble prophylaxis, let me remind you that a trend towards "ameaningful thinking" does not mean an accretion of new substance in the universe, but rather, an increasing incidence of a level of functioning which has always characterized *most* of man's cognitive effort. We have perhaps not sufficiently emphasized that in a very wide range of contexts ameaningful thinking can be and is adaptive; ameaningful thinking is distinctly not *meaningless* thinking.

Contrariwise, human nature is such that the occurrence of meaningful thinking, in the sense described, is rare at best. The problem is one of relative incidence of these two modes of function, and the trend we decry is perhaps better stated in terms of a decreasing incidence of the *meaning-*

ful — especially in those contexts of inquiry which traditionally have prospered only when approached at the highest and most passionate levels of meaningful function.

My natural history of ameaning sees it developing to levels which give a new and deleterious twist to the sensibility of man throughout the nineteenth century, and becoming stabilized in a way which colors ideologies concerning the nature of knowledge in all areas, towards the end of the century. This movement towards ameaning can perhaps most clearly be seen on the one hand in the development throughout the century of positivistic thought and, on the other, in the development of Marxist and cognate theories of history and society. Its deeper impetus, which in turn motivated the movements just mentioned (and others), springs from many circumstances, among which the following two seem especially important:

1. The rapid growth throughout the century in the complexity, differentiation, and unmanageability of knowledge. It would appear that deep threats can be posed by *knowledge itself,* merely as a function of cumulating to an immensity which precludes the possibility that individual intelligence can view it in a way at once synoptic and with fidelity. Such a state of affairs in itself produces bewilderment, bafflement, estrangement, alienation, fear. It is natural, then, for man to search for sets of rules, methodologies, devices which will give security, absolve him from the ardor of meaningful thought. This brings method-fetishism. And a-ontologism is implicit in the correlative disposition not to admit defeat. Meaningful thought cannot *always* be relied upon to give answers — ameaningful can. Given a set of devices which *preguarantee* accumulation of knowledge, aesthetic artifacts, etc., a-ontologism is already with us. We can epitomize these considerations by saying that given some critical degree of bewilderment in the face of the very complexity of knowledge, man takes refuge in the *coziness of ameaning.*

2. Many other factors building up through the nineteenth century that impel man to embrace the coziness of ameaning. Of pervasive and weighty importance are, of course, the direct and indirect consequences of the *industrial revolution.* The attendant crumbling of accepted and traditional values, the erosion of religion, the counterposing of certain as yet unstable articles of faith (e.g., Marxism, positivism, evolutionary progressivism, psychoanalysis, etc.), fall into a pattern with certain of the factors already adumbrated. Certainly the social dislocations and readjustments precipitated by the industrial revolution have brought man an uneasiness, relative

to his place in the universe, which renders the cozy allures of ameaning ever more attractive.

All this may seem incompatible with the image of the Victorian nineteenth century as an intensely "optimistic" period. There are no monolithic answers to these questions, but is it not possible that there was something rather driven about this optimism? After all, it was precisely this "optimism" that we have seen to be responsible for the legislation into existence of the psychological and social sciences, and, more generally, the idea that knowledge can be beckoned into being by administrative plan.

I think it would be most revealing if we could trace the development of scientism, method-fetishism, and a-ontologism—and the attendant disorderly cluster of such attitudes as simplism, reductionism, a-historicism, autistic activism—through such movements as the Marxism and positivism of the nineteenth century. I have gone back to a little of the relevant history and am amazed at the shock of recognition imparted by a new perspective.

It is profoundly instructive to consider the role of Marxism in the development of ameaning. *History* (which as is often said was discovered by the early nineteenth century) soon, via Hegel, was dissolved into its own philosophy, a philosophy from which the universe as given can readily be recomposed in a modest number of logical steps. Marxism proceeds to convert this philosophy into a tool for social action. In this conversion—a process sanctified with the iconography of scientism—the *content* of history is displaced, first by a method, then by a monolithic metaphysic, then by an activism, then by a religion. And, inevitably, as socialist thought moves through the century, its simplistic schematisms act as a reducer, distorter, homogenizer of history. Ultimately we see these schematisms calling the turns for the rewriting of history. History, discovered early in the century as food for man's imagination, ends it as an invention of man.

With regard to nineteenth-(and in fact, twentieth-) century positivism, it would be possible to suggest some instructive parallels—so far as I know not generally recognized—between *it* and Marxism. But here I would at least like to suggest that something highly instructive might ensue if a little more attention were given to Comte who, after all, was the *founder* of positivism in the formal sense of the position. Though not unremembered in sociological scholarship (he "founded" sociology, too), I have the impression that he is held rather distinctly in the background in twentieth-century positivistic writing. If you do not already know the answer, I ask you to find out why (cf. Mill 1865).[2]

We now modestly turn to the situation in twentieth-century science and in the humanities, respectively.

Science

It is no secret that the dominant tendency in thought about the nature of science since the late nineteenth century has been, broadly speaking, positivistic and that positivism has seen science mainly under the aspect of method and as being ontologically neutral. From the late nineteenth-century positivism and pragmatism, on through the successive phases of logical positivism, of neo-pragmatism, and of English analytic philosophy — and not excluding the activities of "methodologists" in the special sciences like Bridgman, the operationist in physics, and Woodger, in biology — there have been certain patent common emphases. Specific doctrines have of course varied in detail over a wide range. But, as is well known, this entire cluster of views reflects an anti-metaphysical bias, sees science mainly as a *useful* and economical tool for anticipating experience or events, stresses the role of stipulation and option in the formal and factual disciplines, makes much of the assumption that a plurality of alternative explanations of any natural domain are always in principle possible, and is preoccupied, sometimes to obsessive degrees, with paradigmatic reconstructions of the rules presumably implicit in scientific practice, reconstructions which soon acquire heuristic force.

I am far from suggesting that positivism as a technical philosophy of science is devoid of contexts in which intensely meaningful thinking has been done, or that it has not made meaningful and valuable contributions to certain of the problems which it has addressed. But the picture that it suggests of the nature of scientific activity is badly off-center. There is a severe defect of balance, of stress. It makes too large a place for method, too little for the human applier thereof; it then turns around and paradoxically makes too large a place for human option, convention, construction, and too little for the universe — which after all has *something* to do with the occasion and object of inquiry, and perhaps even with its answer. That

---

2. As he notes at the beginning of chapter 4, Koch believed that the answer can be traced to the fact that "Comte . . . after founding the *science* of sociology on a strict positivistic basis, proceeded, some time later, to found what was possibly the most obsessively rule-saturated *religion* in all history." *Eds.*

positivism, even at *technical* levels, has encouraged tendencies towards a-ontologism and rule-fetishism, few would deny. The best confirmation comes from philosophy itself, which is currently seeing a massive revolt against precisely such trends — a revolt in which former logical positivists, or residual ones, are enthusiastically participating. But it is at non-technical levels that positivism has worked most profoundly towards an ameaningful conception of the scientific enterprise.

The typical working scientist of the twentieth century has tended to hold positivistic *attitudes* even when totally innocent of the details, or even the existence, of positivism as a philosophical tradition. He has tended to hold a grossly instrumental conception of the nature of knowledge, to be rule-bound, methodologically monolithic, to believe that any question is answerable given the requisite material and collaborative facilities for research, etc. He has tended (at least until instructed to the contrary by Snow) to see science as morally neutral, and to look upon it as more or less inexorably cumulative, progressive, and so on. Note, I do not say the *exceptional* scientist; I say the *typical* scientist. And another qualification should be noted: even the typical scientist *knows* at some level that these attitudes are not tenable. But this he is incapable of hooking up with the rest of himself. Such attitudes are no doubt held more widely and intensively by psychological and social scientists than by other scientists; and by applied scientists than by pure scientists. Amusingly, these attitudes are rather less prevalent among physicists — the members of the very science on which the methodic reconstructions of technical positivism were most closely based — than among members of any other group. But the attitude-complex I have in mind has been widely diffused among scientists throughout the twentieth century. Combining with the specialism in the milieu of modern science, it has tended to support a disdain for non-scientific knowledge, often so marked as to involve a generalized bellicosity towards the rest of "culture."

The popular, or public, image of science has varied in detail over the century, but in all of its forms it has tended to see science as some kind of infallible information-processing mechanism. Science is seen as technology, technology as gadgetry, and gadgetry as resulting from automation. In its more recent versions, scientists are seen as the proletariat of the factory of science. They tend the machines, they work in teams under the guidance of their foremen. The endless flow of their produce either in gadgetry or information can be accelerated or decelerated at will by planning, administration, by order of industry or the military, by act of Congress. They are an efficient proletariat, having gone long to school and learned well the rules. The *rules* are infallible. Perhaps even more important than the rules is "apparatus." This is the machinery of the factory of science tended, according to the rules, by the workers.

The Humanities

When first thinking about trends towards ameaning, one is tempted to see its burgeoning mainly in connection with certain aspects of the development of science. But one can find the *same* tendencies at work in the recent history of the humanities. Here I can offer only a few bare associations having to do with the creative arts and criticism (points more fully developed in the next chapter).

From the late nineteenth century on, art and its evaluation have been tied to special aesthetic rationales, movements, schools, tendencies, as never before in history. These sub-ideologies have in each case had an essentially restrictive effect on the aesthetic outcome, and almost progressively so over much of the century. One finds this restrictive tendentiousness to be almost equally at work in the visual arts, music, and literature, not to mention such applied arts as architecture, industrial design, etc. The "experimentalist," "workshoppy" imagery which has been prevalent in the talk generated around the edges of art in itself reveals a kind of dilute scientism, but though the pressure towards ameaning exerted on art by science is of considerable importance, I believe that the trend towards ameaning was independently imposed on both science and the arts by common historical factors, such as those I tried to identify in discussing the "coziness" of ameaning.

Art, being in its nature concerned with the maximization of certain varieties of meaning, does not succumb as readily as science to a grossly instrumental conception of the nature of knowledge. But it is susceptible to method-fetishism, and certain kinds of a-ontologism can be even greater in it. And it can, despite all, do a pretty good job of succumbing to instrumental use in the interests of a special activism — as is evident by the virtual domination of world literature in the thirties by Marxist aesthetics, and the long-term responsiveness of Soviet literature to the Party line.

Twentieth-century aesthetics and the quasi-aesthetics of literary criticism have been dominated by a collection of the thinnest kind of schematisms. And these theories of art, criticism, taste, have been buttressed mainly by a combination of sententiousness and arrogant preciosity. Take, for instance, the supercilious, intransigent "difficulty" of modern verse, and its sustenance by a coterie of critics and a readership that have taken high pride in defending the irrelevance to poetry of certain forms of meaning, sometimes all forms. Consider, for instance, the "new criticism" with its mystique concerning the absolute non-paraphrasability of poetry, the irrelevance of inferences concerning aesthetic intention (the aesthetic *problem*), the vulgarity of referring to *any* factors extrinsic to the poem. Currently such attitudes are, of course, coming under attack, but one can doubt that the proffered substitutes are appreciably less obscurantist. A happy note was, however, struck by the resurrection of a profound early twentieth-century movement known as "Spectra"—perhaps the one highly tendentious literary movement which brought something truly and deeply instructive to the modern world. This, as I am sure most of you know, was a movement in poetry, prismatic with metaphysical insight, launched in 1916 by Emanuel Morgan and Anne Knish, two utter unknowns at the time. This movement, which was in fact a hoax perpetrated by two poets known in their less inspired moments as Witter Bynner and Arthur Davison Ficke, was taken with absolute seriousness and, in some cases, high intellectual excitement, by literary critics for several years (Smith 1961).

Throughout the century, avant-gardism, "Modernism," has stood for constriction, simplification, de-differentiation of the resources brought by the artist to the generation of *meanings*. In one imposing instance in which experimentalism *did* involve a passionate attempt to extend the boundaries of both language and human experience, the intention ultimately boomeranged. The trajectory of Joyce's career from *The Dubliners* to *Finnegans Wake* is the example I have in mind. With respect to *visual art*—I will restrict myself to asking you to conduct an experiment: juxtapose a visit to the Metropolitan Museum in New York to one only a few blocks away—the Guggenheim.

The special case of the *direct* impact of science on art and its evaluation in the twentieth century is, of course, a most instructive story in itself—the influence, say, of scientific philosophy and the ideology and methods of linguistic analysis on people like I. A. Richards and Empson, or the rather less direct influence on the new critics.

Perhaps the best way I can convey the "atmosphere" re ameaning in the humanities is via a remark addressed to me by a literary critic with whom I once participated in a symposium. I had said that one of the obvious functions of criticism is explication and that, since the critic in so doing is asserting relations between specifiable properties of the art object and of experience, he necessarily makes *some* statements of empirical psychological import. His response was to assure me, with great hauteur, that criticism is and *only* is *one thing,* namely "literature." Naturally, this produced in me a blinding flash of insight, and I was thoroughly grateful to be freed of my confusion. I had foolishly thought that literature was *about* something; and that criticism was conceivably literature about literature.

My sketch of ameaning has, of course, been ridiculously selective. I will be told that different selections from the modern history of ideas would give *quite* different trends. Of course. But I *think* this trend towards ameaning is a dominant one. I will be told also that there have been developments which pose counterforces to ameaning — say, the flurry of interest in "creativity," "excellence" and related matters, the mass art and symphony movements, changing emphases in philosophical and other scholarly thinking. Such developments *could* be counterforces, but it is my contention that to contain ameaning *effectively,* we need a far more precise localization of its contours than is implicit in these developments, far more precise than *any* that has been yet made.

I will also be told that the existentialists, the Zen Buddhists, the professional social critics, the Neo-Kantians, and many other groups and individuals have said these things. In some sense, this may be so, but I think in a way which leaves at least *one* important difference. *They* do not see the problem of ameaning (or whatever alternate cry of pain they register) as an *empirical psychological problem,* as one rooted in certain lawful regularities of human cognitive function. Nor do they perceive that one can *narrow down* with precision on the conditions of meaningful vs. ameaningful thought only by psychological modes of analysis.

The latter oversight is not the less intelligible for the fact that *psychology* is indeed that area which has succumbed more fulsomely to ameaning than any other in the scholarly community. But — paradoxically — it is this very circumstance that could give it a purchase on its own cure. In cognitive pathologistics, as in medical pathology, advanced diseases can bring to the surface symptoms, detection of which is but a step away from cure.

If psychology is to live up to the promise of its very definition, then it must sooner or later rise to such challenges as that provided by the problem of ameaning. In so doing, it will be playing its proper role in setting right the deficiencies in man's conception of his own knowledge. It will be helping to place into proper registration our currently non-fusing images of science and the humanities. Most importantly, in so doing psychology will be by way of facing—for the first time without embarrassment—its proper task: the understanding of man in all contexts of his functioning, not excluding those in which he and his artifacts are most noble, beautiful, or profound.[3]

3. What, then, did Koch make of *post*-modernism—as it came to be expressed in the 1980s and 1990s—and the particular ways it sought to blend science and the humanities? In his postscript to the reprinted edition of *A Century of Psychology as Science* (Koch 1992b), he noted the growing view that "nomothetic psychology requires supplementation by a psychology analogous to Wundt's *Völkerpsychologie*—indeed, that laboratory psychology has no meaning unless it is contextualized and qualified by cross-cultural and historical concerns" (964–65). Koch then offered these observations, ending with a terse, typically trenchant critique:

A subgroup within social psychology that had already by 1979 been making more radical suggestions concerning the historicity, context-dependence, and socially constituted character of *all* matters bearing on human activity, has grown appreciably in influence. This subgroup forms a cluster with many European psychologists, and many who implement cognate views in the social sciences and humanities.

There are few overarching agreements, other than a largely shared critique of conventional psychology, and indeed "post-enlightenment" science in general. Their dominant ideas, both substantive and methodic, derive largely from structuralist and post-structuralist theories in the humanities, from "hermeneutics" as developed by Gadamer and successors, from modern incarnations of rhetoric, and from the traditions of "narratology" and "discourse analysis" (especially as developed in recent years). They are likely to call themselves "social constructionists"—which can mean many things, but at the extreme entails a view that envisages the "self" as a semitranslucent, historically and interactionally plaited discursive knot within an immense but time-bound matrix of social "discourse." Most have been influenced by Derrida and like to perform "deconstructions" on all positions in the history of thought other than their own. They are, of course, hospitable to the use of qualitative methods, and indeed have influenced the growing interest in such matters. Most like to characterize their positions as "postmodern," and like to deconstruct the ahuman consequences of the "Enlightenment Project."

In this brief Postscript, I can only identify—not assess—the trend at issue. Because their most prized concepts are derivative from the literary humanities, and because they would align psychology (and related social sciences) primarily with the humanities, I suppose I should be pleased. I am. But in my now ancient invitation that psychology, in many humanly relevant areas, pattern itself more on the humanities than on the sciences, I was thinking of different strands within the humanities. I was also suggesting that psychologists be selected and trained relative to humanistic sensibility rather more than has been the case. I think it more important to be deeply conversant with a few great texts than to proclaim that human beings can be read as texts. Or that they *are* texts! (Koch 1992b, 965) *Eds.*

8

Ameaning in the Humanities

Foreword

This chapter extends the analyses of the preceding one to the arts and humanities. In effect, it is an extended critique of "modernism" — seeking to show that the modernist impulse, as it has unraveled throughout the century, is a manifestation of the very same tendencies toward ameaningful modes of thought that have been at the basis of the scientism so broadly evident in the psychological and social studies.

The chapter derives from a longer paper prepared in 1967 for presentation before the Program in Criticism at the University of Texas at Austin. It was written towards the end of my stay at the Ford Foundation as Director of its Program in the Humanities and the Arts, and in part reflects my experience in that capacity. I attended the conferences which comprised the basis of "exhibits" 1 and 2 in this chapter as a representative of the Foundation. Indeed, it was my office that subsidized the exhibit 2 conference on structuralism, held at Johns Hopkins in 1967 and issuing in the book, *The Structuralist Controversy: The Languages of Criticism and the Sciences of Man,* edited by R. Macksey and E. Donato (Baltimore: Johns Hopkins University Press, 1970). The symposium on "The Morality of Scholarship" that formed the basis of exhibit 1 celebrated the inauguration of a Society for the Humanities at Cornell University in 1967; the proceedings were published in the volume *The Morality of Scholarship,* edited by M. Black (Ithaca: Cornell University Press, 1967).

The present form of the paper was adapted from the 1967 draft, and used as the basis for my presidential address to Division 10 (Psychology and the Arts) of the American Psychological Association in 1969.

I. Introduction

I am a member of an interdisciplinary group concerned with issues relating to the "unity of knowledge." We are a motley collection of philosophers, humanists, scientists, and even one lonely artist, united mainly by anti-scientistic and anti-reductionist sympathies. Over three years, we have been having sporadic meetings looking towards an epistemological synthesis which might help reintegrate our fragmenting culture. But I have long felt that the trouble is not *mere* fragmentation; the fragments themselves are succumbing to catabolic and value-depleting forces.

In a recent act of desperation, I suggested to the group that we turn our attention to clinical appraisal of the state of certain of the fragments. The first of my specific proposals was a conference on "The End of Art?" I defined the issue in these restrained and Apollonian words:

> The significance of the restrictive and art-defiling aesthetic mystiques now so prevalent has been explored in adequate depth by no one: The meaning of the "non-isms," "anti-isms," phony experimentalisms, and assorted nihilistic posturings; the theater of shock and nudity; the new horizons of "expanded consciousness" and exploded form in literature; the visual arts of the "minimal" which track their target so effectively as to approach the delineation of pure nothing; the "underground" and "art" cinema; the developments in rock, electronic, and modern music; the proliferation of new "forms" in every field, the single intent and entire force of which is to perform a gigantic act of defecation upon the past. Are there not a dozen people in the world with something significant to say?

Cant thinking applies the term "value free" (*Wertfrei*) to the sciences and leaves the impression that the phenomena, principles, and standards of value are firmly ensconced in the arts and the humanities. But the strange history of the arts and humanities in this century suggests a sense in which value freedom has obtained in those areas, as well: a sense something like "value-anarchy." It is not only that subjectivistic, relativistic, and "emotivist" theories of value have been dominant during much of the century; what is worse is that even those artists and humanists who have seen value as objectively grounded have in theory and in practice made such arbitrary, restrictive, simplistic, casual, and even whimful identifications of the conditions and range of value phenomena as to make subjectivistic thinking seem ever more hygienic. These circumstances invite ardent and serious concern with the theory of value, and I am disposed to think that psychological modes of analysis must be the criterial ones, if only for the undeniable circumstance that the phenomena at issue are ubiquitous to human experience and implicated in all action.

By "psychological modes of analysis" I do not mean the conquest of value by application of some handy weapon in psychology's extant armamentarium of theory or method. I mean something at once more humble and difficult: a disposition to essay open-minded and painstaking phenomenal analyses of value-suffused segments of experience in a way informed by (but not controlled by) relevant psychological knowledge. Moreover, if the context be *aesthetic* value, I do not think any psychologist — save the extraordinary one who is also an artist, or perhaps critic, of great refinement — can go very far unaided. The stagnancy of philosophic and triviality of experimental aesthetics — as these have been practiced in the past — cannot be unrelated to the circumstance that so few of their practitioners were expert in the artistic domains they sought to illuminate or order. Whatever one's altitude as philosopher or scientist, one cannot explicate what one cannot discriminate! Significant work in the psychology of art, especially on such central and subtle problems as those associated with "value," will necessitate a partnership between the psychologist and the artist or explicative humanist. In this province, the primary tool of discovery can only be relevantly specialized and high-order sensibility. We must look forward to a tradition of research in which artists and humanists, preferably of unusual creative and analytical powers, cooperate with the psychologist, both as collaborator and subject.

I had planned to discuss an analysis of value which creates a context for the kind of cooperation I have just suggested. Central in this thinking is a notion of "value properties" which, if just, makes it difficult to doubt that differentiated value events occur as *objective* characters of experience, and are related in lawful ways to the biological and, ultimately "stimulus" processes of which experience is a function (cf. Koch 1969d; chapter 6).

But I have changed tack! I think it feckless to dwell on the *theory* of art, when the *fact* of art is in such grave jeopardy. To do so would be in violation of the very same admonition I made to my colleagues in the group concerned with the "unity of knowledge." Besides, is not the theme of this convention "Psychology and the Problems of Society"? If pollution be one of them, its *chemical* form does not exhaust the genus.

I shall therefore talk about the state of the arts and humanities. In effect, I will be talking about that state of world-sensibility known as "modernism." I will proceed impressionistically and tendentiously, but as a *psychologist*. For my concern is with a lawful tendency of human cognitive function which is implicated, and I think centrally so, in the "modernist" impulse. I call this tendency, "ameaningful thinking" (cf. chapter 7). For tactical reasons, most of my illustrative materials will derive from the critical and explicative humanities — the talk generated around the edges of art — rather than the arts directly. Thus, my title for the day: "Ameaning in the Humanities."

In previous writings (e.g., Koch 1965, 1969c), I have traced some of the manifold expressions of ameaning in twentieth-century attitudes towards (and theories of) science, and especially in the "scientistic" governing assumptions and framework commitments of the psychological and social studies. I have given especial attention to the relations between ameaning and the epistemology of behaviorism. At this juncture, I shall try to widen the case to the humanities!

II. The Humanities

From the late nineteenth century on, art and its evaluation have been tied to special aesthetic rationales, movements, schools, tendencies, as never before in history. These sub-ideologies have in each case had an essentially restrictive effect on the aesthetic outcome and progressively so over much of the century. One finds this restrictive tendentiousness to be almost equally at work in the arts, music, and literature, not to mention such applied arts as architecture, industrial design, etc. The "experimentalist," "workshoppy" imagery which has been prevalent in the talk generated around the edges of art in itself reveals a kind of dilute scientism, but though the pressure towards ameaning exerted on art by science is of importance, I believe that the trend towards ameaning was independently imposed on both science and the arts by common historical factors, such as those I tried to identify in referring to the "coziness" of ameaning.

Art, being in its nature concerned with the maximization of certain varieties of meaning, does not succumb as readily as science to a grossly instrumental conception of its own nature. But it is susceptible to method-fetishism and certain kinds of a-ontologism can be even greater. And it can, despite all, do a pretty good job of succumbing to instrumental use in the interests of a special activism — as is evident by the virtual domination of world literature in the thirties by Marxist aesthetics, and the long-term responsiveness of Soviet literature to the Party line.

Twentieth-century aesthetics and the quasi-aesthetics of literary and "art" criticism have been dominated by a collection of the thinnest kind of schematisms. And these theories of art, criticism, taste, have been buttressed mainly by a combination of sententiousness and arrogant preciosity. Take, for instance, the supercilious, intransigent "difficulty" of modern verse, and its sustenance by a coterie of critics and a readership which have taken high pride in defending the irrelevance to poetry of certain forms of meaning, sometimes all forms. Consider the "new criticism" — with its mystique concerning the absolute non-paraphraseability of poetry, the irrelevance of inferences concerning aesthetic intention, the vulgarity of referring to *any* factors extrinsic to the poem. Currently such attitudes are coming under attack, but one can doubt that the proffered substitutes are appreciably less obscurantist. They may "liberate *from*," but do they liberate?

It is unfair to single out literary criticism, for the situation has been immeasurably worse in those arts in which the job of the critic is to deploy words about objects which are not verbal. In the criticism of music, the visual arts, architecture, the dance, not only is there the formidable difficulty of explicating in words the properties and laws of structures of experience which are not mediated by words, but the derivative difficulty that there is likely to be a stauncher wall (sometimes an impenetrable one!) between the critic's sensibility and technical knowledge on the one hand and that of the victim of his professional solicitude on the other. Both circumstances conspire to make the allures of ameaning even more seductive. The critic or theorist is even more likely to adopt an arbitrary simplism, a trusty canon, a pet fad, and to apply it unrelentingly to every work that he addresses — or, be he of less systematic cast, to adopt a limited array of gamesmanship clichés and use these "contextually," which is to say "eclectically," which is to say randomly. Visual art and performing arts criticism has thus given us one of the great running joke-books of our century: a joke-book only because the utter destructiveness of its message reveals something so ludicrous about the human condition.

Lest these remarks seem to discriminate too much against the critic and theorist, let it quickly be noted that the artist has something to do with the fate of art. Our century has posed problems which make the security-crutch of ameaning somewhat more like an inevitability for the artist than for any other member of the intellectual community.

There are forms of specialization in which a scientist committed to the pursuit of meaning may take refuge. There are no "specialties" *in the same sense* in art. There are fields of science in which one may operate in intensely meaningful ways upon symbols the experiential "meanings" of which are not only thin and inferentially remote, but so fully "absorbed" by the symbols as to make their unpacking irrelevant for most purposes, should this indeed be possible in principle. The artist, however, works close to experience at all times. In creating, he orders experience and what he creates mediates a structured experience in others. However much he may abstract (and he always does), it is perforce from *his* experience, the experience posed by his world, his time.

The same historical tendencies that work towards ameaning in the sciences, then, assail the artist more inescapably—and more ferociously. That the artist is impelled towards the coziness of ameaning is in some sense more forgivable, more poignant. That he embraces philosophies, mystiques, rationales, "directives," for his own work which simplify the terms of the aesthetic problem, which call upon a narrowed range of technical or imaginative resources, which provide or suggest what may seem a "methodology" for creation, which permit a constriction of objective—all this is understandable. What is less understandable is that the century has not been devoid of giants who have withstood such blandishments of ameaning absolutely. And it should be added that neither in science nor in art is creative practice ever fully constrained by its methodic rationale; and less so in art than in science. Any cultural history of the twentieth century which did not see its art at every phase as belying both in diversity and richness its own philosophic and procedural slogans would itself be ameaningful.

It is, nevertheless, no trivial circumstance that throughout the century *avant-gardism, modernism,* has worked towards constriction, simplification, de-differentiation of the resources brought by the artist to the generation of *meanings.* The early part of the century saw a reassessment of the past animated by a degree of self-consciousness and hostility towards tradition without precedent in the efforts of previous ages to find their identity. In many fields, the search for a "modern" idiom was regulated by the imagery of a kind of dilute scientism, a desire at once to mitigate and exploit the circumstances of a mechanized culture, and a conception of "integrity" that tended to find complexity of aesthetic means or ends suspect, and to value stylized and simply structured forms. The "modernist" impulse was quick to find broad segments of the past no longer viable: quick to diagnose forms, genres, styles, qualities of sensibility—especially of the nineteenth century—as dead. It was quick to search for attitudes appropriate to the new conditions, and to "experiment" with novel technical resources. Often it was sufficient to experiment.

The trajectory of the modernist impulse in its responses to the grotes-queries unfolded by twentieth-century history is not easily plotted. Nor is anything like a final plot possible, least of all by me. It would take the resources of a Kandinsky to diagram this vast, erratic, quasi-curve with its peaks and valleys, and peaks within valleys, and topological regressions upon itself.

There are, however, obvious inflection points on the location of which most of us would agree. For example: the search for metaphysical "sub-structures" that was early "non-objective" art; the driven, naughty boy, heady nihilism that was Dadaism; the rule-bound decomposition of the perceptual ecology that was Cubism; the exposure of the archetypal, magi-cal, extra-rational to the glare of an obsessive realism that was the special joke of Surrealism; the peaceful, equilibrated, prosy dynamics of Imagism and Objectivism in poetry; the abrogation of prosodic resources for the stereotyped freedom and the intellectualism of the Free Verse movement; the selective re-animation of tradition in the service of the low-key, con-tained, rejective anatomizing of culture of *The Waste Land* school. To con-tinue, one might note the reaction at a certain phase to earlier philosophies of spareness and limitation by the pursuit of "ambiguity" and "complex-ity" (or the theory advocating that pursuit); the pursuit (over an interval that overlapped the preceding and virtually every other phase) of social responsibility via formulae deemed salubrious by Marxism for the current state of its own metabolism; the exegesis of the phenomenology, philoso-phy, and humble pleasures of "alienation" (also a trend overarching many of the special movements). At this point I begin to flag; the picture be-comes more homogeneous: in overview, the explosive proliferation after World War II of a congeries of "philosophies" and trends which seek to purify art and its beneficiaries by one or another strategy of defilement, to enrich art by a policy of total impoverishment—to generate new and subtle species of "meaning" from a compost of the random, the arbitrary, the reduced, the de-differentiated, the distorted.

It is this last category of trends—the "anti-isms," "non-isms," "ab-surdisms" that preempted most of the map of the arts at the end of the 1960s—with which we all, perforce, must come to terms. These trends are in such continuity with the most restrictive of the earlier aesthetic ideologies of the century as almost to justify being thought regressions. But they are caricatures of their precursors and the force of the caricatures is that they take the process of constricting the objectives and resources open to the artist working under their sway to something like a vanishing point.

The early twentieth-century non-objectivism finds its reduced and distorted echo in a gamut of recent tendencies ranging from the abstract expressionist through the barely visible austerities of "minimal art." The aesthetic of early objectivist poetry finds its parody in the presuppositions of the *nouveau roman* and the anti-novel. The principles of the "early" collage as practiced by Braque, Picasso, and others meet a debased application in the three-dimensional junk collages, constructions, "assemblages," of much recent sculpture. And Dada—Dada is everywhere. But with a terrifying difference. It is the difference between witting nihilism and the unwitting kind in which the joke is on the agent of the enterprise. In some instances, it must surely be a difference between two kinds of *witting* nihilism: the former pure, rather loving, and committed; the latter, entrepreneurial.

It does not elude me that the line between such immense generalizations as the preceding and platitudes is a dim one, if at all existent. More to the point would be concrete examples of that type of method-dominated thinking, analysis below and belying the call of duty, intellectual tunnel-vision, gimmickry-freighted "spontaneity," etc., that can be thought symptomatic of ameaning. My difficulty is that I come by way of too many examples. Perhaps I am the victim of my own febrile conceptualization and have become a filter through which only ameaning passes. I can arrive at no principle of selection, not even that of the dramatic, the splendrous instance.

I can resolve this difficulty only by being arbitrary. I shall segregate a few examples of ameaning from the history of its impingements upon me. They will be sufficient, I hope, to show the extraordinary pervasiveness and viability of ameaningful thought patterns in the very areas of the culture which, by historic intention at least, are most directly concerned with the maximization of meaning.

I shall choose the examples mainly from the explicative and critical humanities rather than directly from the arts on which they bear. Because art, even when imperfect, is an ardent enterprise, I dislike making allegations about limitations of particular works in a context which does not permit detailed analyses. It is important to note that I will not be choosing *extreme* examples: the points are better made in the context of serious endeavors; not transparently zany ones!

Exhibit 1

I recently attended the inauguration ceremonies for a "society for the humanities" at one of the many forward-looking universities now seeking to "reinvigorate" the humanities. The topic of the inaugural symposium was "The Morality of Scholarship" and I went with high interest, not only because of the glittering reputations of the participants, but because as a scientist and sometime philosopher of science, I had long been exercised about the exceedingly superficial treatment in those areas of the relations between values and science, and had long believed that the corrective could come from re-examining scientific practice in the light of scholarship in general. From this point of view, sensitive and differentiated analyses of the morality of humanistic scholarship could go far towards clarifying one of the most grievous areas of confusion in the modern ideology of science. The keynote speaker, whose paper was to form the basis of the day's discussion, slaked my curiosity in his first two paragraphs:

> In the eighteenth century there was some confidence that, in Samuel Johnson's words, no new discoveries were to be made in the field of morality. But new discoveries continued to be made elsewhere, most remarkably in science, and these have had their effect on our conceptions of morality as well. The development of science emphasized the value of the "scientific method," but most expositions of that method turn out to be, not so much methodologies, as statements of a moral attitude. To achieve anything in the sciences, one needs the virtue of detachment or objectivity. One starts out with a tentative goal in mind, but on the way to it one must consider evidence impartially and draw only the strictly rational conclusions from that evidence. Cooking or manipulating the evidence to make it fit a preconceived idea works against detachment. And though we may say that detachment is an intellectual rather than a moral virtue, it becomes increasingly clear as we go on that such a distinction is without meaning. The persistence in keeping the mind in a state of disciplined sanity, the courage in facing results that may deny or contradict everything that one had hoped to achieve — these are obviously moral qualities, if the phrase means anything at all.
>
> The triumphs of these virtues in modern civilization have naturally, and rightly, given them a high place in our scale of values. They are most clearly displayed in the physical sciences,

which are so largely informed by mathematics, but as the social sciences developed, they too felt the powerful pull of detachment, and so they became increasingly behavioristic, phenomenological, and restricted to what can be observed and described. At present it may be said that the principle, which is also a moral principle, that every discipline must be as scientific as its subject matter will allow it to be, or abandon all claim to be taken seriously, is now established everywhere in scholarship. (Frye 1967, 3–4)

The skein of grotesqueries embedded in these two paragraphs could not be unraveled by an entire army of analytic philosophers, even in a ten-year campaign. Even highly scientistic scientists are beginning to become aware of the existence of extra-rational determinants of the scientific enterprise — of the importance of decisions, options, and processes that cannot in principle be constrained by rule — and are willing to locate these "extra-rational" determinants within themselves. And, at least in some scientific quarters, an imagery of passion, commitment, identification, is beginning to vie with the stale and evasive imagery of "objectivity" and "detachment." For "disciplined sanity," some few scientists would be willing to substitute "disciplined madness," and one or two might go so far as "Pythagorean ecstasy" or "Dionysian surrender."

This is no place for an elaborate excursion into epistemology. But the emphasis of Polanyi and others on the personal coefficient in all knowledge — the responsibility of the knower (in or out of science) for the content of his knowledge rather than of the rules which he has creatively applied or evaded (as the case may be) — has not gone unheeded. For myself, I would go further in holding there to be an utter interpenetration between what philosophers have been wont to call the "realms" of "fact" and "value" (cf. chapter 6). I think that any just reanalysis of the processes of science would show the options, decisions, actions, of scientists at every phase of inquiry to be as much based on judgments or assertions of value as on cognitions of fact (inclusive of the "transmitted" cognitions from prior or "received" knowledge) and, further, that the very process of cognition always rests partly upon the perception of objective value properties.

I recognize the last statement for the monstrously abstract shorthand that it is, but what it implies is easy to say. The modal conception of the relation between science and value is that the scientist is a double personality: in the laboratory, a rule-regulated automaton, and outside it, a citizen who happens to be a "good Joe." The part that is citizen — as Mr. Snow is quick to inform us — learns a respect for telling the truth, absorbs the future into his bones, and even is less likely than most (so Snow tells us) to undergo divorce or be indifferent to the poor. However these latter virtues be interpreted, the extra-laboratory person wires this citizenly respect for the truth into the laboratory person and then proceeds happily to automate in a way which precludes fudging data or lifting his ideas from junior colleagues.

My counter-theory says that the scientist is not necessarily a saint, but that he need not be thought in need of constant constraint by a sub-assembly of ethical transistors. The matter is at once more simple and more complex. Our concept of human nature need not be so cynical as to preclude the possibility that there are levels of cognitive hunger which, by the laws of their own workings, cannot be sated by ersatz food — that there are potentialities for meaningful thinking such that the thought process will move passionately towards the apprehension of the object of inquiry and not find surcease in a pseudo-solution, a role-playing solution, a concocted solution, a stolen solution. If the morality of scholarship be thought of in the global sense here at issue ("respect for the truth"), what needs explanation is not the morality of scholarship but its frequent immorality: the factors in history, society, and ultimately the individual which curtail the incidence of meaningful thought episodes and reinforce ameaningful or, indeed, worse tendencies.

To return to our symposiast's confident paragraphs: no "new discoveries" have been made about morality in science; on the contrary, what was known about morality by the time of the eighteenth century has thus far only been obfuscated and scrambled by science. The symposiast interprets "most expositions" of the "scientific method" as "statements of a moral attitude." He has misread those expositions! Conventional formulations of scientific method do not at all invite the exercise of a "moral attitude." Instead, they project a view of the inquirer as a *scoundrel* who must be protected from his tendencies towards motivated mis-perception, the manufacture of data, and generalized lying by an externally imposed set of constraints.

It is often said (and I was once among the sayers) that scientific methods are essentially a set of checks against the "fallibility" of the human being as an agent in the establishment of knowledge. The still-regnant the-

277

ories of science present so rule-saturated a picture of its processes that one can only suspect their authors to regret anything so unhygienic as the human being to be implicated in those processes. They do not perceive that the kind of morality required in science (or any *meaningful* intellectual activity) — unlike the kind germane to a law court — cannot be legislated, and cannot be policed. Still more do they fail to perceive that the attempt to do just this can only backfire and lead to its opposite: a pseudo-morality, a role-playing morality, a morality which relegates its good works to the rules, a morality which *at once* fosters the inquirer's conception of himself as a base and unsavory participant in the scholarly enterprise and brings him comfort in the belief that the *rules* will protect the world from his own perfidious tendencies.

As a coda to this "exhibit," it may be added that during an entire day's discussion, involving the participation of three other distinguished humanists as speakers and a large number in the audience, not a single presumption within the paragraphs I have quoted was questioned.

Exhibit 2

Another conference that I recently attended had also an inaugural objective: in this case to launch the movement known as "European structuralism" on the sea of American scholarship. I was irresistibly drawn to this rite, not only because of my general interest in the foundations of knowledge but because of vertiginous bemusement over the phenomenon of a group of European humanists wishing to integrate the methodological foundations of the humanities with those of the social sciences. I had naïvely thought that the salvation of the social sciences at this phase of history lay in their humanization! I was, incidentally, no keen student of this movement; nor am I now. In offering the following impressions, I must thus draw copiously on the courage of my philistinism.

The conference was indeed a sparkling affair. Some dozen scholars were imported, mainly from Paris, to present the structuralist case — rather contrapuntally, as it turned out. A large group of American scholars, most of them distinguished, came for the three days of discussion. The most heavily represented fields were the romance languages, comparative literature, linguistics, and literary criticism. The excitement ran high. Most of the delegates had been reading the structuralist literature like mad, but — because of the high social standards of Gallic scholars — had never expected to meet their heroes. I was informed repeatedly that the conference could well prove to be the most important event in American scholarship for the next fifty years.

I shall not attempt a vignette of the structuralist "position," for even at *my* level of innocence, it would require a million words. For those who have not followed the efforts of these doughty thinkers — who find their inspiration in Lévi-Strauss and, beyond him, in radiating lines of influence which ultimately comprehend all who have ever used the word "structure" or a synonym — I quote the following paragraphs from the editor's introduction to the double issue of the *Yale French Studies* on structuralism (Ehrmann 1966):

> What is structuralism? Before being a philosophy, as some tend to see it, it is a method of analysis. Even as such its many facets and different uses make it a subject of various interpretations, debate, even polemics. No simple or single definition applies to it except in very general terms. One could say a structure is a combination and relation of formal elements which reveal their logical coherence within given objects of analysis. Although structuralism can hardly be subsumed in some overall formula, or be given any label which will identify it for public consumption, we can say it is first of all, when applied to the sciences of man, a certain way of studying language problems and the problems of languages. Initially it was concerned with the structure of languages (*langues*), an area first explored by linguists whose interest developed the methods under study. It was then applied to anthropological inquiries, and in particular to the study of myths which are of the nature of a language (*langage*). The structural method also extends to the structures of the unconscious, as they are apprehended in psychoanalytical discourse, to the structure of the plastic arts with their language of forms, to musical structures where Lévi-Strauss believes he finds the very type of structural activity, and to the structures of literature since literary language, drawing upon ordinary language, transforms it into *langage* par excellence (from the point of view of the literary critic, at least!).
>
> Thus, structuralism attempts to uncover the internal relationships which give different languages (*langages*) their form and function. On a broader point of view, scholars are now trying to lay the bases for a science of signs — semiotics — which would include not only these languages but also any system of signs. Without pursuing this tangent, we can simply say that

since languages have in common their function as communication, it is impossible to overestimate the degree to which each discipline—the social sciences especially, but the natural sciences as well—can profit from the methods of neighboring disciplines. (7–8)

Returning to the conference, I can only say that in the mind of one American scholar bemusement subtly gave way to obfuscation, which stealthily expanded into amazement, which rapidly gave way to convulsive shock. In the collective definition of the speakers (and often in the confines of a single presentation) "structuralism" emerged as a rubbery, cosmic mélange of components of the following order: descriptive linguistics (inclusive of randomly chosen elements from phonology and morphology), generative grammars; cybernetics, information theory, elements of the theory of finite automata, and points West; elements of the C. S. Pierce theory of signs, the Charles Morris revision thereof, and thus scrambled appropriations of elements loosely subsumable under each of the three divisions of "semiotics"; garbled borrowings from *Principia Mathematica,* Polish semantics, I. A. Richards–style semantics, Carnapian semantics, and logical syntax; winnowings from the epistemology of logical positivism, analytic philosophy, and physical science methodology; a dash of Marx, a dash of Hegel; aspects of American structural anthropology and sociology (each a very mixed bag); diverse ingredients from psychoanalysis and other depth-psychologies, Gestalt psychology, behaviorism; a discrete dollop of Merleau-Ponty; a baker's dozen of approaches to myth criticism; random segments of formalist, contextualist, neo-critical, and neo-Marxist literary criticism and aesthetics.

The elements of this extraordinary, open-ended mélange are, of course, non-enumerable in principle. Certain generic attitudes of those who have erected this "structure" are, however, easily inferable from it, and these attitudes were expressed with high élan by the speakers. Obsessive scientism, of course—but to a degree that often made the logical positivism of the early thirties seem romantically libertarian by contrast. Though the positivists often seemed a bit oppressed by finding themselves in the lingua-centric predicament, these men behave as if there could not be a more congenial prison. Being Gallic, they will occasionally note that it is very sad, very poignant, that there is nothing but language, but not without an overtone of relish in these very perturbations.

The experience of those three days was one of constant *déjà vu.* Tatters and fragments of long-relinquished theses of early logical positivism, classic neo-pragmatism, operationism — of a kind of aggressive and hard-nosed scientism that has been, in the Anglo-Saxon countries, in process of defensive dissolution for many years — kept being ebulliently spewed forth by speakers who apparently regarded them as new and timely inventions. One heard that the sciences already formed a unitary language, that the future of scholarship depended on the integration of *all* knowledge into one cosmic linguistic structure; one heard theses that sounded much like physicalism and radical conventionalism; one's ears were assaulted by all the ancient imprecations against metaphysics and other forms of linguistic dysfunction. It need hardly be added that often the speakers seemed not very clearly to know the origins of certain of these motifs, nor was I content that the level of mastery of the materials borrowed from the newer developments in structural linguistics and other scientific and formal disciplines was uniformly high.

I think my point by now sufficiently well documented to present it: we have in structuralism an exquisite example of an unconquerable tendency in the modern history of ideas that can only be called "dynamic stasis." The logical positivism that issued from the Vienna of the twenties as perhaps the most ameaningful codification of the nature of knowledge in human history spread rapidly to most countries of the Western world and, by the mid-thirties or a little before, had become the dominant philosophic outlook in the Anglo-Saxon countries and not a few others. (Germany was able to resist these ideas by the not very creditable expedient of burning the books that conveyed them.) France, however, by virtue of preoccupation with a Teutonically inspired phenomenological tradition which was soon to receive indigenous coloration, was not especially responsive. We thus (to simplify) get the well-known "two world" situation in Western philosophy over a large segment of the century: the Anglo-Saxon countries being dominated by positivism and cognate positions, and the French pursuing a modified phenomenologism which by the forties assumed whatever contour the "existentialist" tradition can be said to have. But in the Anglo-Saxon countries, positivism and its relatives have been in an almost constant process of liberalization and retreat for not a few years. At the present time, some would argue that a critical turning point is within sight in the Anglo-Saxon countries and that *what* will be turned *to* — if it be not existentialism in any of its extant forms — will at least be strongly conditioned by phenomenological modes of analysis.

Meanwhile, at the École Pratique des Hautes Études, certain denizens have surmounted a crisis of restlessness: they have had a hypersufficiency of turgid Sartrean rhetoric; they cannot bear the instability of his middle terms and the frequent inaccessibility of his premises; they wish an end to all that and a return to the pristine clarity of Gallic rationalism. And thus does France *re*-discover *positivism*.

The "structure" underlying all this circumstantiality is, of course, that of "musical chairs." The fact that in this instance it is danced to a minuet should not prevent us from seeing such a structure as definitive of the history of ideas in our century. And we should note that the pattern is self-perpetuating. One game leads to another on a second structural principle: that of the impotent spiral, the would-be spiral that cannot rise. For note that structuralism is re-exporting positivism to American humanists who, until now, had been protected from its impact by virtue of specialization, at the *very* time that positivism and its offshoots are on the verge of being left in dereliction by the technical philosophers and scientists who were the chief developers and promoters of the position in the first instance. Ameaning is a redoubtable enemy!

Exhibit 3

I was a member of a club of two, which we called variously "The First Act Club" and "The 10 O'clock Marching Society." We had a very limited program, which was to attend the truly serious plays in New York City. The club met, aperiodically, for two years. Throughout, the members were impelled to behave with remarkable stereotypy: they marched down the aisle at the end of the first act, never to return to their seats. Lest I be thought a negativist on principle, may I note that my club-mate was a professional theater person, equipped with one of the most open, loving, and philosophically probing minds in American theater. Only now do I have the courage to say that some time ago we effected a post–first act termination of our contact with Pinter's *The Homecoming* (Pinter 1966), leaving behind a rapt and straining audience, from which randomly spaced peals of Method-laughter had been emerging with high frequency.

We were annoyed — indeed, insulted — by the play, in that we felt the author had let his considerable gifts down, not to mention letting us down, and even his generally appreciative audience. I do not propose to violate my intention of *not* directly addressing particular works of art in this talk. I am here concerned primarily with the ameaningful reaction to Pinter's play and not the play. This will necessarily involve a few comments bearing on very general properties of his work, but these will not be pejorative and are not offered as a substitute for the detailed analysis which alone can justify a pretension to critical judgment.

My club-mate and I feel that Pinter comes through superbly in certain of his short plays. His forte is that of a certain kind of prosy, naturalistic, low-key, "business-as-usual" *accommodation* of the extra-logical, the unpredictable, the grotesque. He places these "two" elements into an apposition, which is yet not a tension: the one is not a commentary on the other; a special, authentic blend, ambience, is achieved. The normal "causal" laws of the social universe, the accepted or received value-universe, the stable contingencies among human actions and events, are suspended, but suspended in an atmosphere of routine run-of-the-mill "normality." Another outstanding quality in Pinter is his profound and comic insight into the *ambivalence* of the human condition: he makes this ramify, often brilliantly, into character, into virtually every sub-unit of utterance, action, and relationship, and into situation.

Both of these qualities are beautifully evident and skillfully deployed in the brief play, *The Collection* (Pinter 1962). The play is an exploration of a kind of simmering, unrelenting, casual, mutual torture-process among four people. But there are odd and rather "disconnected" elements of attraction and zany good fellowship, too; these occur unpredictably and yet not surprisingly, and manage to convey much about the human condition. The play has its own logic of tone (of a sort derivative from such general traits of Pinter's approach as have been noted), but also a logic of emotion, and a logic of progression. The play reveals something of the human condition that makes *sense* (which is *not* to say that the play is its paraphrase), and the whole play reveals something that would not be revealed with comparable efficacy by its parts (though this latter may be questioned within limits).

To return to *The Homecoming*, it can be said that the general "qualities" of the Pinter approach are apparent: the tensionless marriage of the extralogical and the matter-of-fact, the witty and sometimes penetrating perception of human ambivalence built into virtually every line. But the play as a whole and its sub-structures of any appreciable "molarity" — the play as a progression, as an unfolding — has no logic other than an arbitrary, and almost random, one. The conjunctive assembly of arbitrary sub-units related on little more than a principle of non-relatedness does not make a work of art (not *one* work, anyway), nor is it likely to result in any kind of object worthy of sustained attention.

The principle of development animating *The Homecoming* is akin to the principle of automatic writing. Automatic writing can result in a work of art, but it is unlikely to. If the outcome has aesthetic integrity, this is more likely to be found in its parts than in the whole. Automatic writing can be highly revelatory of processes within its author. But even this virtue cannot be imputed to *The Homecoming*, in that its method of composition was almost certainly not that of automatic writing, but only like it. Whatever the method of composition, the product can be characterized only as ameaningful in the extreme, and I think we are entitled to infer that certain of the premises of its author were ameaningful, however sincerely held. *The Collection* is not comparably ameaningful, and proves that its author is capable of entertaining somewhat different premises. Its superiority is partly in its brevity (the characteristic Pinter "qualities" tend to pall as a function of length), but also in the fact that it cumulates into a meaningful pattern rather than mere yardage.

It is, to repeat, the critical reaction to *The Homecoming* that I wish to address rather than the play. The reviewer for *The New York Review of Books* is thrilled by the fact that in it "there is no tendency to the moralistic italicizing that marks the American theater." Further, Pinter "avoids exposition in the ordinary sense and is not seduced by affection for pieties: *The Homecoming* is indeed difficult, and one of the most interesting works to reach New York in some time." The reviewer rightly resonates to the quality of Pinter's dialogue, but quotes the following as an example of his "poetry of bare, insistent repetition":

> How are you Uncle?
> Not bad. A bit tired.
> Tired? I bet you're tired. Where you been?
> I've been to London Airport.
> All the way up to London Airport?
> Yes, all the way up there.

I think this a rather substandard selection and would like to propose, though they are less poetically repetitive, the following lines, which are rather great:

> Mind you, she wasn't such a bad woman. Even though it
>   made me sick just to look at her rotten stinking face, she
>   wasn't such a bad bitch. I gave her the best bleeding years
>   of my life, anyway.
> Plug it, will you, you stupid sod, I'm trying to read the paper.

284

> Listen! I'll chop your spine off, you talk to me like that! You
> understand? Talking to your lousy filthy father like that![1]

But the *New York Review* reviewer proceeds, after her selection, to an unassailable statement of its rationale:

> It may be that the justification for his dialogue lies in the strange statement of Ruth, the young woman of the play. "My lips move. . . . Perhaps the fact that they move is more significant than the words which come through them. You must bear that . . . possibility . . . in mind."

Indeed, here she has isolated one of Pinter's central premises for the play, a premise which *he* was apparently so eager to make plain that even he performed the unpardonable sin of saying rather than showing. It is, of course, the premise of *ameaning* — too thin, in my opinion, to warrant a two-and-a-half-hour implementation in a work of art, even if it *can* support an interminable lecture.

1. After writing the section on *The Homecoming*, I found that these same lines were quoted with approbation by Richard Gilman in a piece called "The Pinter Puzzle," *New York Times,* January 22, 1967 — one of the few evidences I have noted of independent observers agreeing on anything *particular* about the play. But this is our *only* point of agreement. Gilman tries to spell out the constrictions of the "conventional dramaturgy" against which Pinter and "all the interesting drama of the past fifteen or so years" have been in revolt. He defines, rather ornately, a view of the drama as an autonomous structure — and implies that what is important is not extrinsic meaning, in the sense of a "realism" for which "life is thought to have provided the model," but internal "substance" (he eschews the word "meaning" in this connection). He advances a theory of Pinter's development in terms of a search for the laws of a "new and substanceful" kind of "drama of his own" and, after an athletic attempt to explain the internal logic of *The Homecoming*, concludes that Pinter has advanced significantly towards some (unspecified) aesthetic target, though his lapse into allegory towards the end of the play is seen as "evidence that Pinter has not yet solved his major problem." The problem is "how to fuse meaning so securely with language, gesture, and setting that it cannot be extrapolated [*sic*] from them. The taints of the old worn-out dramatic procedure — characters who represent, action that points to something else — are still discernible in his work."

Mr. Gilman writes as if "theater of the absurd" and its derivatives represented the first exploration in history of the ancient theory of art as autochthonous — varying forms of which have practically preempted the theory and practice of the arts throughout this century. If a work of art *is* an autonomous system (and I would think it at *least* that), it would follow that the "laws" of such systems can be differentially rich in their capacity to generate internal meanings (and value properties which I take to be "parameters" of meanings). Moreover, it must be recognized that the character of these internal meanings cannot be *wholly* determined by the system per se, for the simple reason (if for no other) that the elements of a work of art are not wholly *constituted* by the art object, but have connections with other contexts of experience. Much art depends on setting the internal and external "meanings" of its elements into controlled relationships — sometimes complex ones. It is exactly this kind of neglect on which ameaning seems to be thriving more vigorously at present than perhaps ever before.

The *New York Times* of Sunday, February 5, 1967, published, under title of "What's Pinter Up To?" explanations of *The Homecoming* by "seven prominent people." One could not conceive of more formidable evidence of the current institutionalization of ameaningful criteria. These sophisticated aestheticians, from various walks of life, almost to a man take pains to point up the substantial irrelevance of meaning "to a work of art" (Larry Rivers: "For me Pinter has written an object"), though some risk admitting that a little meaning is an engaging bonus. Six of them, nevertheless, proceeded to give their own readings of "*the* meaning," sometimes three or four alternate readings. Naturally, the consensus was remarkable.

One of the participants (Isaac Bashevis Singer) finds that:

> While arbitrary distortion of nature and human behavior may occasionally succeed as a caricature and a curiosity—as it does in "The Homecoming"—sooner or later it evolves into a mannerism and a bore.

He later points out:

> There is room for only one Kafka in a century. A multitude of Kafkas is bound to cripple the art.

I can only think that a multitude of *Kafkas* would be extraordinarily welcome, but even more extraordinarily improbable. Amusingly, some time before seeing those words, I had written out a set of notes which also compared Pinter with Kafka. For a contrast between the two reveals precisely the difference between two authors of superficially similar "approach," one of whom is ameaningfully disposed, while the other is passionate, almost suicidally unrelenting, in his determination to maximize meaning. There is, of course, by now an extensive strand in modern literature of which the apposition of the extra-logical or fantastic, with a low-key acceptance thereof, is a definitive trait. Kafka's writing is the supreme example and to a large extent the originating one.

A comparison of *The Homecoming* with such a story as *The Metamorphosis* (Kafka 1952) is instructive. In this story, the only element of the fantastic is in *one* assumption—not an unduly arbitrary one considering that the story makes it quite plausible that man in fact *is* an insect (though none the less man, for that!). From the moment of Gregor's inconvenient transformation into a cockroach, the story is an inexorably logical calculation of the consequences for the victim, his family, and the network of relations in which they are embedded; a logical calculation most of the accessory premises of which are based on a matter-of-fact and even relaxed acceptance of the extra-rationalities of modern life, and of the strange admixture of the grotesque, the cowed, the gallant, and the loving that inhabits the human soul. It is an enterprise very much like the construction of a non-Euclidian geometry: one accepts all the premises of a given, familiar system except one. This one is replaced by a startling and "contrary to fact" contrary. One then proceeds to unpack the meaning of the altered axiom set, by a relentless derivation of consequences according to all the "normal" rules of inference. An intensely meaningful enterprise!

Assuming that ameaning is dominant in the modern world, and that the writer perforce must come to terms with it, one can make the following contrast: Pinter and the genres of recent dramatic writing to which his work may be ordered, in effect seek (whether wittingly or no) to reduce ameaning by ameaning. Unfortunately, this can have the consequence of multiplying the ameaning in the universe — while leaving its quota of art pretty much unaltered. A writer like Kafka forges meaning from ameaning.

Exhibit 4

To derive salubrious amusement from visual-art criticism is anyone's game, and virtually any specimen will render a rich return. But I cannot resist brief reference to one of my stable sources of comfort over the years, a 1962 article in *Encounter* by Clement Greenberg. This precious artifact entitled "How Art Writing Earns Its Bad Name" appeals to me because of its membership in that vast class of modern phenomena that might variously be called "ameaning at *n*th remove," or "ameaning as instanced by a root paradox of modern thought: viz., contumelious critical protestations that fall under the range of their own application."

The author attempts to chart the cascading flow of gibberish generated by art writers on the theme of post–World War II abstract art. In particular, he examines the twists and turns of art critics' attitudes towards "action painting," since the launching of the movement (at some causal distance, it would seem) by Harold Rosenberg in a well known 1952 article in *Art News*. It is Greenberg's contention that Rosenberg developed an absurd and pretentious quasi-existential, anti-art rationale for certain work then being done by Jackson Pollock and confreres, one which represented the "covered canvas" as "unmeaning aftermath of an 'event' (an event of pure doing); the solipsistic record of purely personal 'gestures,' and belonging therefore to the same reality that breathing and thumb prints, love affairs and wars belong to, but not works of art."

The alleged East Hampton athletes of the adventitious found, according to Greenberg, this interpretation ludicrous: they were very much interested in the "product," and rather hoped it would be found to be art. Rosenberg's article had a limited impact until the British critic Lawrence Alloway, two years after its appearance, "set its ideas and terms in effective circulation." Alloway became an ardent and voluble champion of the nonexistent movement (apparently a true "non-movement") and "propagated Mr. Rosenberg's notions with such conviction and verve . . . that 'action painting' became current overnight in England, as the authorized brand name and certified label of the new abstract painting from America." Apparently this wave of titillation washed across to the Continent and then back to America, and had the consequence finally of rescuing from the null-class an *actual* movement of action painting around New York and elsewhere. The confused exponents naturally bought Mr. Rosenberg's analysis — at least as modified by Alloway and other mediators — as rationale for their efforts. Meanwhile, Pollock, de Kooning, and the other inadvertent primal-fathers continued in the pursuit of their subtle and self-determined labors and prospered madly by virtue of the noise. What seems to appall Mr. Greenberg to the roots of his being is the unauthenticity of all this, the multiple perversions that have been introduced into the history of ideas.

For himself, he sees Pollock, de Kooning, and associates as giants, but not on the distorted grounds developed by people like Alloway, Monsieur Tapie, and others who stand on *their image* of the fraudulent shoulders of Mr. Rosenberg. He refuses to be consoled by the fact that all this has meant money in the bank for the pseudo-fathers. He refuses *also* to generate a single hint, intimation, hypothesis, guess, or line of prose about the true (Greenbergian) grounds of their greatness!

There are many other evidences of the vulnerability of Greenberg's analysis to its own strictures. One of his central points, for instance, seems to be that the critics, in their naïveté, see each tendentious ripple on the tide of modern art as something sui generis, without precedent. Contrariwise, Mr. Greenberg fails "to discern anything in the new abstract painting that is that new." He continues: "I can see nothing essential in it that cannot be shown to have evolved out of either Cubism or Impressionism (if we include Fauvism in the latter), just as I cannot see anything essential in Cubism or Impressionism whose development cannot be traced back to the Renaissance." Since this weighty thesis is not further developed, it is at least fair to observe that "tracing back" is a very general class of operations, and it is therefore difficult to know what such an assertion proves, or is meant to mean. For example, the Renaissance *could* be thought a necessary condition to the eventual destruction of what it had learned about painting. Is that what Mr. Greenberg means? Again, there are shapes and colors in Renaissance painting (also pigments and canvas), and these elements still seem in some sense present in de Kooning. Perhaps it is this!

Again, in a spirit somewhat inconsonant with the point just examined, Mr. Greenberg addresses himself to the following large questions:

> Why is art writing the only kind of writing in English that has lent itself to Existentialist and Phenomenological rhetoric? What is there about modern art itself that leads minds like Herbert Read's and Harold Rosenberg's astray? The answer is not one, I think, that reflects on modern art. It has to do with the speed with which modernist painting and sculpture have outrun the common categories of art criticism, invalidating them not only for the present or future but also for the past. (This has not been a revolution; it has been a clarification.) (71)

Once more our author remains coy. *What* has been clarified?

But my favorite sentence in the article, and one that should surely go down in history as Greenberg's Canon, is the following: "It is discovered that flung paint can be as thoroughly controlled and as carefully manipulated as patted or stroked paint." Perhaps I am a pathological risk-taker, but I challenge Mr. Greenberg, or any of the artists in his stable, to fling me a "City of Toledo." I even rather doubt that it can be flicked, poured, sprayed, swabbed, sponged, or mopped.

My sketch of ameaning in the modern history of the arts and humanities has, of course, been ridiculously selective. I will be told that different selections would give different trends. Of course. But I think the trend towards ameaning a *dominant* one.

I will be told that people (that is, at least some) have been predicting the end of art throughout the century, and that it has not died. But that does not preclude the possibility that it has been dying, and the present symptoms offer thin ground for reassurance.

But some—who agree with the trend of the present diagnosis—will say: "Why worry? Things will soon be put right. The assumptions of modernism, of avant-gardism are now under widespread rescrutiny. Has not

Irving Howe, one of the old-line (or "mid-old-line") New York critics, admonished his colleagues to re-examine their modernist premises (Howe 1968)? Has not John Weightman, an influential English student of French literature who tracked the trajectory of the *nouveau roman* with some respect, been led to raise some queasy questions about the entire concept of the avant-garde (Weightman 1969) — as a result of vertigo prompted by the emergence of the *nouveau-nouveau roman?*

I certainly welcome these and other dissents. But, given sufficient time, I think I could show that the *analyses* in which many of them are housed — and the "solutions" often offered — are as ameaningful as the phenomena which occasion them! Most of these dissenters do not see the problems of modernism in empirical, psychological terms; as rooted in certain lawful regularities of human cognitive function. Nor do they see psychological modes of analysis (in *some* sense of psychology) as among the important paths towards the *liberation* of world-wide sense and sensibility from their present ameaningful constraints.

In conclusion, may I assure you that today's concern has been a thoroughly scientific one. The independent variables have been people, artifacts, situations, institutions and history. The dependent variable has been the appalled experience of one, hopefully human, being.

9

Psychology and Its Human Clientele: Beneficiaries or Victims?

Foreword

This chapter considers the impact of scientific psychology on its eager lay consumership or — in the prejudgmental terms commonly applied to such issues — on "human welfare." I had long wished to demonstrate the vacuity of the presumption that scientific psychology is a font of great "gifts" (actual and potential) to the human race, and to show — via *particular* illustrations — that the force of modern psychology has been to coarsen or, indeed, obliterate many of the insights concerning the human condition which have slowly emerged in the history of the humanities and, more generally, within human praxis. A strategic opportunity for such an endeavor arose when I was invited to participate in the first of the University of Houston symposia on "Psychology and Society," held in 1978 (Kasschau and Kessel 1980). This symposium was given to a reanalysis of issues that George Miller had raised a decade earlier in his presidential address to the American Psychological Association. Miller's (1969) address — "Psychology as a Means of Promoting Human Welfare" — had become something of a classic in relation to its theme — but had always impressed me as a classic in another sense: that of an exercise celebrating the mainstream pretensions and objectives of a flawed and turmoiled discipline. As such, Miller's paper is an irresistible datum for analysis by the cognitive pathologist — it provides a rich source for the isolation and assessment of ameaningful profession-centered simplisms bearing on a very grave set of issues. It is to be emphasized (and I think this evident in the text) that my paper is not an attack on Professor Miller. The intention is to approach

Miller's address as an impersonal artifact that is highly revelatory of the beliefs and values of many psychologists (as would seem to be confirmed by the wide resonance elicited by the artifact in question).

Introduction

In 1930, one of the most rigorous English literary critics of the century, F. R. Leavis, was eager to show in an essay on D. H. Lawrence, whose novels he much respected, that there are worse things in this world than Lawrence's admitted extravagances in his treatment of certain psychological topics. To illustrate, he quotes the following passage by another author:

> Is it too unattainable a social ideal to believe that every man, woman and child should be trained about his own organism as thoroughly as the last boy was trained about the clock? We could very quickly teach children enough anatomy to give them a thorough working notion of their body, nervous system, heart, lungs, liver, kidneys, glands, sex apparatus. . . .
>
> Next we should teach the rudiments of hygiene (what may be called "mental hygiene"), show them in the simplest kind of terms how infantile unverbalised behaviour arises, and how it is carried over into adult life; teach them about fear, love, and anger reactions, work out with them how the individual behaves in depressions. Teach them what exhibition behaviour is like, how easy seclusion behaviour develops, about invalidism and other nascent psychoses. Teach them first to spot these reaction patterns in others, and then, most important of all, how to spot them in themselves by watching and tabulating their own behaviour. What boy or girl taught in this way could not check his own behaviour three or four times a month? "For days I have fought with my parents — two or three times in the last week I have been depressed and have tried to find excuses for not going to school and doing my work." . . . Or once more, "I find that I am going with girls much less than I used to and that I have begun to gang up with boys in the neighbourhood."
>
> Having taught individuals to observe their own behaviour in this way, as they observe the behaviour of others, can't we next teach them what to do when their records show that they are getting into jams? In other words, give them the essentials of corrective hygiene. For example: "All my work has slowed down. I am lacking in pep, don't care whether I go to see any-

body or not; I have been leading a humdrum existence, things haven't gone right at home. I guess I'll talk to my physician. He will probably tell me I had better pack up and go for a week's fishing or hunting, and that when I come back I'd better change things around a bit and try to do some interesting jobs, get some hobbies going that I have been flirting with for a long time, and to reach some satisfactory decision about my sex life which has been bothering me lately."

I would give this training before the fourteenth year, since at this age the great mass of our population gives up its schooling. Can young children get all this? I am hopeful of it. My business experience has opened my eyes to how simply things can be put to the public — how in homely words nearly all the worth-while truths of science can be set forth.

Among Leavis's comments, he points out that:

Dr. Watson, of course, is an extreme instance, but he has great influence in America, and it is not for proposals like the above that he is regarded in England as a crank. They merely represent in a pronounced form certain tendencies that are general in the West. . . . Civilised life is certainly threatened with impoverishment by education based on crude and defective psychology, by standardisation at a low level, and by the inculcation of a cheap and shallow emotional code. (Leavis 1930, 30–32)

Little did Leavis know at this time that, far from Watson's continuing to be looked upon as a "crank" in England, a second behaviorist revolution — deeming itself more sophisticated than Watson's but in no wise embarrassed by his priority — would be staged twenty years later by Oxford philosophers!

When I arrived in England in 1952 to commence a Fulbright year, I was amazed to discover that British psychologists were beginning a frenetic love affair with Hullian theory, especially in that this was precisely the juncture at which Hull's influence had begun its rapid decline in America. That circumstance, incidentally, was not a little embarrassing to me, for I had just completed a massive critique of Hull (Koch 1954) which did nothing to mitigate the erosion of his influence.

Dr. Miller's (1969) invitation that psychology be given away was fulsomely realized long before he had issued it. Is this not the psychological — nay, the psychologist — century? Who, these days, would consort with a friend, lover, relative — even dog, cat, or horse — who was not a psycholo-

293

gist? Who, in recent decades, has eluded teachers, preachers, friends, parents, bosses, colleagues, brokers, bankers, salesmen, air hostesses, who do not *treat* one rather than ply their respective crafts in the scientifically unillumined modes of olden times?

Throughout this century (and before), psychology *has* been under gracious dissemination — whether in school, bar, office, or bedroom; whether by book, magazine, electronic propagation, or word of mouth — to a voracious consumership. People everywhere have been given, gratis, revolutionary reconceptions of the nature of man — reams, truckloads of them — all based on cogent and valid *scientific* evidence. They have been analogized, even hypostasized, as cockroaches, dogs, monkeys, and especially rats; as telephone exchanges, computers, or colligations of billions of the latter; as configured systems of protons, electrons, neutrons, and neutrinos, or as epiphenomena of direct current distributions in electrolytes, or as code-bearing macromolecules; as products of insufficient prophylaxis, or of neurobiotaxis, homeostatics, conditioning, reinforcement contingencies, cognitive maps, cell assemblies, TOTE hierarchies, or computer programming lists; as empty intersection areas between S's and R's, topologically differentiated Jordan curves, collections of exponential functions, or schematic sowbugs; as cybernetic mechanisms, information-processing entities, or finite automata; as utilities optimizers, game strategists, pleasure-principle protagonists; as mutual voyeurs, ego titillators, or masturbators; as collectivities of traits, attitudes, dispositions, instincts, or factors; as reactors, agents, achievers, self-realizers, autonomy maximizers; as id-ego-superego structures, orgone receptacles, plastic-phallus copulators, vibrator cohabitators; as elements of group mind, filings in social force fields, cooperating or competing or reinforcement bartering *socii*.

These are but a few of the revolutionary conceptions freely available in the public domain — and mankind has listened reverently. No matter if sometimes the mind of the eager apprehender will spin a bit. The revolutions are sufficiently graded in difficulty to make at least a few accessible to everyone. "Everyman" has been well served! And indeed, each ardent seeker of a theory of himself will do everything possible to conform his person to the theories that come his way (for the truly diligent, that *could be* all of them), even if he understands them not at all. "Everyman" is grateful!

In his 1969 paper, Dr. Miller does seem a bit vacillatory as to where the great thrust of psychological philanthropy should be localized. He does, in all fairness, seem to favor a conception of man as self-therapist rather than patient. But his somewhat inconsonant emphasis on the need for augmenting our cadre of human and social *engineers* seems to leave a place for problem-oriented troubleshooters. If this indeed be "giving psychology away," it can be said that at this prosier level of dealing with particular personal problems (if they ever *are* particular), psychology has been distributed with immense abandon, even if a bit less cheaply. Who among us has not been psychoanalyzed, encounterized, non-directive counselorized, professionally humanized, Tao-or-Zen or transcendental meditationalized, reality or sexuality therapized, biofeedbackized, behavior modified, drug cathecticized, transorbitally leucotomized, lobotomized; or merely tranquilized and/or shocked; massaged and/or Rolfed; group nudified and/or "crotch-eyeballified"?

In short, I fear that by 1969, when Dr. Miller was making his invitation, he was calling for a policy that had been under massive and explosively cumulating implementation ever since that glorious moment in the history of civilization when psychology discovered itself to be a science. Lest any perverse hypothesis be formed that Dr. Miller's invitation *turned off* this policy in the years after it was made, may I refer the potential contrarian to the following culling of titles of books reviewed in the fat December 1977 issue of *Contemporary Psychology: Attachment Behavior; Schizophrenia: The Sacred Symbol of Psychiatry; Increasing Leadership Effectiveness; Stay Slim for Good; Stop Smoking for Good; Take It Off and Keep It Off: A Behavioral Program for Weight Loss and Healthy Living; Permanent Weight Control; Alternatives to Alcohol Abuse; Take Charge: A Personal Guide to Behaviour Modification; Learning to Use Extrasensory Perception; Marital Communication and Decision Making; Hypnosis and Behavior Therapy; The Naked Therapist: A Collection of Embarrassments; Human Sexuality in Four Perspectives; Androgyny: Toward a New Theory of Sexuality; The Intensive Group Experience: A Guide; Interpersonal Living: The Skills/Contract Approach to Human-Relations Training in Groups; The Powerholders; Psychosexual Problems: Psychotherapy, Counseling and Behavior Modification; Psychology of Women: Behavior in a Biosocial Context; Exploring Sex Differences; Barred from School: Two Million Children; Marriage and Alternatives: Exploring Intimate Relationships; Beyond Intellectual Sexism: A New Woman, A New Reality; Learning to Teach: A Decision-Making System; In Search of Identity; Children and Television; Drug Education: Results and Recommendations; The First Encounter: The Beginnings in Psychotherapy; Korotkyi psykhologichnyi slovnyk* (Short Dictionary of Psychology in the Ukrainian); *Psychology and Consumer Affairs; Psychology of Sport:*

The Behavior, Motivation, Personality, and Performance of Athletes; Love and Hate on the Tennis Court: How Hidden Emotions Affect Your Game; Death, Society, and Human Experience; Mutual Criticism; Behavioral Psychology for Teachers. I would estimate that of the 110 (or so) books reviewed in this issue of *Contemporary Psychology,* perhaps twenty-five could be thought addressed to a technically or professionally qualified audience. Let us be generous about the matter and set the "giveaway" ratio as 4 to 1. If *any* man has a basis for complaint, it surely cannot be Everyman!

Leavis's appalled demur to Watson is but one ripple in a flow of critical concern with the massive dehumanizing impact of certain aspects of science and technology that has extended throughout the century. This phenomenon (whether its manifestations be phrased as the simplification of sensibility, homogenization of taste, attenuation of the capacity for experience, or in some other way) has formed the basis for that continuing chorus of pain in which every sensitive critic of twentieth-century culture — whether he be writer, artist, humanist-scholar, or scientist — has participated. One can doubt that there has been a period in history in which the style and message of its intellectuals have been so uniformly rejective.

Of one thing we can be sure: However the symptoms of dehumanization be phrased, they are certainly in the first instance psychological symptoms. Coarsening of discrimination, simplification of sensibility, homogenization of taste, whatever their far-flung dependencies, are matters which certainly seem relevant to psychological concern. One would expect that psychologists and social scientists would be more deeply concerned with such trends than members of any other group in the community of scholarship. Have they been? Far from it. Though some secret part of many psychologists must surely be troubled by these trends, few have given this part of themselves a hearing.

But that is not all. There are some — mainly outside psychology — who would maintain that modern psychology, far from developing a counterstress to the dehumanization process, had itself contributed to it. Such diagnoses have not been uncommon in the past four or five decades. Though the details of the argument vary widely, the pattern is familiar: Psychology has projected to the world a simplistic and demeaning image of man (as we have seen, a generous plethora of such!); modern man, rendered especially vulnerable to the authority of science by the many social and historical factors which have exacerbated his need for security, embraces these images and happily compresses himself to them. A seemingly absurd argument, and one often made by absurd people! But it is disturbingly true that some form of it is often made as well by minds who are among the most brilliant and intellectually responsible of our time: literary, philosophical, *and* scientific. *Could* such an argument, when properly spelled out and qualified, contain a germ of truth? Even a germ of such truth would entail a terrible responsibility.

Apparently, Dr. Miller senses some of the horror that critics seek to convey by such attributions as "dehumanization." In his paper there is strong evidence of unrest over one common presupposition of many of the images of man in wide currency—namely, their definition of man as *object*. Along with Kingsley Davis, Dr. Miller does not wish to treat human beings as "pure instrumentality." He "agree[s] with Davis that behavioral and social sciences cannot be applied to people and institutions in the same way physical and biological sciences are applied to objects and organisms." Nor does he claim to like the notion of *control* as a goal for the applied psychological enterprise. He would "prefer to speak of understanding and prediction" as the major routes towards implementation of the psychological "revolution." Moreover, the "heart of the psychological revolution will be a new and scientifically based conception of man as an individual and as a social creature." Indeed, this revolution is not altogether "pie in the sky," it is "already upon us" and its furtherance requires us not merely to "strengthen its scientific base, but we must also try to communicate it to our students and to the public." Furthermore, the "enrichment of public psychology by scientific psychology constitutes the most direct and important application of our science to the promotion of human welfare."

I am agreeably impressed by aspects of Dr. Miller's paper, both in the letter and in the spirit, but more so in spirit than letter. What is attractive about the spirit is a certain tentativeness, humility, even irresoluteness of the sort that betokens deep perturbation over the tendency of our discipline. But these very qualities of spirit tend to cloud the contours of letter. Then, too, Dr. Miller's mood oscillations are engaging but do not enhance univocality: When he renders judgments that he labels "optimistic," I sense a weaker registration of conviction (and a stronger one that he is in the course of a presidential address) than when he counterposes his doubts and reservations. In short, this is a difficult paper to deal justly with but, to my mind, is sufficiently fraught with dangerous profession-centered simplisms and autisms to merit analysis even at the risk of some injustice.

Take Dr. Miller's abrogation of "control" as the objective of the psychological enterprise: I am delighted to find him saying that "changing behavior is pointless in the absence of any coherent plan for how it should be changed." And he is on solid ground when he suggests that detailed reinforcement-contingencies demonstrated in animal behavior studies may prove but tenuously extrapolatable to the human case. But it is worrisome to find that his "concern has nothing to do with the validity of these ideas." I am impressed when he advocates the principle of "habeas mentem" and adds that if "we really did have a new scientific way to control human behavior, it would be highly immoral to let it fall into the hands of some small group of men, even if they were psychologists." But I flag a bit when the ground for rejection becomes "there is a better way to advertise psychology" in that "reinforcement is only one of many important ideas that we have to offer."

The succubus of *control* is not, however, easily exorcized! After "giving psychology away" in the form of a new "paradigm" for the conduct of social life, we find Miller discovering the need for scads of human and social "engineers"—for "many more psychological technologists who can apply our science to the personal and social problems of the general public." Though this psychotechnological troubleshooting is to be mitigated by shaping it to "the *perceived* needs of the people who receive it," it is nevertheless to include such matters as teaching supervisors "how to write a job description and how to evaluate the abilities and personalities of those who fill the job"; also, "perhaps we should teach him the art of persuasion, or the time and place for positive reinforcement." Moreover, why not pass on the "many obvious and useful suggestions that we could make" to *non*-psychologists; as, for instance, "principles governing the design and evaluation of programmed materials," psychometrics, interview methods, etc. Indeed, the "techniques involved are not some esoteric branch of witchcraft . . . reserved for those with Ph.D.'s in psychology. When the ideas are made sufficiently concrete and explicit, the scientific foundations of psychology can be grasped by sixth-grade children." As a matter of fact, "if we psychologists are ready for it, we may be able to contribute a coherent and workable philosophy, based on the science of psychology."

I will note only in passing the striking similarity of Dr. Miller's tone (and argument-line) to that of Watson. But are we not here in the ambiance of a Russellian "type"-paradox? *Control* has been abjured. We do not impose our *own* solutions on the personal and social problems that we address. We allow the subject to suffer his problem, define it (though for *that* he'll probably need our expert help), and even decide it (though, there too, we're certainly on the ready). All we as psychologists do is provide the "scientifically valid" technology—based on the latest Ph.D. dissertation and saturated with the authority of Science—which will convey the inept lout to a solution. We refrain from controlling the subject; we control the subject's control of the subject. "We are," in the words of Dr. Miller, "proposing to tamper with the adaptive process itself." Did I say "subject"? Or are we already in the presence of an "object"?

And similarly, Dr. Miller fails to see that the revolutionary reconception of the nature of man that he will be gallantly offering the world—whether in the guise of paradigm 2 or paradigm 42—will, by the very rhetoric of its proclaimed "scientific validity," its linkage with the iconology of science, have the force of making, remaking, steering the development of its beneficiaries. Did I say "beneficiaries"? Or are we already in the presence of "victims"?

Some Deeper Problems in Dr. Miller's World View

There are some assumptions built into Dr. Miller's conception of the human applicability of psychology which are deeply revelatory of the superficiality, ahistoricism, and, indeed, hubris of the modern psychological enterprise. These assumptions—or at least the cognitive scotomata that foster them—will emerge from an analysis of Dr. Miller's *central* examples of actual or potential gifts that scientific psychology can make to the world. I am prepared to argue that *every one* of Dr. Miller's illustrative "gifts" is either (1) of dubious efficacy, utility, or truth value; or (2) *not* uniquely attributable to the exercise of psychological method or to the power of the technical psychological imagination; or (3) *not* uncontestable by alternate analyses or insights (sometimes a large plurality of such) that have emerged in the rangy history of observation and cerebration essayed by humanists and other scientifically illiterate citizens. I will scrutinize, however, only two major examples: his Varela-based paradigm "of the social nature of man," and his speculations on the import of what might be called the "pupil-contract" approach to the teaching of reading developed by Ashton-Warner. Because of the complexity of the issues raised by these examples, my discussion will necessarily be a glancing one.

The Varela "Paradigm"

The Varela conception of man—which is "based on psychological research" and is to bring about the brave new world that Miller would like to foster—is developed in contrast to "a set of assumptions on which our social institutions are presently based." It is necessary that I quote Miller's précis of these two paradigms.

The Current Social Paradigm

All men are created equal. Most behavior is motivated by economic competition, and conflict is inevitable. One truth underlies all controversy, and unreasonableness is best countered by facts and logic. When something goes wrong, someone is to blame, and every effort must be made to establish his guilt so that he can be punished. The guilty person is responsible for his own misbehavior and for his own rehabilitation. His teachers and supervisors are too busy to become experts in social science; their role is to devise solutions and see to it that their students or subordinates do what they are told.

Varela's "Revolution"

There are large individual differences among people, both in ability and personality. Human motivation is complex and no one ever acts as he does for any single reason, but, in general, positive incentives are more effective than threats or punishments. Conflict is no more inevitable than disease and can be resolved or, still better, prevented. Time and resources for resolving social problems are strictly limited. When something goes wrong, how a person perceives the situation is more important to him than the "true facts," and he cannot reason about the situation until his irrational feelings have been toned down. Social problems are solved by correcting causes, not symptoms, and this can be done more effectively in groups than individually. Teachers and supervisors must be experts in social science because they are responsible for the cooperation and individual improvement of their students or subordinates.

It would require a ten-year seminar to disentangle the skein of intellectual grotesqueries contained in this contrast. Looking first at the second paradigm (the Varela-Miller universe), it can be said that not a single one of the beliefs there set forth is historically recent, nor was "psychological research" required for its discovery. Cognate views emerge from many strands (some of multi-millennial length) within the humanities and, in the broadest sense, the social studies (e.g., social philosophy, philosophy of history, etc.). And there are cognate strands within social doctrines associated with major world religions. The history of utopian thought alone will provide a hypersufficient basis for every one of these ideas, and the history of utopian *experimentation,* even if restricted alone to the some two hundred utopian communities established in this country during the nineteenth century, has involved the embodiment of such ideas in multiply permuted combinations. Moreover, it is in these humanistic and practical contexts that such ideas and their cognates have received their most powerful and subtle formulations. It is dubious that the psychological research has strengthened or clarified these "insights."

In the very same breath, I must add that not a single component of this paradigm is non-problematic (whether as formulated, or on the presumption of the best conceivable formulation), and not a single component, in all probability, will ever achieve preemptive or totally general warrant. Finally, looking at these word-strings as given, some are truistic or even tautologous, and some are plain silly. Let us consider these statements one at a time, and point merely to the most obvious objections or qualifications that a non-psychologist human of average critical intelligence would raise.

That "there are large individual differences . . . both in ability and personality" is a truism to which few demurs have been registered in the history of the world *except* by psychologists afflicted with rampant environmentalism. Fortunately, with the demise of classical behaviorism, this quaint disease has largely disappeared, but it must be added that in the opinion of many, the psychology of individual differences has had a scandalously deleterious impact on human welfare throughout the century.

That "human motivation is complex and no one reacts as he does for any single reason" is a truism few persons who have led normal lives could have doubted, but has been brought under question only by the rhetoric of certain of the simplistic drive theories that dominated certain areas of psychology over a wide time-swath in this century. It is, however, the humanist — and especially the more exalted masters of such forms as drama and the novel — who has documented the complexity, indeed, the antinomal character of human motivation at the most profound and subtle levels, and has massively conveyed and evidenced a human truth to which psychologists have given little heed: namely, that the complexity of human motivation can be such as to render the *meanings* of action inherently ambiguous and unrecapturable, that man (when conceived as agent, not object) can never finally adjudicate the question of self-sincerity, or attain final and cozy confidence in his appraisals of others.

Are "positive incentives . . . more effective than threats of punishment"? Mankind did not wait upon psychologists to perceive that often this is so. Often it is not so. I doubt that psychologists can define the differential conditions for selecting and applying the one technology of influence as against the other with any greater nicety than ordinary mortals of perspicacity and sensitivity. In this century, modal practice has certainly moved towards a preference for use of positive incentives in many of the institutions which seek to guide and influence human beings. But it is possible to argue that there have been intervals and contexts in this century in which permissiveness has been practiced to a fault.

The assertion that "conflict is no more inevitable than disease" is both false and silly. Of course, modality judgments (in the philosophers' sense) are notoriously dangerous. Yet the distinguished microbiologist and pathologist Dr. René Dubos in fact believes that disease is here to stay. And *conflict* — in some ample subset of its infinitude of forms — is not *merely* inevitable; it is a definitive condition of life in the absence of which no experience or action could have meaning, structure, or value. That particular conflicts "can be resolved" and even "prevented" is news to no sentient creature.

How "a person perceives the situation" *has* to be more important to him than the "true facts" if only for the reason that consensual truth cannot be persuasive upon one who, by hypothesis, is no party to the consensus. Of course, there have been "cosmic eye" theories of truth throughout the history of epistemology, but side by side with these have been theories stressing the perspectival and observer-dependent character of "truth." That a person "cannot reason about the situation until his irrational feelings have been toned down" is my candidate for a niche in a Hall of Fame dedicated to the housing of tautologies. On a kinder interpretation, this word-string can be seen as registering the view that emotion or affect distorts reason — a view which is assertable but, in my opinion, unless considerably qualified and specified, wrong.

As for the insight that "social problems are solved by correcting causes, not symptoms" — it can be said that the lexical constraints upon "cause" and "symptom" are such that the correction of a symptom *cannot* entail the correction of its cause. Are "social problems" solved "more effectively in groups than individually"? A sane, even if scientifically illiterate, response would have to be: that depends on cases.

The final element of the "paradigm" ("Teachers and supervisors must be experts in social science because," etc., etc.) has the weird property of being contraindicated by every preceding assertion, on the assumption that the asserter is a social scientist.

If we turn now to the initial paradigm, the bad one, the contrast case

302

descriptive of current social dynamics which must be replaced, it can be said that not a single component is determinately more anemic in truth value, or necessarily more counterproductive in its bearing on social life, than is its putative contrary in the second paradigm. I quail before the project of a sentence-by-sentence analysis. Let us be content with a sample.

In relation to the first sentence ("All men are created equal"), the presumption is apparently that such an assertion is disconfirmed by modern differential psychology. But, of course, the literal fact of variance has no bearing on such a statement when read in the light of its historical and normative context. It is embarrassing to have to point out that for several hundred years it has been evident to most humans, however psychologically misinformed, that it is "equality of rights" that such a statement predicates of man, and not equality of ability, hair color, nose shape, personality, or any other psychic or physical trait. The widely prevalent (and indeed, persuasive) reading is, of course, that there is a range of rights, considerations, entitlements, which all human beings can claim by virtue of their membership, *as such,* in the human race. Under law and God. It should be news to no one that there is a large and respectable body of literature — within social philosophy, law, ethics, theology — addressed to the identification, specification, and adjudication of these rights, a vital task, even if resistant in principle to full and final resolution.

Few reasonable men believe that "one truth underlies all controversy," but one would be hard put to find a reasonable man who does *not* believe that "one truth" underlies *some* controversy. What is implicit here is a regrettable belief, widespread among behavioral scientists and among do-gooders of fuzzily egalitarian proclivity, that "truth" is an epiphenomenon of a vested interest. The view that "unreasonableness" is *not* "best countered by facts and logic" can be seen as reflecting another pseudo-sophisticated stereotype within the behavioral science Weltanschauung. Committed or tendentious persons *may,* in fact, be refractory to "facts and logic." Changes of attitude and belief *may,* in fact, be more easily facilitated by therapy, bribery, flattery, and other extra-rational modalities of persuasion than by rational means. Whether even *this* will be so will depend on person and context. But note that what is considered naughty in this plank of the paradigm is the view that unreasonableness is "best" countered by "facts and logic." Certainly there is a wide swath of mankind — inclusive of the community of all genuine scientists and all genuine scholars (in contradistinction to the pseudo case) — who believe that the best antidote to unreason is reason, in any normative sense of the word "best."

Note the statements concerning "guilt" and "responsibility." I shirk differentiated analysis of the pattern of assumptions from which the proscription of such beliefs (e.g., that the "guilty person is responsible for his own misbehavior and for his own rehabilitation") issues. But I would certainly rather read Dostoevsky on guilt, responsibility, and rehabilitation than Miller, or even than Freud. I would rather read Kant on these matters than Watson, Skinner, or even the most able management theorist or the most streamlined penologist.

I apologize for this painfully literal analysis. It is even in some respects unfair. Mr. Varela may indeed be a superb manager. But so was Robert Owen, in his management, at the very beginning of the industrial revolution, of the factory, schools, and associated community, at New Lanark—and *he* was able to set his utopian microcosm into effective operation without the help of a single scientific finding from industrial, social, or general psychology.

As for Dr. Miller, it must be acknowledged that the context of his presentation permitted him but the barest adumbration of his two paradigms, and that he modestly indicates that "no doubt other psychologists would draw the picture somewhat differently." But Dr. Miller addresses a large and grave issue when he proposes to promote human welfare by giving psychology away, and the potential recipient has a right to expect that even illustrative tidbits of the beneficences to be vouchsafed by this general policy make sense. We psychologists have held forth to humanity some of the most grandiose promissory notes ever issued by a field of scholarship. What we have thus far delivered is miles and miles of half-meaningful prose which has conveyed quarter-truths and eighth-truths and untruths concerning the human condition in a sordid patois of tarnished scientistic imagery. Our "gift" has been a progressive obfuscation of what man already knows about his own condition.

Pupil-Contract versus Pupil-Contact in the Teaching of Reading

Dr. Miller's second major illustration of the kind of gift that mankind can expect from psychology is the approach to the teaching of reading developed by Ashton-Warner. In brief, this is a "contract" approach such that the child is asked what words he wants. The

> children ask for . . . words that are bound up with their own loves and fears. She [i.e., Ashton-Warner] writes each child's word on a large card and gives it to him. . . . And he learns to read them almost immediately. It is *his* word, and each morning

he retrieves his own words from the pile collected each night by the teacher. . . . Given this start, children begin to write, using their own words, and from there the teaching of reading follows naturally. Under this regimen, a word is not an imposed task to be learned with reinforcements borrowed from some external source of motivation. Learning the word is itself reinforcing.

Dr. Miller proceeds to link this method with White's conception of "competence motivation," which suggests the "use" of "psychology to give people skills that will satisfy their urge to feel more effective." He is enthusiastic over the possibility that "some might want to learn more about the science that helped them increase their competence." In other words, "competence motivation" is a good thing for the world and a good thing for psychology, which, in turn, entails more good news for the world. It is the thin end of a wedge which will insert psychology right into the action—we will be in a position to "do something practical for nurses, policemen, prison guards, salesmen—for people in many different walks of life."

May I first note the curious fact that the Ashton-Warner example is an obvious counter-example. It flies in the face of Dr. Miller's thesis that scientific psychology has profound resources of knowledge to give away. The seminal method that he proposes to give to the world was discovered right in that world *not* by a psychologist but—as he himself records—"by an inspired teacher in a small New Zealand school."

There is, however, a plexus of deeper issues here; I can only scratch their surface. John Stuart Mill was subjected to an extraordinarily pressureful and hyper-disciplined education by his father, James, who assumed the role of tutor when his son was a virtual infant. The story is told in detail in J. S. Mill's autobiography, and the tale is more or less of an archetype of the genesis of a child prodigy. As we further learn in Mill's autobiography, he went through a period of deep and sustained melancholia as a young man, and it is easy to discern a relation between this and the mode of his early education. Many writers have pitied Mill for the severity of his training, but Raymond Williams has pointed out that it did, after all, eventuate in a very fine mind and a very fine person. It clearly would not be sensible to universalize upon such an educational model. But are we to create the conditions that would disenfranchise the very possibility of such exceptional modes of education? Shall we not be permitted to have *occasional* prodigies like Mill?

The institution of the English public school has been characterized by a degree of discipline and pressure that verges, in the opinion of many who have been exposed to it, on brutality. Some of its products, like George Orwell, have expended much of their adult psychic energies on the effort to recover from their school experiences. Yet this system has had a very high success ratio in turning out persons of exceptional intellectual altitude, refinement, and cultural literacy.

Despite the harsh rigors of their early educations, a John Stuart Mill and a George Orwell have not, one can guess, had to depend on extrinsic motivation for the functioning and development of their rather high-order linguistic skills. It can only be assumed that even within the pressureful context of their early training, intrinsic motivation soon came to their aid! It is well to note, also, that the intrinsic interest ("grab-value," "value-property saturation") of certain ranges of intellectual material can only become evident on the assumption that the material is encountered. It is unlikely that pupils who learn reading on a contract basis will stipulate words from Homer, or even Virgil.

What I have said is certainly not to be interpreted as a rejection of the Ashton-Warner method. It could well be a method of choice for some persons in some contexts. As a generalized pattern for the human race to be implemented by all schools tomorrow on the say-so of "scientific psychology" it must be adjudged highly questionable.

Dr. Miller could have found better examples from ordinary human experience of the importance of—and even the developmental conditions of—"competence motivation." To suggest that scientific psychology has a larger or deeper range of insights into the conditions which promote particular competences (or the illusion thereof) than what is already known by sensitive and intelligent teachers in every field—or by summit-level possessors and practitioners of every complex skill in the human gamut—is simply counterfactual.

An Alternate View of Psychology

So much for an analysis of Dr. Miller's highly philanthropic proposals of 1969. I, too, am a philanthropist. In sum, I believe that the most charitable thing we can do is not to give psychology away, but to take it back. Such a program of reverse philanthropy, however, would require the efforts of a far larger workforce than we now have for at least the next century. And even that effort would fail, for Dr. Miller's "revolution" is already in place. Modern man now *wishes* to be an object: it is deeply reassuring to think oneself mendable, calibratable, lubricatable, and refinishable like any other machine. Our victims are so convinced that they are beneficiaries that they would no doubt reconvince us.

Views as to the applicational potentialities of psychology, the promise of the field (if any) for human welfare, depend, of course, on one's positive conception of psychology. My own perspective has been developed in previous chapters, particularly chapters 4 and 5. Relative to the aspirations of psychologists who wish to hoist man to a new and revolutionary conception of himself on the petard of a science that can be rendered fully intelligible to "sixth-grade children," the notion of the psychological studies presented there will be seen to entail but modest promises to the human race. The psychological studies, when significantly conceived, will be seen as immensely challenging, immensely difficult, and very possibly in some ranges entirely refractory areas of *scholarship*. As is the case in other serious and dignified fields of scholarship, knowledge exceeding in precision and differentiation what the human race already knows will be won only by the ardent and creative efforts of relevantly equipped and sensitive persons who proceed with a minimum of public-relations fanfare. Psychology has been flagrantly and vulgarly oversold. In my view, it will find its dignity only to the extent that it retracts the feckless promises, pseudo-conceptualizations, and corrupt technologies it has flung out upon the world, and succeeds in reestablishing authentic continuity with the Western scholarly tradition.

My view proposes a relation of partnership between the psychological studies and the human race, rather than patronizing handouts of counterfeit knowledge, or even the variant of the latter implicit in Mr. Miller's policy of palsy, "on-the-line" troubleshooting. The partnership that I propose would see the best efforts towards specifying man's inner universe (and his condition) of the most sensitive and prehensile minds in history as *already* part of the *tissue* of psychology. It would see those efforts as criterial in respect to the assessment of "new" psychological knowledge.

In this connection, I have devised a classificatory test (Koch 1976a; cf. chapter 5) for conceptual frameworks (or more pretentiously, "theories") in the psychological studies — a test which I believe to provide a central criterion in so-called issues of "theory choice" or even in absolute judgments of significance. This handy epistemological device can, if you will, be seen as a kind of consumer protection law in relation to the marketing of psychological wares. My perceptual theory of definition — which sees so-called empirical definition as *real* definition — entails that the knowledge coded in natural language and internalized in human sensibility gives us a kind of ontology of the human universe. On this basis, it becomes possible roughly to distinguish three kinds of theories or conceptual frameworks within the human studies: some that are *ontology-distorting,* some that are *ontology-respecting,* and some that are *ontology-revealing.* My theory of definition permits me to call any technical framework which obliterates or does not permit us in some way to "recapture" the network of epistemically rich concepts in the range of natural language bearing on its domain, *ontology-distorting.* A frame which merely "respects" such distinctions but does not (by processes of metaphor, etc., as I have analyzed them) permit the sharpening, extension, supplementation, or enrichment of natural language knowledge is *ontology-respecting.* A frame which *does* permit such sharpening, supplementation, or enrichment of the natural-language knowledge is *ontology-revealing.* At any given time it is, I think, possible to find within the gamut of the psychological studies conspicuous instances of frameworks within each of these categories. Regrettably, however, a frequency distribution of the frameworks currently comprising the substance of the psychological studies, as conventionally conceived, would be savagely skewed towards the ontology-distorting category.

My sense of partnership means also that we must relate to gifted humanists, artists, scientists, possessors of special skills and forms of connoisseurship in every field (not excluding managers, political leaders, planners — yes, and salesmen, nurses, and automobile mechanics, too) as allies and collaborators. We can expect no "technical" insight, or more refined insight than nontechnical mankind already has, into complex and subtle and humanly important phenomena until we address those phenomena. We do *not* address such phenomena when we inferentially recompose them from the activities of rats, college sophomores, or even computers. In every human area we must use high-order, refined, and relevantly specialized sensibility as a probe into the structure and dynamics of its own operations. In every field individuals of summit-level attainment must be assumed not only to generate the most interesting phenomena for study but must be assumed to know (in some sense of that slippery word) most about those phenomena. We should not be inhibited by the stereotypic belief that ownership of a process or skill disqualifies the owner as an explicator thereof. Though we must presume an ultimate core of ineffability in respect to all "tacit knowledge," we may also presume that the boundaries of what is tacit at any given time are larger than that core, and can be made to recede. The history of reflexive awareness is not, after all, a totally barren one. *Our* role as investigators must be to facilitate a recession of the tacit. To this we bring some slender but actual resources — at the minimum, a deep sense, derived from our own past failures, of the complexity of those factors of which action (or experience) is a function, and a bit of wisdom, similarly derived, about the criteria for an informative analysis. On this view of partnership, in which the target phenomena are located in other persons, it should be stressed that those persons are more properly to be construed as co-investigators than as subjects.

What does my conception of psychology say about the currently institutionalized implemental areas: the so-called applied fields which render formal services to our human clientele? It says, somewhat trivially but wholly confidently, that any analogy of their status to that of an applied natural science is obfuscatory, and remains so even when bearing in mind that the division between pure and applied science is nowhere a well-defined one. Further than this, it says that the various psychological studies of implemental cast would have to be addressed one at a time. To take one large case: My theory of definition suggests there to be severe and *principled* constraints to fullness and univocality of communication within such fields as clinical psychology or psychopathology (cf. chapter 5). I suspect, for instance, that not only do no two psychoanalysts *do* psychoanalysis in the same way (a fact granted by virtually everyone) but that no two of them "speak" psychoanalysis in sufficiently similar ways to warrant the conclusion that they hold the "same" theory. Yet the various theories or conceptual frames within clinical psychology do loosely influence the professional sensibilities of their followerships, and feed and guide their therapeutic practices, but differently so for each member. Clinical work is necessarily an *art* which must tap the resources of the entire person. It is well that clinical training involve broad exposure to the differentiated and subtle knowledge of the human condition embedded in the humanities (I would exclude only the one known as "humanistic psychology"), and perhaps even a soupçon of involvement in extra-academic and extra-professional life.

And what does my view say — more generally — about the relations between psychology and human welfare, the services that we can render, the gifts that can be given? Very little — in the space available. But I would build my answer around one pregnant, but no doubt opaque, concept which we need to dwell on and proceed to unpack in a particulate and experientially informed way: the concept of *disciplined connoisseurship*. Bertrand Russell once gave a characteristically simple and wise answer to a questioner who wished to know *how* he had arrived at the formidably differentiated, intellectual structures of *Principia Mathematica*. He replied merely that he had found that if he allowed his mind to dwell on a matter for a sufficient length of time, he began to see distinctions. Psychology may not yet have any large body of significant and humanly applicable principles of coded and general character: "laws." It *certainly* has *no* self-applying algorithms, or deep insights that can attach to quiddities by easy target-detecting "operational definitions." What it does have is many individuals, both in professional and more abstract research areas, whose minds have dwelled for long periods — in disciplined and passionate ways — on certain realms of human phenomena. Assuming relevant observational sensitivities and analytical powers, such minds inevitably form distinctions, detect patterns, develop implemental skills. The owners of minds so schooled are disciplined *connoisseurs*. Much of their knowledge is tacit, some of it is explicit: all of it may prove helpful to fellow human beings whose minds have not been comparably immersed in the same domains. The best way to provide psychological services would be to provide, where relevant, *human beings* (as consultants, therapists, etc.) in the many contexts involving human welfare; to provide psychologists as human beings who may be *disciplined connoisseurs* of certain ranges of human action and experience. The point to stress is that we do the world a great injustice if we unleash upon the world a corps of putative "technicians" who, under a cloak of scientific impeccability, have everything to offer but wisdom and understanding.

Not all human predicaments are resolvable, not even in principle. An ounce of mitigation is therefore preferable to a pseudo-solution weighing a ton. My modest conception of psychology can have, at best, only small and slow mitigative consequences.

Throughout the writing of this chapter, I have been obsessed by an image of gauges: billions of them reproducing at bacterial speed and threatening the residual space in the ecosystem. Hundreds of gauges are protruding from the orifices and integuments of each inhabitant of the world. The rational biped who used to stride through the world in quest of experience has become the sedentary reader of gauges and oscilloscope displays which monitor his condition. Do I feel elated or depressed? What does my electronic sphygmomanometer say? Better peep at my portable biofeedback module and get a fix on my brainwaves, too. And why not make an early appointment with my psychiatric team for a good going over? Better remind them to send me over to Neurology for a CAT scan.

The same interposition of gauges between events and our apprehension of them qualifies our reading of the social world. What is happening out there in the society at large, the body politic, the economy, or just merely in our own micro-world (whether it be General Motors or Blowing Rock State Teachers College) is totally obscured by a miasma of gauges, computer readouts, sociometric indicators, surveys. Reality is not merely displaced—indeed, rendered superfluous—by these instruments, but the surrogate reality is rendered even more perversely chaotic and unpredictable than the initial one by virtue of the "self-fulfilling-prophecy" impact of *each* reading. The trouble is compounded by the fact that most of these scale-faced beings are merely mock-ups, sans sensors.

The behavioral and social sciences have set a generous fraction of these instruments in place. Is it not time to relent? It will be painful while these quills are being retracted, but is it not possible that we gauge-bearing porcupines can yet rediscover our humanity?

10

The Image of Man in Encounter Groups

Foreword

This paper was written in c. 1969 for presentation before a "convocation" at a liberal arts college in Albion, Ohio. In searching for a theme that might be of interest to so mixed a group (the entire student body and faculty), I fixed upon my appalled reaction to the encounter group movement. The movement had come to national prominence during my stay (in the mid-1960s) in the Ford Foundation when I was out of contact with psychology. By 1967, when I returned to scholarship, the movement had not only attracted the broadest consumership in the history of psychotherapy, but had captured the involvement of virtually all psychologists of "humanist" leaning. One of the central ironies that engaged me was that the "humanist" wing of psychology—which had emerged in the mid-1950s as the first protest group of appreciable size to the behaviorist hegemony of the preceding forty years—had embraced a conception of man which, if anything, was *more* reductive, demeaning, and callow than that of behaviorism: another example of the too familiar phenomenon of *ameaning* finding a more impregnable housing within the very "critiques" meant to supplant its first-order artifacts.

My modest paper, written casually in a two- or three-day interval, had entirely unanticipated consequences. Word of the talk at Albion somehow got around—over the next few years I was invited to present my views on encounter groups at many universities and before several organizations. Even the leaders of the encounter movement themselves invited me to appear before the national convention of their organization (the Association for Humanistic Psychology), where they tried at once to mollify me and cure me of my "misapprehensions." Versions of the paper were published by invitation in three sources, and excerpts from these were quoted and commented upon in a motley variety of other sources (the oddest of which was the magazine *Money Sense*). In the course of my giving the talk at York University (Toronto), it was taped by the Canadian Broadcasting Company for broadcast over its FM network, and apparently was used frequently for a number of years. I have received possibly a thousand requests for reprints, and have also been the lucky recipient of scores of letters from encounter-victims. These circumstances say something about the dispersion of interest in the encounter movement then prevailing. They say something also about the quiet desperation experienced by a scholar who may prefer to rest his reputation upon less modish, if more technical endeavors. This chapter is based on the version published in the *American Scholar* (Koch 1973a).

«

Many social critics have been concerned about the tendency of modern man — especially American man — to prize images, pictures, more than the realities for which they "stand." Some fifteen years ago, I had the melancholy accident of falling through a then prevailing picture of psychology– one that contained some of the cant premises of what I now think to be the bad metaphor of "psychological science." Like most images, this one got out of phase with reality, and with its initial intention, almost as soon as it was formed.

Scientific psychology was stipulated into life in the late nineteenth century. That intensely optimistic age, understandably dazzled by the apparent cognitive and technological fruits of the natural sciences, decided to try out a hopeful new strategy: that of extending the methods of natural science to all human and social problems. At the very beginning, there was some degree of realism about the magnitude and difficulties of such a task. But the *image* had been created, and in almost no time at all the ever-autistic character of man under challenge asserted itself. The hypothesis was soon prejudged! The *hope* of a psychological science became indistinguishable from the *fact* of psychological science. The entire subsequent history of psychology can be seen as a ritualistic endeavor to emulate the forms of science in order to sustain the delusion that it already *is* a science.

As a result, the inability of anyone — whether psychologist or his grateful lay victim — to fix the limits of the metaphor known as "psychological

313

science" has, in my opinion, been close to catastrophic throughout the century. Strange things happen when image is seen as fact! Numbers are assigned to hundreds of millions of people in the line of intelligence, personnel, or educational "measurement" with little regard for their meaning and none for their effects on the dignity, self-image, or practical fate of the victims. Vagrant guesses about the importance of permissiveness, fondling, breastfeeding, social reinforcement, and the potentialities of teaching machines or computerized instruction, are allowed to influence whole eras of parental and educational practice. Dime-a-dozen "breakthroughs" are applied wholesale to the "cure" of the mentally disturbed: exotic little interventions like partial destruction of the frontal lobes with an ice pick, malarial-, insulin- or electro-shock. For the less refractory disorders, or just for soul-expanding kicks, psychological "science" has available its endless armamentarium of "psychotherapies," most of them devised with minimal concern for whether the presumably neurosis-free or expanded person who emerges has not also been freed of large areas of his personhood.

But what is perhaps worse than any single symptom of psychological science is the demeaning image of man himself at the basis of its presumably tough-minded conceptualizations, an image that mankind cannot but accept and strive to emulate because of its association with the iconology of science. In its austere form, it depicts man as a stimulus-response mechanism or, worse, a mere mathematical point of intersection between stimulus and response processes, and steered by socially "manipulated" rewards and punishments. According to this form of the image, the laws of human and social "behavior" can be derived from rigorous study of the variables controlling the rate at which a hungry rat in a small, dark box presses a lever to obtain tiny pellets of food. The more sophisticated and recent form of the image holds man to be an information-processing entity operating on the principles of a binary digital computer programmed to conform to payoff criteria similar to the rewards of the previous case.

Both of the "images of man" that I have just sketched (and other slightly varied ones) are products of the tradition of *behaviorism*, which for sixty years has maintained hegemony, especially in this country. The first of the images mentioned is representative of what might be called *explicit behaviorism*, while the second — which is now beginning to supplant older forms of behaviorism — might be called *crypto-behaviorism*. The behaviorisms are an especially pure assertion of man's reality-defiling propensities in that they achieve (by arbitrary stipulation) the complete liquidation of psychology's subject matter: the elimination, as legitimate or even meaningful objects of study, of both experience and mind. Even the brain is proscribed, as unclean and somehow fictive, by certain long-influential forms of behaviorism, including Skinner's. The computerized version restores a brain in some sort, but tidies it up by insisting that it be reduced wholly to transistors, magnetic "cores" and miles of interstitial wire.

By the mid-fifties, an appreciable number of psychologists had become restive over the behaviorisms and were searching for more significant professional and human commitments. At about this time, Abraham Maslow, who had long complained about the "means-centeredness" and scientism of psychology and who was discovering existentialism, called for a "third force" in psychology. Fairly soon, such a group — calling themselves "humanistic psychologists" — began to emerge. Initially, it seemed a motley group with heterogeneous interests.

By a process that no one has yet chronicled in a coherent way, the interests of this group soon began to concentrate on various of the approaches to group therapy, which had been multiplying profusely since the twenties. The pre-"humanist" tradition in group therapy took its conceptual inspiration primarily from psychoanalysis and various of the "depth" psychologies. By the mid-fifties, however, a number of group approaches to therapy (or therapy-like changes of individuals and groups), based on principles of "group dynamics" and other non–depth psychological schemes, were in the air. Drawing their ideas from these and other scattered sources (especially, a variety of loose interpretations of existential philosophy, but also client-centered therapy, psychodrama, sensitivity training, dance therapy, Gestalt therapy, relaxation methods), the humanistic psychologists proceeded to experiment with an ever-widening range of eclectic mixes.

Today the group movement has become the most visible manifestation of psychology on the American scene. Carl Rogers (1969) has said that the encounter group may be the most important social invention of the century. Within psychology, it has captured the interest of an overwhelming majority of the students and investigators who wish to maintain contact with a human subject matter. It is tremendously important that we assess its message, impact, meaning — its "image of man."

It is my assessment that the group movement is the most extreme excursion thus far of man's talent for reducing, distorting, evading, and vulgarizing his own reality. It is also the most poignant exercise of that talent, for it seeks and promises to do the very reverse. It is adept at the image-making maneuver of evading human reality in the very process of seeking to discover and enhance it. It seeks to court spontaneity and authenticity by artifice; to combat instrumentalism instrumentally; to provide access to experience by reducing it to a packaged commodity; to engineer autonomy by group pressure; to liberate individuality by group shaping. Within the lexicon of its concepts and methods, openness becomes transparency; love, caring, and sharing become a barter of "reinforcements" or perhaps mutual ego-titillation; aesthetic receptivity or immediacy becomes "sensory awareness." It can provide only a grotesque simulacrum of every noble quality it courts. It provides, in effect, a convenient psychic whorehouse for the purchase of a gamut of well-advertised existential "goodies": authenticity, freedom, wholeness, flexibility, community, love, joy. One enters for such liberating consummations but settles for psychic striptease.

There is no question of *proof* in relation to such matters. It is a question of *seeing*, of the fidelity of our perception of the human condition — and this kind of question is as old as the history of man and will never be finally resolved. But the history of the humanities has already given us many differentiated, sensitive, ardent visions of the human condition. All of us, I think, are capable of significantly sharing in, and even extending, this noncounterfeit kind of vision — but that only comes the hard way, the way that involves fear, trembling, loneliness, discipline, gallantry, humor, and a loving, if ironic, sense of the dimension of human imperfectibility.

The autisms of those who want it the *easy* way have put them out of touch with the differentiated content of the significant visions in man's heritage; worse, they are out of contact with the intricate and delicately contoured meanings of some of the best — as well as some of the plainest — words in our language. They nevertheless use these words incessantly, with the best of intentions, but in debased, vulgarized, schematic ways. For them, words like openness, honesty, awareness, freedom, trust, growth, feeling, experience, form a simplistic conceptual abacus which they manipulate and apply in mechanical, repetitive, incantatory fashion. To convince people who reside within this framework of its impoverished character is like asking for a change of sensibility.

I *could* start with a collection of horror stories about the grave human crises, indeed tragedies, that have been precipitated by membership in one or another kind of "human potential" group, but that is not my main concern. In "Group Therapy: Let the Buyer Beware" (one of the most reasonable articles about the movement I have seen), one group leader, E. L. Shostrom (1969), presents a roundup of representative suicides, breakdowns, and divorces precipitated by injudicious shopping. He proceeds to develop seven guidelines for the floundering shopper in the form of specific "nos" that should discourage him from either joining, or remaining in, an encounter group. These "nos" cut a very wide swath indeed, and call for exceptional discriminative powers, if not prescience, on the part of the intending grouper. One of the "nos," for instance, "Never join an encounter group on impulse," explains to the shopper that any "important crisis in your life . . . deserves reflection" and enjoins him to be "doubly cautious" if "you are sanely suspicious of your grasp on reality" (Shostrom 1969, 38). To apply such a rule effectively presupposes a remission of the condition that invites its application. Were such a criterion met, I would still doubt that the shopper, or even a committee consisting of his mother, psychiatrist, and priest, could make this discrimination with accuracy.

What concerns me about the group movement far more deeply than its toll in human crises is the image of man it has purveyed to man. The central horror of the history of psychology is that distorted images of human reality are soon accommodated by the reality that the images distort. Perhaps more frightening than the failures consequent upon participation in groups is the rich reported yield of "successes." The principal toll of the movement is in the reducing and simplifying impact upon the personalities and sensibilities of those who emerge from the group experience with an enthusiastic commitment to its values.

Perhaps the best way for me to explicate this judgment is to present excerpts from a vignette of my impressions upon accidentally wandering into a national meeting of the American Association for Humanistic Psychology in 1968. I had left psychology for foundation work some four years before and had not kept in touch with the group movement. I included this vignette as a coda to my article on the general plight of psychological science, which was published in *Psychology Today:*

> I caught up with the "humanistic psychologists" last fall at the annual American Psychological Association meeting in San Francisco. Here scholarly exposition must give way to reportage. . . . A bit of investigation established that these were members of the Association for Humanistic Psychology, which had been holding its own pre-convention for two days. I learned further that the Association now has some 1,500 members and that there are no professional requirements for membership.

The humanistic fervor of the group has been channeled into one activity, variously designated as group therapy, sensitivity training, encounter groups, human potential groups, et cetera.

. . . With curiosity thus reinforced, I attended all the humanists' activities that I could at the A.P.A. Convention proper. [I had arrived at the very end of the humanists' separate meeting.] It was not easy because every humanistic audience spilled over into the corridors, unlike the sullen, spare audiences at the non-humanistic events.

By far the largest audience showed up at a symposium in which Paul Bindrim, the originator of "nude-marathon group therapy," spoke and showed a film. Reprints of a magazine report on Bindrim's "breakthrough" were made available. Bindrim had wondered whether what he calls a man's "tower of clothes" is not only a safeguard for privacy but a self-imposed constraint to keep out people he fears. If so, a man who disrobed physically might be better able to disrobe emotionally. The modest Dr. Bindrim refuses to take sole credit for this hypothesis and wishes to share it with Abraham Maslow. Dr. Maslow had speculated that with nudity in groups, "people would go away more spontaneous, less guarded, less defensive, not only about the shape of their behinds, but freer and more innocent about their minds as well."

Bindrim's methods, for the most part, are the standard devices of group therapy. He was enthusiastic at the symposium, however, about a therapeutic intervention of his own inspired coinage that he calls "crotch-eyeballing." The crotch, he notes, is the focus of many hang-ups. In particular, three classes: (1) aftermath difficulties of toilet training; (2) masturbation guilts; (3) stresses of adult sexuality. Why not blast all this pathology at once! Thus two group members aid in (as Bindrim says) the "spread-eagling" of a third member and the entire company is instructed to stare unrelentingly and for a good long interval at the offending target area. Each group member is given an opportunity to benefit from this refreshing psychic boost. . . .

Admittedly, Bindrim's is only one of many approaches within the group movement. But all these methods are based on *one* fundamental assumption: that total psychic transparency—total self-exposure—has therapeutic and growth-releasing potential. More generally, they presuppose an ultimate theory of man as socius: man as an undifferentiated and diffused region in a social space inhabited concurrently by all other men thus diffused. Every technique, manipulative gimmick, cherished and wielded by the lovable, shaggy workers in this field is selected for its efficacy for such an end.

This entire far-flung "human potential" movement is a threat to human dignity. It challenges any conception of the person that would make life worth living, in a degree far in excess of behaviorism. . . . The "human potential" movement obliterates the content and boundary of the self by transporting it out of the organism—not merely to its periphery, but right out into public social space. The force of behaviorism is merely to legislate the inner life out of existence for *science,* while allowing the citizen to entertain the illusion, perhaps even the reality, of having one. Even Skinner gallantly acknowledges a world of "private stimulation."

The "human potentialists," however, are saying in effect that a world of *private* stimulation is unhealthy. They generate a militant rhetoric of anti-rigor and are derisive about the "up-tight," whether in scholarship or life. But as fix-it men to the up-hung, they have a passion for the unending collection and elaboration of group engineering *methods.* They have a barrel of them for every type of hang-up. Have hope!

The moral and logic of the foregoing vignette are too obvious. "Humanistic psychology" started as a revolt against . . . fifty years of reductive behaviorism. In no time at all it achieved a conception of human nature so gross as to make behaviorism seem a form of Victorian sentimentality—which perhaps it was. We have come farther than full circle. (Koch 1969c, 67–68)

Note that this brief characterization uses a strategy that verges on caricature. But let there be no mistake about what "caricature," when responsibly practiced, is: it seeks to reveal *essential* characters of its subject by selection and even exaggeration; it is not a *literal* mode; indeed, it seeks to be in some sense more "true," more revealing, than literal representation. I was certainly not attempting a *summary* of the mountains of prose generated by groupers about their rationale and practice. As I read that literature, I occasionally run into isolated, *en passant* warnings about "overexposure." But very seldom. What I do run into, however, on almost every page, are recommendations, advertisements, celebrations, hymns about the cosmic values of openness, disclosure, exposure, honesty, directness, "letting oneself be known," transparency, and so on. The force of most of the theoretical rhetoric, of virtually *all* of the group-engineering devices, of the experience-protocols of group leaders and members, creates an inescapable conclusion that a belief in the growth-releasing potential of self-exposure is a dominant and pervasive premise of the movement. "Self-exposure" *functions* very much like a therapeutic absolute in the work of the movement.

An article in *Psychology Today,* "The Group Comes of Age," by Carl Rogers (1969), which seeks to focus on "certain threads that weave in and out" of "the rich, wild, new tapestry that is the intensive group experience" is an impressive case in point. The threads that he singles out and presents in the rough order of their emergence within the rich, wild tapestry of a group's life (for example, Milling Around, Resistance, Recalled Feelings, Lashing Out, Revealing Self) make it quite clear that in the mind of the thread-unraveler the group process is seen as a kind of Pilgrim's Progress toward the stripping of self. Many of the other "threads" identified by Rogers either have the character of basic changes that are consequent upon the process of psychic stripping (for example, Cracking Masks, Basic Encounter, Positive Closeness), or facilitate the stripping performance (Here-and-Now Trust, Feedback).

I find this same iterative and echolalic concentration upon self-disclosure as the hub, nub, pivot, and growth-releasing agency of the group process in the writings of other leading encounter theorists such as Frederick Stoller, Jack Gibb, or William Schutz — in fact, in all accounts of encounter rationale, or method, that have come my way. Indeed — if one disregards terminological embroidery and differential turgidity — most accounts of the therapeutic rationale turn out to be remarkably uniform. Growth toward freedom, autonomy, authenticity, spontaneity, expressiveness, flexibility or realization is released by self-disclosure in a group situation in which all of the atmospheric variables militate toward mutual self-definition and the "direct" expression of response (whether hostile, loving, or other) by all members to any given member who is in the process of disclosing. When theoretical analysis is attempted, it is customary to point to the joint interplay of reinforcement and feedback in shaping each individual's movement through the group experience. Such variables may be supplemented, in some accounts, by postulating natural healing tendencies that are liberated in individuals by the group process. That is about the size of the rationale, whatever the yardage in which it is conveyed.

Some idea of the fruits of facilitating these growth-releasing dynamics may be derived from Rogers's description of that tapestry thread of his called "Cracking Masks":

> In time, the group finds it unbearable that any member should live behind a mask or a front. Polite words, intellectual understanding of each other and of relationships, the smooth coin of tact and cover-up—amply satisfactory for interactions outside—are just not good enough. . . . Gently at times, almost savagely at others, the group demands that the individual be himself, that his current feelings not be hidden and that he remove the mask of ordinary social intercourse. In one group there was a highly intelligent and quite academic man who had been rather perceptive in his understanding of others but who had revealed himself not at all. The attitude of the group was finally expressed sharply by one member when he said, *Come out from behind the lectern, Doc. Stop giving us speeches. Take off your dark glasses—we want to know YOU.* (Rogers 1969, 31)

Rogers reports that the man looked on the verge of tears during the lunch hour. Then triumphantly: "When the group reconvened the members sensed this and treated him most gently, enabling him to tell us his own tragic personal story, which accounted for his aloofness and his intellectual and academic approach to life."

Is it too much to hope that some may see something frightening going on here? Is not the group a bit lecherous in its pursuit of its payoff? Is it not possible that this "perceptive" and contained man was pressured into relinquishing something gallant and proud in his makeup? Is it not conceivable that even *if* disclosure had made him *feel* somewhat better, he had *become* somewhat less?

Some profound questions are raised by this example (incidentally, an innocuous one in comparison to many in the group movement literature). Are all so-called "facades" phony and psychically crippling accretions? Are all surface traits facades? If there is a distinction between a surface trait and a facade, who is to make it? Is every individual or reference group equally competent to do so relative to a given case? Who is qualified to tell Proust to get rid of his fur coat and his hypochondria; Eliot to ditch his reserve; Mann his rather bourgeois surface rigidities; Gide his exhibitionistically asserted homosexuality; Joyce his propensity for occasional fugues of high living; Dylan Thomas his alcoholism and arrogant scrounging? Is the "facilitator," "change agent," "therapist" to be the chap who shouted, "Come out from behind the lectern, Doc"? Is it to be Carl Rogers?

But there are deeper problems here. The concept of *transparency*, as applied by our promoters of human potential, serves grotesquely to mask certain of the most pervasive and potent conditions constitutive of value. Total transparency is constitutive only of nullity, and human beings in the process of approximating or sustaining transparency are among the most boring phenomena in creation. We all have run into those bores who want to apprise you of the entire content of their souls, not to mention the consistency of their feces and their taste in deodorants, within five minutes of having met them. We usually feel guilty over such boredom, for we know that they are sick. Or again, what could be more boring, and even sordid and life-denying, than a spouse, lover, or friend who wishes to pass half of each day in salubrious examination of "our" relationship? But the point I am trying to get at is far more subtle and important than such illustrations convey.

We often talk about prizing "depth" rather than "transparency" in people and their artifacts, and elsewhere. But "depth," too, is a rather coarse-grained and unilluminating concept, as generally used. A little reflection will show that what we tend to prize maximally in our perception of people, or of art, or the natural world, is a special, difficult-to-specify relationship between surface qualities and interior or depth qualities. Really a *class* of such relationships, for there can be all kinds of complementarities, interactions, stresses, distances, degrees of clarity or of ambiguity in the surface-to-interior relations. Whatever the ultimate analysis of such matters, we are so constituted perceptually and affectively as to derive intense and differentiated value from carriers of such relationships. To take a simple perceptual example, most of us differentially value a color that somehow mysteriously emerges from the depths of an exquisite gem (say a fine tourmaline) as against a color of similar spectral properties in the form of a pigmented surface patch. In every form of art, what we maximally respond to — when we respond competently — is a set of special and complex relationships between surface and interior properties. The much prized "ambiguity" that has been a dominant (but inadequately explicated) aesthetic canon over much of the century probably points to a particular subset of such relations.

Until recently, most of us recognized such qualities of human beings as the charm of certain forms of reticence; the grace of certain kinds of containedness (which need not mean stiffness or rigidity but which *can* be definitive of dignity); the communicative richness of certain forms of

322

understatement, allusiveness, implicativeness; the fetching quality of the kind of modesty that is the outward form of the capacity to prize person-hood and to love directionally rather than diffusely. Some of us even used to be charmed by the kind of "openness" that is not transparency (a quality that renders even glass only utilitarian) nor yet hearty and robust explic-itness (which is superficial) but, rather, a capacity to focus sensitively, pre-cisely, and even vulnerably upon value-laden human and natural objects, and an analogous gift for allowing the self to emerge into focus, without surrender of dignity or modesty, for valued others. When I attempt such baroque specifications of the ineffable, the encounter groupers I know have a propensity for saying, "That is precisely what we mean." They will never convince me — for everything they *do* with groups can only obfus-cate, belie, and ultimately destroy such distinctions. In this endeavor, they can count on plenty of support from other agencies in our culture.

The pursuit of "openness" via self-revelation before an adventitiously assembled group of strangers centers the process of individual self-definition much too heavily upon group response. We have here a simplis-tic and crass "solution" to the immensely complex and delicate question of the relation of man and society, one which (despite all loving intentions to the contrary) assigns as much weight to the *social* shaping of the individual as do the most rigid theories of social determinism. I suspect that lurking under all this is a deep misconstrual of the concept of democracy — a per-version of it which is widespread in the culture at large. This is the sense of the democratic process as an egalitarian merging of happy, well-met, mutually voyeuring "people," rather than a system of agreements guaran-teeing maximal dispersion of social control and minimal invasion upon both self-determination and privacy.

The tendency of encounter groupers to engineer individuation via "feel-ingful," "direct," and "honest" feedback has already been illustrated by Carl Rogers's description of the archetypal professor who was savagely denuded of his lectern and then gently restored to "health." As another example, I quote an instructive paragraph from an article, "Marathon Group Ther-apy," by Frederick Stoller:

> When time is compressed as it is in the marathon, the conse-quences of one's behavior are placed in greater contiguity to the behavior itself. Both the individual and the other with whom he is involved have the opportunity to specify why he

invites his particular fate. The assumption is made that the marathon group represents a sample of the world, and one's behavior within the group represents a sample of one's behavior in the world. (Stoller 1968, 60)

This differential assessment of the force and value of real life experience as against encounter group experience is frequent in the group literature. Up to a point it is correct, but this constitutes one of the very grave threats of the group movement. What Stoller says about the force and immediacy of group feedback, under the prevailing conditions of member motivation, group objectives, and the leader's structuring, cannot be denied. But it is a dangerous thing for an adventitiously selected group to have this degree of force in controlling the individual's self-image. As we have already seen, the assumption seems to be that any old kind of feedback is fine — regardless of the degree of sensitivity, general quality of sensibility, et cetera, of the feeders. The literature is not encouraging concerning the evidence for such qualifications, whether of the member-feeders or the leader-feeder. The chances for simpleminded, callow, insufficiently considered or reductive shaping of the individual are high.

The obvious defense against this argument is: Are the chances any better in actual life? This is superficial. The chances of winning sensitive "feedback" (I loathe the word) are probably pretty meager, at best, in any context. But in "ordinary" life we are most of the time recipients of multiple and disparate feedbacks; we are protected by this very dishomogeneity from the sense that our essence has been caught and fixed by our assessors. Besides, any given assessment is less likely to be perceived as peremptory; we tend more readily to assess our assessors. We do not "enter" ordinary life, as we do an encounter group, with pat and virtuous expectations of self-clarification or improvement; usually we are merely *there*. In life we may pay for our follies, but we do not commit the folly of buying feedback, at so much per yard, from our friends. Indeed, the dynamics of friendship are such that people receive much of their feedback from individuals of comparable or higher sensitivity, rather than lower. Most persons need heroes in their lives, and there is at least a faint correlation between admiration and admirability.

However inefficient the ordinary conditions of character formation, it is diabolical to make these contingent on group engineering. Moreover, it is the very "effectiveness" of the group situation that is its great danger. The ambiguities and delays in feedback in normal, nonengineered life are safeguards — guardians of the significant (not nominal) form of authenticity that can only be achieved by allowing intrapersonal factors the fullest possible play in development. The capacity for individual transcendence of the group is perhaps the most value-charged gift of the human station.

I have repeatedly made reference to the gross and debased ways in which encounter groupers use certain humanly precious words of our language. I hope it can now be appreciated that this deficiency is no mere matter of literary or conversational inelegance. If an image of personhood be specified in coarsened terms, then that image is a coarsened one in comparison to the image that might be specified via more sensitive (thus richer) use of the self-same terms. When this degraded image now becomes criterial with respect to the desirable directions of personality change, we can anticipate only a degrading of personhood in the course of efforts to move the person toward such "ideal" qualities.

The words of our language stabilize hard-won insights — sometimes extraordinarily salient and delicately contoured insights — into the universe, both the inner universe of experience, and the outer universe. The discriminations presented and transmitted by natural language form the matrix of all the knowledge that we have. Even the technical languages of science have grown out of natural language, and their interpretation continues to depend on discriminations within the natural language. From such considerations it follows that if a word has stabilized a salient, delicately bounded, and humanly valuable discrimination with respect to the universe, then a coarsening or degrading of its usage will entail a loss of actual knowledge. An individual's conception of the application conditions for a word is a fact of sensibility. Coarsening of language means coarsening of knowledge, and a language community that uses language in a coarsened way is a community of coarsened sensibility.

The low-level, mechanical way in which the groupers use glitter-concepts like authenticity, love, autonomy, and the rest in the inflated rhetoric that passes for their theory, but that nevertheless controls the selection of their methods and practice, at once reveals and promotes a serious impoverishment of sensibility.

I will conclude with one final example of such crippled and crippling uses of language. In encounter group parlance, "trust" is that homogeneous, gelatinous enzyme secreted by a group that catalyzes the process of self-exposure by decreasing the apparent risk-contingencies. The person will "let himself be known" because his share of the collective ambience of trust gives him a sense of safety. And our perspicuous savants have developed certain subtle laws of trust: for instance, if X trusts Y, Y is more likely to trust X, or if X trusts Y, Y is more likely to like X, or again if X trusts Y, Y is more likely to please X (whether by services rendered or in some other way).

I will spare the reader a serious analysis of "trust" and merely indicate that it is no simple notion. Even in the sense that our groupers have somewhere in mind, "trust" (a dictionary form of which is "to do some action, with expectation of safety, or without fear of the consequences") is not an undifferentiated, global matter. I can *trust* someone's good intentions, or his friendliness, or that he will not steal from me, or poison my shredded wheat, or that he will not covet his neighbor's wife, or covet mine, yet *distrust* his capacity to perceive me, or me him, or them or it with clarity, delicacy or precision. Again, I can trust X's ability to see me with nicety and depth, but (perhaps) not his ability or disposition to respond in a way congruent with his perception, or to use his perception of *my* trust in any way that may be congenial, constructive, or safety engendering from my point of view. Again, I can trust X to be generally, or in the long run, or fundamentally, decent (or honest), but not that he will not try to work me for all sorts of short-term and local advantages. "Trust," when asserted as between X and Y, is not truly a two-termed relation; when the word is used sensitively, there is actually a third relatum that may appear explicitly or be implicitly conveyed by context. This reflects the human reality that when X trusts Y (and assuming that X can satisfy some weak criterion of rationality), he does so with respect to some finite class of Zs.

More revealing, however, than the groupers' *general* theory of trust is their understanding of it as signalized by one of their favorite "nonverbal communication methods." You all know the device: "trust" is presumably instilled by asking members of a group to fall backward on the assumption that another member stationed behind the faller will catch him. Now, to my febrile mind, this may instructively serve as a screening device for detecting whether the presumptive catcher is a psychopath, but it has nothing to do with trust. Any designated catcher who played the wry practical joke of allowing the faller to crack his head on the floor could justly be thought the owner of a character defect. A catcher, however, who did carry out the prescribed function of catching could only be thought, by an intelligent faller, to be a man capable of playing a meaningless game according to prescribed and easily applicable rules, or one minimally equipped with concern for the survival of his fellows quite outside the context of those rules, but the faller would have no warrant for regarding the receiver trustworthy as a recipient of psychic confidences.

The "operational" (or essentially mechanical) definition of trust conveyed by this example exhibits, in especially witless fashion, the deficiency of most so-called "operational definitions." These are essentially definitions by "symptom," and cannot be expected to hold for the relational pattern of symptoms actually constitutive of any reasonably abstract or general concept. All other methods in the copious armamentarium of the encounter groupers have this same garbled relationship to the notions of which they are the purported realization, and thus to the states of affairs that it is hoped they will bring about.

The encounter process is in fact an *extraordinarily ritualized kind of game.* The attempt to accelerate, in the artificially engineered ways at issue, what in real life might be the inefficient but *meaningful* process of self-definition imposes on leader and group members alike a tendency to perceive (that is, to interpret and assess) psychodynamic and internal states in essentially *symptomatic* modes. The range of "evidence" afforded by this artificial situation over its limited time course, and upon which the group must base its shaping and modulating influences, is so *thin* as to enforce the rapid adoption of a crass and simplistic lexicon of symptom-meaning (or phenotype-genotype) correspondences. The essential complexity, indeed ambiguity, of the meanings of human actions and expressions, thus of personhood, is damped out.

Such "simplistic lexicons" may vary in content from group to group, but there are many broadly constant lexical units. Thus, in many encounter groups *joking* or *wit* may automatically be seen as *evasiveness; sleepiness, boredom,* or *torpor* as *withdrawal;* a *raised voice* must mean hostility (rather than, say, passionate concern); *blocking* must be *defense* (rather than the stumbling desire to achieve a clear articulation of the complex). More widely *abstract statement* must mean a form of *intellectualistic concealment* or "mindfucking"—despite the fact that a responsible abstraction can be seen as a perceptual disembedding of a *highly specific,* if widely instantiated, character from the concrete (a point recognized in much Western philosophy and in most of the great Eastern systems of thought). Still more widely, *love* may be seen as a *barter of reinforcements; honesty* as *transparency,* and so on.

This "most important social invention of the century" that we have been considering carries every earmark of a shallow fad. Yet the impetus behind it is poignant and powerful, and permanently embedded in man's condition. Man's search for egress from the cave, platonic or other, is rendered especially frantic in such times as ours. However compelling its impetus, this fad will soon — as historic time is measured — fizzle out. But its *effects* need not.

When value-charged discriminations drop out of man's ken, there is no certainty that they will be rediscovered. We transmit to the future what we are. We may be what we eat, but we are also what we image. If what we are has been reduced by shallow or demeaning images, that impoverishment will persist in the world long after the images that conveyed it have gone their way.

11

Clark Hull and Psychology's Age of Theory

Foreword

As the century draws to a close, it is grotesque to contemplate that among *all* academic psychologists, John B. Watson, Clark L. Hull, and Burrhus F. Skinner have had the greatest impact — certainly in their own time — upon both their profession and perhaps even the world at large. (If we go *outside* the academy, they would be outranked only by Freud.) It is deeply significant that behaviorism — which can be defined (as I once did) as a "poignant lament that anything so refractory to the assumptions and methods of 18th century science as the *person* should clutter up the world-scape" — has elicited so joyous a resonance from the clutterers.

The present chapter is a very brief and general assessment of Hull's contribution to the "pathology of knowledge." Though I think it will serve its purpose, it is ironic that this should be the shortest chapter in the book, in that I have written more extensively on Hull than on any other topic. I was a close (though progressively disabused) student of his work over the first decade of my career, and in 1954 — when my disabusement had become utter — published as section 1 (Koch 1954) of *Modern Learning Theory* an analysis of Hull's theory which is the longest and most muscular piece of critical writing I have ever done. This gigantic article (actually book-length at 176 pages) is thought by some to have had something to do with the demise of Hull's theory. Whatever its interest as a historical artifact, it could hardly be included in the present collection. The short chapter that follows does at least convey the gist of my 1954 conclusions concerning the inadequacy of Hull's theory and environing metatheoretical commitments, and it assesses certain of my 1954 predictions concerning the destiny of his theory against the actual psychological history of the subsequent fifteen years. And, in a general way, it sets Hull's effort — which was an ardent and poignant one — into historical perspective. This latter objective I deem important. Due to the ahistoricism of current psychological education and the tendency of Skinner and his followers to rewrite psychological history, most younger psychologists are unaware of the extent to which Hull's work dominated the theoretico-experimental psychology of the 1930s and 1940s.

This chapter is a composite from two sources: (1) a contribution to a 1969 APA symposium on "The Hullian Impact on Psychology" and (2) a paper entitled "Theory and Experiment in Psychology" (Koch 1973b), deriving from a 1972 AAAS symposium on "Case Studies on the Relationship Between Experiment and Theory."

«

Clark Hull's work was invited into existence by an acute phase of a predicament endemic to "scientific" psychology. This is the requirement that psychology become a cumulative and shareable knowledge-finding enterprise in the same sense that the natural sciences are believed to have these traits. The history of psychology, ever since its stipulation into existence as "science," may be seen to stem from a succession of proposals as to how attain these and other traits thought to be definitive of successful natural science. Nineteenth-century "experimental psychology" proposed to emulate the *experimental methods* of science via a paradigm such that the stimulus be controlled and specified in physical terms, while the dependent variable constitute an experiential report rendered reliable by use of a set of simplistic descriptive categories ("elements") and appropriately trained "observers." Early behaviorism proposed a stricter emulation of physical-science experiment: namely, that bodily *response* be substituted for the experiential dependent variable, thereby rendering experimentation homogeneously "objective."

But the strategy of classical behaviorism resulted in scattered and particulate findings, most having little interest. Also, disagreements — both conceptual and empirical — persisted in the same static, time-marking way as previously; behaviorism was merely one among a large number of "schools," all transfixed in an endless moment of internecine polemic. This stifling situation led to a new stage in which the hope was that a *decision procedure* could be made available by emulating the *theoretical* methods of natural science. Hull may be seen as the person who advocated and explored such a strategy in the most self-conscious, unrelenting, and dedicated way of anyone in his time.

The yearning for a decision procedure which would liberate psychology for dependable, cumulative advance had become obsessive and widespread by (circa) 1930. The search did not have far to go! For philosophy, in response to a similar and more ancient inner-necessity, had entered a phase in which its quest for the rule and paradigm of significant knowledge had begun to focus on a new codification of the nature of science. By the early thirties that codification had begun to stabilize in the formulations of logical positivism, neopragmatism, and operationism. This "new view," if it may be called that, was being exported with missionary zeal to the general scholarly community at precisely the time that psychology's need was coming to be felt as critical. Hull was not alone in his preparedness to discern the heady prospect of psychology's salvation in this apparently new formulary of the scientific enterprise.

In Hull's case, the strategy of salvation became that of implementing what he thought to be the promise of classical behaviorism, by translating its as yet thinly developed orienting commitments into the sinewy idiom of hypothetico-deductive method: a strategy that soon became known as that of *neobehaviorism*. More generally, the tendency, from the early thirties onwards, of theorists of divergent leaning to be controlled by aspects of the "new" view of science makes it possible to identify the fundamental psychology of the period as "the Age of Theory." I have written widely (e.g., Koch 1959a, 1964, 1965) about the definitive attributes and history of this period, but in this brief presentation must assume that something of my point of view is known. Whatever else can be said about Hull's place in history, he is, and will remain, the prototypical "Age of Theory" theorist.

In 1954 I published the most sustained assessment of Hull's theory that has yet appeared: if I may make bold with myself, perhaps the most obsessively detailed analysis of a psychological, or indeed scientific, formulation that has ever been written. The primary questions I sought to answer were: "What kind of a theory can Hull be said to have; what are the orienting commitments and methods which underlie its construction; what is the degree of correspondence between Hull's theoretical objectives and the resulting theoretical structure?" (Koch 1954, 3). As I then saw it, "the single greatest barrier to an appreciation of the need for reassessment of where we stand today is the belief that the heroic era [the "Age of Theory"] has given us one formulation which is a *theory* in the most rigorous natural science connotation of the word. Curiously enough, Hull's followers are likely to agree that, even if Hull is wrong, he *at least* has a determinate theory, while opponents are likely to urge that Hull must be wrong, *because* he has a determinate theory" (3).

My general conclusions were stark. Many pages later, I found myself saying:

> We have raised, in some form, most of the types of questions that can be asked in characterizing the status of a scientific theory. We have inquired into the adequacy of all classes of definition of all classes of the theoretical variables. We have inquired into the postulated interconnections among all classes of variables. We have looked into the methods of postulate construction, of quantification, of derivation. We have examined the induction basis, and the general state of evidence, for certain of the assumptions. Under close scrutiny, not a single member of a single class of such theoretical components satisfied the requirements for rigorous scientific theory of the sort envisaged within the theorist's explicit objectives. More importantly, many of the detailed solutions embodied in the theory of major problems in the methodology of psychological theory construction — e.g., the techniques employed for the "measurement" of independent and dependent variables, the techniques for the construction of quantitative, or even qualitative function forms — prove to have little merit within their concrete theoretical context, however suggestive certain of them may be in defining the problems that behavior theorists must face. (159–60)

In assessing Hull's future impact, I said: "His future influence, while it will probably be less direct than he might have wished, can be expected to remain far-reaching. How salutary this influence will be depends more on what the future does with his formulations, than on the formulations *per se*." I suggested further the strong unlikelihood that the behavioral theory of the future could be an elaboration of the Hullian postulates, "or even written within the Hullian idiom" (164). Nevertheless, I indicated that, "embedded in the massive bulk of Hull's formulations," there were many ideas and hypotheses, the fruitfulness of which was independent of the integrity of their theoretical context. These (e.g., the "sensitizing" effects of drive on habit structures, the explanatory potentialities of r_G for aspects of "complex behavior," the notions of indirect and "secondary" stimulus generalization, etc.) would, I predicted, engage the interests of many workers for a long time to come. I anticipated also that other hypotheses with "more limited chances of ultimate survival" would remain of continuing interest: e.g., the drive reduction treatment of reinforcement, the principle of secondary reinforcement, the principle of primary stimulus generalization, and a two-component analysis of inhibition.

It is certainly now possible to say that these anticipations have withstood the test of time. Even within the ranks of neobehaviorists, anything resembling the articulated corpus of Hullian theory has become a dim memory, while modification and attrition of the core hypotheses has been incessant. And the ideal of strict, explicit hypothetico-deductive procedure, if not entirely renounced, has certainly been practiced by few who have worked within the Hullian tradition. There is also among this group a markedly chastened attitude towards the prospects of strong degrees of quantification of lawful relationships, and a more modest assessment of the actual and feasible generality-limits of behavioral functions.

Since my 1954 analysis — if prophetic — has hardly been *that* influential, what has caused so marked a change? A series of earth-shaking crucial experiments? Not a likely route to the demolition of a "theory" which can have no strict entailments. The emergence of a better theory: an alternate systematization of the same or broadly overlapping domain having greater predictive power? In actual fact, no. What has happened is very complex and can only be summarized as a partial return to sanity. It is perhaps not overoptimistic to assert a statistical law of human cognition such that illusion, even when sustained by an overarching autism, tends to become self-liquidating after burgeoning to some threshold dimension within a large group of inquirers. However sanguine this law of cognitive teleology may seem, it does *not* imply that what replaces a given self-liquidated illusion is nonillusive.

If we address the facts rather than the laws of psychological history, it is worth noting that the most productive interests since the mid-1950s have been pursued outside the neobehavioristic confines and have, at least in my reading, been utterly at variance with the premises of Hullian or any other form of behaviorism. The revolutionary advances of biological psychology and the neurosciences have increasingly revealed the grotesquerie of peripheralist and "empty-organism" biases. This flow of bad news can no longer be curtailed or concealed by semantic readjustments of S and R, even by "functional" redefinitions thereof which deploy S's and R's and r_G's and s_G's into every micronook and minicranny of the nervous system. There are other floods of bad news which will not be calmed by any amount of further lubrication of the slippery S-R concepts. Ethological research has increasingly generated findings which strain any imaginable version of behavioristic drive theory, which elude meaningful interpretation in categories that do not directly acknowledge complex perceptual and cognitive processing, and which make ever more obvious the inappropriateness of the classical conditioning *and* instrumental learning situations as induction bases for general laws of learning. The new horizons in the theoretical and empirical study of language punctuate the utter futility of an approach in the idiom of S and R (with or without "reinforcement"). Most of what has seemed illuminating in studies of cognitive development could only be vulgarized and distorted by translation into an S-R vocabulary. Even the mathematical modeling of learning has become increasingly hospitable to cognitive categories, while the computer models of mind have become so centralist as to make one nostalgic for the days when minds were peripherally embodied. Many more flood tides which converge on the inundation of behaviorism could be mentioned, but even I can become wearied by the rhetoric of iteration. At least some of these lines of work are more problem centered, and imbued with greater intrinsic interest and human relevance, than anything done in the ambience of the Hullian framework.

But how account for the rapid acceptance of Hull's theory and the long period of its hegemony? My answer may seem paradoxical. Men were insulted and bored by their role as dustbowl experimentalists — as rat-runners, memory-drum operators, brass-instrument calibrators whose main function was to generate a rhetoric of "just-like-physics" objectivism. They were tired of the fetishistic pursuit of trivial, isolated, arbitrary problems selected on no basis other than amenability to some rudimentary experimental design. The promise of a lawful, rigorous hypothetico-deductive ordering of the entire domain of psychology was to these men a promise of meaning, significance, direction, purpose, interest, intellectual exaltation — all of this to be rendered accessible by the harnessing of action to a sure-fire set of rules. At bottom, they were drawn to the Hullian framework by the same passionate thirst for illumination, for intoxication through the apprehension of cognitive symmetry — the same wish to surrender to the value symphony potentiated by insight — which animated a Kepler. That this heady gift was in reality a shoddy, inflated, arbitrary, non-meaningful, malproportioned blueprint for an altered form of scientistic role-playing, they resisted seeing — with every fiber of their souls — for periods up to twenty years and longer. The same may be said of the author of the theory, a man of admirable diligence and poignant commitment to a significant psychology.

Perhaps the most compelling allure of the Hullian approach was in fact the promise of a determinate and meaningful linkage between experiment and theory. To get this issue straight for psychology, it is worth looking into the form of this aspect of the Hullian promise.

According to Hullian metatheory, experiment is to be related to theory both inductively and deductively by a schema that can be called the *intervening variable paradigm*. First introduced in the early thirties by E. C. Tolman as a modest device for illustrating how analogs to the subjectivists' "mental processes" might be objectively defined, the concept of the intervening variable was soon thereafter elaborated by Tolman and others into a paradigm purporting to exhibit the arrangement of variables which must obtain in any psychological theory seeking reasonable explanatory generality *and* economy. In the late thirties, Hull adapted the intervening variable paradigm to his own ends: his entire theory was projected as a complex chain of inferred intervening variables linked, on the one side, to a set of independent variables representing the antecedent conditions of behavior and, at the terminal end, to four response measures which served as systematic dependent variables. It is a leitmotiv in Hull's writing that intervening variables must be "securely anchored on both sides to observable and measurable conditions of events." A related caution states the need for "a grim and inflexible insistence that all deductions take place according to the explicitly formulated rules stating the functional relationships of A to X and X to B," A and B, of course, being independent and dependent variables respectively, and X being the intervening variable or chain of such. Given these putative conditions, it is easy to see that we have the basis not only for a theoretical *decision procedure* but for a theoretical *construction procedure*. The paradigm seemed to render into orderly and intelligible terms the problems confronting the psychological theorist: e.g., he needed three classes of variables; he needed the interconnecting "functions"; he needed a mode of inferring or constructing those functions; etc. Naturally, such a schema was readily reconcilable with elements of the hypothetico-deductive view of science. The demand for explicit linkages with observables could be equated with *operational definition*. The statements interlinking the three classes of variables could be asserted as *postulates*. If the theorist was courting mathematical levels of determinacy (which in those days all theorists were), this became the quest for mathematically specified intervening variable functions. And so on.

Best of all, the intervening variable schema was associated with a strategy for manufacturing intervening variable functions. In briefest terms, this strategy was to select or design a series of *defining experiments,* the variables of which would be placed in correspondence with (i.e., "represent" or "realize") the theoretical variables whose relationships were under determination. Standard curve-fitting techniques were to be applied to such experimental results. The resulting equations or curves were then presumably to hold for the theoretical variables whose relations were in question.

Even from this inadequate description, it should be clear to any sentient scientist that the procedures suggested by this intervening variable doctrine could only lead to results which are question-begging in the extreme, and so truncated in their generality as to be local to the conditions of the defining experiment (if valid even for those). There are many ways of showing this: I will dwell on only one, involving a distinction between *systematic* and *empirical* independent (and dependent) variables which I found necessary to make — to the edification of no one in particular — a long time ago. Such formulations as that of Hull's 1943 theory and Tolman's early systems had tended to represent the antecedent and consequent conditions discriminated by the theory as direct "observables." But the stipulated independent and dependent variables were in fact far from this: such notions as Tolman's "past training," "maintenance schedule," and "heredity," or Hull's "S," "C_D" (conditions constitutive of drives), and "G" (reinforcement in several vaguely specified senses) can be seen to discriminate enormously broad and heterogeneous classes of possible operations and/or observations. They are therefore *systematic variables* in the sense that they clearly represent rather complex epistemic constructions made within the *system language* of the theory in question. The numerous *individual* operations and/or observations designated by each systematic variable would, in the terms of my distinction, be called *empirical variables.* Now if one examines closely the lists of independent and dependent variables given for such theories, it should be clear that the stipulated theoretical laws are making enormously general commitments — from the magnitude of which the theorist himself was often protected by the tendency to *equate* his systematic antecedent and consequent variables with "observables" (i.e., *empirical* variables). In this way it was easy to overlook the fact that, say, an intervening variable function based on (or verified by) values of the *specific empirical* variables manipulated and recorded in a single experiment was often formulated in such a way as to assert this function for huge and indefinite classes of empirical variables (i.e., merely by transposing the function into the corresponding *systematic* terms of the theory language).

From such considerations it will be seen that Hull and other Age of Theory systematists came close to suggesting that highly specified laws of unrestricted generality (across indicators, measures, situations, individuals, groups, species, occasions, and other conditions) could be had almost by fiat.

I had hoped to concentrate, in one-to-one fashion, on the orienting attitudes of Hull's neobehaviorism, and to show how whatever could have been thought the rational grounds for each have been progressively disenfranchised by (a) the results of their theoretical entertainment over time, (b) the (by now massive) accumulation of new and unanticipated psychological knowledge, and (c) more penetrating philosophical analyses which have revealed, to the satisfaction of virtually all philosophers and most scientists outside of psychology, the thinness and distortion of those rule-saturated models of science on which behaviorist epistemology and method were grounded. Within the brief confines of this chapter, I cannot. If by virtue of this, I have seemed to deal cavalierly with Hull's bequest to the future, that was no part of my intention. When younger, I dwelled for more than a decade within some part of his assumptional system, and full well knew the power of its claims upon many ardent men of those times.

The orienting assumptions of neobehaviorism — its methodological objectivism; S-R orientation; peripheralism; belief in the conditioned response or law of effect "situation" as providing insight into the fundamental laws of learning; corollary belief in the extensibility of such laws to all psychological processes and events; belief that these manifold consequences could be deductively generated by an axiomatic theory, the intersubjective applicability of which was to be guaranteed by explicit and quantitative rules — all of these grew out of strange necessities produced by psychology's entire history as a science, and by certain pervasive developments in extra-psychological history as well. It was inevitable that these assumptions be widely entertained. It was *not* inevitable that they be entertained as steadfastly, responsibly, even imaginatively as by Hull.

His gallant effort will stand as something like the apogee of a certain kind of scientism in our field. His contribution was the critical demonstration of the *infeasibility* of achieving a significant psychology on the basis of that form of scientism. The lesson of Hullian theory is rendered the more poignant by the talent that went into the effort. The lesson is deeper, I think, merely than the failure of a particular set of epistemological and quasi-substantive judgments that at one time appealed to many as a plausible basis for psychology. The lesson bears on the nature of the endeavor called "psychology," and the permanent limits upon its objectives and stratagems.

12

Skinner's Philosophy of Behaviorism

Foreword

This short chapter derives from a review in *Contemporary Psychology* (Koch 1976b) of Skinner's book, *About Behaviorism* (1974), which seeks to address the philosophical presuppositions of "the experimental analysis of behavior." It is, in fact, the most serious and comprehensive effort he made to explain, justify, and defend his position of "radical behaviorism" and, in general, to establish his place in the historical (and cosmic) order. My review was terribly constrained by the allotted space, and I took enormous pains to write in a condensed way. Despite the space limits, I sought to hoist the author on the petard of his own multivocal, inconsonant, and just plain silly assertions — which meant that I allotted virtually as many words to the author as I did to myself. I think that the imposed brevity did not prevent the review from revealing the ameaningful character of Skinner's formulations. Skinner (1977) wrote a formal rejoinder to the review, and I a rejoinder to that (Koch 1977a); these appear following my review.

«

Though this book rings no changes upon the Skinnerian cosmology, it is the most focused effort the author has yet made to deliver a coup de grace to "mentalism." In line with his familiar thesis that "behaviorism is not the science of human behavior; it is the philosophy of that science," he fashions a kind of philosophic capstone to "the experimental analysis of behavior." The book commences with brief paraphrases of twenty commonly held demurs to behaviorism that the author believes to represent "extraordinary misunderstanding[s]." It ends with a chapter of point-by-point rebuttals. In between are deployed the grounds for these rebuttals: thirteen chapters which address such far-ranging matters as "The Causes of Behavior," "The World Within the Skin," "Perceiving," "Verbal Behavior," "Thinking," "Knowing," "The Self," etc.

The point of the exercise is to state the rationale for *radical behaviorism* which, unlike *methodological behaviorism,* "does not deny the possibility of self-observation or self-knowledge . . ., but . . . questions the nature of what is felt or observed and hence known." Such a position "does not insist upon truth by agreement and can therefore consider events . . . in the private world within the skin (Skinner 1974, 16)." Moreover:

> . . . what is felt or introspectively observed is not some non-physical world of consciousness, mind, or mental life but the observer's own body. This does not mean . . . (and this is the heart of the argument) that what are felt or introspectively observed are the causes of behavior. An organism behaves as it does because of its current structure, but most of this is out of reach of introspection. At the moment we must content ourselves . . . with a person's genetic and environmental histories. What are introspectively observed are certain collateral products of those histories. . . .
>
> Our increasing knowledge of the control exerted by the environment makes it possible to examine the effect of the world within the skin and the nature of self-knowledge. It also makes it possible to interpret a wide range of mentalistic expressions. (17)
>
> I consider scores, if not hundreds, of examples of mentalistic usage. . . . Many of these expressions I "translate into behavior." I do so while acknowledging that . . . there are perhaps no exact behavioral equivalents, certainly none with the overtones and contexts of the originals. (19)

So staccato and dense a text results from objectives of the sort at issue that any brief review must be more than usually confined to a few impressionistic generalities.

Selectivity of scholarship. The author is as much concerned with establishing his uniqueness within the behaviorist tradition as with the demolition of "mentalism." This joint aim has led to extraordinarily casual scholarship.

Complex positions are often reduced to a few magisterially dismissive sentences (or less). For instance, Michael Polanyi (along with Percy W. Bridgman) is said to "have insisted that science is inexorably personal" (144). But "it is absurd to suppose that science is what a scientist feels or introspectively observes" (145). The reading of Polanyi that is implicit here could have been based only on the title of his book, *Personal Knowledge,* not its content. For the purport of that book was to explore and reconcile the apparent conflict between the personal (and largely non-rule-subsumable) bases of scientific discovery and assessment and the indubitable objectivity (indeed, "universality") of scientific knowledge. Again, the rangy entanglements of logical positivism and operationism with behaviorism are scrutinized in two paragraphs (14–15). Not only is the ancient tendency of amateur psychological methodologists of the thirties to identify these two topics resuscitated (e.g., "Logical positivism or operationism holds that . . .") but the representation of the joint position bears a coincidental relation to either component.

Though the book is *About Behaviorism,* non-Skinnerian behaviorism is present only as a dim foil to the author's position and receives but brief and enigmatic treatment. The only behaviorists mentioned by name are Watson and (in one sentence each) Max Meyer, J. R. Kantor, and Edward C. Tolman. The readings of Watson are questionable in several respects, one of them being the hoary misrepresentation of Watson as "arguing that thinking was merely subvocal speech" (6). (Watson, in fact, included abbreviated or "implicit" nonverbal acts of any type in his conception of thinking, just as does Skinner!) The widely varied positions (inclusive of the neobehaviorisms) lumped by Skinner under his rubric of "methodological behaviorism" are given cavalier and often misleading treatment. Thus it is alleged in a discussion of "covert behavior" that "it was a mistake for methodological behaviorism and certain versions of logical positivism and structuralism to neglect it simply because it was not 'objective'" (103–4). But of course, from Watson on, no behaviorist has neglected "covert behavior"; the sheer necessities of peripheralism have enforced acknowledgment of some such concept. Hull's subspecifications of "covert behaviors" into an ornate range of concepts such as r_G, the "pure stimulus act," the "receptor exposure act," etc., and his long-term interest in exploring their role for behavior dynamics, were conspicuous in his theorizing. And a patent feature of post-1950 neobehaviorism was the broadened attention given these and cognate notions in efforts to arrive at more differentiated analyses of perception, thinking, and other "higher" processes.

Bivocality of the Exposition. The author's tendency to address the same issues in different connections at varied confidence levels, and in accents ranging from the inconsonant to the incompatible, is confusing. At the most general level, such inconstancy is evident in the author's attitude towards his own position, which ranges from near-humility to Messianic optimism. On page 3, we find him conceding that "some of these questions [concerning the 'science of behavior'] will eventually be answered by the success or failure of scientific and technological enterprises," but noting that "provisional answers are needed now." Moreover: " . . . I am not speaking as *the* behaviorist. . . . [The] account . . . reflects my own environmental history" (18). On page 250, however, we find the author complaining that "not a single behaviorist in the strict sense" had been invited to a recent International Congress on Peace and concluding that the "currency of mentalism in discussions of human affairs may explain why conferences on peace are held with such monotonous regularity." The book's final sentence goes a bit further: "In the behavioristic view, man can now control his own destiny because he knows what must be done and how to do it" (251).

A substantive illustration of this multivocality may be found in varied assertions concerning the central topic of the book: the "inner world," "mental events," "introspection" — acknowledgment of which is the definitive trait of radical behaviorism. One confronts a dizzying love-hate dialectic concerning such matters, which can be only thinly sampled. Page xii informs us that "a small part of that inner world can be felt or introspectively observed, but it is not an essential part . . . and the role assigned to it has been vastly overrated. . . ." By page 15, methodological behaviorism is being rejected for ruling "mental events . . . out of consideration." On pages 16–17, radical behaviorism is being advertised for its interest in such matters. By page 18, "mental events" reappear as "mental fictions." On page 104, the topic of thinking is introduced as follows: "Mental life and the world in which it is lived are inventions. They have been invented on the analogy of external behavior occurring under external contingencies. Thinking is behaving." Nevertheless: "No one can give an adequate account of much of human thinking. It is, after all, probably the most complex subject ever submitted to analysis" (223).

At times, multivocality is transcended by downright incoherence. What it means to say that "covert behavior is . . . easily observed," I cannot guess; the further contention that "no one has ever shown that the covert form achieves anything which is out of reach of the overt" (103) seems equally strange — nor does this oddity decrease when it is conceded that the "great achievements of artists, composers, writers, mathematicians, and scientists are no doubt still beyond reach" (223). Not infrequently, however, it is the search for "consistency" that creates absurdity. For instance, since the position does not permit imputation of causal significance to "inner events" (the "causes" of these *and* of correlative overt behavior are "in" the environment), one "need" not presume that a particular symphonic theme came to Bruckner because of sadness at the thought that Wagner would soon die; rather, "certain circumstances (news of Wagner) produced the conditions felt as sadness *and* induced him to behave musically in a special way" (158–59). The treatment of "cause" is itself one of the central incoherences of the book, for — though the word is used repeatedly with an insistent (and arbitrary) restriction to antecedent conditions in the environment — it is argued that physiology will one day enable more detailed causal analysis of behavior in terms of an organism's "current structure." Despite this, the motley collection of positions (inclusive of those that distinguish between learning and performance) that Skinner assigns to "structuralism" (cf. 11–12, 64–68) are rejected on grounds that they "abandon the search for causes" (11). And, despite many statements that celebrate the theory's unique concern for causal analysis (its capacity for prediction and, above all, control), the theorist occasionally makes it quite plain — for readers who may be in doubt — that his adventures into "reinforcement history" can result, at best, in tenuous and gappy probability relationships and, indeed, that "there may be something about the human organism which makes indeterminacy relatively important" (236).

The "Translations." This issue requires close attention, for behavioral "translation" is, after all, Skinner's main device for repairing "the major damage wrought by mentalism" (17). The point of the endless behavioral lexicon is apparently to demonstrate that "causal" analysis of complex human behavior wholly in terms of manipulable environmental variables describable in a "physical thing language" is possible, and that such analysis is adequate to all meaningful discriminations that can be made about the "inner world."

A random sample of translations follows: "'I miss you' could almost be thought of as a metaphor based on target practice, equivalent to 'My behavior with respect to you as a person cannot reach its mark'" (50–51). Similarly, a "'lovelorn' person is unable to emit behavior directed toward the person he loves" (59). Purpose and intention are handled by noting that "operant behavior is the very field of purpose and intention. By its

343

nature it is directed toward the future: a person acts *in order that* something will happen . . ." (55). Moreover, "the basic fact is that when a person is 'aware of his purpose,' he is feeling or observing introspectively a condition produced by reinforcement" (57). Motives are dispatched by noting that "when we reinforce a person we are said to give him a motive or incentive . . ." (51). Shame, guilt, and sin form an orderly phalanx: "If he has been punished by his peers, he is said to feel shame; if he has been punished by a religious agency, he is said to feel a sense of sin; and if he has been punished by a governmental agency, he is said to feel guilt" (62). One can now move easily to morality and justice: "The behavior we call moral or just is a product of special kinds of social contingencies arranged by governments, religions, economic systems, and ethical groups" (244). Bravery, courage, audacity are comprehended by "behavior which is strong in spite of punishing consequences" (64). Imagery: "When a person sees a person or place in his imagination, he may simply be doing what he does in the presence of the person or place" (82)—no copies, "iconic representations," "data structures" need be invented. Moreover, "If there are no copies of things inside the body at any time, then all that can be seen introspectively is the act of seeing" (86). As we have already seen, "thinking is behaving" (104)—covertly, of course. Analyses are given of two senses of faith: Qua confidence, "frequent reinforcement . . . builds faith" (58); within Skinnerian theology, however, "Faith is a matter of the strength of behavior resulting from contingencies which have not been analyzed" (133). Understanding is partly conveyed by: "I come to understand a difficult text . . . when, by reading and rereading it, I acquire a stronger and stronger tendency to say what the text says" (141). A summation of the position is implicit in the definition of a person: "A person is not an originating agent; he is a locus, a point at which many genetic and environmental conditions come together in a joint effect" (168).

Literate persons will note the magnitude of the distortions perpetrated upon some of the most intricately contoured and rich discriminations achieved within the natural language. But they will be told that they have missed the point! The translator has not sought "exact redefinition" and "there are perhaps no exact behavioral equivalents." What is at issue is a "causal" analysis of behavior, the technical terms of which need not capture the phenotypic properties of its explicandum. But if it be granted that significant features of the explicandum have been effaced in such "translations" or "interpretations," the operative question becomes whether these are in any sense recapturable or recomposable from the analytic categories of the "behavior scientist." Considering the poverty of a conceptual abacus that would phrase the entire psychological ontology within three or four enormously general and contextually rubbery concepts (e.g., "operant behavior," "past contingencies of reinforcement," the "current setting," "collateral products" of reinforcement history), the prospects for such recapturability would seem very limited. The translations promise to be unidirectional — and final. We are threatened with a type of translation that is more like transmogrification or traduction. One's fears are not diminished when the author says, "Some [mentalistic expressions] can be 'translated into behavior,' others discarded as unnecessary or meaningless" (17).

The status of Skinner's extrapolations. This is a book that offers a portentous redefinition of man and society on the basis of no discernible arguments — save a form that might be called "perseverative asseveration" — intrinsic to the text. Authoritatively but distantly in the background, however, is "the experimental analysis of behavior" — a repository of hard knowledge constantly alluded to by the author as the scientific bedrock of his assertions. To rebut frequent charges that the laboratory generalizations are but vaguely extrapolated when applied to "daily life," the author argues that "the laboratory analysis makes it possible to identify relevant variables and to disregard others which, though possibly more fascinating, nevertheless have little or no bearing on the behavior under observation" (229). But this will simply not do! Insofar as such notions as "operant" response, "reinforcement" and its "contingencies," behavior "strength," etc., have a determinate meaning, this is rooted in the foundational data. It is one thing to identify an "operant" (like lever depression) in an experimental setting in which the range of response topographies "strengthened" by a "reinforcer" is sufficiently limited by the setting to make it plausible to assign them to the same class (and in which the "similarity" of consequence-instances allows comparably unambiguous identification of the reinforcer); quite another when the operant is a putative unit of complex human behavior like "Hitler prolong[ing] the Second World War for nearly a year" (60), "the behavior involved in musical composition" (159) (which is what was "strengthened" when Bruckner completed his Seventh Symphony), or even "com[ing] to understand a . . . text" (141). The remarkable detail in which "schedules of reinforcement" and other rate fluctuations of the bar-pressing and key-pecking behaviors studied in the foundational experiments should not mask the astronomical analogical distances between the "laws" and such contexts of application. One can generate metaphorical extensions of *any* notion ad libitum but there are good and bad, illuminating and obfuscating metaphors — a circumstance, incidentally, which could not be inferred from Skinner's bare representation of "metaphor" in terms of "stimulus generalization" (93).

Prevalence of pseudo-explanations. By now it should be clear that the book is replete with pseudo-explanations — often of complex and humanly precious phenomena, processes, or events. Each of the "translations" is a pseudo-explanation: a reduction of matters meaningfully (if not always precisely) distinguished and specified in natural language to a definition base that can only be characterized as scientistic babbling. But there are many "explanations" of important contexts of human activity that so thoroughly sidestep the relevant questions that one can only wonder why the topic was broached. Two examples follow.

The large topic of "creative behavior" is handled by noting that: "Operant conditioning solves the problem more or less as natural selection solved a similar problem in evolutionary theory. As accidental traits, arising from mutations, are selected by their contribution to survival, so accidental variations in behavior are selected by their reinforcing consequences" (113–15). The suggestion that there are "happy accidents" (114) in creative work is true, even if it be news to no one; and to draw an analogy between such accidents and "mutations" is anyone's option (though a questionable one). But to offer these trivial observations as any large part of the explanation of creative effort is only to evade — or obliterate — the topic. If, however, "our analysis of the behavior called thinking is still defective," it is in part "because great thinkers . . . have been led to report their activities in subjective terms" (118). Now that these "great" (but obviously confused) thinkers have been cured of their mentalist propensities, we shall simply have to await their "mutation" biographies!

That the author is in touch with the finer things is attested by his attempt to interpret what is meant when it is said that an artist has "extracted the essentials": "The artist who paints photographically is under the powerful control of his model but, if he can bring his personal history into play, his work can show a kind of generality. . . . He will have 'extracted the essentials' by attenuating the control exerted by the current setting" (178). But of course such an analysis says nothing about extracting *essentials* or significant abstraction; it is merely a near-tautology asserting that isomorphism between "picture" and model will decrease to the extent that painting is "controlled" by something other than the model. Bringing "personal history into play" *may* conduce towards extracting "essentials" or as well towards extracting superficialities — or retreat from the model via the substitution of a symbol (whether for a meaning, a concurrent mood, or nothing). Picasso's contour drawings of bulls are often quintessentially bullish in a way in which a canvass covered with black pigment is not a significant abstraction of a face, even if the pigment matches the color of the blackhead on the model's nose. The interesting questions concerning abstraction in art have to do with the intrinsic character and revelatory force of what is abstracted.

Skinner generously permits us to continue to enjoy "the warmth and richness of human life" (5) for "there is nothing in a science of behavior or its philosophy which need alter feelings or introspective observations" (245). There is an obvious sense in which no theory (or "science") of man would be worth writing if it did not have such an influence, and a conceivable one in which this could be said of even a physical theory. In psychology, though, a theory of any generality becomes in effect a part of its domain. A theory that teaches man that his mind is an "invention," and rescues him — via such "behavioral" translations as have been sampled — from the complement of "mental fictions" that have fogged up his world could, if it failed to alter "feelings and introspective observations," only be said to have failed. A person's reading of himself is powerfully affected by what he believes himself to be. What persons believe themselves to be is powerfully affected by what authorities — including "behavior scientists" — tell them they are or are about. It is cynical for the promulgator of "the most drastic change ever proposed in our way of thinking about man" (249), the engineer of communal motel life (as prefigured in *Walden Two*), the prophet of behavior modification, to argue that "scientific" analyses of man, even false ones, do not alter the realities they structure!

Reply to Professor Koch

I suppose that I should be glad that Professor Koch is willing to review *About Behaviorism* simply as "more verbal behavior from Dr. Skinner,"[1] but he has not singled out the more important variables of which that behavior was a function. He has, so to speak, criticized the author rather than the argument. I was not writing a history of behaviorism nor was I summarizing the positions of recent or current behaviorists. I was addressing myself to a number of ways in which a widely accepted view of the behavioristic

1. This was the original title of Koch's review. *Eds.*

position is misunderstood. (Much of this was brought home to me by reactions to *Beyond Freedom and Dignity*.) I list twenty misunderstandings at the beginning of the book and take each of them up in detail at the end. Professor Koch tells the reader that I do so, but he does not identify a single example. Instead he confines himself to "a few impressionistic generalities" about my behavior as a scholar and writer. My style is staccato and dense; I am multivocal, cavalier, misleading; I am guilty of misrepresentation and downright incoherence; and so on. As evidence, he supplies a number of quotations, some of which, necessarily out of context, are indeed strange and even amusing. I hope that interested readers will put them back into my text and discover what I am really saying. I do not "dispatch" motives with the phrase Professor Koch quotes, I do not interpret "Hitler's prolonging the Second World War for nearly a year" as one operant, I should puzzle no one when I say that "covert behavior is . . . easily observed"—*by the behaver,* and so on.

Professor Koch's adhominemity also pervades his style. There is a delicate mocking irony. "Skinner," he says, "generously permits us to continue to enjoy 'the warmth and richness of human life.'" As to scholarship, he says that my reading of Polanyi "could have been based on the title of his book, *Personal Knowledge,* not on its content." I assure any reader who concludes that I have not read the book, that I have done so, and that the position I attribute to Polanyi is the one for which he was widely known. Percy W. Bridgman reached the same position, alas, toward the end of his life, and not only have I read Bridgman, I had something to do with what he wrote (see *The Way Things Are* [Bridgman 1959], vi).

So much for the author. I wish you would now find someone to review the book.

B. F. Skinner
Harvard University

A Text in Search of an Author

1. I have "criticized the author rather than the argument." Well yes, but only to the extent that it is legitimate for a non-behaviorist to infer that someone (probably Skinner) wrote the text. My review is pure textual analysis: it contains, perhaps, more of the text's words than my own. Sometimes I attribute quoted word-strings to "the text," sometimes "the author" or "Skinner"; readers who feel it base to presume that verbal "behavior" may be referred to the agent thereof are invited to substitute

"behavior" for every occurrence of "author" and "Skinner." As for "the argument," I observed (p. 345) that there are "no discernible arguments . . . intrinsic to the text." (The text is essentially a sequence of assertions — e.g., behavioral "translations" of "mentalist" terms — the rational basis for which is alleged to lie outside the text within "the experimental analysis of behavior.")

2. I supply quotations, "some of which, necessarily out of context, are indeed strange and even amusing." Here I *am* in a bind, for I do not have the space to show that they are even stranger and more amusing — at least until exasperation intervenes — when read *in context*.

3. I did not suggest that Skinner had not read Polanyi (a fact obscured by Skinner's omission of "only" from my phrase "could have been based only on the title"); merely that his "reading" (i.e., interpretation) was a passable paraphrase of the title but not the book. Nor do I see why Skinner emitted his retrospection concerning Bridgman, for I raised no issue as to whether he had read *or* misconstrued that author (cf. 340–341). Skinner indeed "had something to do" with *The Way Things Are* (Bridgman 1959); the "many illuminating conversations" with him that Bridgman acknowledged on page vi made it "evident that the behaviorists were not capable of talking my language" (vii), and, one can infer, helped fuel Bridgman's unsympathetic assessments of behaviorist epistemology (cf. 200–248).

4. A small erratum. I did not say that Skinner's "style" was "staccato and dense" but made these attributions to the "text" (p. 340) in a context (not enough space to cover all issues broached) over which it would be odd to take umbrage.

Sigmund Koch
Boston University

13

Karl Edward Zener: A Contrast Case

Foreword

This essay may be seen as a foil to the massive documentation of ameaningful tendencies in psychology and the culture at large provided by the preceding six chapters. It is a description of a not widely known man who withstood the blandishments of ameaning absolutely. I knew Karl Zener — initially as my teacher and then a close colleague — over a twenty-five-year span. In my opinion, he was one of the most penetrating — indeed profound — psychologists of this century. He was also the most admirable person I have known. Lest such judgments be thought wholly to reflect idiosyncratic sentimentality, I should add that *all* who knew Karl Zener — a group of not negligible size — would be likely to make a similar assessment. Since, for reasons which my essay suggests, he left few *written* artifacts, I deem it important to memorialize him as a kind of reminder that intensely *meaningful* thinking (and personhood) is never wholly absent in history, even the recent history of psychology. Though (as I somewhere suggest) history is not its record, it is important that a Karl Zener enter the record.

The paper was written for presentation at the dedication of the Karl E. Zener Auditorium (Duke University) on March 8, 1968. A shortened version of it was published in the *Journal of Personality* (Koch 1969b).

«

It is not always evident when we are in the presence of the great. For many years in this department, we were in the presence of a great man — very simply, a man who overlapped and outranked us in generosity, humility, penetration, profundity, and energy. Proximity is not a good vantage from which to identify the great. Nor does it help when the bearer of the quality has limited respect for the standard stigmata of "distinction," is modest to the point of self-effacement, has not a shred of the histrionic in his makeup.

Our time does not conduce towards connoisseurship in recognizing the great. It gives us a definition biased towards somewhat ordinary forms of the extraordinary. Karl Zener was extraordinary in an extraordinary way. The memory of *such* a person cannot be adequately celebrated, however ardent the effort. The language of professional assessment will not suffice; nor will that of formal eulogy. I offer, therefore, a memoir in the language of friendship, for in that idiom the reporter can be authentic, and in that idiom his own limits can emerge.

But I must begin with the bare facts of my friend's biography. Since these do *not* speak for themselves (facts rarely do), I can then feel free to speak about him as a living man, for, with me as with those of you who knew him, he surely lives. I give this bare outline mainly as I wrote it for the newspaper obituaries on the bleak morning of September 27, 1964, a few hours after this vigorous and healthy man had died of a heart attack:

Karl Edward Zener was a man of unusual depth and scope as scholar, administrator, and human being. His scientific interests during his career ranged over most of the fundamental fields of psychology: psychophysics, learning, motivation, conditioning, perception, and aesthetics. To each of these fields he brought originality and a disposition to do full justice to the phenomena being studied, whatever their complexity. In a period of psychology in which the tendency has been to court the forms of science more than its content, Karl Zener was steadfast in the profundity of his questions and the meaningfulness of his answers.

Born in Indianapolis, Indiana, on April 22, 1903, he was the son of the late Clarence and Ida Zener. His wife, the former Miss Ann Adams, survives, along with two sons, Dr. Karl A. Zener and Dr. Julian C. Zener. A third son, Wilfred Zener, died in a drowning accident in 1956. Also surviving are his sister, Mrs. Katharine Humiston, and brother, Dr. Clarence Zener.

He received the Ph.B. degree from the University of Chicago in 1923, and the M.A. from Harvard in 1924. After doing a doctoral dissertation at Harvard on the psychology of music (Ph.D., 1926), he spent the year 1926–27 as a National Research Council Fellow at the University of Berlin, where he worked closely with Wolfgang Köhler and Kurt Lewin. Some feeling for the spread of his interests can be derived from the fact that he had been an accomplished musician since childhood, and, during this postdoctoral year in Germany, was in conflict as to whether to continue with psychology or become a concert violinist.

In 1927, he went to Princeton University as instructor of psychology. There, in collaboration with E. G. Wever, he did research of great originality in psychophysics (1928, 1929).

Coming to Duke in 1928 at the invitation of Professor William McDougall who was then, as founder of the Duke Psychology Department, in search of the most brilliant younger talent in the country, Dr. Zener soon commenced an ambitious program of research on the conditioned response. For a period of ten years, he maintained one of the few Pavlovian conditioning laboratories in the country. But this was a unique conditioning laboratory in that, by a long series of subtle experiments, in which he measured many aspects of his animals' behavior of a type that Pavlov had neglected in the hope of finding simple laws, Dr. Zener was able to establish that in many respects Pavlov's formulations were inadequate. He was, in fact, able to show with great plausibility that the animal acts as if it were intelligently *expecting* or preparing for the unconditioned stimulus (e.g., food) upon presentation of the conditioned "signal" (e.g., buzzer), rather than — as represented in standard accounts — being passively subject to the formation of a new stimulus-response bond (e.g., 1933, 1934, 1936, 1937, 1938, 1939, 1949; see also Beck 1939).

Concurrently with his conditioning work, and for some years later, Dr. Zener was interested in problems of motivation, especially in its relations to learning. From the early Duke years onward, he also worked in the experimental psychology of perception (e.g., 1943, 1946b), and maintained a constant interest in neurophysiological and psychobiological problems. His research on perception and learning took on a practical slant during World War II, when he conducted a series of studies on the analysis of aerial gunnery skills (1946a).

His interest in phenomena and theories of personality was reflected in his translation (with D. K. Adams) in 1935 of Kurt Lewin's important *Dynamic Theory of Personality,* and in his editorship over a period of twenty years of the journal known initially as *Character and Personality* and later as the *Journal of Personality* (cf. 1945).

These many interests found their coherence in a continuous and deep concern with problems of psychological theory and methodology (e.g., 1958).

During the last fifteen years of his life, he tended to concentrate his research more and more upon problems of human perception (e.g., 1952,

1953, 1959; Zener and Gaffron 1962). He was in course of formulating a bold and comprehensive theory of perception which, unlike most contending ones, sought to do justice to the finer and more significant aspects of experience, as, for instance, the perception of visual and other art objects. This work, done in collaboration with Dr. Mercedes Gaffron, had already identified important, though subtle, aspects of visual experience which had not been discriminated in the previous history of psychology or, indeed, any other area. The Zener-Gaffron theory combined with its analysis of perceptual experience important ideas based on recent findings concerning nervous and brain process; the theory led to a broad range of implications spanning phenomena both of biological science and the humanities; indeed, it suggested a radical and liberating re-conception of the task of psychology. A breakthrough promising new research vistas had come about with the development of a technique for measuring complex eye-movement patterns of the sort involved in the viewing of paintings just a few weeks before Dr. Zener's death.

At various times, he rendered distinguished service on national professional committees. From 1958 to 1962, he served as member and, finally, Chairman of the consultant group of psychologists to the Training Branch of the National Institute of Mental Health. From 1952 until his death, he was on the advisory panel of the project (Project A), jointly sponsored by the National Science Foundation and the American Psychological Association, which resulted in the series, *Psychology: A Study of a Science.*

He was the recipient of grants from several foundations, the last of which was unique in that it was the only grant ever made by the Ford Foundation Program in Humanities and the Arts for psychological research. This award enabled him, in 1962, to go to Egypt to test certain comparative-cultural implications of his and Dr. Gaffron's theory of perception.

Throughout his career at Duke, he was actively involved in departmental administration and constantly prepared to lend his effort to the general development of the University. For twenty years, he was Director of Graduate Studies in Psychology. He was appointed Chairman in 1961, and during his brief tenure did much to develop the department into the outstanding and rather special center that it now is. The department's tradition for responsible heterodoxy of thought, for breadth of purview, for allegiance to the significant rather than the fashionable, was well served during his leadership. To these administrative efforts he brought not only vision but deep humanity, endless generosity and patience, and an ability to bring out the finest intellectual and personal qualities of his colleagues. By them he is sorely missed, as by all who knew him.

I first met Karl Zener on a train between New York and Ithaca a few days before New Year of 1939. We were en route to one of the annual meetings of a small group of psychologists interested in the work of Kurt Lewin. Though I was then a first-year graduate student in philosophy at the University of Iowa, I had been taking a seminar with Lewin and I was proudly reading the galleys of his new book which he had lent me. A young man sitting near me — apparently having noted the book — fell into a pleasant conversation with me. I judged him another graduate student, perhaps somewhat younger than I. The name did not register, but I knew that the appearance would prove indelible: the piquant combination of angularity and delicacy of feature, the classic forehead and slanting, outward thrust of lower face; a physiognomy at one moment sharp, poised for knifing into truth, then recomposed into a foreshortened expression of intense, seemingly embarrassed puzzlement. The body was well formed and wiry and, like the face, incessantly motile, each movement being staccato yet somehow graceful. The impression was one of startling charm. I do not remember our conversation — only that we were soon joined by another man, one who later became one of the most renowned psychologists of his generation in every measurable way. What I do remember is that two days later the first of these men gave a lengthy, ardent, groping talk involving many slides, reams of supplementary data which appeared out of a battered briefcase, incessant blackboard scribbling. The talk, which was on conditioning research with dogs, was received with great respect and met with much discussion — but it went completely over my then wholly philosophical head.

I somehow never got the name of that man straight, but when I came (now a psychologist) to Duke in the fall of 1939 to commence work towards my Ph.D., I saw him again. His name was Karl Zener. He became one of my teachers and, not too long thereafter, one of my colleagues. My respect for him was immediate and continued to grow, but it took ten years for me to perceive (or perhaps admit to myself) that this man was the most profound and admirable person I had ever known, and would probably remain so, whatever my future course. Over the fifteen years that yet remained of our relationship, my amazement over his inexhaustible multidimensionality never ceased.

In this day of instant liaisons and lightning disaffections, I think it instructive to note that some friendships may require a ten-year gestation. No person is an "open book," but there are even open books of which we may win but little of their meaning after ten years' study. There can be orders of dimensionality, levels of depth, in people and their artifacts the discovery of which must await the growth of our own resources. The young are handicapped in their choice of heroes. They want heroes desperately—but intelligible heroes. In my graduate student days, those of us who studied with Karl Zener had but the vaguest impression of what was happening to us. In a part of ourselves, we knew that we were somehow being enriched in a way which would remain forever viable and yet which we could not specify. In every conventional sense, he was a flagrantly maladept teacher. He was hesitant, fumbling, often close to incoherent (though there were occasionally surprising flights of hyperfluency, too), and *seemingly* "unprepared," at every meeting of a class. There were also strange periods of abstraction—as when once, in a session of our experimental psychology class, he broke off in the midst of a very athletic blackboard-analysis of a table of data (from the Von Restorf experiment, as I recall), walked abruptly into an adjoining apparatus-storage room (for what purpose, one will never know) and remained incommunicado for at least an hour, each fifteen minutes of which he punctuated by opening the door, staring at us rather strangely, and saying: "Well, yes."

Naturally, these traits provided rich materials, at least in my day, for that academic genre known as the student "in-joke." But our joking on this theme had about it two revealing qualities: it was affectionate in tone, and it preempted so large a part of our pooled output of wit as to suggest that Professor Zener was reaching us very deeply. In some inchoate way, we all knew we were working with a man who had an absolute disposition to exhume every molecule of meaning in anything that he considered; that, in fact, we were, during each funny meeting of his classes, in contact with the raw immediacy of an authentic creative process. We knew, further, that it was important to seek to understand him: rather more important than the objective of one of *his* constant endeavors, which was to seek—patiently and nonjudgmentally, whatever our naïveté—to understand us. But we resented rather the constant challenge he posed to our own youthful simplemindedness; resented also that he could be subsumed under no schema, no image, of the teacher or scholar that we had yet developed. It thus gave us comfort to undervalue him, or to try to, and certainly we had not the resources to have more than a feeble intimation of his dimension.

It has been my lot in recent years — both in and out of the Ford Foundation — to hear much grave and pompous talk about the "problems" of teaching in the American university. How to improve it, how to assess it, how to "turn out" (as the phrase goes) more and better teachers. During these dull moments, my reveries dwell on the best teacher I ever had, and I wonder about what niche the talker would provide for such a man. I can only hope that we remain sufficiently unsuccessful in our educational engineering to leave room for the Karl Zeners. But this is a divigation.

It was a slow process, then — and one presupposing a degree of maturation which itself would have been unlikely without the influence of this man — to come to the beginning of insight into Karl Zener's true stature. And how can that slowly won vision be conveyed?

His mind was unlike that of any other person I have known. It seemed to shatter any problem, any issue presented to it, into its maximum number of *meaningful* units, and then somehow spread them out into a spatial manifold, and proceed simultaneously to pursue, via its entire repertoire of experience, the requirements of each unit and of various tentatively entertained alternative patterns of them. I can think of no simpler way even to begin to characterize this remarkable apparatus. It was a mind that sucked dry of meaning each word, phrase, sentence, problem which came its way; unpacked a linguistic communication, a table of data, a scientific graph into a lattice of coexisting ramifications of great density. To vary the metaphor, it was a facet-seeking mind which expanded each object of thought or experience into its maximally faceted configuration.

As my metaphors suggest, the style of thinking, of cognitive processing, was essentially visual. The *input* to this mind was filtered through an observational sensibility of awesome powers. The man was the most ardent, acute, analytical, loving observer I have known. He saw with delight, and to see him see was an experience. Whether it was a face, an art-object, a landscape, or a flower upon which he lighted, he would seem to view it, study it, with such passion as to drain it of its essence for all time.

In talks with Karl, one often felt brighter than one was. For he would see seven or eight implications of each remark one made, however pedestrian, and automatically reject all but the least crass of those meanings. From the point of view of the other, a conversation with Karl could rapidly become more fundamental than it had any right to be. All of us in the department were accustomed to the profitable, if humbling, outcome of discussing research findings with him. Whether the context were our own research, or membership on a common dissertation committee, the result was standard: Karl would take one look at an obtained curve, or a data distribution, and see anywhere from three to several baker's dozens of implications which had eluded *us,* even if *we* had been collecting and pondering the data for a year or two. Often this kind of edification was less than welcome, for Karl was uncanny, despite an almost total ignorance of advanced statistics, in his ability to spot inadequacies of design, the absence of needed controls, unwarranted generalizations; indeed, every context in which the investigator, through insufficient perspicuity or sloth, had not done justice to the inherent meanings of the problem.

Language is a linear thing and no language could conceivably absorb the layered and differentiated complexity of such a mode of mental processing as I have tried to describe. For any of us, the difficulty of speaking or writing—especially at phases of high creative fluency—is largely a matter of re-coding a volumetric, rather river-like flow into a linear representation. Language—that is, socially standardized, natural language—is an enemy to a mind like that of Karl Zener. I think he hated it rather—persisting in a gallant refusal to surrender the complexity of his thought to the swindling and crass schematisms of language. His apparent "inarticulateness" was one side of a coin of which the other was stubborn refusal to sacrifice any of the quiddity he so keenly saw: his only course was continually to challenge the limits of language. This he did, when speaking, via strange involutions of syntax, concentrically structured compound sentences containing a multitude of parenthetical sub-sentences, odd but pregnant elisions, private shorthand devices, semantically charged idiosyncrasies of tone and inflection. And there was much supplementation of speech by gesture. These may *seem* to be symptoms of inarticulateness. They were actually symptomatic of—more properly, means of—unusually rich communication. The inarticulateness was in the hearer, especially he who had not learned Karl Zener's language. Poets and philosophers alike, in our time, have tended to make language an absolute, and have celebrated few things so much as *its* power; *its* richness. Civilization owes much to those compelled to resist the easy and meretricious "order" offered by the ready-made categories of language. Indeed, only in this way are properties of the universe overlooked by language brought ultimately within its ken.

With regard to writing, Karl Zener came to a different solution. He wrote as little as possible. For him, writing was more than a torture; at some level he must have seen it as the ultimate dishonesty—rendered the more grievous by its permanence. What he did write was thoroughly lucid but not easy. *His* form of dishonesty had far too much integrity for ease.

In consequence, nothing that he wrote was not utterly fundamental. His ten years of research on conditioning resulted in two major publications (1937, 1939), instead of the twenty or thirty that this rich research sequence would have justified. But they are among the most profound publications that have emerged from the five or six decades of research in this intensively ploughed area. His article with Gaffron — really monograph — on perception in volume 4 of *Psychology: A Study of a Science* (1962) is, in my opinion, one of the fundamental psychological documents of the century.

Two of Karl Zener's favorite adjectives tell much about what he stood for as a scholar. They are: "differentiated" and "significant." With him it was a first principle that knowledge — that is, *significant* knowledge — must in some way bear on *reality*. This is a belief more radical than it may sound, if one considers it in relation to the temper of psychology in our time. But for Karl, for *his* sense of fascination and awe before the universe, it was not enough that knowledge merely acknowledge reality (i.e., address and conserve significance in some loose and general way); still less was it sufficient to court reality by a rhetoric of respect for what are sometimes called "the higher things." It was Karl's unceasing compulsion to know and specify reality in a *differentiated* way. To arrive at *stable laws,* per se, was of little moment. What mattered was to strive towards functional relationships, the elements of which were sufficiently determinate and congruent with the structure of the subject matter to permit generalizations that were at once particulate and illuminating. He carried forward a lifelong offensive against the lazy, role-playing practice of erecting laws of unbridled generality on the basis of local and situation-bound evidence; laws the scope of which remains cosmic until one asks what their terms may mean for any situations or events outside their locus of discovery. At the same time, he had equally little respect for that chest-thumping espousal of particularity which proclaims that the terms related in a generalization speak only for the corresponding "experimental operations," and that the experimental operations speak only for themselves.

To assert such a philosophy of research is one thing; to live by it unrelentingly is another. Karl Zener did. And the man who did this living was possessed of a vast curiosity. He was unique in my acquaintance as a psychologist who took seriously, almost literally, the *calling* of a discipline, the awesome purport of which is no less than the study of all experience and action. Every segment of his experience, every moment of it, spurred his curiosity as man and scientist; he was equally enticed towards reflection by the experience of others. In professional contexts, this insatiable curiosity even extended to scientific problems seen as significant by colleagues with whose viewpoint he utterly disagreed. However misconceived the problem by his *own* standards, however remote from his immediate concerns, he could not but listen, question, surrender to a dialectic which swept him towards an isolation of its kernel of meaning, or the meaning of why no such kernel was isolable.

In the twenty-five years of our acquaintance, I do not recall an interval in which Karl was not doing research (formal research) in at least three or four fields of psychology, sometimes distantly deployed ones. In any one of these intervals, he might be embarked on six to a dozen problems, some pursued wholly by himself, others with the collaborations of colleagues, students, or assistants. Though his mode was very much to work with and through others, it was *not* the mode of the "research team" or the "Ph.D. mill." He tended to relate to each of his co-workers separately, privately, and intensively. Moreover, one with *his* philosophy of research could not stay himself from ardent involvement in the research processes connected with each problem. He had to *experience* the laboratory setting, procedure, and "dependent variable"–phenomena at each phase; he had to gaze long and hard—with screwed-up face and quizzical eyes—at the recorded data of each day's work, at the pooled and transformed data at each phase of their processing. I doubt if many of the people who worked with him were aware of the range and variety of other research commitments he was pursuing with equal energy at the same time. And each of these problems he embraced with the same passionate disposition to disembed differentiated meanings that characterized all his work.

Despite what I have already said, some might still be baffled at the circumstance that this remarkable volume of professional energy has left so few tangible marks on the pages, the actual journal-pages, of history. Yet— quite aside from Karl's special attitude towards writing—it is hard to see how matters could have been substantially different. And it is important to see this because it can show us something about the predicament of psychology in our time.

Psychology is a hard subject: so hard that it may remain forever blocked from going much past what might be learned about the human condition without its aid. The refractoriness of psychological problems to *genuine* advance soon led scientific psychologists to a strange compromise: they settled largely for spurious advance, for the illusion of forward motion that can be engendered by decorating the arbitrary or the obvious with the iconology of science. By this point in history, we know more than we ought about the mass delusion-systems that can arise in certain fields of scholarship, and gradually come so to dominate inquiry as to alienate it from its subject matter, indeed, cut it from its original impetus or any rational purpose. The saving grace in such eras is the phenomenon of individual transcendence. Karl Zener was such a phenomenon.

His passion for meaning had to confront not only the appalling first-order difficulty of achieving an analysis of experience and action in some sense finer and more determinate than man, in his many creative excursions, had yet accomplished, but the additional (and asphyxiating) one of communicating to those living within the delusion-system of modern psychology that our field is nothing unless some such aim be addressed. He who would maximize meaning in the circumstances of our field must be not only a self-determining and profound scholar, but a prophetic rhetorician. And he must face the additional problem of separating his own subtle—and thus not too sharply contoured—views from those of the many self-appointed "transcendors," the spurious prophets who tend to be bred in such times as ours.

Men who genuinely transcend their time confront strange necessities. They may find it necessary to spend a decade of their lives doing polemical research—i.e., research calculated to penetrate a group delusional system by laboriously showing the untenability of its premises through reanalysis of the very phenomena on which they are claimed to rest. Karl Zener spent ten years of his life on exactly such a project in his conditioning work. What prompted his choice of the conditioning situation was the need for reanalysis of Pavlovian phenomena of the sort used as basis for the then dominant neobehavioristic theories of learning. Had this objective not seemed to him desperately necessary for the liberation of psychology, he might have pursued his then current interest in developing a cognitive theory of action in a research context better calculated to yield constructive knowledge. Or he might have been able to devote much more time and energy to the human perceptual problems in which he had already established an interest and which, as we know, ultimately became his dominant concern.

Moreover, a glance at the two major articles (1937, 1939) reporting aspects of this research will go far towards showing why he did not write the other twenty or thirty substantial papers which the entire research sequence could have generated. One will be struck by the pages of laborious qualitative description of details of the behavior in the conditioning situation which *should* have been obvious to the hundreds of investigators who had been working in that field for many years. One will note also the many laborious (and brilliant) analyses of inconsonances between the obtained data and particular theoretical "mechanisms" and "principles" which had been "grounded" on conditioning data by behavior theorists.

Turning to another phase of his career, one must see the difficulty of communicating novel phenomenal dimensions of visual experience (discovered in the work with Gaffron; cf. Zener and Gaffron 1962), subtle experiential distinctions which had not been achieved in all human history, *as compounded* by the resistances and observational limitations of an audience that had learned not to trust individual experience (their own or others'). Indeed, this was an audience that considered it a mark of professional sophistication to proscribe experience as a legitimate scientific datum.

A man has only a small finitude of choices. Who is to say that it is not more dignified and somehow purer to borrow time and energy for the wider deployment of curiosity, even at the expense of withholding results from the historic record. History, after all, is not its record.

I have tried to characterize Karl Zener's mind and some of the emphases of that mind. That the mind is not distinguishable from the man, especially in the case of this mind, this man, is already clear. But I should like to dwell a bit further on Karl Zener's qualities as a person in relation to other persons, whether colleagues, students, friends, or relatives.

The quality of his concern for others is as unique and difficult to convey as is the quality of his intellect. How to start? He was always late for an appointment. The volume of his scholarly and formal administrative commitments might itself have accounted for this, had Karl been an ordinary man. He was not. His range and level of involvements with people was incredible. When X found him late or unavailable, he was usually with Y. His tendency to surrender lovingly and utterly to the immediacies of a human problem made "termination" for him close to impossible. And he could not resist the impulse to help, to nurture, constructively to shape.

I have heard him make cynical judgments of people, but hardly ever express dislike. He had a remarkable insight into the disorderliness, the cross-purposefulness, the inherent uncontrollability of the human world, and yet this somehow prompted him all the more to want to straighten things out, to intervene, to avert, to ameliorate for the good of all. If he heard that even a remote acquaintance was in the hospital, he was forthwith on the phone speaking to the doctors, then to the family and, if possible, the patient, and from this point on, he would continue to track the process, help in every way, subtly and shrewdly advise. In the case of any human problem of graver import, his concern was absolute, his head cool, his purview of the situation broader than anybody's, and his ministrations and help inexhaustible. In every poignant or tragic situation that arose in the department, during my twenty-five years' stay, Karl took leadership. When a former student's wife died, Karl Zener rushed to New York to speak at the funeral. A graduate student or colleague facing divorce, illness, an anxiety attack, or mere worry about his work, had Karl Zener's instant sympathy and help.

His patience with people was formidable. He could not bear to allow a misunderstanding, whether between another and himself or between others, to go unmitigated. If he felt that a colleague or friend misperceived him, or he they, or anybody anybody, he would spend hours and sometimes years trying to achieve a constructive resolution. He had a touching — and usually well-founded — faith in the maturational process; a confidence in the potentialities of young or not fully formed people. He could be deeply troubled by the occasional crassness shown towards him, say, by a young and still insensitive colleague, but he would seek in every way, if necessary for years, to foster the person's development. Not a single one of us who joined the staff as young men failed to learn much in a human way, and usually a professional way, from Karl — and this not merely by being in his ambience, but through his active concern.

His interest in administration reflected his deep commitment to the future of psychology, his yearning that there be institutional forces which press the field towards its potential dignity, but it was also a corollary of his concern for people. All of his life he maintained a far greater burden of responsibility for others than any man I have known. When he became Chairman, that burden expanded. It was a burden he loved, but it killed him.

I have re-studied all of Karl Zener's publications in hope of giving an account of his major ideas. I soon concluded that the ideational richness is such that any brief précis in a talk of this sort would be a disservice to the author. A man's work is first and foremost the man himself, and it has not been easy to begin to characterize the manner of such a man.

A glance at Karl Zener's last publication — his 1962 contribution (with Mercedes Gaffron) to *Psychology: A Study of a Science* — will show why any summary could only be a mark of disrespect. These densely packed one hundred pages project a view of the field of perception which at once seeks to salvage all significant lines of inquiry in this area and to open up a radical new perspective. As I have already indicated, what emerges in the course of this analysis is an essentially new and liberating view of psychology.

The importance of the article is two-fold:

1. It develops an extraordinarily clarifying framework for the study of perception which straightens out many of the traditional and recent muddles in this field, and yet manages to accommodate most of the significant research that has been done. This so called "phase analysis" of perception is unique in its acknowledgment of the complexity of psychological processes in their joint interdependencies with the world and the biologically describable events of a real (rather than hypothetical) organism. It acknowledges also and elucidates with great power the critical role of experience and its analysis in the study of perception. In my estimation, from this time forward it would be a salubrious exercise for workers in perception and other fundamental fields to test their own conception of their research objectives against the rigorous and differentiated requirements of this framework. Indeed, graduate students and others contemplating a career in psychology might well use this framework as a vocational screening device: if they cannot face the kind of complexity here seen as endemic to psychological analysis, perhaps they should choose a different career.

2. It contains the most detailed descriptions yet made of the "novel" dimensions of visual experience that had been isolated by Gaffron and Zener over their ten-year collaboration. These subtle phenomenal properties had emerged from the infinitely dedicated and patient comparison of art objects, photographs, and natural objects in their normal aspect as against their mirror-image reversals, inversions, and partial rotations. Differing clusterings or organizations of these properties are shown to depend on variations in looking or survey-behavior, quadrant of the visual field under survey, indices of hemisphere dominance, and other factors. Plausible inferences are made from these discoveries as to the character of the central processes that could mediate them. A major conclusion is that there may be a limited number of alternative processing systems favoring different organizations of the same visual input. If so, our entire mode of conceptualizing and investigating problems of perception would have to be realigned, on this ground *alone*.

The happiest outcome of my talk would be if it motivated psychologists who have not yet read this article to do so. It has been good to come by way of evidence in the past few years that it has become something of a classic. This is deeply reassuring in that the view of psychology projected by the article entails that the calling of psychologists, when significantly pursued, be the most agonizingly difficult of any in the gamut of scholarship. It entails also that if psychology not shirk its historic mission as the discipline which seeks empirical insight into all human experience and action, it must permanently remain the most conceptually heterogeneous, and systematically the least unitary, of the sciences. It entails that the workforce of psychology comprise individuals not only of high intellectual capacity but marked openness and sensitivity to their experience, and that this force include sub-groups of individuals differentially equipped by background and sensibility to cope with *all* areas of human phenomena, not excluding those traditionally in the province of the humanities.

A few months before Karl Zener died, he gave a talk on graduate education. Its final paragraph is probably the last paragraph he ever wrote for a formal purpose and it says, better than anything I could say, what his life was about:

> In a long perspective which includes the recent accumulation of specific scientific knowledge of man set against the accumulated wisdom of the ages, it is *in fact* challenging to believe that to the combined attack of courageous investigators of acumen, sensitivity, and integrity, the way may be clearing for a truly unified understanding of the nature of man — that in principle such a unification may not be impossible — and that in such an understanding the truths and the beauties of both the scientific and the humanistic pictures of the human reality might be transformed into an integrated perspective. In such a space, the psychological investigator could indeed attack his problems with the total resources of his person and an additional factor favoring contact with significant reality would have been added. In such a space, graduate education in psychology could indeed engage the resources of the total person. (1964)

If the way *is* "clearing for a truly unified understanding of the nature of man," no one in our time had worked more gallantly to clear that way than he who wrote those lines.

Karl Zener died in mid-course at a phase when he was more resolved within himself, more enthusiastic about his work, than I had ever known him to be. There were evidences that this very ardor would have impelled him more and more to write, whatever the compromises for a man of his special cast. But his form of greatness could not have been registered to the world by an infinite number of words. Much that the world needs, that psychology needs, went out of the world with him.

The challenge of his last paper has already been taken up. Phenomenal research using picture rotations is already going forward at several centers. Mercedes Gaffron is continuing in the tradition she shared with him. And whatever his many students have done, and will continue to do, is perforce his work. His impact on me was such that had I been Plato he would have been my Socrates. But I am no Plato. Nevertheless, for decades I have not been able to judge where his thinking stops and mine begins. What haunts me is that whatever part is mine is not worthy of him, and may become less so without his guidance.

I said that when I met him on the train to Ithaca on that bright December day of 1938, we were for a while in the company of another psychologist. And I noted that the man in question had subsequently become one of the most renowned psychologists of his time. I mean no disrespect to that bright and productive man in using him, at this moment, as one term in an invidious comparison. Karl Zener was a great man; *he* is a merely successful one. I think this a happy thought, for it must surely mean that there is in history a larger supply of the great than we have any basis for knowing.

14

Psychology's Bridgman versus Bridgman's Bridgman: A Study in Cognitive Pathology

Foreword

Since its inception as science, psychology has generated a rhetoric of "rigor" concerning the ideal characteristics of its inquirers. An early emphasis on experimental exactitude expanded, by the 1930s, to a conception that saw the first-year graduate student also as a mature theoretical physicist, logician, and (when required) carpenter. By the 1960s, the student was expected also to be an expert in "computer science," and an adept in esoteric speciations of probability mathematics. Consistently missing from these autistic job specifications have been such trivial matters as the ability to read, to report reliably on what has been read, and to write. As for the more sophisticated hermeneutic and analytic skills of scholarship, *these* have apparently been seen as positive threats to scientific purity. This chapter illustrates the consequences of the divorce between psychology and even minimal requirements of the Western scholarly tradition. The doctrine of "operational definition" (or "operationism") has been a central strand in the official epistemology governing psychological method for nearly sixty years. Despite a large literature of stipulation and pseudo-exegesis of operational procedure, it can be shown that any demand that "variables" or "concepts"—whether of psychological theory or experiment—be operationally defined in the senses advocated would, if literally construed, confine psychological discourse to matters so fragmented and trivial as to be worse than empty. The doctrine of "operational definition" in psychology was presumably based on the methodic thinking of the distinguished Harvard physicist, Percy William Bridgman, who, in many writings over some forty-six years, elaborated a way of explicating the meaning-contours of concepts *already in place* within physics and other contexts — including that of natural language. He called his method "operational analysis" and did not suppose that he was stipulating any canonical schema for *definition*. The total misconstrual by psychologists of Bridgman's "critical concern," and the evidence suggesting that they had based their "reading" of Bridgman's position on little more than a single slogan taken out of the context of the very paragraph in which it had occurred (at the beginning of his first book on general methodic issues, *The Logic of Modern Physics* [1927]), provides a dramatic case study of the quality of scholarship that has long prevailed in psychology.[1]

«

Should there be any confusion about the title, let me explain that I am the founder of the new science of "cognitive pathologistics." My claim is modest, for the field as yet has but one practitioner. Its objective is the diagnosis of the many epistemopathies that pervade modern scholarship. On the therapeutic side, I have found the logical scalpel to be of little avail, but a form of exorcism, leavened by an effort to make evident the ludicrousness of the sufferers' symptoms, sometimes helpful. A forty-year application of this method has met moderate success in curtailing that epistemopathic epidemic known as "behaviorism." But, strangely, a coordinate campaign toward exorcising one of behaviorism's main methodological supports — the doctrine of "operational definition" — has had no effect whatsoever.[2]

1. Koch's initial exploration of this terrain — under the title, "The 'Operational Principle' in Psychology: A Case Study in Cognitive Pathology" — took place in Boston in April 1982 as part of a AAAS Centenary Symposium on Bridgman. Revised versions were presented at two subsequent conventions of the American Psychological Association — in 1985 and in 1991. The present chapter is drawn from "Psychology's Bridgman vs. Bridgman's Bridgman: An Essay in Reconstruction," *Theory and Psychology* 2 (1992): 261–90. This foreword is, in fact, the abstract of that paper. An excerpt from the paper was published in *Recent Trends in Theoretical Psychology*, vol. 3, ed. H. J. Stam et al. (New York: Springer-Verlag, 1993). *Eds.*

2. Some readers may feel that "operational definition" is no longer a live issue in psychology in that the practice of ritualistically labeling specifications of the application conditions of formal theoretical concepts and/or research "variables" as "operational definitions" is not as broadly evident in recent psychological literature as it was a decade or two ago. But the presumption of some form of an "operational paradigm" can be shown to lurk but slightly beneath the surface in the implicit or explicit rationale for the choice of research variables, and in the practices associated with the linkage of such "empirical" discriminations to some broader problem context (read "hypothesis" or "theory") to which the research is presumed relevant. Indeed, any psychologist who has read yesterday's Ph.D. dissertation will know that students are still told that they must "operationalize" their concepts and give explicit

The notion, as it now functions in psychology, is part of an empyrean of jargon that instructors can draw upon in order to give students the illusion that they are studying a *science*. It is conveyed sans historical context (I doubt that most undergraduates would recognize the name Bridgman), and without much content in excess of the admonition to make sure that "variables" be "testable" or "measurable." Psychology is now widely taught in high schools, and perhaps the best way to convey the fate of the operational prescription may be to quote from a lavishly illustrated 1980 high school text:

> OPERATIONAL DEFINITION
> It is very important to all scientists that their work be objective, and that events being studied can be observable—by you, by me, by anyone who's interested. It makes it easier to specify what is being studied and how. These events must also be repeatable. That assures that you can study an event whenever you want. Events must also be testable and measurable. . . .
> The easiest way to achieve all this is to define events operationally. An *operational definition* means simply that any concept

---

"operational" specifications for anything in their head that may be permitted to filter into their professional discourse!

The sophisticated reader may also know that analyses of meaning (and definition) in philosophy of science, philosophy of mind, formal linguistics, psycholinguistics, semiotics, the hermeneutic studies, etc.—though the analyses are now so intricately speciated as to defy classification—have, in almost all cases, left simplistic paradigms like the psychologist's version of "operational definition" (and most meaning-criteria that propose a reduction of lexical units to any predetermined "base" of epistemic or linguistic "simples") in distant dereliction. The trend in linguistics and formal semantics has been increasingly to see the semantic "dimension" of natural language as resistant to algorithmic treatment. Knowledge of such developments is certainly in the command of some psycholinguists but *they* are not in command of psychology!

Some may have the impression that reliance upon psychology's "operational paradigm" has waned in the wake of the "cognitive revolution" in that certain cognitivists (whether Piagetian, Chomskyan, or of the "cognitive science" ilk) have been disposed to launch large speculative guesses concerning, say, innate linguistic and/or cognitive "competence" rules, processing strategies, etc.—formal structures which are often but tenuously related to "performance." It can be shown, though, that much of the *psychological research* within these traditions is still heavily constrained by the presumptions of operationism. By now it is hardly original to note that the American addenda to Piagetian theory have largely been efforts to *operationalize* what are presumed to be loose or free-floating elements of his conceptualization. And much of "cognitive science" presumes that one is not playing ball scientifically if one cannot reduce (or equate) assertions concerning mental states or processes to a machine-programmable algorithm. (The algorithm is the concept!) A large part of "cognitive science" can indeed be seen as a deperipheralized form of methodological behaviorism: a presumably impregnable new stronghold for "objectivism."

is identical to its operations. For example, if you talk about the length of your father's moustache, how are we going to measure it? To find the length of an object we must perform certain physical operations with a tape measure or yardstick. . . .

What do you mean when you say "I love you" to your boyfriend or girlfriend? Many things are involved in that statement, but if a psychologist is to study "love," the term must be operationally defined. If you're in love, it is likely that (1) you seek the company of that individual before anyone else; (2) you will give gifts, such as birthday presents or Valentines; (3) you will date that person; and (4) you will do many other such things. Maybe this is just describing the obvious, but it should also be obvious that if those behaviors aren't there, you probably aren't in love. The operations, then, define the concept. (Kasschau 1980, 27–29)

Though the foregoing presentation may average a syllable per word less than the characteristic treatment of operational definition that might be directed at a contemporary graduate student, pretty much the same archetype would emerge from the two accounts.

In this article I hope, first, to restore the dignity of a fascinating (if erratic) thinker by establishing the total unrelatedness of operationism in psychology to anything Bridgman had in mind; second, to convey a little of the historical context in which the debased and vulgarized versions of his "critical" concern entered and captured psychology; and, third, to outline a way of looking at problems of so-called "empirical definition" which is at once an alternative to the lore concerning operational definition as stabilized within psychology *and* not inconsonant with important but neglected aspects of Bridgman's thinking. In a fourth section, I seek to identify certain of Bridgman's interesting and/or viable emphases which have been either not noticed or misconstrued in the psychological literature.

1. Psychology's Bridgman versus Bridgman

P. W. Bridgman (1882–1961) was an experimental physicist who specialized in the physics of high pressures over a long career at Harvard. He became a Nobel laureate in 1946. His "discussion of the operational technique" emerged *after* ten years of "pondering . . . what was really happening in branches of physics that puzzled" him (in particular, dimensional analysis, electromagnetic field theory, relativity theory "and those parts of quantum theory which had been developed by 1926") (1938b, 2). This

369

"critical" interest (as he called it) in "the foundations of our physical thought" was first asserted in a 1916 paper, and, by 1922, a stance that presaged what he later called "operational analysis" was evident in his first book, *Dimensional Analysis*. His operational viewpoint received its first explicit and general formulation in the second and most widely known of the six books given to his "critical" concerns, *The Logic of Modern Physics* (1927). The method therein employed for the analysis of a large range of concepts in classical and modern physics ("operational analysis") increasingly appealed to him as having broad significance not only for physics but for the philosophy of all science (natural and social), for education, for social ethics, for issues of national science policy and, indeed, for the maximization of human intelligence in such a way that the *individual* could fully "emerge" — for the first time in the history of the race — from the homogenizing pressures of society.[3]

Within *psychology*, Bridgman was *used*, not read. The "middlemen" who, in the mid-1930s, began to inform their colleagues about the timeless virtues of something called "operational definition" or "operationism" were interested *not* in Bridgman's ideas but, rather, in the *authority* that he could seem to lend to a set of loose decisions concerning the desirability of a

3. Bridgman's corpus of writings is enormous, comprising (on the count of his student, Gerald Holton) 260 articles and four books (plus the posthumous seven-volume *Collected Experimental Papers*, 1964) bearing on his experimental and technical concerns, and sixty articles and seven books on his "critical" concerns. (The seven "critical" books — included in the references of this book — are those of 1927, 1936, 1938a, 1950, 1952, 1959, 1962.) No comprehensive bibliography of his works is in print, but fairly complete listings are contained in entries for "Percy William Bridgman" in the *Biographical Memoirs of Fellows of the Royal Society* (Newitt 1962) and the *Biographical Memoirs* of the National Academy of Sciences (Kemble and Birch 1970). The texts of the memoirs of Bridgman in these volumes are important reading for anyone who might wish to get his ideas into focus.

Of course, the present article can in no way *repair* the atrociously distorted representation of Bridgman's views within psychology; it can only identify and suggest the magnitude of the distortion. There is a large secondary literature on Bridgman in a number of fields other than psychology (e.g., philosophy, sociology, and, of course, physics). I have made no effort to represent this extra-psychological literature in the references except for one useful work by a philosopher: *Operationism*, by A. Cornelius Benjamin (1955). In it will be found both a recapitulation of Bridgman's views of greater accuracy than anything to be found in the psychological literature, *and* summaries of the positions of several so-called "operationists" in psychology and sociology. It contains also a useful bibliography. The work is limited, however, not only by the fact that Bridgman's thinking continued to evolve after its publication, but — more seriously — by its disposition to align Bridgman with standard philosophic position-categories and issues of a sort alien to the texture and style of his "critical" project (cf. note 9).

wholly "objectivist" epistemology that had been advocated by classical behaviorists like Watson twenty years earlier, and that had become congealed articles of faith among the majority of psychologists for at least the preceding decade. Experimental psychologists have traditionally suffered from a syndrome known as hypermanic physicophilia (with quantificophrenic delusions and methodico-echolalic complications), and the impression that a distinguished physicist was seeming to confirm certain of their homespun epistemological beliefs was intoxicating. Bridgman was filtered through the frame of these beliefs, and there resulted a collectivity of methodic stipulations and stereotypes bearing only a vague phonetic similarity to a few statements that Bridgman had made.

"Bridgman in psychology" could form a peculiarly revealing chapter in the history of ideas! It would require more than a small book to correct the misinterpretations that have congealed in the psychological literature. May I summarily suggest the magnitude of a few:

1. Bridgman was not in any focal sense "anti-metaphysical," as he himself makes clear as early as page xi of *The Logic of Modern Physics* (1927). He was fairly constant in taking a dim view of speculative philosophy, but did not ground this on any litmus-paper criterion meant to predetermine the boundaries of the "meaningful." Though he distrusted concepts smacking of apriorism, "essences," and intrinsic "properties"—and had no patience at all for "absolutes"—he acknowledged at many junctures (early and late) metaphysical implications of certain of his analyses, and presumed a kind of physical realism in his recognition that significant operations in physics evolve out of age-old backgrounds of "real physical experience." Indeed, we can find Bridgman embracing—however grudgingly—a form of the Kantian project in the last sentence of his introduction to *The Logic of Modern Physics:* "In spite, however, of the best intentions, we shall not be able to eliminate completely considerations savoring of the metaphysical, because it is evident that the nature of our thinking mechanism essentially colors any picture that we can form of nature, and we shall have to recognize that unavoidable characteristics of any outlook of ours are imposed in this way" (1927, xi).

2. The paragraph in *The Logic of Modern Physics* (5–6) from which Bridgman's famous "criterion" ("the concept is synonymous with the corresponding set of operations") is taken gives as much importance to "mental operations" as it does to "physical operations." Moreover, if ocular fatigue does not prevent the reader from finishing the paragraph, one will

encounter the sentence: "It is not intended to imply that there is a hard and fast division between physical and mental concepts, or that one kind of concept does not always contain an element of the other." Though neither of these operation classes was treated with ultimate clarity in Bridgman's writings, this hardly justifies the usual tendency wholly to elide "mental operations" in accounts of the "operational principle," or to assign them some minor, if not supererogatory, status. It is to be emphasized that the famous "criterion" on page 5 is perhaps the most uncouth and ill-considered sentence that Bridgman ever wrote;[4] nevertheless, it seems to mark precisely the point at which most psychologist students of Bridgman terminated their study. Even in the body of this early book — the purpose of which was to carry out detailed explications of fundamental physical concepts in light of the new physics — the page 5 criterion is often violated by the acknowledgment of modalities of meaning other than the "corresponding operations."

And, in his many writings over the next thirty-four years, perhaps the bulk of Bridgman's methodic thinking was given to further specification and revision of particulate problems that were either mooted or created by the initial rough-and-ready formulation. Quite early on, for instance, the force of the notion of operation seems to shift from a set of activities *constitutive* of the "meaning" of a concept to ones which help us *find* the meaning. Also, from an early point on, Bridgman repeatedly indicated that operations are necessary conditions for meanings, not *sufficient* ones. Moreover, he *stressed* — constantly and emphatically — that he was not advocating a theory or method of *definition* (or, still less, of concept formation), but only a method for analyzing, perhaps sharpening, the meanings of concepts *already in place.* He did not advocate "operational *definition*" but rather "operational analysis," or "operational method."

Questions having to do with concept generality, alternate operations leading to the "same terminus," good vs. poor operations, "introspective"

4. Within days after writing this sentence, I came across the following passage in Bridgman's 1938 paper, "Operational Analysis": "the statement 'meanings are operational' comes to be used carelessly as a *sufficient* description of the whole situation. In fact, I myself have doubtless gone further in some of my printed statements than would be justified when the statement is taken out of context. For instance, my statement on page 5 of *The Logic of Modern Physics* that *meanings are synonymous with operations,* was obviously going too far when taken out of context; it was in any event going further than necessary. My own dictum is applicable to this statement of mine, namely that what a man means by a term is to be found by observing what he does with it, not by what he says about it" (1938b, 5).

operations, the meaning of "same" operation, and many others, are embraced and reembraced with increasing specificity in the sequence of Bridgman's writings. "Introspectional terms" were analyzed in extenso in later writings (e.g., 1959).[5] They were seen as "relational terms" in that the referent varied for each user (e.g., he proposed "mescious" as a revealing surrogate notion for "conscious"). The "operation" for understanding another's introspective report was that of "projection."

Again, operations are to be viewed as "consciously directed activities." *Concepts* are "frozen nodes of experience," which we have noted relative to our own purposes and which recur in never precisely the same way. Moreover, neither our "concepts," our "operations," nor our "experiences" are ever ultimately sharp; they are always surrounded by "a penumbra of uncertainty," a "haze" (cf. 1927, 33–36). Another of his emphases is that operations are not necessarily describable in terms of "simpler" ones — often more complex operations have to be used in elucidating "simpler" ones. Also, at best, operations are but loosely communicable by *language;* often they can be learned only by "imitation" (note the foreshadowing of Polanyi, and of Kuhn's borrowings from Polanyi, here!).

Though ultimately the bare notion of operation becomes, on the one hand, so general and, on the other, so intricately qualified as to render the concept useless as a foundation for epistemological analysis, in the *course*

---

5. The importance attributed by Bridgman to the distinction between "introspectional terms" and others of more "public" character is suggested by the following passage:

> In the class of operations performable by only one person there is a subclass which is so sharply set off from all the others that I think it demands special treatment — this is the subclass of operations which only I can perform. The dichotomy between the operations by which I decide that I am having a toothache and any of my neighbors is having a toothache is so sharp and spectacular that it is to be emphasized by every means in my power. This dichotomy is the most insistent and uncompromising of the characteristics of my world — I do not see how I can neglect it and possibly hope to give an adequate description of what happens to me, or to adapt myself to living in the world. (1959, 217)

This passage falls toward the beginning of an extended analysis in which Bridgman considers in detail the meaning of key "introspectional words" (216–43). He leaves no ambiguity concerning the position that serves as foil to his arguments: "It is not meet that an outsider like me should question the judgment of the psychologist that he can at present spend his time more profitably on more public matters than introspectional report, but as a physicist I may be permitted to express a mild surprise that this should be made so much a matter of principle by the behaviorist, or that any method should be discarded which might conceivably help in unraveling the incredibly complicated maze of present psychological phenomena" (1959, 241). Sentiments of this sort had been expressed earlier by Bridgman (e.g., 1940b, 43–61; 1945, 36–42).

of these increasingly differentiated analyses Bridgman spins off many original, useful, and even profound insights into the nature of inquiry and knowledge.

3. What is often referred to (if referred to at all) as a minor and regrettable foible of Bridgman's — his so-called "solipsism" — is indeed a central aspect of his thinking (as it would *have* to be if the diagnosis were true). The diagnosis is, of course, no more "true" than it would be in relation to *any* empiristic epistemologist or, indeed, anyone who gives emphasis to the perspectival and sensibility-dependent character of knowledge.

In any event, we find Bridgman unembarrassedly "accept[ing] as significant our common sense judgment that there is a world external to us" as early as page xi of *The Logic of Modern Physics* (1927). The more closely he scrutinized the meaning of "operations," in the sequence of his writings, the more he came to stress that operations are always *someone's* operations, and that the importance of acknowledging this dependency of an operational statement on "first-person report" increases as one ascends from physics to the biological and social sciences. By 1936 (*The Nature of Physical Theory*), which was exactly the year that "operationism" entered into prominence in psychology, the problems suggested by this experientialist emphasis had become his dominant interest. In *The Way Things Are* (1959), the "fact that operations are performed by individuals" and that "we cannot get away from ourselves" can be said to set the context of the entire discussion. An almost existentialist emphasis on the need to restore what he calls "freshness of perception" in science (and elsewhere) is often registered in that work. Naturally, Bridgman was not sympathetic to behaviorism — which he suggested was "riding for a fall" (42) in the 1945 *Psychological Review* symposium on operationism in psychology, and which he subjects to extended criticism in *The Way Things Are* (1959, 200–248) — nor could he at any time have been sympathetic to the garbled use of his ideas by behaviorists!

2. The Larger Historical Context

The history of psychology, ever since its stipulation into existence as "science," may be seen to stem from a succession of proposals as to how to attain the status of a cumulative and shareable knowledge-finding enterprise in the sense thought to be definitive of successful natural science. *Nineteenth-century "experimental psychology"* proposed to emulate the *experimental methods* of science via a paradigm such that the stimulus be controlled and specified in physical terms, while the dependent variable constitute a report by an appropriately trained "observer" upon a correlative subjective change — a report presumably to be rendered reliable by use of a stipulated set of descriptive categories.[6] Despite some success in areas like sensory psychophysics, forty years of "brass instrument" introspectionism did not seem to bring psychology much closer to the realization of its scientific objectives. Early behaviorism proposed a *stricter* emulation of physical-science experiment: namely that bodily *response* be substituted for the subjective dependent variable, thereby rendering experimentation homogeneously "objective." Thus *both* the independent and dependent variables of lawlike statements were to be restricted to publicly observable events, and the so-called psychological "subject" was to be treated as an "input-output" system in the terms of stimulus and response.

But the strategy of *classical* behaviorism (as promulgated by Watson in 1913 and rapidly accepted and pursued by others) resulted in scattered and particulate findings, most having little interest. Also disagreements — both conceptual and empirical — persisted in the same static, time-marking way as previously; early behaviorism was merely one among a large number of schools, all transfixed in an endless moment of internecine polemic. Moreover, the aseptic "objectivity" and determinacy vouchsafed the observation base of psychology by Watson's strictures were soon contaminated by his (and others') penchant for reinstating virtually every mentalist category in the history of thought via the arbitrary invention of one or another type of "implicit response." Still less satisfactory was the dizzying ambiguity in the definition and application of the basic notions of S and R evident in the analyses of the classical behaviorists: witness Watson's vagrant fluctuations as between molar and molecular criteria for both. Finally, there was — to some — a disturbing admixture of the methodological and the metaphysical discernible in the classical behaviorists' rationales for "objectivistic" policy.

Within the interval 1925–1930, there is much evidence to suggest that psychology was once again seeking a methodic panacea for its long frustrated scientistic hopes. The stifling dysfunctionalities that I have just hinted at led to a new stage in which a *decision procedure* that might ensure "progressive" status was sought in two (not unrelated) directions: (1) the emulation of the *theoretical* methods of natural science, and (2) the implementation of responsible and univocal concept formation (and the conjoint final laying of the metaphysical ghost) via a more rigorous and effec-

6. This is but a rough generalization — which needs qualification in relation to some versions of "nineteenth-century 'experimental psychology.'"

tive way of ensuring that concepts be linked to publicly checkable observations.

This yearning for a decision procedure which would liberate psychology for dependable, cumulative advance had, at least in some minds, become obsessive by the early 1930s. The search did not have far to go! For philosophy, in response to a similar and more ancient necessity of its own, had entered a phase in which its quest for the rule and paradigm of significant knowledge had begun to focus on a "new" codification of the nature of science. By the early 1930s that codification had begun to stabilize in the formulations of logical positivism and neopragmatism. And of course, Bridgman's writings on the conceptual analysis of physics had attained "visibility" by the late 1920s. Since there was a family resemblance between Bridgman's conception of operational analysis and the logical positivists' approach to the analysis of "empirical definition," and since the positivists tended to be assimilative, it was not long before some of them — and particularly Moritz Schlick, Herbert Feigl, and Carl Hempel — began to import aspects of Bridgman's thought into their own rather more ambitious efforts toward a "rational reconstruction" of the nature of scientific theory. In this way, a certain melding of what came to be called "operationism" with logical positivism began to take place — a circumstance which later caused much confusion among the consumerships of the two components. Be all this as it may, the "new view" of science, if it may be called that, was being exported with missionary zeal to the general scholarly community at precisely the same time that psychology's need was coming to be felt as critical.

As is well known, the interaction between the logical positivist view of scientific theory and the orienting attitudes promulgated by classical behaviorism formed the basis of a strategy that soon became familiar as *neobehaviorism*. Clark Hull's hypothetico-deductive theory of adaptive behavior (e.g., 1930b, 1943) was the initiating — and long dominant — archetype for this kind of formulation. More generally, the tendency, beginning in the early 1930s, for theorists of divergent leanings to be controlled by aspects of the new view of science makes it possible to characterize the ensuing period in fundamental psychology as an "Age of Theory." I have written widely (e.g., Koch 1959a, 1964, 1971, 1992a) about the definitive attributes and history of this optimistic and autistic period (which may be crudely bounded by 1930 and 1960) but the charting of that "Age" can be no large part of my story here. The six-volume American Psychological Association–sponsored assessment of the status of psychology that I directed at midcentury was essentially a detailed analytical survey of the Age of Theory as seen through the eyes of its molders and major contributors (cf. Koch 1959b, 1962b, 1963).

Bridgman's influence on the presuppositions of that period was mediated partly through logical positivism, and partly in a less indirect fashion. The story is complex and ironic. Through no fault of his own, his impact proved to move psychology in a direction diametrically opposed to his deepest commitments. And his occasional efforts to correct or mitigate the situation were characteristically met by therapeutic efforts to bring him into line with the therapists' own misconstruals of the earliest and crudest version of his position. It is a sufficiently weird story to merit detailed study by a battalion of cognitive pathologists. But here I must limit myself to a few highlights.

A spate of articles concerning the virtues of "operational definition" began to appear in the psychological literature circa 1935. The initial prophets were S. S. Stevens (1935a, 1935b, 1939) and E. G. Boring (1936), both of whom had been introduced to the ideas of their own physicist colleague, Bridgman, by Herbert Feigl, who spent the year 1930 at Harvard immediately after his departure from the Vienna Circle (cf. Boring 1950, 656 ff.). The Stevens-Boring enthusiasm for the operational prescription (as they understood it) was boundless: they saw it not only as a fail-safe tool for ensuring the sharpness and univocality of psychological discourse, but as in some sense implying a definitive program for the entire psychological enterprise. Stevens, in particular, envisaged a psychology which would be wholly dedicated to establishing precise functional relations between precisely operationalized concepts. But he helped Bridgman out a bit by positing that the ultimate "verifying" operation must be the "discriminatory response." He was so obsessed with the need to ensure the "publicity" of science that he felt it necessary to conceptualize the "observer" as a "physical system" whose status as such was guaranteed by an *equation* of "experience" with the "discriminatory response." In this way, argued Stevens, it was permissible to study "attributes" of sensory dimensions, images, feelings, etc., in wholly objective terms. It was necessary merely to perceive that the operation *is* the construct. And, to keep matters tidy, Stevens (at least for a while) proposed that psychology be defined as the science of *discrimination*.

Other votaries for one or another form of operationism soon emerged: a motley group, including psychologists as varied in viewpoint as E. C. Tolman (e.g., 1935, 1936a, 1936b), Carroll Pratt (1939), A. G. Bills

(1938), J. R. Kantor (1938), Kenneth Spence (Bergmann and Spence 1941; Spence 1944) — even a dismally callow version of Sigmund Koch (1941a, 1941b). And, of course, those logical positivists who felt it their special mission to help psychologists see the methodological light — especially Herbert Feigl and Gustav Bergmann, but also Carl Hempel and others — addressed their own clarifications of the operational principle to a psychological audience. By the early 1940s, a substantial methodological literature on operationism in psychology had been accumulated: it continued to burgeon over the next decade. But this large cluster of detailed (and sometimes tortured) analyses was hardly a precondition to the broad *acceptance* by psychologists of the "operationist" patois. Within a year or two after the *word* was first heard (probably via one of Stevens's 1935 articles), virtually everyone in psychology — not to mention their relatives and their dogs — was some kind of operationist. It was as if the adjective "operational" had become cemented to the noun "definition."

Though the hermeneutic shadings of "operationism" were virtually infinite, two broad versions of the role of operational definition in respect to the objectives of psychology soon emerged. One of them insisted that the task of psychology be wholly pursued via the determination of functional relationships between carefully specified experimental operations. On this view, all legitimate concepts of psychology must be operationally defined — and, indeed, the concept *is* the operation. Generality, in respect to a given concept, is to be purchased only by the empirical "discovery" of further operations which co-vary with (or are "equivalent" with) the initial one. The Stevens-Boring brand of operationism, and, in some respects, Skinner's (e.g., 1938), were of that ilk.

The second grouping — and for a long time the dominant one — comprised approaches based on dimly apprehended versions of the logical positivist view of theory as an "interpreted formal system" (cf. Koch 1941a, 1941b). On this view, operational definition is one component of a hypothetico-deductive system. It is that form of definition which relates concepts *implicitly* defined within the axiom set to "empirical states of affairs," thus transforming the formal system into an empirical theory. (A number of other names had been used by the neopositivists for this handy type of definition, as, for instance, empirical definition, coordinating definition, etc.; they were now generously willing to assign similar force to "operational definition.") On this view, then, in an adequate scientific theory the meaning of a concept is (at least in principle) not uniquely constituted by its "operational definition," but is also determined by its relations to other concepts within the postulational network and (indirectly) by other factors such as explicit definitions and inference rules. Most psychological theorists of the Age of Theory presumed some such model as their ideal, and then proceeded to put forward a vague blueprint or plan for such a theory—in most cases managing soon to believe that they had proffered the genuine theoretical article.

However, theorists of this ilk accepted a proposal that E. C. Tolman had made in the early 1930s that any psychological theory of reasonable generality *and* economy take the form of a chain of "intervening variables" interpolated between a set of measurable antecedent conditions and the final dependent variable of "behavior." Since the *meaning* of the intervening variables was usually held to be uniquely constituted by their functional relations ultimately to the independent and dependent variables discriminated by the theory, the presumption was that the intervening constructs were thereby *operationally* defined.[7] However, among the many things that

7. Such "unique" determination of the meaning of intervening variables by the associated independent and dependent variables was the typical metatheoretical position during much of the Age of Theory. It was easy to see, however, that some of the theorists had "surplus meanings" in mind for some or all of the intervening variables: i.e., conceptual properties reflecting a plausible basis for the choice within, say, neurophysiology, or indeed any domain including commonsense phenomenology, which provided an intuitive rationale. In an important article, "On a Distinction between Intervening Variables and Hypothetical Constructs," MacCorquodale and Meehl (1948) analyze in depth the point here at issue. I think it important to note that even theorists who asserted a "pure" intervening variable position (e.g., the Hull of 1943) were presuming easily detectable "surplus-meanings," and thus using "hypothetical constructs" (cf. Koch 1954).

The MacCorquodale-Meehl article stimulated many efforts during the 1950s (and later) to reconcile the hoped-for generality of intervening variables, or "theoretical constructs," etc., with the specificity suggested by a tight construction of the intervening variable paradigm. This type of concern is broadly evident throughout the approximately five thousand pages of *Psychology: A Study of a Science* (Koch 1959b, 1962b, 1963). The decisive words were, however, generated by the author of the "intervening paradigm for theory construction," E. C. Tolman, who concluded that intervening variables, as he had used them, were "merely an aid to thinking ('my thinking,' if you will)"—"a tentative logic (or psychologic) of my own, for predicting what the dependent behavior should be and how it should be affected by variations of such and such sets of independent variables" (Tolman 1959, 148; also cf. 147 and earlier in the same chapter).

Tolman's reconception of the intervening variable as a personal heuristic device is buttressed by Neal Miller's assessment, in the same volume, of the "experimental design required but seldom used to justify intervening variables" (Miller 1959, 276–80). On the modest assumption that there must minimally be *two* independent experimental "operations" and *two* "measures," he concluded that "there are relatively few experiments which use the design required," and this even at *qualitative* levels (278).

See *Psychology: A Study of Science* (Koch 1959b, vol. 2), for analyses which converge with those of Tolman and Miller in the contributions of E. R. Guthrie and others. See also my

eluded the intervening variable theorists was that their independent and dependent variables (which they held to be "direct observables") were themselves complex epistemic constructions in their system languages, and of such a character that each would require multiply disjunctive operational definitions of infinite length. Contemplate for a moment the list of Tolman's independent variables of 1936 (1936b): "Environmental stimuli (S), physiological drive (P), heredity (H), previous training (T), and maturity (A)." *These* are "direct observables"! A list of Hull's systematic independent variables (cf. 1943, 383) would be equally instructive.

From these considerations alone, it should be clear that the intervening variable theories of the Age of Theory were as free-floating as the wildest speculations of a pan-psychic philosopher, and that the quest for the unambiguous linkage of psychological concepts to an "intersubjective" observation base was no more successful when decorated with the heraldry of Bridgman and Carnap than it had been in the earlier history of psychology when conducted sans such authority. And even the relatively atheoretical applications of the operational principle can be shown to have had a most obfuscatory and trivializing impact on the vast volume of research carried out under its aegis, and a simplifying impact on the scientific (and general) sensibility of investigators. I think these generalizations hold true right down to the present day.

---

epilogue to Study I in volume 3 of the same series (Koch 1959a) for discussion of the bearing of that study on the intervening variable paradigm and related issues.

Finally, it is not within the province of this chapter to discuss the almost endless speculation of "meaning" analyses within the philosophy of science, linguistic and/or analytic philosophy, and related areas in linguistics, semiotics, etc. that has been taking place at accelerating pace during the second half of the century. Suffice it to say that by the early fifties the neopositivists themselves had "liberalized" their meaning criteria far past any approach that could have seemed consonant with *psychologists'* interpretations of Bridgman's "operationism" (*sic*). In the mid-fifties, Carnap, Feigl, Hempel, and others were giving far more attention to the "nomological network" (or postulate set) in determining the reference of theoretical terms than to direct linkages with an "observation language." In volume 1 of the *Minnesota Studies in the Philosophy of Science,* Feigl (1956) strikes the keynote by emphasizing that "the more liberal meaning criterion permits the abandonment of phenomenalism and radical operationalism" and that knowledge, "both on the level of common sense and that of science, is now being regarded as a network of concepts and propositions tied in only a few places to the data of immediate experience, and for the rest a matter of 'free construction'" (16). Carnap, in the same volume, develops a similar position in characteristically formal and sustained manner within his chapter on "The Methodological Character of Theoretical Terms" (1956, 36–78). His analysis and that of Feigl and other contributors to the *Minnesota Studies* entail the acceptance of certain classes of metaphysical statements as meaningful.

3. Meanings, Operations, and an Unbowdlerized Bridgman

I now want to suggest that a serious reading of Bridgman will show that what *he* calls "operational analysis" is consonant, almost point by point, with the "perceptual" account of definition I have tried to convey in chapter 5.[8] He was shocked by the practices attached to the label "operational definition" in psychology—and, I suspect, in several other disciplines.

Perhaps I can render this plausible by an analysis of one of the critical differences between Bridgman's and most psychologists' interpretations of "operational" practice. The difference I have in mind may not be conspicuous in the Bridgman of 1927, but clearly emerges as early as 1934 in his article "A Physicist's Second Reaction to *Mengenlehre*." There he suggests that operations are necessary conditions for meanings, not sufficient ones, and that meanings are "to be *sought* in operations" (103, italics added). And, in later writings, he not only immensely broadens his conception of operations but repeatedly says things like "the operational aspect is not by any means the only aspect of meaning" (1952, 257).

The characteristic assumption of the psychologist is that all falls into simplicity and order when one equates or *identifies* the operations and the meaning. Thus matters get snug and cozy if:

"Experience" *becomes* "the discriminatory response" (Stevens).

"Learning" *becomes* "a measurable change of performance with practice."

"Response" *becomes* its objective indices (e.g., latency, probability, amplitude, resistance to extinction, etc., as in Hull).

"Retention" *becomes* "the number of nonsense syllables recalled (or recognized, etc.) after X number of practice repetitions of a list."

"Reasoning" *becomes* a particular machine-programmable algorithm.

"Intimacy" *becomes* "the duration in a situational sample in which A gazes directly at B (or stands within a certain distance of B)."

8. "Consonance," of course, is not identity. I am using this term to suggest a relation somewhere between "family resemblance" and consistency. To be consistent with my account would presuppose that both Bridgman's and mine were internally consistent. We already know that Bridgman's was certainly *not*. (As for my own, it is not meet for me to judge!) But I hope that even the limited compass of this chapter can make it evident that the dominant contours of Bridgman's viewpoint are *far* more consonant with such an account of definition as I have developed than with the central tendency of psychologists' reading of Bridgman. Much fuller evidence for this contention than I can give in the text may be found in Bridgman's differentiated (and insightful) presentation of his mature position on "words, meanings and verbal analysis" in chapter 2 of *The Way Things Are* (1959, 13–36).

"Morale" *becomes* "the incidence of AWOL's (or letters home, etc.) in a military unit or a summer camp."

"Rat emotionality" *becomes* "defecation in an open field" (so-called).

And, presumably, generality is purchased by the "positing" (or "discovery") of additional operations that systematically co-vary with the *initial* operation (or group of such) which "*is*" the concept — or so it would be claimed by those who do not take the extreme position of one operation–one concept. On the assumption, then, of "co-varying" or "equivalent" operations, the *meaning* of a concept *is* the *totality* of the corresponding operations.

But if we accept Bridgman's suggestion that "operations" are cues which help us *seek*, locate, perceive the meaning of a concept, we have a very different situation: an "operational definition" may then be held to instantiate, exemplify, or guide the addressee toward the meaning of a concept, and not comprise or constitute that meaning; in other words, an "operational definition" becomes something much like what I have called a "perceptual display." Moreover, this would remain true for concepts having multiply disjunctive operations or single operations. And indeed, if we consider what is involved in epistemically rich concepts of great generality, we would soon see that the meanings (or "meaning profiles") discriminated by an appropriately sensitive language-user can and do "generate" very large classes of "symptomatic" instantiations — indeed, a practical infinity of them, if analysis be pushed sufficiently finely. Moreover, some of these symptoms or symptom-subsets can mark out relatively clear paths toward the meaning contour or profile, some but indistinct paths, whereas still others can utterly mislead.

Bridgman came to see all these complexities (and more) as he dwelled on the operational principle — and, more generally, on language and meaning — over time. For *him*, "operational analysis" became ultimately a kind of no-nonsense, hermeneutic analysis, but he persisted in the use of his original nomenclature, as people tend to do when experiencing the dissolution of a long-held position by virtue of increasingly refined and differentiated pursuit of its initial intent. If, in his mature use, the adjective "operational" did retain a coherent core of meaning, it was something like a marker for his insistence that it is more important to pay attention to what a user (or definer) *does* with a concept than to what the user *says* will be done (i.e., via the general statement of application conditions). In this — as in other aspects of his thinking — we can discern Bridgman's close affinity with pragmatism. We can also align this attitude with an old and more general philosophic precedent: the preference of philosophers here and there for *definitions in use*.

In psychology, however, to this very day there has been little erosion of the tendency to *equate* operations and meaning. The principle is brought into the field as a reassurance fetish — and it remains just that. Now the equation of symptom and meaning has far more drastic consequences for a field like psychology than it does for physics. Thus, even in the early period, when Bridgman was suggesting (or could be read as suggesting) an equation between symptom and meaning, it was possible for him to analyze certain conceptual problems in physics and not produce total obfuscation (far from it: some of the specific 1927 analyses are luminous). But if it be seen that the *task* of psychology can only be that of refining and extending the psychological knowledge already embedded in natural language, then psychology must commence with (and in all probability stay with) concepts of a far more "open horizon" character — thus concepts discriminating far more complexly contoured and ramified meaning fields than in physics. The fact that a game is played such that these meaning fields are not even explored (or, indeed, looked up in a good dictionary), but are *equated* with presumably objectively definable and technically manageable "operations" bearing an arbitrary, selective, or vagrant relation to the concept in question, prevents the serious business of psychology from getting started.

4. Bridgman's Actual Bequest

Bridgman's significant contributions are to be found in certain general attitudes that remained relatively stable in his writings, despite an extraordinary number of changes in their verbal housing, and, indeed, in the substance of his ideas. The attitudes are perhaps rendered all the *more* compelling and vivid by virtue of their habitation in a body of writing characterized by flagrant inconsonances, ardent overstatements, and marked changes of position over time. It was Bridgman's great good luck *not* to be freighted with philosophical erudition, or constrained by the philosopher's drive toward "system."[9] In these ways he was like Witt-

9. It is important to stress that to categorize Bridgman's "critical" effort as formal "philosophy of science" is to obscure — and perhaps derogate — the character of his contribution. Even worse is the tendency of most commentators to "place" him relative to standard philosophical tradition-labels. Bridgman was an *original* — barely conversant with formal philosophy, and little impressed by it within the range of that conversance.

If his emphasis on *activity* and on experience as an active process be seen as suggestive of the pragmatic tradition, there is little evidence that he had studied the writing of pragmatists

genstein—a free spirit unencumbered by the usual craft barriers against authenticity. I should like to identify a few of his emphases that I think permanently viable.

1. *A supremely sensitive awareness of the relations between knowledge and its generative conditions.* His contribution in this regard is not to be found in his sometimes inept generalizations concerning the "operational method" or in his sometimes convoluted struggles with the meaning of "operation," but in his differentiated and clear illustrations of such dependencies via the analysis of many particular concepts and issues of physics and of other fields, including psychology. Others in the history of thought have been apprised of the dependence of knowledge on its generative methods, but have not given us the kind of authentic, expert, and illuminating case studies that Bridgman has provided.

2. *A persistent and instructive effort to curb the overgeneralizing tendencies of the human mind.* Some may think he went too far in this effort—but from a certain point of view it is impossible to go too far. He had a keen appreciation of the autistic component in "man thinking," whether in daily life, science, or even the formal disciplines. He saw with clarity the dangers implicit in the fact that "man has never been a particularly modest or self deprecatory animal" (1936, 135), and is afflicted with "incorrigible optimism" (136) to boot. His "recognition that the only possible attitude toward the future is one of unreserved acceptance, no matter how distasteful

---

in any detailed way. He was a self-dubbed "empiricist" (1927, vi), but obviously his own kind of empiricist—if only for his emphasis on the active "apprehension of meaning" by relevantly competent individuals rather than on some canonical class of sensory or phenomenal inputs—as basis of and warrant for "knowledge." (It is a very special kind of empiricist who will claim that "[t]here is no unique operation of verification, and the concept is not sharp—in fact, it is an unusually fuzzy concept" [1959, 56]!) He has often been aligned with the positivist tradition (whether early or "neo"), but no diagnosis could be more wrong-headed! Scientific assertions were reducible neither to sensations, phenomena, protocol statements, nor an "observable thing" language. In fact, there is no significant sense in which they are "reducible"; their origin and meanings could be *explicated* via the associated "directed activities" or practices, and it was a prudent condition of intellectual hygiene that such activities be identified as clearly as possible. Nor was he a logical or ontological reductionist: effective and legitimate explanation could come from "above" just as well as from "below."

In the preface to *The Logic of Modern Physics* (1927, vi), he identifies "Clifford, Stallo, Mach, and Poincaré" as previous writers on "the broad fundamentals" of physics, but he "believe[s] a new essay of this critical character needs no apology." Furthermore: "None of the previous essays have consciously or immediately affected the details of this; in fact I have not read any of them within several years." In subsequent "critical" writings, Bridgman rarely aligns his position with other traditions or persons; indeed, they are virtually devoid of references.

or contrary to expectations" (30) could provide potent cognitive therapy—*if* such an attitude could only *prove* acceptable.

3. *An ardent effort to restore science to its human agency—to subvert the recently prevailing tendency in philosophy and elsewhere to analyze and represent science as if it were a disembodied rule structure.* His constant emphasis on such matters as the importance of "first-person report" (indeed, *dated* first-person report) and the fact that "we can't get away from ourselves" (cf. 1959, 1–11 and elsewhere in this fascinating book)—however abhorrent such considerations may have been to those whose religion is the "publicity" of knowledge—were among his most valuable offerings to the human race. He luminously anticipated the tendency to acknowledge the sensibility-dependent character of all knowledge, in or out of science. It is ironic that his views were interpreted by so many during his time as consonant with, or even on some issues identical to, those of logical positivism. His project is better understood as a war of attrition against the neopositivistic enterprise. On this score, no further evidence is required than his passionate address—"Science: Public or Private?"—to the Fifth International Congress for the Unity of Science in 1939. Bear in mind that he was speaking to persons who were already using him as authority for their own emphasis on a "physical thing language" as the reduction basis for all of science. Imagine the consternation that must have been created among an assembly of logical positivists from all corners of the earth by the following magnificent paragraph:

> The process that I want to call scientific is a process that involves the continual apprehension of meaning, the constant appraisal of significance, accompanied by a running act of checking to be sure that I am doing what I want to do, and of judging correctness or incorrectness. This checking and judging and accepting, that together constitute understanding, are done by me and can be done for me by no one else. They are as private as my toothache, and without them science is dead. (1940b, 50)

Bridgman's sense of the "privacy" of the processes of science comprehended an element which, if it was perceived at all during his time, was probably perceived as so shocking that it was repressed: an illustration of this is his oft-reiterated emphasis upon the privacy of *proof.* The following quotation from a 1940 article gives the gist of his position:

> The sciences have been contaminated by this over-emphasis on the social factor no less than have the other disciplines: it is very much the fashion at present to say that science is essentially "public." In fact, the name of science is often applied, by definition, only to that which is publicly demonstrated and accepted. But what does one find when he examines what he actually does? In making this examination, it will be sufficient to typify science by logical reasoning, since logical reasoning is part of all scientific activity. The value of logical reasoning lies in the assurance of correctness of the conclusion that one has when he has properly gone through the logical processes. Now everyone knows that the conviction of the correctness of a proof or an argument can be obtained only by oneself, after he has made and understood the proper analysis. No one else can make me see or understand, no matter what pressure he may exert on me. I may *say* that I understand when I do not, in order to silence too vociferous an instructor, but "he who consents against his will is of the same opinion still." The feeling of understanding is as private as the feeling of pain. The act of understanding is at the heart of all scientific activity; without it any ostensibly scientific activity is as sterile as that of a high school student substituting numbers into a formula. For this reason, science, when I push the analysis back as far as I can, must be private. (1940a, 71–72)

It is fair to say that even if such a position would not yet command universal assent, its shock value must now be considered negligible relative to the climate of philosophic thought concerning foundation problems of logic, mathematics, and science.

4. *A recognition of the extra-articulate aspect of language-use* (cf. 1959, 12–36), *the dependence of a theory on a "text"—explicit or implicit—* (cf. 1936, 60–71) *and the dependence of the use of the text, ultimately, on unspecifiable skills learned via ostension or imitation* (e.g. 1959, 41). His sensitivity to such matters shows a sophistication sadly lacking in the positivistic philosophy of science of his day—and leads toward a much more informative picture of scientific and non-scientific communication than was then regnant. In these (and other) connections, he converges in a remarkable way with central emphases of Michael Polanyi (cf., especially, Polanyi 1958).

5. *An emphasis on the primacy of the individual (both in and out of science) vis-à-vis the "social."* Bridgman's principled insistence upon the centrality of the individual in the metabolism of science (which anticipated by decades

Polanyi's emphasis on the "personal coefficient" of knowledge) was paralleled by an almost obsessive critique of the tendency of all societies, including modern democracies, to eradicate the "distinctions between mine and thine" (1945, 36). He sees this as a kind of societal conspiracy:

> The entire human race, ever since the appearance of articulate speech, has been so conditioning itself to suppress the difference between me and thee that most members of the race have lost any capacity they may ever have had to recognize even the existence of the issue. Simple observation shows that I act in two modes. In my public mode I have an image of myself in the community of my neighbors, all similar to myself and all of us equivalent parts of a single all-embracing whole. In the private mode, I feel my inviolable isolation from my fellows and may say, "My thoughts are my own, and I will be damned if I let you know what I am thinking about."
>
> All government, whether the crassest totalitarianism or the uncritical and naïve form of democracy toward which we are at present tending in this country, endeavors to suppress the private mode as illegitimate, as do also most institutionalized religions and nearly all systems of philosophy or ethics. Yet the private mode is an integral part of each one of us, ready to flare into action under the stimulus of any new exploitation of the individual. I believe that no satisfactory solution will be found for our present social and political difficulties until we find how to handle together as of equal importance the social and the private modes of each of us. Each of us, in moments of clarity or stress, reverts to the private mode in spite of millennia of exhortation and instruction. In these moments of clarity we know that the private mode is as justifiable as the social mode and even more inescapable. It seems to me that only when I deal with both modes do I become capable of achieving complete rationality. (1945, 39–40)

Thus, individuals, qua members of interest groups or governments, feel free to apply to others pressures ranging from well-intended exhortation to naked force, in that they fail to distinguish between "my thoughts and your thoughts," "my feelings and your feelings." They are blind to the "spectacular" operational differences between an inwardly experienced state of affairs and the *uncritical* (and unwitting) attribution, by projection, of the "same" state of affairs to another. Bridgman's intensive interest in the analysis of "introspectional terms" can be seen to spring from the depth of his concern for bringing about a proper appreciation of the individual — indeed, for militating toward his or her "emergence." His social ethics (e.g., 1938a, 1938b, 1940a, 1959) is directed toward assuring that the "inner freedom in virtue of which every individual leads his own life eternally free from his fellows within the walls of his own consciousness" — that this "elemental fact" which society tends to obscure — be rendered explicit and palpable (1940a, 62).

Bridgman's concern for a rational social ethics which could adequately resolve the "duality" of the "public" and "private" modes was so persistently and passionately pursued as to suggest this to be an animating motive of his interest in "operational analysis," rather than a mere corollary. This theme is adumbrated in *The Logic of Modern Physics* (1927, 32), and addressed with increasing specificity in many subsequent writings. His ultimate position may be found in the penultimate chapter of *The Way Things Are* (1959, 249–314), in which the central issue is characterized as "the most important new moral problem in a modern democracy": "the ethics which should control me in my capacity as a member of a majority, actual or potential, in my exercise of compulsion on my neighbor."

His answer — in terms of a "minimum social code" based on a principle of "fair exchange" — will be seen by many as itself problematic in certain of its details, and his *applications* of this "answer" to particular social issues as varying from the noble, to the eccentric, to the downright harrowing. But it is hard not to conclude that in tendency and tone these analyses add up to one of the most ardent, if cantankerous, critiques of societal interventionism mounted by any modern writer. It is clear that as early as the 1930s and 1940s this formidably sensitive individualist was combating conformity-pressures within civil and scholarly communities, simple-mindedly egalitarian construals of democracy, and incursions upon privacy of the sorts that have steadily increased to their present epidemic proportions![10]

10. Votaries of the current trend toward "diffusing the content of the individual into social space" (a phrase I once used to convey the essence of encounter-group ideology; cf. Koch 1973a [chapter 10]) will see Bridgman's conception of the "individual" vis-à-vis society as unspeakably naïve — an unreflective registration of a historically dated mode of commonsense discourse. For this very reason, I think it refreshing and timely to recirculate Bridgman's antediluvian emphasis upon the centrality of the individual. "Social constructionists" and "post-structuralist" discourse theorists who prefer to dissolve the individual into a set of "positions" in "discourses" about that unhygienic non-entity are — by virtue of their own principles — invulnerable to rational argument. An occasional bit of counter-rhetoric can therefore harm no one. Amusingly, Bridgman was in partial agreement with the "social construction-

6. *An ardent championship of "integrity."* This theme, which emerges often in his writing—and to which he devotes the coda of *The Way Things Are* (1959, 317–25)—is the key to what "operational analysis" was about. It was also the substance. He seems at the end to be saying that his entire superstructure of recommendations and analyses was, in effect, a kind of sprawling, asystematic, sometimes inconsistent but occasionally beautifully on target, and always passionate, panegyric to integrity. But he meant "integrity" in no simple sense.

For Bridgman "integrity" was not a homely matter of a sort comparable, say, to C. P. Snow's celebration of the scientist's disposition to tell the truth (cf. 1961). He meant something far more complex than encompassed in the entirety of the last chapter of *The Way Things Are* (1959, 315–25)—which I can here but sample via two brief quotations:

> For me, integrity in the individual implies intellectual honesty, but it is more than this. It is a frame of mind. Integrity demands that I *want* to know what the facts are and that I *want* to analyze and to understand my mental tools and know what happens when I apply these tools to the facts. . . . [T]here is one thing which I may not do and retain my integrity—if I have a new vision of something which I did not appreciate before, I may not try to put the vision back and pretend that I did not have it and refuse to admit that there may be consequences. . . . And it is continually to be kept in mind that new visions do occur, both to the individual and to society. Intellectually the human race is still quite young, and . . . it has many new intellectual experiences ahead of it. (319)

Bridgman then proceeds to "consider in detail some of the mental tools . . . which I have received from society which make it difficult for me to practice intellectual integrity." Yet the final paragraph of the book makes it clear that such societal impediments to integrity are not the ultimate ones:

> Intellectual integrity is always an affair of the individual. For the individual, that is, for me, there are other situations in which the practice of intellectual integrity is incomparably more difficult than in the situations presented by society. For I know that my intellectual tools are defective, but I have to con-

---

ists," though the two viewpoints are temporally and valuationally out of register. *He* felt that the individual had not yet arrived, but lamented that circumstance. *They* feel that the "individual" has had its day, and see its "deconstruction" as good news.

tinue to use them. What am I to do in a situation like this? This book is part of my answer. (325)

There is, of course, in all of Bridgman's allusions to "integrity" an *aesthetic* undercurrent: an implicit encomium to sound craftsmanship — craftsmanship that pursues its objective over and above the call of duty, but by the sparest possible means. And — when added to his constant celebration of openness to future experience, preparedness for surprise — it invites one to put together the two "halves" of Bridgman: Bridgman the physicist, and Bridgman, the generalist-commentator on science and society.

His early choice of high-pressure physics for his specialty can be seen as no mere accident, but reflective of special and permanent aspects of his sensibility. A conviction that the future may hold surprises — and a combination of high curiosity with a zest for adventure — can certainly fuel an interest in what happens to "laws" of nature under *extreme* conditions such as very high pressures. Bridgman approached this challenging but largely open field very much in the tradition of the scientific "loner" who assumes full individual responsibility for everything from the design and construction of instrumentation, to the manipulation and control of independent variable "values," to the final dependent variable measurements. He was a superb apparatus designer with equally superb mechanical skills, and was able to build a series of instruments (on spartan resources) capable of generating pressures several orders of magnitude greater than previously achieved (in the late stages of his program, 100,000 atmospheres in a mechanism driven by a hand pump!). Via such means, he investigated the effects of high pressures on hundreds of specimens — ranging from pure elements to compound substances to liquids — uncovering in this endless stream of experiments many polymorphies and unexpected discontinuities in the properties of the test materials. Only when well into his career did he acquire "a couple of assistants" and, throughout, his mode was to leave the few graduate students he accepted into his laboratory to their own devices, preferring to advise — rather than work *through* — them.[11]

11. Bridgman describes his mode of work interestingly in a short paper based on "remarks" he made at a 1947 dinner celebrating his receipt of the Nobel Prize (1950, 293–302). Characteristically, his theme was "Science and Freedom." It will come as no surprise that he was an extreme libertarian in his conception of the relation of science and government, and lamented many of the consequences of "the increasing trend . . . to large-scale cooperative enterprises among physicists." He was especially concerned that the younger physicists who had been drawn into large team enterprises during World War II ("with the consequent and necessary submergence of the individual") would form the nucleus of a new generation of

It is clear, then, that the "integrity" that he preached was the integrity that he practiced, and that there is an organic relationship between his conception of the nature, constraints, and responsibilities of the scientific enterprise and the particularities of his own experience qua scientist. Bridgman's "critical" writings may thus be ranked with the confessional literature of gifted scientists: that rivulet of protocols which bear authentic witness to how science is done (rather than how the philosopher or externally situated student of science imagines it ought to be done). The Bridgmans, Polanyis, Heisenbergs, Bohrs, and the small cohort of other contributors to this confessional literature stand as our only protectors from the professional "methodologists."

No one in psychology—and few, so far as I know, outside of it—has perceived the overarching personal meaning of Bridgman's mission. The font is, of course, his "conviction" (as expressed in 1959, 1) "that there is some fundamental ineptness in the way that all of us handle our minds." That conviction was nourished, and perhaps initiated, by his experience as a physicist—a point that is difficult for my colleagues in psychology to perceive because of their "physicophiliac" obsessions: physics and heaven being "operationally" synonymous. From such a viewpoint, Bridgman's persistent concern with how "to render unnecessary the services of the future Einsteins" (which is registered as early as 1927, on page 24 of *The Logic of Modern Physics,* and oft reiterated in other writings) may seem wholly inexplicable.[12]

---

physicists "who have never exercised any particular degree of individual initiative" and "who have had no opportunity to experience its satisfactions or its possibilities." On the more general matter of his deep concern for protecting the freedom of the scientist from governmental influence, his paper on "Scientific Freedom and National Planning" (1950, 320–31) should prove enlightening.

12. There was a part of Bridgman that was appalled at the circumstance that classical physics required such radical revision merely by virtue of the Newtonian concepts of space and time not being adequately tied to their modes of measurement. Einstein's reanalysis of both concepts in terms of the conditions of their measurement formed the *central* animating model for Bridgman's "operational" program (cf. 1927, 1–9). Considerably before 1927, he had become obsessed by the need to ensure that the "quantities" in physical equations be linked to the conditions of their experimental determination. As Bridgman points out in a manuscript of September 1922 (quoted by A. I. Miller in the introduction to the second edition of *A Sophisticate's Primer of Relativity,* 1983): "The general goal of criticism should be to make impossible a repetition of the thing Einstein had done; never again should a discovery of new experimental facts lead to a revision of physical concepts simply because the old concepts had been too naïve. . . . A program of consideration as broad as this demands a critical consideration not only of the concepts of space and time, but of all other physical concepts in our armory." It was to the implementation of this program that *The Logic of*

I am perhaps the only non-applied psychologist alive willing to confess a massive ignorance of physics, but am at least apprised that Bridgman's life was coextensive with the most stressful and dynamic interval in the history of modern physics. As an exceedingly sharp scientist *and* an exceedingly sensitive human being, Bridgman must have been amused and bemused by the evidence in his own rigorous field of humankind's extraordinary reluctance to vacate conceptual boxes which had long given shelter, and by the fecundity of the arguments that certain inhabitants can generate to the effect that the box is weather-tight long after the lid has been blown off.

From this stressful core of professional experience it must have been easy for Bridgman to infer that the human mind could well be in trouble in areas other than physics, perhaps even in the world beyond the cloisters. His long-term extra-laboratory project thus became that of seeking a wise policy for the management of mind. Earlier in this article I alluded to Bridgman as having embraced a form of the Kantian enterprise. But he was situated in an era which invited a realignment of the Kantian priorities: the concern with what the mind contributes to the structure of knowledge was perhaps exceeded by a concern with what the mind does to foul it up. I rather fear I shall have to acknowledge that it was Bridgman who founded the science of "cognitive pathologistics."

Modern Physics was directed. Often thereafter Bridgman was to make reference to the goal of rendering future Einsteins unnecessary. Yet, another part of Bridgman—especially as it matured—saw such a goal as absurd, and indeed makes explicit mockery of it in *The Way Things Are*.

As for Bridgman's effort to unleash the "operational method" upon Einstein himself and to arrive at a "minimum point of view" which would read unnecessary ontological components out of both special and general relativity—that issue is beyond the compass of this paper. Bridgman's pursuit of such a project commenced in the early 1920s and culminated in his *A Sophisticate's Primer of Relativity* (1962). This strand of his thinking shows little concordance with his general development of the operational viewpoint (from, say, the mid-1930s onward). Though the wielding of the operational principle is nowhere so Occam's-razor-like as in his critique of relativity, the distance between this context of application of operational method and the psychologists' view of "operationism" is still astronomical.

CODA

15

The Limits of Psychological Knowledge: Lessons of a Century qua "Science"

Foreword

This chapter is drawn from my essay "The Nature and Limits of Psychological Knowledge," published in *A Century of Psychology as Science*, edited by S. Koch and D. Leary (Koch and Leary 1992). That in turn was based on my presidential address to the Divisions of General Psychology and of Philosophical Psychology at the 1979 annual meeting of the American Psychological Association. It picks up much of the rationale of the critique of psychology that has been developed throughout this book, and seeks to extend it to "deeper" levels. The paper is certainly the most "all-stops-out" message I have ever communicated to my psychological confrères, and I delivered it not without trepidation. I was therefore surprised when one of the editors of the *American Psychologist* invited me to submit it for publication; they published it in 1981 (36:257–69). I was even more surprised by the response to the article; apart from my paper on encounter groups (chapter 10), I have never had more requests for reprints. And nothing I have ever done seems to have elicited comparable *international* interest.

«

Throughout the nineteenth century (and indeed, before) an independent scientific psychology was vigorously invited. Toward the end of that century (in 1879, according to prevailing legend), an independent, scientific psychology was bestowed upon the world by the founding of a laboratory and further consolidated some two years later by the inauguration of the first journal for the "new" psychology which, somewhat ironically, was entitled *Philosophische Studien*. And, as we are certainly aware, over the next one hundred years an "independent, scientific psychology" has been enthusiastically enacted by a burgeoning workforce that by now constitutes one of the largest groupings within contemporary scholarship. But the frenetic activity of the past hundred years has left the issue in doubt!

If we are "independent"—which, in historical context, is intended to mean aseptically free of philosophy—then why have psychologists been impelled to borrow chapter and verse from one or another presumably authoritative philosophy of science (or indeed, nonscientific philosophy) for every definition of a "proper" subject matter, every procedural or metatheoretical proposal, every substantive conceptual net put forward *throughout* our century of happy autonomy? If psychology is *a* science, then why have our posits in each of the foregoing categories been so multifarious on each day of that century? And what kind of "science"—independent or otherwise—can we have achieved when it be considered that though our century-long cumulation of a vast technical literature may contain several thousand (perhaps million) law-like statements, not a single such statement can yet be counted a *law,* whether on criteria definitive of lawfulness in the natural sciences that we have been emulating *or* in the simple sense of commanding universal assent?

I am not a historian. But I have lived through more than half a century of psychological history from the vantage of a participant-observer whose arrogant construal of his calling has been to explore the prospects and conditions for a significant psychology. At some point near midcareer, I began to feel that my calling had rendered me a human and scholarly cipher in all respects save one: I had developed an uncanny connoisseurship concerning the fine structure and dynamics of pseudo-inquiry, the seamy vicissitudes of the phony scholarship that has characterized so much of the "activity" in my own field, and indeed others, in this century. I became, in fact, the modest founder of a discipline given to the study of misfirings of the scholarly and creative impulse: the field soon to be widely known as the science of "cognitive pathology," the metatheory of which is "epistemo-pathologistics."

I have tended to be somewhat secretive about this new enterprise. But a few years ago, in the course of an intellectual autobiography I had been asked to present to the APA Divisions of Philosophical Psychology and of the History of Psychology (Koch 1977b [chapter 1]), I permitted a brief glimpse of the noble architecture of this discipline. The glimpse apparently piqued curiosity, for after the talk representatives of the same divisions asked whether I would consider giving an "advanced course" in the new discipline on another occasion. That occasion has arrived. What could be a more appropriate one than the centennial of scientific psychology?

Space limits will permit only a précis of the advanced course. But I hope to be able to develop the powerful theoretical structure of this new discipline sufficiently to exhibit certain constraints on the character of the knowledge claims made by the psychology of the past century, as well as some constraints on the character of psychological knowledge in principle. After that, I close with a brief confrontation of the theme of the centennial by asking whether, after the century-long march of psychology under the banner of "independent, experimental science," the field actually is (1) *independent* and (2) a *science*.

The Pathology of Knowledge

Decades of inquiry into the inquiry of others — and into germane processes inside my own head — have induced in me a sense of awe at the plenitude of our gift for the mismanagement of our own minds. It is perhaps the ultimate genius of the race!

If you are a psychologist or social scientist, test any systematic formulation of your choice (whether learning-theoretic, systems-theoretic, information-theoretic, cognitive-genetic, cybernetic, or, indeed, phenomenologico-hermeneutic; or, just maybe, behavior-therapeutic) against the following "epistemopathic" peregrinations of the inquiring impulse. (Those who assign passing grades I shall have to presume either the owners of the formulation under test or first-year graduate students!)

1. Jargon and "word magic."
2. Single-principle imperialism.
3. Substitution of *program* for performance.
4. Tendency to make so restrictive a definition of the field of study as to render the study beside the point or, indeed, finished before begun.
5. Facilitation of progress by making a set of arbitrary and strong simplifying assumptions (e.g., imaginary "boundary conditions," counterfactual assumptions re mathematical properties of the data), proposing an "as if" model observing that set of restrictions, and then gratefully falling prey to total amnesia for those restrictions.
6. Tendency to select — usually on extraneous bases like amenability to "control" or to contemplated modes of mathematical treatment — a "simple case" and then to assume that it will be merely a matter of time and energy until the "complex case" can be handled by application of easy composition rules.

7. Tendency to accept on authority or invent a sacred, inviolable "self-corrective" epistemology that renders all inquiry in the field a matter of application of rules which preguarantee success.

8. Corollary to the preceding, a view of all aspects of the cognitive enterprise as so thoroughly rule-regulated as to make the role of the cognizer superfluous. The rule is father to the thought—and mother, too!

9. Tendency to persist so rigidly, blindly, patiently, in the application of the rules—despite fulsome indications of their disutility—that the behavior would have to be characterized as schizophrenic in any other context.

10. Tendency to accept any "finding" conformable to some treasured methodology in preference to "traditional" wisdom *or* individual experience, no matter how pellucidly and frequently confirmed the nonscientistic knowledge may be.

11. Epistemopathy No. 10, at a certain critical-mass value, results in the *total abrogation* of the criterion that knowledge should *make sense* and in an ultimate distrust of one's own experience. If a finding does make sense, one distrusts *it*.

12. An exceedingly strong reluctance to reinspect one's deeper epistemological and/or substantive commitments. This, in effect, is the theory of truth by individual consistency over time.

13. Ergo—a remarkable and telling disproportion between the attention given to the foundation commitments of one's work and that given to superficial or pedantic details of implemental character. One dwells happily within the "superstructure," however shoddy or wormeaten the "substructure."

14. Tendency to buy into stable or fashionable profession-centered myths with a minimum of prior critical examination, to accept congealed group suppressions concerning bypassed problems or data; or alternative theoretical possibilities; or intrinsic (and sometimes patent) limits on the scope, analytic or predictive specificity, and so on, attainable in the field in question. Ergo, a disposition to become a "central tendency" creature, to hold in check (or happily suffer a reduction of) one's imaginative and critical resources.

The preceding sampling is necessarily a limited exercise in elementary cognitive pathology. My object here is to try to make plausible a large generalization that has come to inundate my mind. It is that there are times and circumstances in which able individuals, committed to inquiry, tend almost obsessively to frustrate the objectives of inquiry. It is as if uncertainty, mootness, ambiguity, cognitive finitude were the most unbearable of the existential anguishes. Under these conditions, able and sincere inquirers become as autistic as little children; they seem more impelled toward the pursuit and maintenance of security fantasies than the winning of whatever significant knowledge may be within reach!

A little reflection will show that such passionately courted cognitive disutilities as these are not exclusive marks of psychological inquiry, but are evident in all contexts of inquiry, both in and out of scholarship. I believe these perversities of cognitive function to be endemic to the human condition, but they have never been manifested more conspicuously (or disastrously) than in our dear century. This darkling hypothesis is not wholly idiosyncratic: It was shared by Bridgman, whose 1959 book, *The Way Things Are,* was animated by a "conviction that there is some fundamental ineptness in the way that all of us handle our minds" (1).

My own epistemopathic observations have not been confined to psychology. Part of my professional commitment has been to philosophy, and I have had a lifelong interest in the arts and humanities. Virtually all fields of cultural life — and too many fields of practical life — are, I think, close to an impasse: an impasse of objective, method, substance, value, and education! Things cannot get much better until we "put our fingers" on the particularities of these blockages. General diagnosis, free-floating existential screams, are not enough.

Localizing the particularities of such blockages against authentic cognition is, of course, an awesome undertaking. Not only are the psychological, historical, and sociological grounds for the ever-accelerating dispersion of epistemopathy vastly ramified and intricately intertwined, but the cognitive pathologist cannot presume to be unafflicted by the disease that he or she seeks to cure. My own feeble efforts have thus far been concentrated on the discrimination of a syndrome that I call "ameaningful thinking" (the prefix has the same force as the *a-* in words like *amoral*) and its detailed contrast to the increasingly rare process of "meaningful thinking" (see Koch 1965 [chapter 7]). I have become so obsessed in recent years with the importance of precise and differentiated analysis of the meaning and referential field of the "ameaning" syndrome that it is meet, before going further, to air the suspicion that my own head may be dangerously afflicted with Epistemopathy No. 2 of my sample list, namely, "single-principle imperialism."

In prior writings, I have sought to delineate the contours of ameaning — and more generally to perform epistemopathic surgery — in a variety of connections. I have, for instance, critically considered *behaviorism* from many angles (e.g., Koch 1961a, 1964, 1971, 1973b, 1976b). Most of these analyses have been trained upon particular formulations and argued in detail. An early artifact of my disenchantment with behaviorism—a study of Hull's systematic work (Koch 1954; cf. chapter 11)—is probably the most mercilessly sustained analysis of a psychological theory on record.

This body of work on the behaviorisms resists summary, but to convey the flavor of the cognitive-pathological enterprise, I can mention the following surgical efforts. I have tried to show the dependence of behaviorist epistemology on philosophies of science that had begun to crumble even before psychologists borrowed their authority and that are now seen as shallow and defective by all save the borrowers. I have given detailed attention to behaviorism's garbled assumptions concerning the workings of language and the nature of scientific communication; to the undifferentiated, rubbery character, impoverished range, and overblown intension of its major analytical terms ("stimulus," "response," "drive," "reinforcement," and the like); to the inconstant, Pickwickian, and (literally) incoherent discursive practices of its theorists and defenders—practices that render its typical argument forms a species of half-studied and half-unwitting double entendre.

I have in many writings (Koch 1959a, 1976a) performed extensive "epistemopathectomies" upon the large segment of twentieth-century psychological history that I have called the "Age of Theory." That happy interval commenced in the early 1930s and may, in modified form, still be with us to this very day. The mark of the Age of Theory, especially in its classic phase (circa 1930–1950), was that all activities were to be subordinated to production of a "commodity" called "theory" *in a quite special sense defined by the Age.* It is as if something called "theory" became an end in itself—a bauble, a trinket—of which it was neither appropriate nor fair, certainly most naïve, to inquire into its human relevance. Indeed, most formulations of the era were based on animal data, and some haughtily claimed a restriction of reference to animal (usually rat) behavior. The overarching cosmology of this interval was based on a loose mélange of vaguely apprehended ideas derived from logical positivism, operationism, and neopragmatism—and, it should be added, *not* from these traditions in their full span but merely from a narrow time segment within the early 1930s. These ideas were construed as providing a formulary for the "construction" of theory. Certain epistemological and procedural agreements were absolutely regulative during most of the Age of Theory: in particular, such matters as the regulation of systematic work by the imagery of hypothetico-deduction, the prescriptive lore surrounding operational definition, the lore concerning the intervening variable, the belief in the imminence of precisely quantitative behavioral theory of comprehensive scope, certain broadly shared judgments with respect to strategic foundation data, and the belief in automatic refinement and convergence of theories by the device of "differential test."

Even in an ahistorical era such as the present, most psychologists know something about these agreements, for some of them are still with us. Nevertheless, much of the rationale of the six-volume project, *Psychology: A Study of a Science* (Koch 1959b, 1962b, 1963), that I directed at midcentury was to test the official epistemology of the Age of Theory via an apposition of the creative experience of the many distinguished participating theorists with the stipulations of regnant canon law. The results made it possible for me to conclude that the study had subjected that body of law to vast attrition. In continued epistemopathic effort, I have succeeded—at least to my own satisfaction—in demonstrating the dysfunctionality of each statute in the Age of Theory code. But apparently not to the satisfaction of all!

A final context in which I have practiced epistemopathic surgery has been in relation to certain of the scholarly and creative mystiques that have been dominant in both the humanities and the arts in this century (Koch 1961b, 1969a [chapter 8], 1969d, cf. chapter 6). I discern in these areas many analogues to the restrictive scientism and rule-saturated ideologies of the psychological and social sciences. I mention this line of interest only to demonstrate that I do not discriminate against psychology.

Despite the extravagant generality into which I am forced by a discussion such as this, I am, by nature and scholarly practice, a particularist. But there is no way of addressing the import of psychology's first century, within a single chapter, particularistically. My only recourse in the remainder of this chapter is to move even further away from the surface details of psychological history. I wish to discuss the human wellsprings of the ameaningful epistemopathy that I believe to be so evident in psychology. I propose to do this in artless and nontechnical terms that address humanity's predicament on this planet. I do not project anything so grandiose— indeed, in my belief, insane—as the determination of the *range* of the knowable. Rather, I am groping toward certain constraints inherent in the human situation which would have to condition the form and texture of any knowledge that reflexively bears on human beings as subjects. Perhaps my groping stems more from hesitation or embarrassment than from the difficulty of discerning answers. For I am discussing matters within the ken of every human being which are disquieting to contemplate or address. Indeed, they are matters in respect to which the history of disciplinary inquiry has to some extent been an evasion. It might almost be said that we are increasingly walled off from the matters I have in mind by the over-confident and often spurious knowledge claims disgorged upon the race by certain of the formal disciplines. It is fitting that so arch an introduction point toward a rather odd title. I turn, then, to a consideration of "The Antinomies of Pure Reason and the Antinomies of Impure Living."

The Antinomies of Pure Reason and the Antinomies of Impure Living

Some years ago, while visiting a small liberal arts college, I was asked to have lunch with the resident philosophers. In the formal discussion session that followed the meal, my first questioner was a young faculty member. The tone of his question suggested his expectation of rapid — and final — edification. "Dr. Koch," he said, "what is your solution to the mind-body problem?" I think I mumbled that despite my Hungarian aura of omni-science, my mind was still open on the issue, and that though I considered it an important and meaningful one, I suspected it was undecidable in principle.

Later, it occurred to me that had the question been put to me some thirty years earlier, I would certainly have been able to untuck from my head a confident and final response. I would have said that *because* the question was asked in ontological form (i.e., in what Carnap would then have called "the material mode of speech"), it was undecidable in principle and therefore meaningless. However, if the *intent* of this pseudoquestion could be extricated from its ontological housing and translated into "the formal mode of speech," then it would become the utterly manageable, and therefore meaningful, issue of the relations between the "language systems" of psychology and physiology. Of course, part of me — even then — was surely apprised that both of these languages were woefully asystematic, mixed, and programmatic and, moreover, that each of the languages was not a single language but rather a congeries of languages, each member of which was shared in the typical instance by one person. But that particular part of me did not speak to the rest of me.

Nor did Immanuel Kant speak to me in an especially persuasive way in those days. In the course of his majestic construction of the critical philosophy, he had perceived that humankind is boxed in a curious way. He had discerned that there is a class of questions which human reason must necessarily confront but which are rationally undecidable. These, as every schoolchild knows, are the antinomies of pure reason—issues such that a thesis and its contradictory antithesis can both be proved. The four particular antinomies Kant considers bear, in the usefully brief words of one commentator (Weldon 1958, 81), on "the infinite extent and divisibility of space and time and also the existence of God and the freedom of the will." Post-Kantian sophisticates are fond of noting that the proofs are not formally unassailable, but the impeccability of the specific proofs has nothing to do with Kant's more general insight that there is a class of questions, intensely meaningful to all human beings—questions over which many experience great anguish—which "transcend the competence of human reason." The questions are meaningful but rationally undecidable in principle.

I suggest that the class of such undecidable yet meaningful propositions is far broader than the four antinomies that Kant thought it necessary to develop in pursuit of his systematic objective—which, in the immediate context of the antinomies, was to demonstrate the inadequacy of *dogmatic* metaphysics and theology. Moreover, if metaphorical extension of the notion be permitted, it rapidly becomes evident that a very broad range of human concerns, and even processes, exhibit, as it were, an "antinomal texture." I should like to identify certain consequences of this widespread "antinomality" for human knowledge and also for some characteristics of psychological inquiry in this century. (To emphasize that I am metaphorically building upon the strict logical sense of the term *antinomy*—and also for purposes of euphony—I have substituted these neologisms for the literally correct constructions "antinomial" and "antinomiality.")

First, I shall call upon Bertrand Russell as witness. The quotation from him may seem a bit long, but it will repay attention in better coin than I can mint. In one of his more inspiring moments, he gave the following definition of philosophy:

> Philosophy . . . is something intermediate between theology and science. Like theology, it consists of speculations on matters as to which definite knowledge has, so far, been unascertainable; but like science, it appeals to human reason rather than to authority. . . . *Almost all the questions of most interest to speculative minds are such as science cannot answer,* and the confident answers of theologians no longer seem so convincing as they did in former centuries. Is the world divided into mind

403

and matter, and, if so, what is mind and what is matter? Is mind subject to matter, or is it possessed of independent powers? Has the universe any unity or purpose? Is it evolving towards some goal? Are there really laws of nature, or do we believe in them only because of our innate love of order? Is man what he seems to the astronomer, a tiny lump of impure carbon and water impotently crawling on a small and unimportant planet? Or is he what he appears to Hamlet? Is he perhaps both at once? Is there a way of living that is noble and another that is base, or are all ways of living merely futile? If there is a way of living that is noble, in what does it consist, and how shall we achieve it? Must the good be eternal in order to deserve to be valued, or is it worth seeking even if the universe is inexorably moving towards death? . . . To such questions no answer can be found in the laboratory. . . . The studying of these questions, if not the answering of them, is the business of philosophy.

Why, then, you may ask, waste time on such insoluble problems? To this one may answer as a historian, or *as an individual facing the terror of cosmic loneliness.*

We will skip the historian's answer and continue with Russell's "more personal" answer:

Science tells us what we can know, but what we can know is little, and if we forget how much we cannot know we become insensitive to many things of very great importance. . . . Uncertainty, in the presence of vivid hopes and fears, is painful, but must be endured if we wish to live without the support of comforting fairy tales. *It is not good either to forget the questions that philosophy asks, or to persuade ourselves that we have found indubitable answers to them. To teach how to live without certainty, and yet without being paralyzed by hesitation, is perhaps the chief thing that philosophy, in our age, can still do for those who study it.* (Russell 1945, xiii–xiv, italics added)

I invite you, in passing, to contrast these attitudes with the following statement by Schlick in the initial paper of the first issue of *Erkenntnis* (1930–1931), the international journal of the Vienna Circle:

I am convinced that we are in the middle of an altogether final turn in philosophy. I am justified, on good grounds, in regarding the sterile conflict of systems as settled. Our time, so I claim, possesses already the methods by which any conflict of this kind is rendered superfluous; what matters is only to apply these methods resolutely. (translated and quoted in Frank 1950, 41)

Schlick's statement is far more characteristic of the dominant tone of philosophy in this century than is Russell's.

It can be seen from Russell's illustrations of "unanswerable" yet, in his view, meaningful and even pressing problems that they include equivalents of Kant's four antinomies but project a considerably broader class. But, if we consider the class of undecidable yet meaningful problems as manifested in the daily preoccupations and concerns of human beings, I think we will all see what we already agonizingly know: that the class is so large as to be nondenumerable in principle. For each of us, of course, there are homely analogues to Kant's four problems and to others cited by Russell; we may not sense them with the finesse of a philosopher, but we certainly feel them in the pit of our stomachs, starting in childhood! And there are others over which we sweat and quake on a day-to-day, or perhaps minute-to-minute, basis.

It does not require an elaborate phenomenological method, but merely honesty, to perceive that very many of the problems—large or small, existential or actional, intellectual or practical—which agitate human beings are indeed meaningful (often intensely so) but undecidable. Moreover, a large fraction of the events, problems, concerns, ruminations, calculations, regrets, evaluations, assessments, projections, and anticipations that populate our existence, whether fleetingly or over a span equivalent to one's biography, are also characterized by something very much like an "antinomal" structure. I do not mean that they pose antinomies in the formal logical sense, of course. What I do mean is that all such moments or units of psychological activity, however configured, involve disjunctive oppositions of meanings, the propositional equivalents of which are not ultimately, or strictly, or even stably decidable. I think I am noting something other than the mere circumstance that decision and action are largely optative or largely determined by "extra-rational factors," or that problem solving, and more generally, the movement of cognition, is probabilistic. I *am* comprehending those things in what I say, but I am trying to convey that the residue of mootness, ambiguity, mystery, is appallingly large. Perhaps the only way to convey what I have in mind is through the cumulative impact of varied examples. These I cannot state in orderly echelons, for the "antinomies of impure living" are not deployed by philosophers. Consider, however, the following array.

Let us commence by noting that the child who experiences night-sweats over a dawning sense of the word *eternity* is by way of discovering the Kantian antinomies, but let us leave aside further discussion of those over-arching issues concerning origin, destiny, and purpose, which torture us throughout our sentient lives.

Consider now the enormous range of ambiguity inherent in the human condition suggested by, say, the unrecoverability of particular motives and, indeed, the principled impossibility of achieving a full motivational analysis of any action; the ubiquitous problems of self-sincerity, altruism versus egocentrism, guilt versus innocence, sinful versus good deeds, personal responsibility versus shaping or control from without; of whether, in particular instances or in general, one is loved or hated, liked or disliked, or perhaps regarded indifferently; whether one is beautiful or ugly or somewhere in between. Moreover, is one beautiful by virtue of physiognomy or personality or both? When is one lying; when isn't one? When is one being lied to; when not? When is one being treated as an object; when as a person? Is it more desirable to project value, ideal, end state X or Y, or Z or . . . ? Is one (whether in general or in respect to particular endeavors) a success or a failure? If a failure, is it by virtue of having successfully sought failure, or by ineptitude, the fault of others, or just bad luck?

"Do I understand this equation (this line of poetry or prose, this view, theory, subject, person, event)? Really understand, or merely think that I do?" "Do I really like X (any object of taste) or only think that I do because I should? As a matter of fact, should I, really?" "Should I wear X or Y today or are they both inappropriate?" "Am I showing favoritism toward one of my children, or is that child the one who needs special attention?"

"Can I sustain this performance? Am I doing brilliantly or did I lose it somewhere? Does the audience resonate to me or does it loathe me? If the latter, does it loathe my person, my ideas, or merely my words?"

"Sometimes I am convinced that they are about to fire me, but five minutes later the same evidence seems to mean that I am on the verge of being promoted."

The examples thus far have been drawn in a rather bold and structural way. Let me now enter the microstructure of a characteristic human rumination sequence and attempt to give something like the formal pattern of the excogitations that we develop around the small issues which preempt so much of our daily round.

406

"A said that B said . . . , but B couldn't have said such a thing. Or could he? I don't think A to be a liar, but I could be wrong. Is A trying to get closer to me by upsetting me over B's inconstancy, or is he really being protective? Or (on the other hand) is B trying to send me a message through A which B is afraid to deliver? But B has never been that kind of person. However, C might have said something to B that changed the way he feels, or maybe B has begun to change because of his relationship with D or that nasty pair, E and F. On the other hand, it's more likely that D is exerting a stabilizing influence on B, that is, on the assumption that D has not been subverted by E and F. But why should E and F, however coarse and vulgar, be so strongly set on changing B, or reaching B through D, when it must be clear to them that there is nothing B can do for them? On the other hand, maybe they don't know that B has given up his connection with G, whom B could indeed have influenced in their favor. But I am not even sure that E and F knew that B ever did have a connection with G. Anyway, I'm not sure that E and F know B at all well or have any basis for wishing to influence him. Now, D, on the other hand, could be changing toward B, not because of the influence of E and F but because. . . ."

These examples are, I think, sufficient to make palpable the awesome dispersion of the antinomal, the problematic, the ambiguous, in human experience. It is no great leap to add that the attendant fear, trembling, and uncertainty are comparably awesome in scope and can, for most of us, at times, achieve an intensity that tests the margins of our sanity. It is no part of our talent to live at utter peace with these pressures — though there are graceful philosophies of faith that can be mitigative and that need not be presumed to be any the less warrantable than, say, the ungraceful philosophies of faith associated with the metaphysics of scientism. And there are other mitigative correlates of antinomality, such as the fascination and intrinsic beauty of the experience of awe and mystery in relation to the universe. But there is no denying that the antinomal texture, the uncertainty of our situation, *can* generate a vast skewing effect on cognition, which can create epistemopathy and sustain ameaning. The ultimate "meaning" of ameaning is indeed that it is a fear-driven species of cognitive constriction, a reduction of uncertainty by denial, by a form of phony certainty achieved by the covert annihilation of the problematic, the complex, and the subtle.

Antinomality, in sum, is at the basis of the endemic human need for crawling into cozy conceptual boxes — any box, so long as it gives promise of relieving the pains of cognitive uncertainty or easing problematic tension. This poignant human need, at any cost, for a frame, an abacus, a system, map, or set of rules that can seem to offer a wisp of hope for resolving uncertainty makes all of us vulnerable — in one degree or another — to the claims of simplistic, reductive, hypergeneral, or in other ways ontology-distorting frames, so long as they have the appearance of "systematicity." Moreover, having climbed into our conceptual box, on one adventitious basis or another, we are prepared to defend our happy domicile to the death — meaning, in the typical instance, *your* death. It is not that we don't want you to join us inside (we would be delighted to accommodate the whole human race); it's just that we don't want you tampering with our box or suggesting — by your location in another one — that there are other places in which to live.

The saving grace of the race is the ability of individuals, occasionally, to climb out of such boxes and look around: to see around the edges of our "received" concepts, our technical constructions, our formal belief systems. When the drive toward easy cognitive assurance remains unchecked and unmitigated, it can lead to something very much like mass insanity.

One might think that all I am doing is addressing the facts of human conflict, which are acknowledged in some form by all psychological theories. If I am, I am addressing them in a special sense and from a special incidence: I am talking about the kind of *cognitive* conflict that paralyzes in the sense that I *know* that I *cannot know*, but somehow am compelled desperately to strive to know. It is a mode or aspect of conflict that is not addressed in theories couched in a language of conflicting drives or needs, conflicting systems of personality, or competing responses.

What I mean by "antinomality" is the kind of conflict generated by a proposition that suggests its contradictory (or the domain of its contraries) as strongly as its own affirmation, at the moment of affirmation. Antinomality, in the sense in which I am employing this metaphor, creates a penumbra of uncertainty around the edges of sentience, such that one can rarely be sure who or what one really is, or indeed what (or which of a class of alternates) one is perceiving, cognizing, or doing. Even when the organization of our mental field seems clear and unambiguous, there is still a faint halo of mystery. On a vast gray area of occasions the organization "wants" to shift into its opposite or some range of alternates, or the field is shadowy, indistinct. And finally, there is that black area of interludes in which something like utter "problematicity," chaos, strangeness, terror, and thus depersonalization supervenes. I am, if you will, talking of something like *metaphysical* conflict and saying that we are all born metaphysicians who are destined mainly to fail when we ply our craft. And I am saying that "conflict" of this sort is far more pervasive in our lives than we tend ordinarily to have the courage to admit, either to ourselves or to others.

When dwelling on the pervasiveness of antinomality, determinate and valid knowledge soon begins to seem a miracle — but no more so than our antinomal presence here on Earth is a miracle. Einstein once wrote that "the most incomprehensible thing in the world is that the world is comprehensible."

I think there are contexts of knowing in which the structures, and relations among disparate structures, in our mental field are defined so perspicuously, sharply, compellingly, as to make "verification" seem superfluous. And indeed, as most great discoverers have reported, nature often says "yes" to such visions when meticulously tested and sometimes continues to say yes over an unanticipated range of their consequences. Taking such occurrences as a prototype case of *meaningful* thinking (as I have previously tried to define it), one should note that approximations of this type of occurrence are within the range of all of us, both in daily living and in moments of "formal" or technical ratiocination. I think that much needs to be said about the human being's capacity for discerning islands of order within the antinomal ocean in which we swim and (in the arts) for creating nobly ordered structures that can transcend or illuminate antinomality. Much needs to be said about such matters, but not in an essay of finite length!

This much, however, has been implicit in all I have said: meaningful thinking, as I have sought to define it, is precisely what cannot supervene when we lack the courage to live with our antinomal uncertainties; it cannot be invited by denial of our situation, but only by a kind of fascinated and loving, if ironic, acceptance.

The twentieth century has been far wiser than Kant — and, in dominant tendency, far wiser than the Russell who spoke in the quotation I cited. (There were many Russells over his long career; he, too, was far wiser over long stretches of it!) A conspicuous strand in the philosophy, especially the scientific philosophy, of the twentieth century has been the view that all questions having presumptive cognitive content but which can be shown to be undecidable in principle are meaningless. They are, in other words, pseudoquestions — linguistically illegitimate question forms. Rational hygiene, therefore, dictates that the human race be freed of such illusory preoccupations. This is the view that received its sharpest (and most incantatory) expression in the various forms of the "verifiability theory of meaning" advanced by logical positivism, but it is prominent as well in pragmatism, operationism, and all *consistent* positivistic and empiricist philosophies. Though not a dominant view in earlier centuries, it was clearly adumbrated in Hume and received something close to its canonical formulation (though not application) in Comte.

In the philosophy of *this* century, unqualified forms of the verifiability theory of meaning began to wane along with the waning hegemony of logical positivism, but some would argue that its imprint was visible well into the 1960s in much of analytic philosophy. This smug and restrictive view of meaning is still, however, implicit in the thinking of most natural and social scientists, while in scientific psychology it remains a devout and irrefragable article of faith.

I should like to suggest that such a view of the range of the meaningful has had, and must have, crippling entailments for the character of the psychological enterprise. If empirical decidability (which, incidentally, itself cannot be *decided in advance*) is the criterion for bounding the meaningful, one then has a perfect rationale for selecting for study only domains that seem to give access to the generation of stable research findings. If any domain seems refractory to conquest by the narrow range of methods (usually borrowed from the natural sciences and mutilated in the process) held to be sacred by the workforce, then, obviously, *meaningful* questions cannot be asked concerning the domain, and that domain is expendable. If one cannot achieve stable findings when the dependent variable is of "subjective" cast, then eliminate such data and concentrate on behavior! Indeed, why presume that mental events or processes exist? Why study the *subject* at all; why not study something else?

Such a view of the meaningful, then, dooms psychology to be an empty role-playing pursuit which, in the course of enacting a misconstrued imitation of the forms of science, gives free rein to every epistemopathic potentiality of the "inquiring" mind. Buttressed by such a view and by the anemic theory of science in which it is housed, psychology has felt justified in fixing upon totally fictional domains as its objects of study (i.e., on arbitrary and schematic models of the person, or even the organism, rather than on the actual entities — say, a *schematized* rat, or dog, or sophomore; or, perhaps, a telephone exchange, a sewage system, a servomechanism, a computer). A related strategy, of course, has been to select a dependent variable category (whether phrased in terms of "behavior" or in some other way) bearing a trivial relation to human—or even sophomore or dog—reality. Some games—even within scholarship—are relatively innocent; the game at issue poses a severe threat to humankind because it links the authority of science with an imagery of the human condition that can only trivialize and obfuscate its beneficiaries.

Now psychology has presumed, throughout much of the century, that its task is the *prediction* and *control* of behavior (or, less frequently, some other member of a limited class of dependent-variable categories, as, for instance, action, experience, cognitive change, attitude change, etc.). But one can well ask what such an objective might *mean* against the background of the antinomal and ambiguous human events of the sort I have sought to illustrate. Does "prediction" mean that we expect to derive, from some nomological net, the behavioral, experiential, or judgmental *outcome* of such episodes in the quasi-logic of antinomality as I have tried to analyze? Does it mean the capacity to generate a lawful technology that will give human beings the tools to resolve their antinomal "problems" with finality and precision? Does it mean a set of normative rules or maxims that will enable individuals better to resolve their disjunctive quandaries?

Or does prediction mean the erection of a scientistic myth which uses the iconology of science to reassure people that their lives are not that complex, their situations not that ambiguous—and that, therefore, if they are able to understand the profound fact that they really are redundant concretions of dry hardware or wet software (or wet hardware or dry software), all they need do is happily percolate in a way determined by the laws of the particular kind of concretion that the lawgiver prefers?

It is incredible to contemplate that during a century dominated by the tidy imagery of prediction and control of human and social events, the perverse cognitive pathology housed in such imagery has not been rooted out. In fact, such notions have rarely been seen as problematic and still more rarely subjected even to perfunctory modes of analysis.

Coda: The First Century?

And now for some easy questions. We are celebrating the first one hundred years of an independent, scientific psychology! It is appropriate to ask: (1) Have we been and are we now *independent* in the sense intended by those who celebrate the adjective, namely, "independent" of *philosophy*? And (2) Is psychology a science?

Independence

We are of course independent in an institutional sense. We have our own university departments, laboratories, journals, professional organizations, and so forth. Are we *conceptually* independent of philosophy? In a word, *no*. That opinion will come as no surprise by this point in the exposition. Most of our ideas have come from the twenty-six centuries of philosophy preceding the birth of our partition myth and, of course, to some extent, from physics, mathematics, various biological sciences, medicine, the social studies, the nonphilosophical humanities, and, yes, millennia of ordinary human experience.

Robinson (1976) has argued that twentieth-century psychology, even in its experimental reaches, is a "footnote to the nineteenth century" and is apprised, of course, of some large continuities between the nineteenth and not a few earlier centuries. Despite the curious size of the footnote relative to the text, I think him essentially correct. I presume he would agree that a footnote need not be merely ampliative, but can contain refinements here and there and even novelty. For even I believe that some islands of penetrating thinking and research have existed in this century.

Though many of us have generated a vociferous rhetoric of independence in this century (especially those of behaviorist persuasion), one and all have of necessity presupposed strong, if garbled, philosophical commitments in the conduct of their work. Psychology is necessarily the most philosophy-sensitive discipline in the entire gamut of disciplines that claim empirical status. We cannot discriminate a so-called variable, pose a research question, choose or invent a method, project a theory, stipulate a psychotechnology, without making strong presumptions of philosophical cast about the nature of our human subject matter—presumptions that can be ordered to age-old contexts of philosophical discussion. Even our nomenclature for the basic fields of specialized research within psychology (e.g., sensation, perception, cognition, memory, motivation, emotion, etc.) has its origin in philosophy. Let us note, also, that even during the period when the claim to independence was most aggressively asserted (the neobehavioristically dominated Age of Theory that I have already mentioned), we were basing, and explicitly so, our "official" epistemology on logical positivism and cognate formulations within the philosophy of science.

We should also bear in mind that there have been many psychologists in virtually every field throughout the century who have been explicit in their use of philosophical materials and in their awareness of philosophical origins. Within this subset fall virtually all of the nineteenth-century "founders" (most of whom — including the newly rehabilitated version of Wundt's ghost — indeed continued to see philosophy as their *primary* vocation, even after the founding); the personalists; Gestalt and field theorists; phenomenological psychologists; transactionalists; and more recently, contextualists, pursuers of a motley plurality of Eastern philosophies, and so forth. And there have been seminal thinkers, standing either alone or not easily assignable to broad movements, who have been explicit about their philosophical interests and dependencies. William James, John Dewey, Wilhelm Stern, William McDougall, Wolfgang Köhler, E. C. Tolman, Heinz Werner, Henry Murray, and James Gibson are names that rapidly spring to mind in this connection. It might also be worth recalling that this very essay is based on an address to the Division of Philosophical Psychology, which is a part — though a tenuous one — of the American Psychological Association.

I should add that no clear line can be drawn between the concerns of philosophy and those of psychology, either historically or in the nature of the case. The ameaningful presumption that a clear line *must* be drawn has fostered much of the grotesquerie in modern psychology. I do not, however, wish to suggest that fuller and more explicit knowledge of our philosophical origins, and of the intertwining of philosophical and psychological modes of analysis, will remove *all* of the blockages that have trivialized psychological thought in this century. For it is part of my position qua cognitive pathologist that one can find forms of epistemopathy in philosophy comparable to those I discern in psychology.

Despite the fact that this ancient tradition — which over history has been the font of every special field of scholarship — has produced many of the noblest achievements of the human mind, the philosophic impulse has at times proven extraordinarily vulnerable to the allures of a specious systematicity and comprehensiveness. For philosophy has also produced many of the kinds of conceptual boxes that promise cognitive reassurance too easily and too confidently. Some of these boxes — as in certain of the post-Kantian idealistic systems — are so expansive as to promote a kind of euphoric hyperventilation of the mind, while others — as in the dominant positivistic philosophies of this century — are so constrictive as to promote a form of cognitive anoxia. There is also a quality of *style* in much philosophical writing that in my opinion puts both reader and writer at epistemopathic risk. This is the implicit assumption that the writer's formulation

413

is *final,* even when the writer knows full well that its claims may be quashed (perhaps even by the writer) next week. This quality of "finalism" is certainly to be found among those *psychological* theorists who view their own work as preemptive, but is not quite so pervasive in psychological writing.

Is Psychology a Science?

I have been addressing this question for fifty years and, over the past thirty, have been stable in my view that psychology is not a single or coherent discipline but rather a collectivity of studies of varied cast, some few of which may qualify as science, while most do not. I have written widely on this theme (e.g., Koch 1969c, 1971, and especially 1976a [chapters 4 and 5]), but must content myself here with a very brief statement of my position, sans the evidence and analysis on which it rests. The reader will be surprised, perhaps, to discover that my proposals are libertarian ones and not devoid of hope.

For some years I have argued that psychology has been misconceived, whether as a science or as any kind of coherent discipline devoted to the empirical study of human beings. That psychology *can* be an integral discipline is the nineteenth-century autism that led to its baptism as an independent science — an autism which can be shown to be exactly that, both by a priori and by empirico-historical considerations.

On an a priori basis, nothing so awesome as the total domain comprised by the functioning of all organisms (not to mention persons) could possibly be the subject matter of a coherent discipline. If *theoretical* integration be the objective, we should consider that such a condition has never been attained by any large subdivision of inquiry — including physics. When the details of psychology's one-hundred-year history are consulted, the patent tendency is toward theoretical and substantive fractionation (and increasing insularity among the "specialties"), not integration. As for the larger quasi-theoretical "paradigms" of psychology, history shows that the hard knowledge accrued in one generation typically disenfranchises the regnant analytical frameworks of the last.

My position suggests that the noncohesiveness of psychology finally be acknowledged by replacing it with some such locution as "the psychological studies." The psychological studies, if they are really to address the historically constituted objectives of psychological thought, must range over an immense and disorderly spectrum of human activity and experience. If significant knowledge is the desideratum, problems must be approached with humility, methods must be contextual and flexible, and anticipations of synoptic breakthrough held in check. Moreover, the conceptual ordering devices, technical languages ("paradigms," if you prefer) open to the various psychological studies are — like all human modes of cognitive organization — perspectival, sensibility-dependent relative to the inquirer, and often non-commensurable. Such conceptual incommensurabilities often obtain not only between "contentually" different psychological studies but between perspectivally different orderings of the "same" domain. Characteristically, psychological events — as I have implied throughout the discussion of antinomality — are multiply determined, ambiguous in their human meaning, polymorphous, contextually environed or embedded in complex and vaguely bounded ways, and evanescent and labile in the extreme. This entails some obvious constraints upon the task of the inquirer and limits upon the knowledge that can be unearthed. Different theorists will — relative to their different analytical purposes, predictive or practical aims, perceptual sensitivities, metaphor-forming capacities, and preexisting discrimination repertoires — make asystematically different perceptual cuts upon the same domain. They will identify "variables" of markedly different grain and meaning contour, selected and linked on different principles of grouping. The cuts, variables, concepts will in all likelihood establish different universes of discourse, even if loose ones.

Corollary to such considerations, paradigms, theories, models (or whatever one's label for conceptual ordering devices) can never prove preemptive or preclusive of alternate organizations. This is so for any field of inquiry, and conspicuously so in the psychological and social studies. The presumption on the part of their promulgators that the gappy, sensibility-dependent, and often arbitrary paradigms of psychology *do* encapsulate preemptive truths is no mere cognitive blunder. Nor can it be written off as an innocuous excess of enthusiasm. It raises a grave moral issue reflective of a widespread moral bankruptcy within psychology. In the psychological studies, the attribution to any paradigm of a preemptive finality has the force of telling human beings precisely what they are, of fixing their essence, defining their ultimate worth, potential, meaning; of cauterizing away that quality of ambiguity, mystery, search, that makes progress through a biography an adventure. Freud's tendency to view dissidents and critics in *symptomatic* terms — and to resolve disagreement by excommunication — is no circumscribed failing, but indeed renders problematic the character of his entire effort, not only morally but cognitively. One is tempted to laugh off the ludicrous prescriptionism of self-anointed visionaries like Watson, Skinner, and even certain infinitely confident prophets

415

of the theory of finite automata, but their actual impact on history is no laughing matter.

Because of the immense range of the psychological studies, different areas of study will not only require different (and contextually apposite) methods but will bear affinities to different members of the broad groupings of inquiry as historically conceived. Fields like sensory and biological psychology may certainly be regarded as solidly within the family of the biological and, in some reaches, natural sciences. But psychologists must finally accept the circumstance that extensive and important sectors of psychological study require modes of inquiry rather more like those of the humanities than the sciences. And among these I would include areas traditionally considered "fundamental" — like perception, cognition, motivation, and learning — as well as such more obviously rarefied fields as social psychology, psychopathology, personality, aesthetics, and the analysis of "creativity."

Conclusion

And so — ponderous scholar and unrelenting epistemopathectomist though I be — I find I have written a sermon. But a moral analysis of the past, by inviting a change of heart, is a surer bridge to a tolerable future than any confident methodological manifesto. I have been inviting a psychology that might show the imprint of a capacity to accept the inevitable ambiguity and mystery of our situation. The false hubris with which we have contained our existential anguish in a terrifying age has led us to prefer easy yet grandiose pseudoknowledge to the hard and spare fruit that is knowledge. To admit intellectual finitude, and to accept with courage our antinomal condition, is to go a long way toward curing our characteristic epistemopathies. To attain such an attitude is to be free.

References

Adams, G. 1931. *Psychology: Science or superstition?* New York: Covici-Friede.

Arnold, W. J., ed. 1976. *Nebraska Symposium on Motivation, 1975.* Vol. 23. Lincoln: University of Nebraska Press.

Attneave, F. 1962. Perception and related areas. In Koch 1962b, 4:619–59.

Austin, J. L. 1962. *How to do things with words.* Edited by J. O. Urmson. Oxford: Clarendon Press.

Ayer, A. J. 1936. *Language, truth, and logic.* Oxford: Oxford University Press.

Bar-Hillel, Y. 1964. *Language and information: Selected essays on their theory and applications.* Reading, Mass.: Addison-Wesley.

Beck, L. F. 1939. Conditioned response behavior (description of research film by K. E. Zener). *Psychological Abstracts* 13:190.

Benjamin, A. C. 1955. *Operationism.* Springfield, Ill.: Thomas.

Bergmann, G., and K. W. Spence. 1941. Operationism and theory in psychology. *Psychological Review* 48:1–14.

Bills, A. G. 1938. Changing views on psychology as a science. *Psychological Review* 45:377–94.

Black, M. 1954. *Problems of analysis: Philosophical essays.* Ithaca: Cornell University Press.

———. 1962. *Models and metaphors: Studies in language and philosophy.* Ithaca: Cornell University Press.

Blanshard, B. 1962. *Reason and analysis.* London: Allen and Unwin.

Boring, E. G. 1936. Temporal perception and operationism. *American Journal of Psychology* 48:510–22.

———. 1950. *A history of experimental psychology.* 2d ed. New York: Appleton-Century-Crofts.

Bridgman, P. W. 1916. Tolman's principle of similitude. *Physical Review* 8:423–31.

———. 1922. *Dimensional analysis.* New Haven: Yale University Press.

———. 1927. *The logic of modern physics.* New York: Macmillan. Macmillan paperback ed., 1960.

———. 1934. A physicist's second reaction to *Mengenlehre. Scripta Mathematica* 2:101–17, 221–34.

———. 1936. *The nature of physical theory.* Princeton: Princeton University Press.

———. 1938a. *The intelligent individual and society.* New York: Macmillan.

———. 1938b. Operational analysis. In Bridgman 1950. (Original work published in *Philosophy of Science* 5:114–31.)

———. 1940a. Freedom and the individual. In Bridgman 1950. (Original work published in *Freedom: Its meaning.* Edited by R. N. Anshan. New York: Harcourt Brace.)

———. 1940b. Science: Public or private? In Bridgman 1950. (Address to Fifth International Congress for the Unity of Science, Cambridge, Mass., 1939. Published in *Philosophy of Science* 7:36–48.)

———. 1945. Some general principles of operational analysis (E. G. Boring, H. Feigl, H. E. Israel, C. C. Pratt, and B. F. Skinner). In Bridgman 1950. (Original work published in *Psychological Review* 52:246–49.)

———. 1950. *Reflections of a physicist.* New York: Philosophical Library.

———. 1952. *The nature of some of our physical concepts.* New York: Philosophical Library.

———. 1959. *The way things are.* Cambridge: Harvard University Press.

———. 1962. *A sophisticate's primer of relativity.* Middletown, Conn.: Wesleyan University Press. (2d ed. 1983.)

Bronowski, J. 1951. *The common sense of science.* London: Heinemann.

———. 1959. *Science and human values.* New York: Harper Torchbook. (Original work published 1956.)

Bronowski, J., and B. Mazlish. 1960. *The western intellectual tradition.* New York: Harper.

Butterfield, H. 1949. *The origins of modern science.* London: Bell.

Carnap, R. 1936–1937. Testability and meaning. *Philosophy of Science* 3:419–71; 4:1–40.

———. 1956. The methodological character of theoretical concepts. In *Minnesota Studies in the Philosophy of Science.* Edited by H. Feigl and M. Scriven, 1:38–76. Minneapolis: University of Minnesota Press.

Cassidy, H. G. 1962. *The sciences and the arts.* New York: Harper.

Cohen, I. B. 1956. *Franklin and Newton.* Philadelphia: American Philosophical Society.

Cohen, L. J. 1962. *The diversity of meaning.* London: Methuen.

Conant, J. B. 1947. *On understanding science.* New Haven: Yale University Press.

———. 1951. *Science and common sense.* New Haven: Yale University Press.

de Jouvenel, B. 1961. The republic of science. In *The logic of personal knowledge: Essays presented to Michael Polanyi on his seventieth birthday, 11 March 1961,* 131–41. London: Routledge and Kegan Paul.

Deutsch, K. W., J. Platt, and D. Senghaas. 1971. Conditions favoring major advances in social science. *Science* 171:450–59.

Dewey, J. 1910. *How we think.* Boston: D.C. Heath.

———. 1917. *Essays in experimental logic.* Chicago: University of Chicago Press.

———. 1938. *Logic: The theory of inquiry.* New York: Holt.

Dubos, R. 1961. *The dreams of reason.* New York: Columbia University Press.

Eastwood, W. 1961. *A book of science verse.* London: Macmillan.

Ehrmann, J., ed. 1966. Editor's introduction. *Yale French Studies,* nos. 36 and 37 (double issue): 5–9.

Eiseley, L. 1958. *The immense journey.* London: Gollancz.

———. 1959. *Darwin's century.* London: Gollancz.

———. 1961. *The firmament of time.* London: Gollancz.

Feigl, H. 1956. Some major issues and developments in the philosophy of science of logical empiricism. In *Minnesota Studies in the Philosophy of Science*. Edited by H. Feigl and M. Scriven, 1:3–37. Minneapolis: University of Minnesota Press.

Feigl, H., and A. E. Blumberg. 1931. Logical positivism. *Journal of Philosophy* 28:281–96.

Frank, P. 1950. *Modern science and its philosophy*. Cambridge: Harvard University Press.

Freud, S., and C. G. Jung. 1974. *The Freud/Jung letters: The correspondence between Sigmund Freud and C. G. Jung*. Edited by W. McGuire; translated by R. Manheim and R. F. C. Hull. Princeton: Princeton University Press.

Frye, N. 1967. The knowledge of good and evil. In *The morality of scholarship*. Edited by M. Black, 1–28. Ithaca: Cornell University Press.

Gellner, E. 1959. *Words and things*. London: Gollancz.

Ghiselin, B., ed. 1952. *The creative process: A symposium*. New York: New American Library.

Gibson, J. J. 1950. *The perception of the visual world*. Boston: Houghton Mifflin.

———. 1959. Perception as a function of stimulation. In Koch 1959b, 1:456–501.

———. 1966. *The senses considered as perceptual systems*. Boston: Houghton-Mifflin.

Gibson, J. J., and E. J. Gibson. 1955. Perceptual learning: Differentiation or enrichment? *Psychological Review* 62:32–41.

Gillispie, C. C. 1960. *The edge of objectivity*. Princeton: Princeton University Press.

Graham, A. C. 1961. *The problem of value*. London: Hutchinson University Library.

Greenberg, C. 1962. How art writing earns its bad name. *Encounter*, December, 67–71.

Guthrie, E. R. 1959. Association by contiguity. In Koch 1959b, 2:158–95.

Hadamard, J. 1945. *An essay on the psychology of invention in the mathematical field*. Princeton: Princeton University Press.

Hanson, N. R. 1958. *Patterns of discovery: An inquiry into the conceptual foundations of science*. Cambridge: Cambridge University Press.

Hare, R. M. 1963. *Freedom and reason*. New York: Oxford University Press.

Hempel, C. G. 1950. Problems and changes in the empiricist criterion of meaning. *Revue Internationale de Philosophie* 4:41–63.

———. 1959. The empiricist criterion of meaning. In *Logical Positivism*. Edited by A. J. Ayer, 108–29. Glencoe, Ill.: Free Press.

Hesse, M. B. 1954. *Science and the human imagination*. London: SCM Press.

———. 1966. *Models and analogies in science*. Notre Dame: University of Notre Dame Press.

Holton, G. 1952. *Introduction to concepts and theories in physical science*. Cambridge: Harvard University Press.

———. 1960. Modern science and the intellectual tradition. *Science* 131:1187–93.

Howe, I. 1968. The New York intellectuals: A chronicle and a critique. *Commentary*, October, 29–51.

Hull, C. L. 1930a. Knowledge and purpose as habit mechanisms. *Psychological Review* 37:511–25.

———. 1930b. Simple trial-and-error learning: A study in psychological theory. *Psychological Review* 37:242–56.

———. 1935a. The conflicting psychologies of learning: A way out. *Psychological Review* 42:491–516.

———. 1935b. The mechanism of the assembly of behavior segments in novel combinations suitable for problem solution. *Psychological Review* 42:219–45.

———. 1943. *Principles of behavior: An introduction to behavior theory*. New York: Appleton-Century.

————. 1951. *Essentials of behavior.* New Haven: Yale University Press.

Johnson, H. M. 1930. Some properties of Fechner's "Intensity of sensation." *Psychological Review* 37:113–23.

Johnson, S. 1755. *A dictionary of the English language.* London: Printed by W. Strahan for J. and P. Knapton.

Kafka, F. 1952. *Selected short stories of Franz Kafka.* Translated by W. Muir and E. Muir. New York: Modern Library.

Kantor, J. R. 1938. The operational principle in the physical and psychological sciences. *Psychological Record* 2:3–32.

Kasschau, R. S. 1980. *Psychology: Exploring behavior.* Englewood Cliffs, N.J.: Prentice-Hall.

Kasschau, R. S., and F. S. Kessel, eds. 1980. *Psychology and society: In search of symbiosis.* Houston Symposium, vol. 1. New York: Holt, Rinehart and Winston.

Kemble, E. C., and F. Birch. 1970. Percy Williams Bridgman: April 21, 1882–August 20, 1961. In National Academy of Sciences, *Biographical memoirs,* 41:23–67. New York: Columbia University Press.

Kerner, G. C. 1966. *The revolution in ethical theory.* New York: Oxford University Press.

Koch, S. 1941a. The logical character of the motivation concept. I. *Psychological Review* 48:15–38.

————. 1941b. The logical character of the motivation concept. II. *Psychological Review* 48:127–54.

————. 1944. Hull's *Principles of behavior:* A special review. *Psychological Bulletin* 41:269–86.

————. 1954. Clark L. Hull. In *Modern learning theory,* by W. K. Estes, S. Koch, K. MacCorquodale, P. E. Meehl, C. G. Mueller, W. N. Schoenfeld, and W. S. Verplanck, 1–176. New York: Appleton-Century-Crofts.

————. 1956. Behavior as "intrinsically" regulated: Work notes towards a pre-theory of phenomena called "motivational." In *Nebraska Symposium on Motivation, 1956.* Edited by M. R. Jones, 4:42–87. Lincoln: University of Nebraska Press.

————. 1959a. Epilogue. In Koch 1959b, 3:729–88.

————, ed. 1959b. *Psychology: A study of a science. Study I: Conceptual and systematic.* Vols. 1–3. New York: McGraw-Hill.

————. 1959c. Towards an indigenous methodology. Invited address presented at the annual meeting of the Eastern Psychological Association, Atlantic City, N.J., April 3.

————. 1961a. Behaviourism. In *Encyclopaedia Britannica,* 3:326–29. Chicago: Encyclopaedia Britannica.

————. 1961b. Psychological science versus the science-humanism antinomy: Intimations of a significant science of man. *American Psychologist* 16:629–39.

————. 1962a. Introduction to Study II. In Koch 1962b, 4:xi–xxxix.

————, ed. 1962b. *Psychology: A study of a science. Study II: Empirical substructure and relations with other sciences.* Vol. 4. New York: McGraw-Hill.

————, ed. 1963. *Psychology: A study of a science. Study II: Empirical substructure and relations with other sciences.* Vols. 5–6. New York: McGraw-Hill.

————. 1964. Psychology and emerging conceptions of knowledge as unitary. In *Behaviorism and phenomenology: Contrasting bases for modern psychology.* Edited by T. W. Wann, 1–45. Chicago: University of Chicago Press.

————. 1965. The allures of ameaning in modern psychology. In *Science and human affairs.*

References

Edited by R. Farson, 55–82. Palo Alto, Calif.: Science and Behavior Books. (Originally a Morrison Lecture sponsored by the Western Behavioral Sciences Institute at La Jolla, California, and presented at the Scripps Institute in 1961.)

———. 1969a. A meaning in the humanities. Presidential address to the Division of Psychology and the Arts at the annual meeting of the American Psychological Association, Washington, D.C., September 1.

———. 1969b. Karl Edward Zener: A memoir. *Journal of Personality* 37:179–89.

———. 1969c. Psychology cannot be a coherent science. *Psychology Today,* March, 14, 64, 66–68.

———. 1969d. Value properties: Their significance for psychology, axiology, and science. In *The anatomy of knowledge.* Edited by M. Grene, 119–48. London: Routledge and Kegan Paul; Amherst: University of Massachusetts Press.

———. 1971. Reflections on the state of psychology. *Social Research* 38:669–709.

———. 1973a. The image of man in encounter groups. *American Scholar* 42:636–52.

———. 1973b. Theory and experiment in psychology. *Social Research* 40:691–707.

———. 1976a. Language communities, search cells, and the psychological studies. In Arnold 1976, 447–559.

———. 1976b. More verbal behavior from Dr. Skinner (review of *About behaviorism*). *Contemporary Psychology* 21:453–57.

———. 1977a. A text in search of an author. *Contemporary Psychology* 22:73.

———. 1977b. Vagrant confessions of an asystematic psychologist: An intellectual autobiography. Invited address to the Divisions of Philosophical Psychology and of the History of Psychology at the annual meeting of the American Psychological Association, San Francisco, August 28.

———. 1992a. Foreword: Wundt's creature at age zero — and as centenarian: Some aspects of the institutionalization of the "new psychology." In Koch and Leary 1992, 7–35.

———. 1992b. Postscript. In Koch and Leary 1992, 951–68.

Koch, S., and W. J. Daniel. 1945. The effect of satiation on the behavior mediated by a habit of maximum strength. *Journal of Experimental Psychology* 35:167–87.

Koch, S., and D. E. Leary, eds. 1992. *A century of psychology as science.* Washington: American Psychological Association. (Original work published 1985.)

Koestler, A. 1964. *The act of creation.* New York: Macmillan.

Köhler, W. 1937. Psychological remarks on some questions of anthropology. *American Journal of Psychology* 50:271–88.

———. 1938. *The place of value in a world of facts.* New York: Liveright.

Koyré, A. 1939. *Etudes Galiléennes.* 3 vols. Paris: Herman.

———. 1957. *From the closed world to the infinite universe.* Baltimore: Johns Hopkins University Press.

Kuhn, T. S. 1962. *The structure of scientific revolutions.* Chicago: University of Chicago Press.

———. 1970a. Logic of discovery or psychology of research? In Lakatos and Musgrave 1970, 1–23.

———. 1970b. Reflections on my critics. In Lakatos and Musgrave 1970, 231–78.

———. 1970c. *The structure of scientific revolutions.* 2d ed. Chicago: University of Chicago Press.

———. 1974. Second thoughts on paradigms. In *The structure of scientific theories.* Edited by F. Suppe, 459–82. Urbana: University of Illinois Press.

Lakatos, I., and A. Musgrave, eds. 1970. *Criticism and the growth of knowledge*. Cambridge: Cambridge University Press.

Lapage, G. 1961. *Art and the scientist*. Bristol, England: John Wright.

Lashley, K. S. 1950. In search of the engram. *Symposia of the Society for Experimental Biology* 4:454–82.

Lazarsfeld, P. F. 1959. Latent structure analysis. In Koch 1959b, 3:476–543.

Leavis, F. R. 1930. *D. H. Lawrence*. Cambridge: Minority Press.

Lenneberg, E. H. 1967. *Biological foundations of language*. New York: Wiley.

Leverhulme Study Group to the British Association for the Advancement of Science. 1961. *The complete scientist*. London: Oxford University Press.

Lewin, K. 1935. *A dynamic theory of personality*. Translated by D. K. Adams and K. E. Zener. New York: McGraw-Hill.

Licklider, J. C. R. 1959. Three auditory theories. In Koch 1959b, 1:41–144.

MacCorquodale, K., and P. E. Meehl. 1948. On a distinction between hypothetical constructs and intervening variables. *Psychological Review* 55:95–107.

Masterman, M. 1970. The nature of a paradigm. In Lakatos and Musgrave 1970, 59–89.

May, R., ed. 1961. *Existential psychology*. New York: Random House.

May, R., E. Angel, and H. F. Ellenberger, eds. 1958. *Existence*. New York: Basic Books.

Merleau-Ponty, M. 1962. *Phenomenology of perception*. Translated by C. Smith. London: Routledge and Kegan Paul.

Mill, J. S. 1862. *A system of logic, ratiocinative and inductive*. 2 vols. 5th ed. London: Parker, Son, and Bourn. (Original work published 1843.)

———. 1865. *Auguste Comte and positivism*. London: N. Trubner.

Miller, G. A. 1969. Psychology as a means of promoting human welfare. *American Psychologist* 24:1063–75.

Miller, G. A., E. Galanter, and K. H. Pribram. 1960. *Plans and the structure of behavior*. New York: Holt.

Miller, N. E. 1951. Comments on theoretical models illustrated by the development of a theory of conflict behavior. *Journal of Personality* 20:82–100.

———. 1959. Liberalization of basic S-R concepts: Extensions to conflict behavior, motivation, and social learning. In Koch 1959b, 2:196–292.

Murray, H. A. 1959. Preparations for the scaffold of a comprehensive system. In Koch 1959b, 3:7–54.

Newitt, D. M. 1962. Percy Williams Bridgman: 1882–1961. In *Biographical memoirs of Fellows of the Royal Society*, 8:27–40. London: The Royal Society.

Oppenheimer, J. R. 1955. *Open mind*. New York: Simon and Schuster.

———. 1962. On science and culture. *Encounter*, October, 3–10.

Pinter, H. 1962. *Three plays: A slight ache; The collection; The dwarfs*. New York: Grove Press.

———. 1966. *The homecoming*. New York: Grove Press.

Poincaré, H. 1913. Mathematical creation. In *The foundations of science*. Translated by G. H. Halsted, 383–94. New York: Science Press.

Polanyi, M. 1951. *The logic of liberty*. Chicago: University of Chicago Press.

———. 1958. *Personal knowledge: Towards a post-critical philosophy*. Chicago: University of Chicago Press.

———. 1959. *The study of man*. Chicago: University of Chicago Press.

———. 1962. Tacit knowing and its bearing on some problems on philosophy. *Review of Modern Physics* 34:601–16.

———. 1966. *The tacit dimension.* Garden City, N.Y.: Doubleday.

Polya, G. 1945. *How to solve it.* Princeton: Princeton University Press.

———. 1954. *Induction and analogy in mathematics.* Princeton: Princeton University Press.

Postman, L. 1955. Association theory and perceptual learning. *Psychological Review* 62: 438–46.

Pratt, C. C. 1939. *The logic of modern psychology.* New York: Macmillan.

Queijo, J. 1987. Inside the creative mind. *Bostonia,* November–December, 26–33.

Robinson, D. N. 1976. *An intellectual history of psychology.* New York: Macmillan.

———. 1998. To practice science: A retrospective appreciation of Sigmund Koch's work (retrospective review of *Psychology: A study of a science*). *Contemporary Psychology* 43:10–12.

Rogers, C. 1969. The group comes of age. *Psychology Today,* December, 27, 29–31, 58, 60–61.

Russell, B. 1945. *A history of Western philosophy.* New York: Simon and Schuster.

Ryle, G. 1949. *The concept of mind.* London: Hutchinson University Library.

Saltzman, I. J., and S. Koch. 1948. The effect of low intensities of hunger on the behavior mediated by a habit of maximum strength. *Journal of Experimental Psychology* 38:347–70.

Schutz, W. 1967. *Joy: Expanding human awareness.* New York: Grove Press.

Shostrom, E. L. 1969. Group therapy: Let the buyer beware. *Psychology Today,* May, 37–40.

Skinner, B. F. 1938. *The behavior of organisms.* New York: Appleton-Century.

———. 1953. *Science and human behavior.* New York: Macmillan.

———. 1971. *Beyond freedom and dignity.* New York: Knopf.

———. 1974. *About behaviorism.* New York: Knopf.

———. 1977. Reply to professor Koch. *Contemporary Psychology* 22:73.

Smith, S., and E. R. Guthrie. 1921. *General psychology in terms of behavior.* New York: Appleton-Century.

Smith, W. J. 1961. *The Spectra hoax.* Middletown, Conn.: Wesleyan University Press.

Snow, C. P. 1959. *The two cultures and the scientific revolution.* New York: Cambridge University Press.

———. 1961. The moral un-neutrality of science. *Science* 133:255–69.

Spence, K. W. 1944. The nature of theory construction in contemporary psychology. *Psychological Review* 51:47–68.

Stevens, S. S. 1935a. The operational basis of psychology. *American Journal of Psychology* 47:323–30.

———. 1935b. The operational definition of psychological concepts. *Psychological Review* 42:517–27.

———. 1939. Psychology and the science of science. *Psychological Bulletin* 36:221–63.

Stevenson, C. L. 1944. *Ethics and language.* New Haven: Yale University Press.

Stoller, F. 1968. Marathon group therapy. In *Innovations to group psychotherapy.* Edited by G. Gazda, 42–95. Springfield, Ill.: Thomas.

Thompson, G. 1961. *The inspiration of science.* London: Oxford University Press.

Tolman, E. C. 1922. A new formula for behaviorism. *Psychological Review* 29:44–53.

———. 1932. *Purposive behavior in animals and men.* New York: Century.

———. 1935. Psychology vs. immediate experience. *Philosophy of Science* 2:356–80.

———. 1936a. An operational analysis of "Demands." *Erkenntnis* 6:383–90.

———. 1936b. Operational behaviorism and current trends in psychology. In *Proceedings of the 25th Anniversary Celebration of the Inauguration of Graduate Studies at the University of Southern California,* 89–103. Los Angeles: University of Southern California Press.

———. 1938. The determiners of behavior at a choice point. *Psychological Review* 45:1–41.

———. 1959. Principles of purposive behavior. In Koch 1959b, 2:92–157.

Toulmin, S. 1953. *The philosophy of science.* London: Hutchinson University Library.

———. 1961. *Foresight and understanding.* London: Hutchinson University Library.

———. 1970. Does the distinction between normal and revolutionary science hold water? In Lakatos and Musgrave 1970, 39–47.

———. 1972. *Human understanding.* Vol. 1. Princeton: Princeton University Press.

Toulmin, S., and J. Goodfield. 1962. *The fabric of the heavens.* London: Hutchinson University Library.

Verplanck, W. S. 1954. Burrhus F. Skinner. In *Modern learning theory,* by W. K. Estes, S. Koch, K. MacCorquodale, P. E. Meehl, C. G. Mueller, W. N. Schoenfeld, and W. S. Verplanck, 267–316. New York: Appleton-Century-Crofts.

———. 1957. A glossary of some terms used in the objective science of behavior. *Psychological Review* 64, suppl. 8: 1–42.

von Wright, G. H. 1963. *The varieties of goodness.* New York: Humanities Press.

Waismann, F. 1951. Verifiability. In *Logic and language* (first series). Edited by A. G. N. Flew, 117–44. Oxford: Blackwell.

———. 1953. Language strata. In *Logic and language* (second series). Edited by A. G. N. Flew, 11 31. Oxford: Blackwell.

Watson, J. B. 1913. Psychology as the behaviorist views it. *Psychological Review* 20:158–77.

———. 1916. The place of the conditioned reflex in psychology. *Psychological Review* 23:89–116.

———. 1919. *Psychology from the standpoint of a behaviorist.* 1st ed. Philadelphia: Lippincott.

———. 1924. *Psychology from the standpoint of a behaviorist.* 2d ed. Philadelphia: Lippincott.

———. 1929. *Psychology from the standpoint of a behaviorist.* 3d ed. Philadelphia: Lippincott.

Weightman, J. 1969. The concept of the avant-garde. *Encounter,* July, 5–16.

Weldon, T. D. 1958. *Kant's Critique of pure reason.* Oxford: Clarendon Press.

Wertheimer, Max. 1945. *Productive thinking.* New York: Harper.

Wertheimer, Michael. 1998. Opus magnificentissimum (retrospective review of *Psychology: A Study of a science*). *Contemporary Psychology* 43:7–10.

Zener, K. E. (with E. G. Wever). 1928. The method of absolute judgment in psychophysics. *Psychological Review* 35:466–93.

——— (with E. G. Wever). 1929. A multiple choice apparatus. *American Journal of Psychology* 41:647–648.

———. 1933. Another attempt at an experimental analysis of the psychological nature of conditioned responses. *Psychological Bulletin* 30:725.

———. 1934. The significance for the problem of learning of conditioned response experiments with human adults. *Psychological Bulletin* 31:715.

———. 1936. Relation of the conditioned salivary response to concomitant overt behavior. *Psychological Bulletin* 33:782–83.

———. 1937. The significance of behavior accompanying conditioned salivary secretion for theories of the conditioned response. *American Journal of Psychology* 50:384–403.

References

———. 1938. An experimental investigation of the role of drive in the acquisition and performance of conditioned responses. *Science* 88:478–79.

——— (with H. G. McCurdy). 1939. Analysis of motivational factors in conditioned behavior: I. The differential effect of changes in hunger upon conditioned, unconditioned, and spontaneous salivary secretion. *Journal of Psychology* 8:321–50.

——— (with W. Bevan). 1943. The effect of past experiences upon limens of visual form perception. *Journal of the Elisha Mitchell Science Society* 59:120.

———. 1945. A note concerning editorial reorientation. *Journal of Personality* 14:1–2.

———. 1946a. Appendix: Analysis of gunnery skills. In *The frangible bullet for use in aerial gunnery training.* NDRC Report No. A-473.

——— (with A. D. Salomon). 1946b. The perception of direction: A quantitative determination of the effects of certain visual factors. *American Psychologist* 1:271.

———. 1949. Individual differences in the functional relationship of conditional stimulus intensity and response magnitude. *American Psychologist* 4:218.

——— (with W. Bevan). 1952. Some influences of past experience upon the perceptual thresholds of visual form. *American Journal of Psychology* 65:434–42.

——— (with R. L. Sulzer). 1953. A quantitative analysis of relations between stimulus determinants and sensitivity of the visual perception of parallelness. *American Psychologist* 8:444.

———. 1958. The significance of experience of the individual for the science of psychology. In *Minnesota Studies in the Philosophy of Science.* Edited by H. Feigl, M. Scriven, and G. Maxwell, 2:354–69. Minneapolis: University of Minnesota Press.

——— (with H. Crovitz and P. Daston). 1959. Laterality and a phenomenon of localization. *Perceptual and Motor Skills* 9:282.

———. 1964. Challenges in graduate education: Comments by a psychologist. Unpublished address given at Duke University, Durham, N. C., September.

Zener, K., and M. Gaffron. 1962. Perceptual experience: An analysis of its relations to the external world through internal processings. In Koch 1962b, 4:515–618.

Acknowledgments

The following materials are reprinted by permission of the publishers: Chapter 2 originally appeared in *Behaviorism and Phenomenology: Contrasting Bases for Modern Psychology* (Chicago: University of Chicago Press, 1964). Portions of chapters 3 and 5 appeared in "Language Communities, Search Cells, and the Psychological Studies," in *Nebraska Symposium on Motivation, 1975*, vol. 23, ed. W. J. Arnold (Lincoln: University of Nebraska Press, 1976); copyright © 1976 by the University of Nebraska Press. Chapter 4 is based on "Reflections on the State of Psychology," *Social Research* 38, no. 4 (1971): 669–709; copyright 1971 New School for Social Research. Chapter 6 is based on "Value Properties: Their Significance for Psychology, Axiology, and Science," in *The Anatomy of Knowledge*, ed. M. Grene (London: Routledge and Kegan Paul, 1969), 119–48. Chapter 7 appeared as "The Allures of Ameaning in Modern Psychology," in *Science and Human Affairs*, ed. R. Farson (Palo Alto, Calif.: Science and Behavior Books, 1965), 55–82. Chapter 9 is derived from a paper in *Psychology and Society: In Search of Symbiosis*, Houston Symposium, vol. 1, ed. R. S. Kasschau and F. S. Kessel (New York: Holt, Rinehart and Winston, 1980), 30–53. Chapter 10 is based on "The Image of Man in Encounter Groups," *American Scholar* 42, no. 4 (1973): 636–52. Portions of chapter 11 are derived from "Theory and Experiment in Psychology," *Social Research* 40, no. 4 (1973): 691–707; copyright 1973 New School for Social Research. Chapter 12 is derived from "More Verbal Behavior from Dr. Skinner," review of *About Behaviorism*, by B. F. Skinner, *Contemporary Psychology* 21 (1976): 453–57, copyright © 1976 by the American Psychological Association; "A Text in Search of an Author," *Contemporary Psychology* 22 (1977): 73, copyright © 1977 by the American Psychological Association; B. F. Skinner, "Reply to Professor Koch," *Contemporary Psychology* 22 (1977): 73, copyright © 1977 by the American Psychological Association, reprinted by permission of the American Psychological Association and the B. F. Skinner Foundation. Chapter 13 appeared in a condensed version as "Karl Edward Zener: A Memoir," *Journal of Personality* 37 (1969): 179–89; reprinted by permission of Blackwell Publishers. Chapter 14 originally appeared in *Theory and Psychology* 2 (1992): 161–90, reprinted by permission of Sage Publications. Chapter 15 is drawn from "The Nature and Limits of Psychological Knowledge," in *A Century of Psychology as Science*, ed. S. Koch and D. Leary (Washington: American Psychological Association, 1992); copyright © 1992 by the American Psychological Association.

Index

theory of definition (*continued*)
phor and, 157–58, 163, 185; natural
language and, 160–62; observation
base of psychology and, 162–64,
163n, 164n, 196; operational definition and, 147–51, 150n, 366–67; perceptual theory of definition, summary
of, 172–73; personal styles and, 156;
psychological language communities
and, 165–68, 166nn. 8, 9; scientific
definition base and, 175–77, 190n; sciences and humanities and, 173–74,
177–78; scientific vs. natural language
and, 153–54. *See also* Bridgman, Percy
Williams; natural language; observation base; theory of definition, psychological studies and
theory of definition, psychological studies
and: anatomizing of experience and,
189; communicative idiosyncrasy and,
181–82, 182–84n; community-
language or "theory appraisal" and,
183–91; comprehensive, "large picture" thinkers and, 183–84n; computer modeling of mind and, 189–90;
definition within language concept
and, 184–85; error detection and,
191; indeterminate classification frameworks and, 189–90, 190n; intracell
communication and, constraints upon,
181–82, 182–84n; leadership in scientific communities and, 181–82;
ontology-distorting frameworks and,
187–88, 191, 308; ontology-
respecting frameworks and, 187, 188,
308; ontology-revealing frameworks
and, 187, 188–89, 308; perspectival
knowledge and, 179; physical stimulus
specification and, 189; psychology
modes of inquiry and, 176–77; pseudoknowledge and, 120, 191; psychological knowledge embedded in natural language and, 184–85, 186–87;
search cells and language incommensurabilities and, 178–80; "theories of
ourselves" concept and, 185–86; visual experience dimensions and, 189
theory of value, 5, 39–40; value properties
and, 40, 43. *See also* Aesthetics Research Center
Thomson, Virgil, 44

Tolman, E. C.: as a behaviorist, 341; intervening variable strategy of, 67, 69,
248–49, 335, 336, 379–80, 379n; motivational work of, 31; objective theory of purposive behavior and, 69;
ontology-respecting framework of,
188; operationism focus of, 377; philosophical interests of, 413; rat behavior focus of, 36, 188, 193; stimulus-
response ambiguities and, 58–59;
value properties interest of, 193
Toulmin, Stephen, 54
"Towards an Indigenous Methodology"
(Koch), 148

value properties: creative activity process
and, 194; experiential sensitivity and,
of humanities, 192, 196; formulation
of concept and, 192; Gestalt psychologists and, 218–20, 219n; J. J. Gibson's
work and, 189, 193, 210, 219n, 220–
23, 223n, 269; human knowledge processes organization and, 193; motivation field and, 196–97; philosophy,
science, and Value and, 192, 223–30,
401; science-humanities relationship
and, 193–97
value properties, motivation studies and:
action-experience syndrome concept
and, 200–201; aesthetic, perceptual
value properties example and, 210–17;
behaviorism and, 196; commonsense
framework of, 198; concept difficulty
and, 206–7, 206n; creative behavior sequence and, 199; differentiated value
events and, 209–11; "directedness" of
experience and action and, 208–9; disequilibrium-equilibrium restoral theories and, 198; extrinsic vs. intrinsic action determinants and, 201–6, 208;
goal-directedness and, 199–200; human discrimination and, 216; "in and
for itself" activities and, 201, 202,
203; interdisciplinary collaboration
need and, 197; "learned drives" and,
208; need-dependency and, 197; perceptual processes and, 209–10; "play"
example and, 202–3; positive vs. negative value properties and, 203, 204–5;
ranges overlap in, 207–8; research
issues and, 216–17; sexual activity